Happiness and P

Edited by Constance Goh and Bernard McGuirk

Critical, Cultural and Communications Press
Nottingham
2007

Happiness and Post-Conflict,
edited by Constance Goh and Bernard McGuirk

Series: Studies in Post-Conflict Cultures, no. 3
Series Editor: Bernard McGuirk
The books in this series are refereed publications.

Cover design by Hannibal.

First published in Great Britain by Critical, Cultural and
Communications Press, Nottingham, 2007.

Publisher's website: **www.cccpress.co.uk**

ISBN 978-1-905510-12-2 (UK)
ISBN 978-1-60271-012-2 (USA)

First edition

Printed by Tipografia Guerra, Viseu, Portugal.

Contents

Histories

Literatures

Acknowledgments

The editors wish to acknowledge the editorial and technical support of Jean Andrews, Beverly Tribbick, Sandi Golbey and Mariana Matoso.

Dedication

This collection of essays is dedicated to Elizabeth Taylor.
Ever striving to avoid conflict, she inspired happiness.

Introduction
On Happiness and Post-Conflict

Constance Goh and Bernard McGuirk

> Wars – hot and cold – are ike love affairs. They don't just end. They fizzle and sputter; sometimes they reignite [...] for a postwar era lasts as long as people affected by conflict employ that painful or exhilarating experience to assess their own current relationship and aspirations [...] the morning after is always an ambiguous moment. What just happened? Who benefited from it?
>
> Cynthia Enloe

There are and will be many mornings after... The series *Studies in Post-Conflict Cultures*, launched in 2006 with *Post-Conflict Cultures: Rituals of Representation*, posed the challenge that has subsequently been taken up in the volumes *Hors de Combat*, *Diasporas* and, now, in *Happiness and Post-Conflict*: how to record, whilst respecting, if not recapturing, those always ambiguous moments – referred to in Cynthia Enloe's interrogative as to "What just happened?" – that resonate sometimes in silence, though often amidst all-too-intensive noises on and off the post-conflict stage? Such inseparable testifying and questioning have been and will continue to be the aspiration of all contributors both to the series and to the present volume. Their re-engagement with the silences and violences residing in the notion of the "post-conflict" exposes further, and plurally, the contradictions always latent, and often lying, within the term as within the spheres of former and ongoing confrontation and struggle. The aftermath, the latter effects, the subsequent to or consequent upon entailed in the "post-" can only be understood, if ever explained, in and by what is veiled by the replays, the deferrals and the slippages of the conflict and its still combative or would-be conciliatory discourses. In other words, the posting of the script will ever gain further momentum in and because of the conflicted space and the conflictual time, whether in aggression, retaliation or reconciliation, in which the embattled subject performs. As Macdonald Daly avers, in his essay on Leon Trotsky, albeit in respect of another time, another place and other circumstances, "we are always in conflict".

Neal Curtis opens a discussion which is lodged necessarily within the interstices of the *economy* (in both the conventional sense and with the Derridan added meaning of differential relations) of ontology and the ontological dimension of economic systems. Curtis argues that economic colonisation, the "attempt to seize and plunder resources", is masked, more often than not, by the rhetoric of neo-liberal and, then, neo-conservative democracy that defines the approach of a West to its Middle-Eastern or Eastern other. The insistence of the United States that the countries of conflict join the "movement of transnational capital", and those countries' compliance to its directive, demonstrate how the economy and politics of those nations are, however vicariously, already and always in the hands and at the mercy of a Wall Street-Washington alliance. Curtis's analysis of the manner in which the democratic superpower conducts the economic war by ontological manoeuvres covers Tony Blair's turn to neo-conservatism after the "infamous 'dodgy dossier' that was the product of incompetent intelligence and political deceit". As "the epitome of liberal democracy", the United States' intervention in Iraq uncannily recalls its "profoundly anti-democratic project" of Vietnam with the same failure – *pace* George W. Bush's belated claim to the contrary – to raise Iraq to the economic stature of a so-called democratised country, resulting in the economic deprivation and political turmoil in the "new" – hardly post-conflict – Iraq.

The anti-democratic phantom lurking behind, or prior to, the United States' democratic stance is invoked by Roberto Grandi's circumspect contextualising of more than a century's interrelations between media and conflicts. Grandi's "On the Promotion of Conflicts: the Media and War" is a critical re-mapping of the ways in which the democratic superpower obtains and maintains the consensus of its population in favour of its war effort through media manipulations, corroborating Curtis's thesis on how media machinations aid in the concealment of the agendas of the hegemonic power-broker. However, as Grandi argues, the media domination of the United States which helps "to maintain a mass consensus for war" occurs "at the cost of censoring and deforming the news". Grandi's exploration starts with the Crimean War and concludes with the post-Gulf War II Iraq conflict in a succinct and comprehensive tracing of the way the media both document and aid the propaganda efforts of the democratic powers. But even media machinations cannot and will not control indefinitely or with impunity the otherwise verifiable documentation upon which authentic journalism is founded – a direct representation of the occurrences in the war zone – not least because of technological advances in mass communication; these can and habitually will be subject not only to manipulation but also to the testing of any suspicions arising from and subsequent interrogations of the ostensible or alleged motives supporting the war effort. Choice? To be Foxed or out-foxed? That is the question.

Constance Goh's discussion of the Danish Cartoons Controversy shows up the contradictions within the power struggle between the Muslim fundamentalists and the Western powers with a focus on form as *technē*. Unwilling and unable to take sides in this supposedly Manichaean confrontation, in a willed and precarious sitting-on-the-fence, she reveals the underlying sameness within the difference between the two opposing parties through a filter of Jacques Derrida's and Jacques Lacan's writings. Goh's argument stems from the dehumanisation implied by global dominance and resulting in the inhuman which takes the extreme form of suicide bombers – the terror from the suicide bombings reflects the horrors of what is known in postmodernity as the other than human. "Country Matters" are demonstrated to be also metaphysical affairs, an oxymoron predicated on a transition mobilised by and within metonymic transferences between writing and being.

The question of violence in post-conflict cultures sees a provisional re-framing in Cristina Demaria's "Reconciliation and Forgiving: the Power of Happy Memory". Closing the theoretical section and acting simultaneously as the pivot that moves the discussion to the section on case studies, Demaria's interrogation of the efficacy of remembrance and forgetting in the form of narratives unveils the ontological destabilisation of historical traumas, extending both Curtis's and Goh's theses that the greatest violence is the aggression found in the universalising tendency of global colonisation, a violence emerging, for example, from a South African apartheid which eventually ends in dehumanising both the perpetrators and the victims, a dehumanisation based on "skin colour". Demaria looks at the possibility of reconciliation as experiencing the impossible, the miracle, in the reconstruction of history in its decapitalised form. The theoretical transition from Curtis's post-Heideggerean take on economic wars to the post-postcolonial letting the oppressed (or repressed) speak, instead of just letting them be, focuses on the effectiveness of the South African Truth and Reconciliation Commission, an emphasis predicated upon Paul Ricoeur's citation of the Derridan paradoxical notion of forgiveness as the ultimate letting go of the unforgivable.

Sturdy support is given to the opening theorectial reflections in the essays on post-conflict architectures and performance art. Michelle Pépin's "Reconstructions and Memories in the Post-Conflict City" turns to the "global cast of 'the city'" with a reading aided by Norberg-Schulz's writing on the interrelations between being and space within architecture. Pépin's comprehensive discussion of the metaphysics underlying environmental images covers a spectrum from the Greek city states to postmodern Berlin. Her argument outlines that hubristic edifice of the City of Man which attempts to override the Augustinian City of God – an intertwining of environmental mastery and cultural identity – and revitalises the symbolic capacity of spatial design to be read as "the expression of these experiences in defining the human being's comprehension of their "beingness", the self in manifestation. More importantly, Pépin's thesis alerts us to the fact that what we see (and hear) is only part of what there is despite the transparency and steeliness of the glitzy postmodern architecture.

Elena Pirazzoli's "Ruins and Reconstruction of the Post-Conflict City: Towards a Poetics of Rubble in the Twentieth Century" recounts the post-conflict rebuilding of cities after the massive environmental upheaval of modern technologisation in its double senses as manifested by the aftermath of World War II. Her essay recalls Derrida's infinite love of the ruin in the "Force of Law: the Mystical Foundation of Authority" with the focus on the wordplay between "ruin" and "rubble", an intersection that reveals the weak cornerstone of metaphysics. Its fall correlates with the cadence found in the rubble of the Third Reich which crescendos to the modern city of Berlin rebuilt from the "ground zero" of Nuremberg – "the destroyed city, the divided city and the capital of reunification" – and corresponds with the multiple "stratifications of History". She moves beyond Pépin's earlier use of

Italo Calvino's literary representation of the city to the filmic level of Tacita Dean's shot of the *Palast der Republik* "in which she registers the light mutation of the orange-brown windows as they gradually gain golden reflections".

Pirazzoli's focus on aesthetics is mirrored by María José Contreras's "Bombs and Poems: The Representation of Conflict through Performance Art" – re-echoing Demaria's notion of the reconstructive possibilities deriving from presentation within representation. Contreras's psychoanalytic reading of the bombardment with poetic book markers of five cities, Santiago, Dubrovnik, Guernica, Dresden and Nagasaki, by the *Casagrande* project, celebrates the memorial reconstruction of the cities affected by various conflicts via the semiotic slippages found in representation; her discussion also draws on Cathy Caruth's speculation as to how the psychological fragmentation of the individual can result from cultural traumas in her exploration of the impact of the remembered confrontation. Alternative recollection opens up a space for the post-conflict cultures to restructure their identity based on a "happy memory" – an expansion of Demaria's, Pépin's and Pirazzoli's reading of the interlacing of the individual and the collective experiences in the active commemoration of conflict through the performative dimension of representation.

Closing this section, Stanislaw Rzyski provides a penetrating look at how the sterile construction of government housing shows the "rift between ideology, planning and the actual completion of these blocks of flats" – the "heritage from the former [Socialist] system and the role of the word 'blokowisko'" – "block estates" reflecting the "lack", akin to the black hole mentioned by Neal Curtis in "Economic Wars and the Myth of Post-Conflict Democracy", within the Socialist *bloc* of the Soviet Union. Rzyski argues that the architecture which manifests the dogmatic ideology of Socialism had a lasting effect on the ontological status of the Polish people. The initial campaign to improve "the living conditions of the working class" by realising "the egalitarian principles of social policy concerning mainly equal access to flats of a uniform standard" cannot, in fact, be *realised* because of the schizoid Real symbolically reiterated by the connotations attached to the word "blokowski". According to Rzyski: "Following the changes to the system in 1989 the estates have become *something unwanted* or at the very least *troublesome*. They are synonymous with the old system, of *mediocrity*, *poverty*, *lack of prospects*, and *deprivation*. The notion of the 'blokowisko' has taken on a pejorative meaning which threatened to become a constituent part of the Polish mentality. Films about the block estates have been made, for example '*Blokersi*' (*The Blockers*) by Sylwester Latkowski of 2001, '*Cześć Tereska*' (*Hi, Little Teresa*) directed by Robert Glińksi of 2001, or '*Dzień Świra*' (*The Day of the Freak*) directed by Marek Kroterski in 2002. All these films portray the traumas connected with the living in blocks on these large estates [...] and strengthen the image of the 'blokowisko' as a *pathological space* which is unattractive and dirty, and which is, furthermore, inhabited by people who live on fringes of society without prospects".

Rui Gonçalves Miranda's "Constructed Happiness: On the Seductions of Messianism" operates as a bridge into "Histories", reading the Portuguese obsession with King Sebastian, nicknamed the "Desired One", as another version of the lure of Messianism. The myth of the valiant King lives on because of the "present absence" at the core of the image, an absence shrouded in multiple narratives reconstructed in different genres – figuratively represented as a fortress of an Empire. Gonçalves Miranda's argument supports Vidal Bouzón's stance that happiness is experienced inversely in the pursuit of the desired object since one cannot completely recuperate something that is dead and lost centuries ago (we are told Sebastian's body was never found). But it is precisely the irrecoverable that prompts these efforts of recovery.

Macdonald Daly's "The Dialectic of Conflict and Culture: Leon Trotsky and Less Fortunate Statesmen" which continues the meditation on histories (and not History) goes hand in hand with both Rzyski's take on ideology and the construction of identity through spatial configuration and Curtis's economic wars conducted via the ontological. It takes further the fundamental thesis of the volume that the strict demarcation between what are apparently oppositional elements is only a matter of convenience for the parties in power and this postulate is made obvious in Daly's sagacious reading of Leon Trotsky, "the seeming combination of man of action with man of aesthetic inclination and intellectual ability", whose *Literature and Revolution* is a figurative correspondence which can be read against the lack of such a phenonomen in British parliamentary history. With a critical analysis of the two histories, that of Russia during the October and February Revolutions and that of contemporary Britain, Daly effectively demonstrates that "the twin foci" of culture as (post)conflict(ed) in Trotsky's Russia and the savoir-faire of a capitalist economy operating in and through culture in modern England are effectively flipsides of the same coin.

Cultural dominance as a form of imperialism is also explored in Stephen Roberts's "Out of the Ashes: Unamuno and Hispanicity post-1898" with the focus turning to the word *Hispanidad*, first popularised by Ramiro de Maeztu, "a justification of Spain's influence on the New World". Roberts's historical account of the Spanish ideological and cultural movement exposes the complexity within Unamuno's cultural aspiration to "a spiritual brotherhood" based on linguistic and literary ties, arguing that his notion of *Hispanidad* cannot be equated with that of Maeztu "firstly because Unamuno always rejected the idea of a Hispanic 'race' and secondly, even at his most 'imperialistic', because he remained a firm opponent of any vestige of the old traditionalist and *casticista* Spanish spirit" and, more importantly, also because Unamuno's *Hispanidad* is not infused with the orthodox Catholic ideals; instead he champions an unorthodox, agonic Christianity which he defined as "a common pagan-Christian conception".

Nicholas Hewitt's "*Le Poids des mots, le choc des photos*: Conflict and the News Magazines: *Picture Post* and *Paris Match*" discusses insightfully the visual impact of war photography. Hewitt relates conflict and news coverage in magazines by looking at the historical development of war and photography. His exploration supports Grandi's political reading of the promotion of conflict in media and war relations.

According to Hewitt, "*Paris-Match* was able to call upon unprecedented resources, both from its own photographers and journalists and from news agencies. Also, in both wars (the Six Day War and the Vietnam War), the magazine was apparently able to break away from some of the controls of embedded journalism which had restricted the operations of *Picture Post* in World War II and which was to become such an issue in the first, but especially the second, Gulf War". He concludes by exploring the complexity inherent in the relationship between the viewer and the object. On the one hand, the pictures are meant to jolt and discomfort the viewer and, on the other, in order to maintain a strong readership, there must be photographs to reassure the readers that the horrors of war visually encountered are external to the happy homes they inhabit, "a complicated menu of concern and happiness which contributed a winning formula".

To close the section on histories, Patrizia Violi's "Remembering the Future: the Construction of Gendered Identity in the Balkans" is a piercing insight into and analysis of the construction of gendered identity based on the diversities discovered in what was formerly known as the Balkans. Violi's stance in terms of identity construction relates to the multiple temporalities which underscore the notion of "memory", as she argues that the past gains significance only in view of the present and, especially, the future. Her psychological study, conducted in conjunction with the Women's Centre of Bologna, includes an archive of thirty-four life stories of Kosovo women of varied origins: Albanian, Serbian and Roma, collected from 1999 to 2000 in Kosovo and Italy. Tying what she refers to as gender competence to genre construction, the autobiographical details can be read as a form of preservation and transmission of the specific culture to which the individuals belong, an elaboration of the theses of the other contributors' concern with identity and cultural reconstructions. What is particularly noteworthy in Violi's astute analysis of the shifting positions in the post-conflict narratives is her emphasis on singularity and her perceptive approach to the unvoiced excesses ever operating at the margins of cultural discourse.

In a movingly personalised reconstruction of the inseparable historical and discursive aggressions to which *Boesman*, *Boer* and *Soutpiel* have been subjected by the predominantly English-speaking hegemonies of both governments and literary representations, Elizabeth Taylor traces the power of condescension towards a supposed "native other" back to Vasco da Gama and the very roots of colonised southern Africa. Cyclical patterns of denigration are shown to have culminated not only in the early use, against the Afrikaner, of concentration camps but also in the very separateness of self and other which, paradoxically, came to underpin apartheid and, more surreptitiously, the fictional representation in southern African literature in English of the ever-recolonised stereotype.

Álvaro J. Vidal Bouzon's lyrical portrayal of Joan Manuel Serrat, with expressions not only about his songs but also the songs about him, continues the section on literatures and his essay is a figure of meta-language itself: the love of and for the other making the agent-writer paradoxically passive. Thus, the object of affection takes centre-stage as the subject of the passive voice. Vidal Bouzón translates Sabina's song on Serrat:

I have a cousin who is a total master
of what's mine, what's yours, what's ours,
a luxury for the soul and to the ear,
a way of avenging oblivion.

What he calls "that way of having revenge" is another way of depicting violence as that space of impropriety which precedes the discourse proper. Serrat, a singer-songwriter who paints pictures with words, speaks of Utopia as a woman, reminding us of the Lacanian phrase for the feminine "the not whole and more", a mirror of the lacuna within the utopic project. Thus, the female is not the "hybrid Nietzschean-Marxist superhuman superproletariat"; she is only a "properly passive" agent who bears the cross of freedom, equality and fraternity. Only as a symbol of the missing link, the female is made dependent on male discourse. Vidal Bouzon, then, in his tribute bears witness to the happiness one gets only with a home and a waiting for the arrival of a certain letter. In the case of Serrat, his is a fortress of solitude.

Colin Wright's perceptive reading of Michael Radford's 1995 *Il Postino*, which is a filmic adaptation of *Ardiente paciencia* by the Chilean writer Antonio Skármeta, focuses on the dialogic possibilities of the literary, a secret link to Violi's take on feminine narratives in the previous section. Drawing on the Derridan motifs of the "postal principle", the patrilineal inheritance and the *unheimlich*, Wright refers to "a necessary contingency in the very operation of language which results from the claim that, contra Jacques Lacan, a letter may always *not* arrive at its destination". The non-arrival can be the result of a conflictual situation that shatters the shelter given by national, familial or racial identity, what Wright calls the "economies of happiness", or a communicative interception as a consequence of the "gap between interlocutors"; because the inherent signifying dissemination allows a disruption of the "proper" transmission of the legacy, a father-son relation which Wright explores through the notion of the countersignature.

Bernard McGuirk's "In Search of Love Past" concludes the volume. His reading of Erri De Luca's *Tre cavalli* interweaves the multiple connotations of Argentina's "dirty war" with a narrative conflict set against the violence of Italy's own troubled Red Brigade past and a far from successfully sublimated shuttling and cross-cultural sexuality. Umberto Eco's "fathoming" of the Argentine press's coverage of the Falkland-Malvinas conflict animates McGuirk's discourse with the figure of the yellow submarine. De Luca's – unintended – crossing of swords with Luce Irigaray is made possible through an uncontrollable poetic deviance – the "*spécule-homme... de l'autre femme*" slipping into the body politic of the Lacanian *hommelette* (the *lamella* as a figure of a "little" man, "an unfulfilled subject's struggling to break out into social reality and out of a curiously isolating amorphousness") – just as the triumph of the bellicose British is enabled by the myths of the "formidable" subterranean warship.

In *Post-Conflict Cultures: Rituals of Representation*, Cristina Demaria and Colin Wright claimed that the most important gesture in circumscribing their – and our – emerging object of study in the series they launched was to surrender to conflict their own theoretical paradigms. What has happened since is that the assembling of the views of international specialists in an unlimited and illimitable range of disciplines has proven the need to think, interpret and understand the possibilities of and for radical intervention in such constructions as happiness, whether as reaction to, antidote for, or concealment of the ever-looming anguish that threatens the very category of "post-".

Part 1
Theories

Economic War and the Myth of Post-Conflict Democracy

Neal Curtis

The official rhetoric surrounding Gulf War II has taken many twists and turns determined primarily by the evaporation of the main justification for the invasion, namely Iraq's possession of weapons of mass destruction. This shift in rhetoric has been especially evident in Britain where Tony Blair has trumpeted his own version of neo-conservatism, something he calls the doctrine of "international community" (Blair, 2005), in order to distance himself from the now infamous "dodgy dossier" that was the product of incompetent intelligence and political deceit. In the US, of course, the threat of WMD was, in the words of Paul Wolfowitz, merely a "bureaucratic" concern used solely for the purposes of achieving consensus. In contrast to the Blair government, the Bush administration had never really been concerned about WMD, the argument had always been for regime change and the "liberation" of Iraq, which, it was argued, would in turn produce a direct broadening of democracy throughout the Middle East. In this regard the argument to invade Iraq was in compliance with the Rogue Doctrine established shortly after the fall of the Berlin Wall to re-establish an enemy for the US in the light of the collapse of the Soviet Union. Here the security threat is understood to be failed states and the wider destabilisation and general anarchy that such black holes in the network of international governance might engender.

This rhetoric of freedom was of course completed by the insistence that along with the establishment of democratic institutions the economic liberalisation of the new Iraq would signal another path to post-conflict peace and happiness. That free trade is a precursor and cultivator of both prosperity and peace has a very long tradition within utilitarian philosophy from John Locke to Jeremy Bentham and Adam Smith. In his study of war Michael Howard writes that liberal thinkers consistently argued that economic rivalry and competition would always contribute to war whereas free trade was closer to the laws of nature, which "dictated harmony and co-operation" (1986, p. 25). This economic version of Kantian cosmopolitan providence "linked mankind by a chain of reciprocal needs which made impossible, *a priori*, any clash of economic interests. It was only a misconception of such interests [...] that led to conflict and war" (*ibid.*). There is, of course, an element of truth in this argument. Those who advocate trade as a significant contribution to peace will note the cultural exchange and awareness that are its by-products and that open borders for trade also offer routes towards a more open society in general. Echoing this sentiment there are those who argued that continuing trade with Iraq, rather than the years of sanctions, would have weakened Saddam's tyrannical rule much faster than the enforced deprivation and starvation of the Iraqi people. The flip-side of this position, however, is that the idealism of British utilitarianism gave way to the realism of British empire with its colonial rule and violent suppression of local resistance.

For many critics of the invasion of Iraq it is this darker side of utilitarianism that is at work in what is little more than an economic war integral to a new formation of empire.

But if Gulf War II is to be taken as an economic war or as an element in an economic war it is necessary to say much more than the invasion of Iraq was an attempt to seize and plunder resources. While Gulf War II did include the plundering of Iraq by opening it up to the movement of transnational capital, economic war is not reducible to the usual understanding of economics as the organisation of productive forces and relations. The economic war currently being fought is primarily an *ontological war*, that is to say, it is a war concerning the definition and organisation of human being, where a supposedly enlightened definition of what it is to be human is systematically imposed on every "backward" country on the planet. In contrast to the humanitarian and humanist rhetoric of liberty and freedom that the leading agents of this war deploy this practice is firmly counter-democratic, or counter-revolutionary (Joxe, 2002); it is less about the spread of democracy and more about the establishment of a new capitalist nobility.

For some time this economic war has gone by the name of neo-liberalism, a doctrine supposedly superseded by neo-conservatism. That neo-conservatism is something different is certain, but quite often this difference is exaggerated because the philosophy that advocated the benign and neutral universalism of the free market often hid the practice of a violent and hierarchical organisation of the global economy that always favoured the most powerful. Neo-conservatism, born out of the confidence afforded by a unipolar world, is the promotion of this hierarchical organisation stripped of its veil, and it deploys "the common sense" of neo-liberalism as a central mechanism to maintain that hierarchy.[1] Of course, it must be noted that neo-conservatism is prepared to deregulate economies by use of military force, where dyed-in-the-wool neo-liberals would rely on the IMF and the WTO, but it is interesting to note that it is precisely at a time when the WTO threatened to become more democratic that neo-conservatism fully emerged to ensure the retention of US sovereignty. It should also be noted that neo-conservatism represents the return of values that exceed the neo-liberal privileging of exchange value; something that is evident in the increased moralism of US rhetoric both at home and abroad. However, this does not mean that the economic war formerly known as neo-liberalism is defunct. On the contrary, the idea of a free market is a central component in the civil religion of the US and it therefore remains at the heart of the current economic war. In fact, without the "common sense" of neo-liberal orthodoxy the rhetoric of democracy that shrouds the occupation of Iraq would be unintelligible. This article will therefore outline the ontological nature of the economic war taking place across the globe and the definition of human being that is at the heart of this "common sense" in order to demonstrate why

---

[1] I have made a preliminary attempt to think through the relation of neo-liberalism to neo-conservatism in *War and Social Theory* (2006). See chapter 8, "Economy and Empire".

a profoundly anti-democratic project can still present itself as the epitome of democratic civilization and the only path to post-conflict well-being.

Before addressing economic war as an ontological project and demonstrating how this project permits firmly anti-democratic forces to present their actions as wholly democratic, it is useful to turn to the conflict in the former Yugoslavia in order to give a sense of the economic war in practice while also exposing the poverty of the democratic rhetoric that surrounded the resolution of the conflict. The war in Yugoslavia and the NATO bombing of Serbia came to be emblematic of the so-called new wars. The term "balkanization" became synonymous with the era of post-nation state wars in which the cause of civil war was often perceived to be religious and ethnic tensions, while the bombing of Serbia was the first incarnation of Blair's doctrine of "international community" that announced a post-Westphalian era of international relations and foreign policy. In keeping with the Rogue Doctrine, after an early period in which the rhetoric concerning the conflict supported EU and US inaction by presenting the complexities and deep history of ethnic tensions, the rhetoric gradually turned to the tyranny of Slobodan Milošević. Both Blair and Clinton were at pains to stress that they were not taking up hostilities against Serbia or the Serbian people, but against a particular regime; rhetoric to be repeated by Blair and Bush in Afghanistan and Iraq. Once again the justification for the bombing was couched in terms of liberty, freedom and the re-establishment of democracy, and yet the discourse of ethnic hatred and tyrannical rule masked the economic causes of the war, causes that should lead us to profoundly question the nature of the democracy under the banner of which the bombing was carried out.

The economic war waged on Yugoslavia can be traced back to the restructuring of the Yugoslav economy by foreign creditors from the beginning of the 1980s, while Yugoslavia's strategic importance and the United States' involvement in the restructuring are documented in United States National Security Decision Directives 54 and 133 dated 2 September 1982 and 14 March 1984 respectively. While Yugoslavia is only indirectly included in NSDD 54, which bears the title "United States Policy Toward Eastern Europe", NSDD 133 directly addresses the "severe financial situation facing Yugoslavia [which] could pose a serious threat to Yugoslavia's ability to maintain those policies which best serve our interests". In both Directives the strategic concern (remembering that these are *security* directives) is to limit the influence of Moscow in Eastern Europe. The best accounts of what took place during the 1980s can be found in Bob Allen's excellent article "Why Kosovo? The Anatomy of a Needless War" (1999), Michel Chussodovsky's *The Globalization of Poverty* (1997) and John McMurtry's *Value Wars* (2002). For McMurtry the success of Yugoslav market socialism necessitated its destruction on ideological as well as strategic grounds. Its rapid economic growth in the 1960s and 1970s presented an alternative to the free market model, but as he notes: "The market God is a jealous God" (*ibid.*, p. 36). This success was, however, fuelled in part by foreign borrowing and by 1980 Yugoslavia had a significant foreign debt. The nature of this debt was worsened by what Allen calls "tight money policies" (1999, p. 11) in the West that forced up interest rates, but for McMurtry these policies were a tool specifically aimed at undermining public spending at home and socialised economies abroad. He notes how Reagan's Federal Reserve Chairman, Paul Volker, claimed that the policy was introduced because "the way to keep government spending [on social programmes] down was not by insisting taxes be adequate to pay for it, but by scaring Congress with deficits" (2002, p. 232). For McMurtry, then, the method deployed by the United States to ensure Yugoslavia did not come under the influence of Moscow was to intentionally produce deficits and force Yugoslavia into the arms of the IMF, the international arm of the US treasury.

As Bob Allen has noted, the reforms enforced by the IMF in return for loans included the cutting of government spending in favour of debt servicing. Importantly, this also included the suspension of federal transfers to republics and autonomous regions, an intervention in the organisation of the Federation that only added to the phenomenon that came to be known as "Balkanization". The country's banking system was to be dismantled and the socially-owned national bank replaced by a system of profit-orientated private banks. This meant that the government was unable to turn to the national bank for credit. Labour-managed firms were to be converted into capitalist enterprises run by private bank creditors. A bankruptcy programme was introduced to shut down the ever- increasing number of insolvent firms, and finally, all trade was deregulated, meaning that imports surged and manufacturing plummeted. The results of the successive reforms imposed upon Yugoslavia were catastrophic.

According to Michel Chussodovsky industrial production in Yugoslavia in the period 1966-79 averaged 7.1%, decreasing to 2.8% during 1980-87, falling to zero in 1987-8 and finally hitting 10.6% in 1990 (1997, p. 245). At that time after further adjustments inflation increased from a staggering 70% to 140% in 1991, and then to 937% in 1992 and 1,134% in 1993 (*ibid.*, p. 246). With wages frozen at 1989 levels it is not difficult to imagine the desperation felt by many of the Federation's population. The sense of devastation is only added to when one learns that after a decade of lay-offs and liquidations 1989 saw the liquidation of 248 firms and 89,400 workers were made redundant, while 1990 heralded a further 889 companies bankrupt and 525,000 people put out of work. As Chussodovsky notes, that is more than 600,000 workers from an industrial workforce of 2.7 million (*ibid.*, p. 249). That this would be traumatic for any society goes without saying, but the cause of the trauma was never taken to be the assault on the economy by the US lead financial institutions. For those who had been party to the IMF deals, including Slobodan Milošević, it was in their interest to divert attention from the economic reasons underlying the trauma and find a scapegoat in the ethnic tensions with which the Federation was rife. The rest is history, or should that read the rest is testament to the forgetting that is history. Interestingly, according to Allen, the situation was made worse by the democratic elections of 1990, which

6

exacerbated the problem because they took place at the regional rather than the national level. The economic reforms had already ensured the Yugoslav government could not provide everyone with economic and social security, which in turn meant that public leaders responded to the insecurity of citizens by advancing the particular interests of the individual republics; and this perspective of individual republics easily slipped into an ethno-nationalist perspective, a problem compounded by the fact that Western governments, in particular Germany in the case of Croatia, were also too swift in recognising the independence of the Republics.

However, aside from these additional political contributions, the social trauma was largely brought about by the imposition of economic reforms, and for McMurtry this production of social trauma by financial technocrats brings this method of economic assault in line with the practice of disconnect that is endemic in the technocratic language of military assaults. For him the "severance of strategic decision from systematic life devastation" (2002, p. 26) is the unifying mind set of the corporate-military system. Where financial technocrats speak of "austerity measures" and "structural adjustments" as euphemisms for destroyed lives, the military technocrats speak of "collateral damage". The question then becomes how, in the light of this intentional production of social trauma, can the leading agents of this economic war deploy the language of democracy without that language collapsing into nonsense. Two obvious answers come to mind immediately. The first would be the active forgetting of the West's capacity for destruction through economic stealth, a forgetting for which we can largely thank an increasingly compliant and corporate-friendly media. The second is the idea that the US, Britain and more broadly the West in general continually make the claim to be the sole representatives and guardians of the Good, the consequence of which is that anything the West does can only be for the good in the long run. This ideology of the West, in its representational and normative modes, certainly helps explain the sleight of hand, but to fully understand the nature of economic war and the great illusion currently being worked in Iraq, for example, we have to think through the ontology of this economic war.

In their seminal, but problematic book *Empire* (2000) Michael Hardt and Antonio Negri argue that the current formation of empire does not follow the old model of imperialism in which an occupied territory is subjugated and exploited by a sovereign nation from which the empire takes its name. The current formation of empire has no national centre but is a networked, transnational sovereignty of capital. Through the mechanism of the free market and the culture of consumption ever new populations are drawn into the marketisation of life through which this new empire practises its biopolitics. While this biopolitics functions through the activation and promotion of difference as varying marketing opportunities, the logic of marketization effectively produces "black holes and ontological vacuums in the life of the multitude" (*ibid.*, p. 389). Biopolitics as the disciplining of individuals and cultures according to the logic of consumer culture erases the complexity of the life of the multitude, or rather reduces it to the differences of production and consumption capacities within the capitalist system, creating a variegated pattern of "lifestyles". In this scenario it is easy to understand McMurtry's claim that the new enemy of civilisation is the non-marketised economy (2002, p. 4) that attempts to exempt itself from the flow and the regulation of this networked sovereignty.

With the global expansion of the capitalist system it is not difficult to understand the threat this poses to human biodiversity. Following Giorgio Agamben's (1998) Aristotelian distinction between *zoē*, the bare life common to all living things, and *bios*, the differing forms of planetary life, it is possible to conceive the complexity of human *bios* being gradually superseded by differing patterns of commodity consumption, leaving behind the black holes in the life of the multitude that Hardt and Negri speak of. And yet to argue that empire functions through the production of ontological vacuums is erroneous. It is more the case that empire and the economic war that is its preferred technology (Nancy, 2000), or means of implementation, functions precisely though the establishment of an ontological foundation and not the production of ontological vacuums. An etymology of the word economic will help us address this.

By far the most important word to be worked through is *oikos*, the primary definition of which is a house, abode or dwelling. It also refers to the affairs of a household as well as its property and goods. When situated with the word *nómos*, which in its primary definition means enactment, ordinance, rule or law we have *oikonomia*, that is, the management of a household, from which our common understanding of the word economic is derived. *Oikonomia*, however, also has the additional meaning in Greek of the management of the state. Thus, when thinking about economic war our first definition would be a war that concerns the management of a household, or possibly more importantly for our purposes here, a war regarding the running of a state. It will be important to return to the Greek word for war (*polemos*) in due course in order to complete the ontological picture of economic war, but for now it is necessary to draw out some secondary meanings from the words *oikos* and *nómos*.

A second level of meaning for the word *oikos* can be found in *oikeo*, which is to inhabit or possess, to dwell or to live, and it is here that the ontological dimension of the *oikos* begins to be revealed. The *oikos* is not only a dwelling but a way of dwelling, a manner of being-in-the-world. *Oikeo* also means to be placed or situated, and in this sense its meaning begins to approach that of *nómos*, which apart from meaning law also means anything assigned or apportioned, stemming from *némo*, to deal out, or distribute. This complementarity between *oikos* and *nómos* is even stronger in *nomós* where the changed accent gives us a word signifying a district, department or province. This definition of the word was of great significance to Hannah Arendt who in *The Human Condition* comments that the law was originally identified with a boundary line, a hedge between two allotted pastures, or the wall that indicated where the laws of the city applied, thereby initiating a political community (Arendt, 1958, pp. 63-4). The *nómos* is also, therefore, the separation of the public from the private, and in many respects this remains a cornerstone of liberal thought; the walls of a person's house signifying a qualified personal sovereignty, while the borders of a geopolitical space function in much the same way for the nation. Of course, Arendt's reading of the *nómos* is profoundly influenced by Heidegger who understood the history of Being as varying economies of presence, where the *nómos* of each historical *oikos* governed what was brought into being, be that the actions of politicians, works of art, buildings, institutions, technologies, cosmologies, legislations, rituals, and so on. Here each age is governed by a law that determines the nature of the world. In the age of late capitalism it is the law of surplus value that currently gives shape to our world, for the production of profit is the principle that currently determines what is and what is not legitimate. In "Letter on 'Humanism'" Heidegger writes: "Νόμος is not only law but more originally the assignment contained in the dispensation of being" (1998, p. 274) and it is in this sense that I would like to think of eco-nomics as the shaping of our being-in-the-world.

To say that the manner of our being-in-the-world is contestable, or that it is continually contested, is to say very little. However, if we are to understand the current economic war it is essential to understand the nature of this contest. Therefore, to complete this preliminary round of definitions and interpretations it is important to say something about the Greek word *polemos*. *Polemos* literally means battle or war, but again it is Heidegger who allows us to see the full complexity of this word and its relation to eco-nomics as the law shaping our being-in-the-world. Using Heraclitus, fragment 53, usually translated as "War is father of all, and king of all. He renders some gods, others men; he makes some slaves, others free" (Heraclitus, 1987, p. 37), Heidegger interprets *polemos* not as war as we commonly understand it, but as the struggle that "allows what essentially unfolds to step apart in opposition" (2000, p. 65). *Polemos* is essentially the emergence of differentiated beings, and Heidegger continues by saying that *polemos* is world-forming; *polemos* "first allows position and status and rank to establish themselves in coming to presence. In such stepping apart, clefts, intervals, distances, and joints open themselves up. In confrontation, world comes to be". To stay with the matter at hand and not become too involved in the many questions Heidegger is addressing here, we must remember that it is only human being for whom being is an issue. Human being is not given but is projected as any number of future possibilities; this is the hermeneutics of human freedom appearing in the numerous discourses that respond to the questions "what should I be?" and "how should I live?". In this sense human being is itself a *polemos*; it is a confrontation concerning both the status of itself and its world. We might, as Gregory Fried (2000) has done, call this an "interpretive confrontation" over what we are to make of ourselves and our world. Drawing out one final important meaning of *nómos*, the root *némo* also means to esteem or to give value, allowing us to think of *polemos* as a conflict over the mode of esteeming or valuing (*nómisis*) that determines the structure of our life.

Most relevant to the structuring of contemporary life are the processes of globalisation; and the dyad globalisation/anti-globalisation gives us some sense of this interpretive confrontation over the structure of our world. We could add to this Huntington's thesis of a "clash of civilizations" (1993), but it is the formation and processes known as globalisation that I think are more redolent when considering our context (a civilisational dispute, apart from being absurd, does not get us anywhere near what is at stake today).[2] Despite the complexities of the concept it is possible to draw out four broad themes within the processes of globalisation: the cultural, the technical, the institutional and the economic; all of which contribute to a number of concerns in the field of global governance. Key to such governance as I have discussed above is the economic doctrine known as neo-liberalism stipulating that the market alone can and should organise the production and distribution of goods, and this market should, of course, be unlimited by either the state or the geo-political borders of nations. However, what is most important about neo-liberalism is not its economic principles of "free trade", privatisation and deregulation, although these principles can hardly be called insignificant, but its ontological underpinnings concerning the nature of human being, for these underpinnings are truly *eco-nomic* in the manner I have sought to define the term above. To understand the ontological principles at the heart of neo-liberalism it is helpful to be aware of the neo-classical economic theory that informs neo-liberal doctrine. The three fundamental propositions of neo-classical economic theory are the "consumption proposition", the "production proposition" and the "scarcity proposition". The "consumption proposition" states that "individuals are endowed with the ability to choose rationally from among the sets of opportunities they confront" (DeMartino, 2000, p. 38), with rationality signalling that individuals will decide according to the opportunity affording greatest satisfaction or utility. This is the simple neo-liberal model for the securing of human happiness. Attached to this assumption is the secondary assumption of "insatiability", meaning that we always prefer more satisfaction or "utility" rather than less. The "production proposition" is that whereby "humans are endowed with the ability to transform elements of nature (through work or labor) so as to produce goods that meet human needs, and they do so rationally" (*ibid.*, p. 40). I shall come back to this. The "scarcity proposition" then states that "all output (in the form of goods and services) requires inputs from nature, and since nature's bounty is finite, output must also be finite" (*ibid.*, p. 40). Economics thus becomes the study of rational choice under conditions of insatiability and scarcity, and it is here that the further principle of competition is hidden, both in the philosophical sense of a Hobbesian state of nature, but also in the bureaucratic sense of competition as a mechanism ensuring the most efficient use of resources.

[2] Huntington's thesis plots a chronology of wars between Princes, wars between Peoples, wars between ideologies, and finally (Post-Cold War) wars between civilisations. The fact that he fails to see neo-liberalism as an ideology that does not reduce to a nicely compartmentalised clash of civilisations significantly lessens the usefulness of the thesis.

The importance of the first proposition lies in the belief that choice is exogenous, that is, prior to or external to social activity. In this sense the question of validity does not appear to enter the equation as the expression of choice is the rational expression of an individual's deepest and most authentic personality. In this way, the market, reflecting as it does the complexity of rational choice, is the standard of our true desires. It is this entirely closed logic of essential expression that prevents contestation of the doctrine. Any notion of asymetrical power and the construction of desire are irrelevant here; and as I have already suggested this is not just economical but eco-nomical defining as it does human nature and the rational means for that nature to be most fully expressed. It is the second proposition, however, that is most important for our analysis of eco-nomics. The second proposition claims that people produce goods to meet human needs and they do so rationally. Again it is the rider of rationality that is the key, for in this instance it means the most efficient technique for producing maximum yield. Of particular concern here is the belief that, let us say, land is used only according to the principal of optimal efficiency, but it should be evident to those who have studied the complexities of any given human culture that the use of land is irreducible to purely economic pursuits. Instead innumerable anthropological and sociological studies offer us a plurality of factors that contribute to the use of land, which in turn give shape to the particular character and form of a culture (*bios*). Neo-liberalism is, therefore, the belief that this unfettered market is the best way for any society to organise itself because it is the ultimate expression of this dual rationality, and because principles one and two bracket out anything contextual in the way of social or cultural determinants the market is believed to be universally applicable, only to be resisted by those who are irrational. This in short is the economic war being waged at present. It is an interpretative confrontation over the nature of human being and the world in which we live, manifesting itself in a profound and deliberate biopolitics. It is, in Nietzschean terms, an expression of the will to power; a structure of valuation (*nómisis*) to be universally applied as neo-liberalism seeks to shape the world in its own image. To return briefly to the qualifications made in the introduction with regard to the relationship between neo-liberalism and neo-conservatism it is possible to say that the structure of valuation favoured by neo-conservatives is the creation of the world according to their vision of the global role of the American nation, which includes within it the principles of private enterprise and a free market. Unlike the abstract, universal and bureaucratic doctrine of neo-liberalism, neo-conservatism is a concrete, nationalistic and messianic doctrine. It still promotes the fundamentalist logic of the free market, but this is now something that automatically comes with shaping the world in the image of America. The *nómos* is now a particular form of American freedom.

That this shaping of the world is imperial, I think there can be little doubt. Of course, those who are best served by neo-liberalism and the military solutions of the neo-conservatives (primarily the rich North) will continue to argue that they are only pursuing the interests of humanity

11

as a whole; but this has always been integral to justifications of empire, and in this the third proposition of neo-classical theory, the scarcity proposition, is especially important, because the notion of scarcity lies at the heart of economic and eco-nomic organisation. From the Roman principle of *res nullius* decreeing that any "empty thing" such as unoccupied land was common property and therefore available to be put to use, to the work of William Petty who in 1691 calculated the value of an "improved" Ireland under an English colonial power, the belief that we must do all we can with scarce resources has been the prime mover for justifying imperial expansion. In a compelling history of empire Ellen Meiskins Wood notes how as early as the sixteenth century the judgement concerning the sufficiently fruitful use of land was made according to the standards of English commercial culture (2003, p. 75). The most notable seventeenth century exponent of this thinking is John Locke, who not only justified imperialism through arguments concerning the damaging effect of unused land, but proceeded to argue against land that was not used *well enough*, an argument that supported enclosure at home and the appropriation of land abroad This is most explicitly stated in §37 of *The Second Treatise of Government*. Having already developed Petty's argument concerning the nature of property stemming from the mixing of labour, he now argues that "he who has appropriated land to himself by his labor does not lessen but increase the common stock of mankind" (1952, p. 22). This is because, Locke continues, enclosed land is worth ten times more than land lying in waste, as he puts it.[3] The logic of this position means that the person enclosing ten acres is in effect giving ninety back to mankind. The crime according to Locke is not the enclosure of land, but waste. The person who gathers fruit and other materials, kills or tames animals, has through his labour acquired a property in them, but if these perish while belonging to him he has offended against the law of nature. The same applies to land. If the fruit planted, or the grass sown perishes, "notwithstanding his enclosure", the land is to be looked upon as open to appropriation. For Wood the key to this justification comes in §40 where Locke stipulates that it is not just labour that produces property but the fact that labour "put[s] the difference of value on everything" (*ibid.*, p. 24). This is a very good example of the eco-nomic war that I am talking about.

This argument concerning the value of land, measured according to the method of enclosure, is the means by which Locke justified the theft of land from the American Indians and the devastation of their culture. The dismissal, or rather the failure to see let alone recognise the manner in which the American Indians attributed value to the land and

---

[3] Locke actually goes on to say that he has "rated the improved land very low in making its product but as ten to one, when it is much nearer a hundred to one; for I ask whether in the wild woods and uncultivated waste of America, left to nature, without any improvement, tillage, or husbandry, a thousand acres yield the needy and the wretched inhabitants as many conveniences of life as ten acres of equally fertile land do in Devonshire, where they are cultivated well" (1952, p. 23).

the place of that land within their world is what Jean-François Lyotard (1988) would have called a differend. It would also be the site of an injustice given that an alien rule of judgment was applied to a way of life incommensurate to that of seventeenth century England. From this point on the value of land was to be judged according to the primacy of *exchange* value (Wood, 2003, p. 97). This same logic of a universal programme being to the benefit of mankind still drives the supposed legitimacy of current global economic practices. The dereliction of local populations and the attack on local cultural practices is still said to be a good; and to return briefly to our three terms, remembering that *nómos* signifies allotment, or in Locke's terms enclosure, we ought to understand the economic war and neo-liberal *oikonomia* as the reduction of the multiplicity of human life forms or cultures, that is, ways of being-in-the-world, to interchangeable components in the global market, and all in the name of rational efficiency. Only now the new method of imperial enclosure is the law (*nómos*) of privatiation and deregulation where public goods, resources and services are appropriated from developing nations through directives set by the WTO and the IMF, precisely the situation that occurred in Yugoslavia and is currently taking place in Iraq.

Despite the belligerence of the neo-conservatives, however, it is important to understand that despite the global military presence of the United States military this does not mean that the economic war and the empire it is forming is an American empire, but this also does not mean that, returning to Hardt and Negri's thesis, the new empire is 'smooth' or without a centre (or what I would prefer to call a centring effect). In terms of global governance we need to think of the current formation of power in terms of transnational realism, that is, thinking the formation of power in terms of transnational actors such as corporations and institutions including the World Bank, the WTO, Davos, etc., but also in terms of the continuing role of the nation state, which the transnationalization of governance was supposed to have superseded. Many theorists including Wood (2003), Wallerstein (1999) and Reinicke (1989), to name only a few, have argued that the nation state remains an important player in this new empire, and that the new imperialism can only be sustained through a network of nation states rather than the total dominance of one

In light of this Leslie Sklair (2001) has argued that global governance is orchestrated by a transnational capitalist class (TTC) comprising the corporate elites of many nations, as well as what he calls the technopols; the politicians, civil servants and bureaucrats who govern and manage their own national economies in the interest of transnational capital. I would add, however, that this class is not equal, and itself comprises a structure of dominance with the US in ascendancy. That the US is hegemonic is not in question, and the anabolic militarism of the neo-conservatives indicates that realism still has a place in the international order. However, for many the question is for how long the US will maintain its dominance and to what extent it is prepared to defend its interests as the dominant agent in the TCC. At present the US can manage the economic war in its own interests and the emergence of neo-conservatism is an attempt to assure America's continuing dominance within the network. The *nómos* of marketisation favours many in the rich North, in particular the US, but David Harvey (2003), for example, has recently argued that US hegemony is about to be challenged by China. The opening up of China means that the Chinese elite, like the elite of the newly "liberated" Iraq, are set to join the transnational capitalist class,[4] indeed are set to become the lead nation in that class as a rapidly growing China becomes what Harvey calls a "spatio-temporal fix" for overaccumulated capital (*ibid.*, p. 122). If there is to be a massive redirection of investment from the US to China as Harvey's analysis suggests it would bring about the kind of structural adjustment in the US currently enforced on lesser nations in the economic war and would bring about the sort of austerity not seen in the US since the Great Depression (*ibid.*, p. 208). The question then becomes whether or not the US will quietly relinquish its position as leading agent in the TCC and governor of the economic war. The foreign policy of the neo-conservatives would suggest not. In this analysis the recent wars in Afghanistan and Iraq can be put down to this threatened shift in hegemony and the threatened loss of control over the resources produced in the ongoing economic war. Neo-conservatives simply want to maintain US proximity to and identification with the new sovereignty of capital. This is quite different from an argument that we are witnessing the birth of a purely American empire.

Iraq, of course, has been the latest country to be liberated/liberalised even though the liberalisation has happened at a much faster pace than the liberation, but this is the point. According to Bush and Blair, despite the daily evidence to the contrary, we are now moving towards a peaceful and democratic post-conflict Iraq. Despite being deeply opposed to the invasion I remain confident that Iraq will, at some point, become more stable and will have all the trappings of a formal democracy. This is largely down to the stoicism and reasonableness of the Iraqis rather than anything the US and the UK have done, a reasonableness that is a great antidote to the West's preferred image of "mad mullahs" and "irrational Arabs". But it will only ever be a formal democracy because it has already been decided that the Iraqis will have no control over their economy. Prior to holding elections Iraq was given observer status at the WTO on 11 February 2004, which preceded the marketisation of Iraq's economy prior to the so-called "transfer of power" in June of that year. This process of marketisation prior to the establishment of elections was detailed in what came to be known as Paul Bremer's "100 orders", orders that were later written into the Iraqi constitution. In the *Los Angeles Times*, of 5 August 2004 Antonia Juhasz offered edited highlights of these orders:

Order No. 39 allows for: (1) privatization of Iraq's 200 state-owned enterprises; (2) 100% foreign ownership of Iraqi businesses; (3) "national treatment" — which means no preferences for local over foreign businesses; (4) unrestricted, tax-free remittance of all profits

---

[4] This argument regarding China and the TCC is not supported by Sklair.

and other funds; and (5) 40-year ownership licenses. Thus, it forbids Iraqis from receiving preference in the reconstruction while allowing foreign corporations — Halliburton and Bechtel, for example — to buy up Iraqi businesses, do all of the work and send all of their money home. They cannot be required to hire Iraqis or to reinvest their money in the Iraqi economy. They can take out their investments at any time and in any amount. Orders No. 57 and No. 77 ensure the implementation of the orders by placing U.S.-appointed auditors and inspector generals in every government ministry, with five-year terms and with sweeping authority over contracts, programs, employees and regulations. Order No. 17 grants foreign contractors, including private security firms, full immunity from Iraq's laws. Even if they, say, kill someone or cause an environmental disaster, the injured party cannot turn to the Iraqi legal system. Rather, the charges must be brought to U.S. courts. Order No. 40 allows foreign banks to purchase up to 50% of Iraqi banks. Order No. 49 drops the tax rate on corporations from a high of 40% to a flat 15%. The income tax rate is also capped at 15%. Order No. 12 (renewed on Feb. 24) suspends "all tariffs, customs duties, import taxes, licensing fees and similar surcharges for goods entering or leaving Iraq". This led to an immediate and dramatic inflow of cheap foreign consumer products — devastating local producers and sellers who were thoroughly unprepared to meet the challenge of their mammoth global competitors. Clearly, the Bremer orders fundamentally altered Iraq's existing laws. For this reason, they are also illegal. Transformation of an occupied country's laws violates the Hague regulations of 1907 (ratified by the United States) and the U.S. Army's Law of Land Warfare. Indeed, in a leaked memo, the British attorney general, Lord Goldsmith, warned Prime Minister Tony Blair that "major structural economic reforms would not be authorized by international law".

We should also add to this list order 81, a very important order pertaining to the patenting and intellectual property on seeds that shifts the agricultural balance of power away from Iraq's farmers and towards multinationals such as Monsanto who can attain a near monopoly on seed production. According to this order it is illegal for Iraqi farmers to save seed from "new varieties" with which the market will no doubt be flooded.[5]

It must surely be self-evident that having marketised a nation's economy prior to giving the people of that nation the chance to vote cannot be democratic. In fact it makes the claims for democracy in Iraq patently absurd. We are now in a situation in which control over a nation's economy is deemed to be outside any democratic accountability and yet this externalising of the economy does not in turn lead us to question the validity of the democracy being pursued. The fact that it does not appear self-evident to a host of mainstream political and legal commentators as well as academics who regularly espouse the values of democracy is, I would argue, down to the

---

[5] For an important discussion of the seed war see Vandana Shiva (2003).

establishment of this neo-liberal "common sense" proposing human nature to have been determined and no longer open to question. What I have attempted to argue in this essay is the idea that the invasion of Iraq and its liberalisation is part of a wider economic war that seeks to tie down the definition of what it is to be human to something that completely naturalises the spread of the free market and makes the running of national economies exempt from democratic accountability. Without an understanding of this ontological project it is hard to make sense of this situation, or at least it is hard to understand how Bush and Blair can still speak about democracy, when democracy in any substantial sense, that is, the people ruling in an autonomous fashion over the shaping of their world, is something that has clearly been consigned to the dustbin of history. Democracy in this sense was only ever an idea and was never really actualised not even in the Greek *polis* that supposedly gave birth to it, but as an idea it still regulated modern thought and practice as something we should strive for. Today the empty platitudes of Bush and Blair signal the death knell of democracy. In fact the economic war I have sought to define here is more in keeping with a form of government we would normally refer to as a plutocracy. The plutocrats keep speaking of democracy. It is mentioned in every news bulletin, written about in every newspaper, referred to in every political speech. We hear the word democracy over and over again, but as Theodor Adorno once wryly noted, when something is constantly spoken about it is probably because it is actually disappearing.

References
Agamben, G. (1998) *Homo Sacer: Sovereign Power and Bare Life*, Stanford, Stanford University Press.
Allen, B. (1999) "Why Kosovo? The Anatomy of a Needless War". Canadian Centre for Policy Alternatives. Available online at **www. policyalternatives.ca/**.
Arendt, H. (1958) *The Human Condition*, Chicago, University of Chicago Press.
Bliar, T. (2005) "Doctrine of the International Community", *Neoconservatism*, I. Stelzer (ed.). London, Atlantic Books.
Chussodovsky, M. (1997) *The Globalization of Poverty*, London, Zed Books.
Curtis, N. (2006) *War and Social Theory: World, Value and Identity*, Basingstoke, Palgrave.
DeMartino, G. F. (2000) *Global Economy, Global Justice*, London, Routledge.
Fried, G. (2000) *Heidegger's Polemos*. New Haven and London, Yale University Press.
Hardt, M. and Negri, A. (2000) *Empire*, Cambridge, MA, Harvard University Press.
Heidegger, M. (1998) "Letter on 'Humanism'", *Pathmarks*, Cambridge, Cambridge University Press.
Heidegger, M. (2000) *Introduction to Metaphysics*, New Haven and

London, Yale University Press.

Heraclitus. (1979) *Fragments*, trans. T. M. Robinson, Toronto, University of Toronto Press.

Howard. M. (1986) *War and the Liberal Conscience*, New Brunswick, Rutgers University Press.

Huntington, S. (1993) "The Clash of Civilizations", *Foreign Affairs* 72(3), 22-48.

Joxe, A. (2002) *Empire of Disorder*, New York and Los Angeles, Semiotext(e).

Juhasz, A. (2004) "The Hand-Over that Wasn't", *The Los Angeles Times*, 5 August 2004.

Locke, J. (1952) *Second Treatise of Government*, Indianapolis, Bobbs-Merrill Publishing.

Lyotard, J.-F. (1988) *The Differend: Phrases in Dispute*, Manchester, Manchester University Press.

McMurtry, J. (2002). *Value Wars: The Global Economy versus the Life Economy*, London, Pluto Press.

Nancy, J.-L. (2000) "War, Right, Sovereignty – Technē", *Being Singular Plural*, Stanford, Stanford University Press.

Reinicke, W. H. (1989) *Global Public Policy: Governing without Government?*, Washington, Brookings Institution.

Shiva, V. (2003) "Food Rights, Free Trade, and Fascism", *Globalizing Rights*, M. J. Gibney (ed.). Oxford, Oxford University Press.

Sklair, L. (2001) *The Transnational Capitalist Class*, Oxford, Blackwell.

Wallerstein, I. (1999) *The End of the World as We Know It*, Minneapolis, University of Minnesota Press.

Wood, E. M. (2003) *Empire of Capital*, London, Verso.

Harvey, D. (2003) *The New Imperialism*, Oxford, Oxford University Press.

On the Promotion of Conflicts: The Media and War

Roberto Grandi

The events immediately following the 11 September 2001 incidents and more recent ones – that is to say those arising from the conflict and the interminable post-conflict in Iraq and other conflicts unleashed in their wake – have made the relationship that exists between Media and Conflict the order of the day in politics, in the media itself and in international public opinion. This relationship throws up both invariables and novelties. The latter involve innovations that have been introduced both in the concept of war itself and in the practice of journalism.

Innovations in war. The wars of the last fifteen years, also called "new wars" or "global wars", can be characterised via a number of different models operating within a framework re-defining the international politics of the West. This new framework attributes to military intervention a function of world-wide public order in the name, time and again, of re-establishing international legality, the reaffirming of human rights or a "lasting freedom" and the fight against terrorism. All this has added up to: a new relationship between the military sphere and civil society; a mass entry of electronics and information technology into the strategy of war that underpins the objective of "no-lose-wars"; a dissemination of the fields of battle in space and time; a greater attention being given to the preparation of conflict and the way in which it is carried out.

Innovations in professional journalism. The introduction of new technologies has changed not only the conception of war, but also that of journalists' professionalism, above all in the phase of the war being waged. On the one hand, the potential of satellite groupings, on the other, the emergence of new all-news television channels, first in the West then also from other cultures, has influenced not only the forms that the news takes, but also the very manner in which news is made and consumed. The media and war relations arising from these changes, however, also re-pose old problems.

How can democratic power obtain the consensus of the population on entering into war and maintain it during the conflict? How can the news remain autonomous and independent when governments put at stake national interests and the very security of the nation? What competences are required in order to comprehend phenomena, such as war, that are projected well in advance via sophisticated instruments of marketing (Rutherford, 2004; O'Shaughnessy, 2004) tied to the hiding of certain events and to the construction of news with the sole objective of influencing the agenda of the media and public opinion in order to maintain the consensus for war?

Ever since the Trojan War, whoever is in power and intends to obtain internal assent to a declaration of war seeks and proposes motives that may come to be seen as plausible by the majority. It is however with the development of the means of mass communication that propaganda and the promotion of conflicts refine their techniques of persuasion. War as product is born, usually, out of a preliminary action that, as

18

much as it retains communicative aspects, is about the preparation of public opinion. In this phase, war is above all the fruit of a discursive competition between interested parties to propose publicly a certain image of reality that justifies it; this activity is rapidly borne forward by those specialist competencies that define the field of action of *public relations*.

Staying within the democracies that we might define as western, it is with the Crimean War, mid-way through the nineteenth century, that journalists succeeded, for the first time, thanks to the use of the telegraph, in having their dispatches get to press in real time (Knightley, 1975). It is said that it was with William Russell, correspondent of *The Times*, that the figure of the war correspondent was born. And soon war news was confronted with the need that democratic countries had to maintain a mass consensus for war, also at the cost of censoring and deforming the news. Not only were the telegraph lines put under the control of the military but the journalists themselves, at the front, encountered strong obstacles to news gathering, as well as official boycotts. Nonetheless, the raw reporting of Russell, that brought to light the shortcomings of the British high command, transmitted a sense of horror in the confronting of massacres and the perception that they were heading towards a military disaster, to the extent that a public opinion unfavourable to war grew and, therefore, was dangerous for the government in power. The official reaction to this loss of consensus on the part of public opinion in confronting war develops on more levels, as we shall find to be the case in subsequent wars. To an ulterior layer of censorship is added the accusation of treachery on the part of Russell because, in his reporting, he was revealing invaluable reserved or classified information to the enemy. One month before the end of the war, the British Government put to the hard test the free exercising of the profession of journalism by passing a law that made it obligatory for journalists to be accredited by military authorities. At the same time, the commanders in the field gave out instructions that prohibited, on pain of the expulsion of correspondents, the publication of details that the commanders themselves might regard as "useful to the enemy".

With the Crimean War, too, war photography was born which, because of its origins, is marked by the difficult relations pertaining between power and the media: photography is documentation but is also explicitly propagandistic in nature. The British Government, in fact, in order to furnish a positive representation of the war, already made unpopular by the journalists' reporting, sent to the front the professional photographer Roger Fenton, under orders not to photograph the dead, the mutilated or the wounded and with the explicit objective of providing a softening and positive representation of the war: photographs that show quiet and gentle valleys more appropriate for holiday making than for the waging of bloody armed conflict (Sontag 2003).

By the time of the First World War, journalists enjoyed a certain freedom of access to the battle zones and to contacts with military sources. It is with the First World War that we witness a mass entry of the State into the world of communications that come to be used to create, before the war begins, a public opinion favourable to military intervention and, successively, one that continues to support war. The correspondents are kept at a distance from the battlefields on all fronts. In the belligerent countries, the offices responsible for censorship have tasks that are both administrative and productive, functioning both as a block and a prompt. Still during the First World War, on the entry of the United States in April 1917, the *Committee on Public Information* (CPI) is constituted as an organ for the federal coordinating of the activities of the United States' public in information and persuasion. The CPI was presided over by George Creel, already a consultant in the electoral campaign for the re-election of President Wilson, who defines his own mission very clearly: "To sell the War to the American public". While censorship is applied by the officers on the battlefields in Europe, the Committee in its propaganda activities adopted, at first, sober and restrained tones, preferring publication to suppression, avoiding censorship, exaggerations and manipulations. After a few months, this soft approach changed, leaving space for the appeals of a nationalism that was more noisy and intolerant. In these circumstances are born either the famous "Uncle Sam Needs You" slogan, designed by James Montgomery Flagg, or the depictions of the invading Hun violating helpless women, the image of the Statue of Liberty in flames, the spilling out of the factories of American workers ready to pour their salaries into the helmet of the victorious German foot-soldier (Taylor, 1990). And, in this period, came the thinking up of the *Four Minute Men* (FMM), trained to make speeches, four minutes long, on any subject concerning bellicose force, in the intervals of cinema programmes. On 16 May 1918 the *U.S. Sedition Act* instituted the Act of Insult to the Nation, to the Constitution, to the Armed Forces, to the Flag and to the Uniform: fines and imprisonment awaited authors of disloyal writings in dealings with the Government. The very techniques of public relations and advertising have been, ever since, added to the other ways in which governments and political systems, in the first place, have related to the system of information delivery in order to condition and, sometimes, control – more or less explicitly – whatever journalists report in words and images.

Censorship, techniques of manipulation, deformation and the hiding of information developed in different ways during the Second World War were applied, at the end of that war, to the confrontation between the West and the Communist East, and the Cold War that developed without the presence of war correspondents, because it was waged, in the main, on a level different from that of direct military engagement on the field of battle. But conflicts are never lacking, and what was fought out in Vietnam in the '60s and '70s was particularly significant, because it was, at that time, the first uncensored war, the first televisual war and the first war that, as sustained above all by the more conservative factions, was lost at home, in those living rooms where the citizens of the United States watched the television pictures.

In 1961, the White House spoke of reinforcing South Vietnam against "communist attack": an intervention – it was said – deemed necessary to defend the free world from the grip of a Communist Block that was gaining hold of Asia. Television and the press did not throw into question the legitimacy of the right of the USA to block Communism, so much so that the images and reporting of the operations remained a function of this divisive subject. News in the United States, except for a few rare cases, was allowed to be critical about internal problematic issues but tended to identify *in toto* with the politics of the military and of foreign affairs policy. War correspondents were free to film military action and send back reports without any kind of censorship, though the Pentagon did have its own news centre with daily briefings for the journalists in Saigon (Hallin, 1986).

It was not always possible however to operate visible and significant measures to restrict freedom of information because the First Amendment only allows them in the case of national emergency, not applicable in the case of the Vietnam conflict, because it was never a declared war. As McLuhan (1968) himself has sustained, thanks to the technical progress of television, this first televisual war carried the battle into the home and made the viewer feel like both a participant and a witness. Some of the televisual characteristics that connoted, in the years to follow, the journalists' reporting of the war were already present in the correspondence from Vietnam: simplifications, represented through the continual reporting of the counter-balance heroes (our men) / anti-heroes (the Reds) and personifications, giving a face, a voice, a story to "our heroes". Television becomes, for the first time, the principal source of information for the majority of the citizens (Arlen, 1982).

The situation that the Pentagon continued to describe, as if it were on the eve of victory, precipitated in February 1968 the US Tet offensive: on all three TV networks images appeared of a group of North Vietnamese who got in, for a short time, to the US Embassy compound in Saigon (Braestrup, 1977). This incursion opened a significant lasting breach in the world of news delivery between the Pentagon and American public opinion, even if it did not provoke the reactions of disillusionment that some people, successively, have wanted us to believe. Doubts, if not disillusionment itself, were indeed widespread amongst both the troops so bogged down in war, that they were not in a state to finish it off, and also in the financial, economic and, in part, the political establishment of the country. The scheme of simplifying the representation of the conflict employed up to this point underwent a partial shift: there was an increase in the images of civil victims and destruction of the local infrastructure and doubts began to slip in about the conduct of the conflict (Cumings, 1992; Hammond, 1988).

The war ended when to the doubts of the *establishment* was added the open opposition of a growing number of citizens inside the United States. The humiliation of not succeeding in defeating the enemy, presented as being ideologically and militarily quite inferior, brought the military and the conservative lobbies not to interrogate themselves over the reasons for such failure but rather to attribute the cause of the defect to the freedom of information allowed to the war correspondents. There emerged what is known as the "Vietnam syndrome" that would mark in later years the relations between news and power: news was considered to be an obvious obstacle to the military operations being waged abroad. The lesson of Vietnam has been studied by the major states worldwide as, in fact, have the Falklands-Malvinas war (1982) and the invasion of Grenada (1983) and Panama (1989), remembered as the first invisible wars of the television era. This result has been obtained thanks to accurate control of the flow of information through the selection of news and the imposition of a patriotic mode of describing the events of war. The Thatcher Government, considering that it was facing an invasion of British territory, even though distant from the mother country, held that it was the duty of all UK citizens, including journalists, to join together in order to win a victory in a "just war". The few reporters, strictly selected, and hosted aboard the British fleet, underwent a double censorship: first when they were transmitting their reports and, then, when the reports were received back home (Adams, 1986; Morrison, 1988). The attack on the Caribbean island of Grenada, officially declared to have been launched in order to save US medical students who happened to be on the island at the moment of a "Communist *coup d'etat*", allowed the Pentagon to apply the strategy already used the previous year by the Thatcher Government: the creation of a pool of journalists, of an official accompanying group and the exclusion from the theatre of armed conflict of other journalists because of the excessive risks they would have been deemed to have run. In 1989 "Operation Just Cause", to remove Noriega from the Presidency of Panama, had no journalist as witness, whilst the interest of the mass media was concentrated on the fall of Communist regimes in Europe.

The first real and proper test of the large-scale focus of the new mode of the representation, or of not allowing the representation, of war came with the First Gulf War of 1991, through the application of mechanisms that rendered this war an invisible one thanks to a coordinated strategy, on many more levels, which started that type of news management which has been repeated, with some variations, in later conflicts (Dennis, 1991; Denton, 1993; Bennet and Paletz, 1994). The two levels of *news management* are: censorship of the sources, and the creation of consensus via the production of ready-made news content to be packaged as the journalists' reported facts for the whole world. These two variables are applied in different ways in news management both before the outbreak of conflict and after the declaration of war has been made. News management before the war is the brain-child of President Reagan's strategies of the 1980s, known as the "control of the news by communicating". Michael Deaver, Ronald Reagan's communications consultant, has repeated that, unlike Kissinger, who released information in dribs and drabs, the Reagan administration thought that the media ought to be fed on what came to them from official sources; their consideration being that as the media would write stories daily, the administration would confect information for them on that basis.

The slogan was: "Manipulation by inundation". The campaign to persuade public opinion in favour of the conflict began well before the wars being waged and those involved were themselves initiated by, on the one hand, the great public relations agencies and, on the other hand, the Pentagon and its *Psy Ops*. The marketing of the war becomes, from then on, one of the specialist areas of US marketing in general. During this phase of preparation of the consensus for war, Craig Fuller, who was Bush's political adviser, became head of the Washington office of Hill and Knowlton. Hill and Knowlton, a US public relations agency officially appointed by the Kuwaiti Government, projected the most effective way to convince public opinion, using marketing techniques, of the necessity and justice of the war, departing from the basis of the results of surveys that indicated that the people did not know Kuwait and that they were, in ever-growing numbers, at the end of October 1990, convinced that military involvement would be a mistake. The methodology used was the traditional one: via *focus groups*, for example, it was recounted that the designation of Saddam Hussein as a new Hitler was the representation that obtained the most indignant reactions. This "manipulation by inundation" through piloted news, manipulated and false, had two objectives: to hide and make the media forget the proofs of the good relations with Saddam Hussein previously maintained by the US and other western governments; to show the democratic nature – improbable – of the Kuwaiti regime; the impracticability of any peaceful solution; the possession of a very significant war capacity on the part of Iraq; the United States as simple executors of the decisions of the UN.

News management before the war obtained the results that the Pentagon expected either because of the professionalism and financial means it used to confect the news or because of the collaboration, often culpable and knowing, of the whole US journalist cohort and of that of the great majority of allied countries. Not by chance, at the end of the conflict, just as has happened at the end of those that followed, the most authoritative US newspapers profess their guilt. In the *New York Times*, Norman Solomon reminds us that "It was above all in the phase preceding the hostilities that the American press abdicated its role". According to reliable calculations, for example, the citations of the *New York Times* in the period prior to the hostilities derived 79% from government sources and only 1.1% from sources hostile to the politics of the Pentagon. Once internal consensus had been obtained in favour of the war, the most significant part of news management was that which arose at the front after the start of the armed conflict on 16 January 1991 (Fialka, 1992; Jeffords and Rabinovitz, 1994).

The "mother of all battles" soon became, via the media system, the "mother of all frauds". The Joint Information Bureau (JIB) in Dhahran, inaugurated in August 1990 during the first US contingents' setting up in the desert, functioned as an enormous control structure for all news through censorship and disinformation, managing to impede any free initiative on the part of the press. Of the 1200 correspondents lodged in military bases in Saudi Arabia, about twenty were chosen daily to receive the news from the Pentagon. All the accredited correspondents associated with the *Joint Information Bureau* in Dhahran, the command HQ of the allied forces, were obliged to sign a document in which they committed themselves to respect certain conditions, on pain of having their accreditation withdrawn. The Pentagon requested all of them to subscribe to security screening of articles: no journalist could supply logistical details on operations and on the make up of troops; none could transmit reports of the arrangements in the front line; the pre-selected ones could go to the front only with a military escort and could not photograph or film the dead and wounded, supply data on allied losses, name the bases that missions set off from, or interview the military without official permission (Mac Arthur, 1992; Taylor, 1992; Kennedy, 1993).

Considering however that the media of the whole world needed news and images, an approach was opted for that was the opposite of that adopted by Thatcher in 1982: the saturation of all channels, of news and news images, giving rise to a kind of "information glut" or "collective intoxication". The great majority of journalists who were not included in the combat pool, or were not admitted to briefings, legitimated the news confected by the Pentagon insofar as, because they could not witness any battlefield action or put any questions, they sent their "war correspondent" reports from next to the swimming pool of the press centre in Riyadh or from the poolside of the Dhahran International Hotel.

The images of this conflict are packed with close-ups and interviews with the military in the absence of long shots and pictures of the wounded or dead. The unfolding of, in the main, aerial shots of the allied conflict, furnish representations, given that they are done by videographic specialists, of a technological and surgical war with targets always hit and collateral damage light. The same acronyms used by the Pentagon in press conferences accentuate the unreal, or rather surreal, character of the discursiveness of the conflict via *warspeak,* the language of war: KIA (killed in action), MIA (missing in action), collateral damage, softening up, intended as the weakening of the adversary with bombings on tap (Kellner, 1992; Mowlana, Gerbner and Schiller, 1992; Smith, 1992).

A different and important source of news in the story of war journalism is represented by three reporters, amongst whom is Peter Arnett, of CNN, who continued to transmit from Baghdad the news that the Iraqi Government allowed to circulate. These services were accompanied by the words "passed by the censor". The visual memory of the First Gulf War is thus tied to the images, also surreal, of a CNN camera that shows from the roof of a Baghdad inn the greenish night crossed by missiles of the Iraqi anti-air defences and the distant dazzling flash, lit up by the missiles of the attackers that were falling amongst the houses of the city. CNN gains legitimacy as a source of reliable journalism, also legitimising the non-stop format with its voracious hunger for images to transmit in an uninterrupted flow. This method of news projection will influence, too, other networks (Arnett, 1994; Gilboa, 2005).

The principal characteristic of what we can define as the first televisual war, even though it looked increasingly like a radio with pictures, is the conjunction achieved, from the point of view of the

Pentagon, between iron censorship and a flood of images. The relation between media and military institutions has given place to a news coverage well represented by the title of an article by Robert Fisk of 4 February 1991 in *The Independent*: "Free to report what we are told". The conflicts that took place in the Balkans, in particular what has become known as the Kosovo War, present a number of interesting aspects from the point of view of news management and of the television experience being re-channelled as *war television*, later perfected during the wars in Afghanistan and in Iraq. An aspect of continuity with the First Gulf War is that of the demonising of the enemy: also the Serb leader Milošević is compared with Hitler. The first novelty concerns the common awareness, on the part of both, of the strategic relevance of communications and propaganda: each image of "collateral damage" caused by NATO bombs put on the air by the Serb media was followed by pictures of common graves or ethnic massacres shown by the allies (Brown, 2002). This ping-pong of horror occurs in the context of the second characteristic of novelty in this conflict: the relevance, in the reporting of war, of the role played by the emotions: a functional role, above all, at the cornerstones of the "Humanitarian War" in which NATO had inscribed the conflict (Carruthers, 2000). This narrative recourse to pathos served, on the one hand, to dissipate any moral doubts about the reasons for intervening and, on the other, to avoid the progressive deadening of the televiewer's sensitivity to a conflict that in reality had become hardly visible and had not itself offered many elements of pure spectacle (Clark, 2002; Halbestram, 2001).

The recent paradigm of humanitarian war, founded on the relevance of sentiment that is turned into denunciation and indignation, finds its correspondence in the posture adopted by the vast majority of European media in support of the thesis of "just war" without the problem of going deeper into, eventually, the subject of justice and the pertinence between the results of what you want and the means used to get it (Berkowitz, 2003). Both the ideology of "no loss" war (for the attacker) and the propaganda about the capacity of missiles and bombs "intelligent" enough to cause only a few victims ("collateral damage") in the civil population, born in the Iraq war and formalised in the RMA (*Revolution in Military Affairs*) that makes electronics and informatics the principal weapons in American military superiority (Joxe, 2002), reach their apogée in the Kosovo War of 1999. The attack of the NATO coalition did not bring a single loss amongst the attackers but there were a few hundred (in fact, possibly several thousand) victims, above all, civilians, amongst the Serbs.

The war in Afghanistan perfected the model of news management that had been imposed in the First Gulf War (van Ginneken, 2003, 2007; Wright, 2006; Woods, 2007) by virtue of the consequences deriving from the destruction of the Twin Towers of 11 September 2001. Bush responded to the destruction with the speech to Congress of 20 September, nine days after the attack. It is a question of a response first of all on a symbolic and emotive level to the attack of 11 September defined, by Bush himself, as "an act of war against our country". The attack is against progress, pluralism, tolerance, liberty, in a word, a fierce attack by barbarians against civilisation. The response of the West, guided by the United States, will not be limited to a series of punitive operations or a pitched battle, but will require a "prolonged campaign", that will need to be extended to various theatres of operation and protracted possibly "even down to the last terrorist group, on a global scale, to be discovered, stopped and destroyed". In this contest Bush insists with force and conviction that the journalists adhere to the defence of the US mission of total war on terrorism, strengthened by evidence, shown by polls, of a public opinion disposed completely to eliminate bin Laden.

Since certain key points of reference, such as the *New York Times* and the *Washington Post* and the TV networks, insisted on the non-contradiction between patriotism and journalistic professionalism and on the competence of journalists to contextualise the news correctly, a climate of self-censorship imposed itself as a pattern on the majority of the media, influenced, too, by the result of the survey to which they themselves had given such great importance (Greenber, 2002; Zeliter and Allan, 2002; Jamieson and Waldman, 2003). To undertake the phase of preparation of public opinion in favour of war, along with appeals to patriotism and the request not to retransmit communiqués and videocassettes of the terrorists, the *Office of Strategic Influence* was set up as part of the US Defense Department with the objective of controlling and coordinating the news produced by the media. Even though, too, the office was closed down after strong criticism, the strategic choice and the financing given to it have been maintained. War news, but also all political communications, of the post-11 September era are caught between the right to information, on the one hand, and the right to protect national security on the other.

In the phase of the war's being waged, the censoring of news in the field is facilitated by the veto on access to the Taliban regime imposed on the journalists who therefore remained and broadcasted camped out in the nation states adjoining Afghanistan. The only voice from the inside was the *Al Jazeera* News which, in conditions of limited freedom as had happened to CNN in Baghdad, sent its news via its own correspondents in Afghanistan with a specific viewpoint and a journalistic approach, giving prominence to packages recorded on the roads of Kabul, showing the sufferings of the population and the damage of the invisible war to everyone else. Al Jazeera transmitted also the appeals of bin Laden that came directly to the station itself but, for that reason, it was accused by the US Government of encouraging anti-American sentiment. On 12 November 2001, the Kabul station was destroyed by a missile launched by a US bomber with the justification that the locale was being used by Al Qaeda terrorists.

The only source of information that, in this conflict, too, tended to satisfy the requests for news and images from journalists from all over the world, was the daily Pentagon briefing and the TV appearances, also daily, of the US political and military leadership: the rhetoric of intelligent bombs that avoided collateral damage and trust in the efficiency of the operations were the leitmotif of everything that was shown.

Despite the fact that the Afghan war was transmitted live, it remains the war that no-one has seen. Even today there has been no credible information as to the number of victims or as to events on the ground and Afghanistan, by dint of continuing to be presided over by foreign troops and being the theatre of deadly armed actions, remains in that part of the world unknown to the media. The Gulf War of 2003 will go down as an important case study in the techniques of the marketing of war used in the pre-war phase. The mechanism through which "wars are sold" is simple and banal in the description of its different phases: construct and then reinforce a sensation of generalised fear; induce, exploiting the fear of terrorist attack, an increase in the proper desire for security with a view to having it reach a level at which strong security measures, perhaps extreme ones, can be imposed even at the cost of the loss of individual freedom, are enforceable; create states of paranoia with a view to creating an acceptance, as generalised as possible, of the idea that only a preventative war can eliminate the danger (O'Shaughnessy, 2004). A potential threat to US security would justify, in this way, in the name of *national security*, a preventative armed intervention with a view to avoiding that threat's being realised. It is clear that in order to ensure that this version be effective it is necessary, in the first place, that the agenda of the mass media and their visions of events coincide as far as possible with the government view, which means thinking up and projecting a continuous and incisive campaign for the consumption of the newspapers and TV channels.

The motivations for the war that the US Government wished to impose on the agenda of the media and therefore public opinion, are: the presence, in Iraq, of arms of mass destruction; dealings, of Nigerian origin, in enriched uranium; the existence of a direct link between Osama bin Laden and Saddam Hussein. These motivations, not demonstrated at the time and successively revealed as false, have become part of the media system, so much so that the link between terrorism, arms of mass destruction and Saddam Hussein has modelled the frame of debate on preventative war, about which no doubt was raised on the part of US news and TV sources towards the end of the summer of 2003, when the most authoritative US newspapers began, as had happened in previous conflicts, to throw into question the truth of the news provided, and apologise to their readers for misleading them.

The technique through which the government achieves adhesion to its own views was also served by leaks on the part of sources said to be authoritative and anonymous which, months later, were revealed as deriving from counterespionage. The most famous victim of these disinformation operations, which ultimately damaged the most prestigious newspapers (therefore the most influential on international public opinion) was Judith Miller, lead journalist of *The New York Times* with direct access to sources at the heart of government, who had legitimated, with her own signature, the conclusions of the Bush administration on the Weapons of Mass Destruction (WMD) programmes of Iraq. After having spent 85 days in prison for having refused to testify to a Federal Grand Jury on her own (leaked) source, on 9 November 2005, she announced her resignation from *The New York Times* at the same time as word got out as to the nature of her sources on WMD: the CIA.

The Second Gulf War, launched one and a half hours after the passing of the ultimatum, took place, whether in the air or on the ground, according to a model of conflict that ought to have lasted for a short time in order not to upset international public opinion and let President Bush negotiate peace. The conflict on the ground did not develop as the US strategists had expected, to such an extent that it passed through at least three phases in a crescendo of protests on the part of troops over both means of support and organisation which was judged to be inadequate. In any case, May 2003 arrived and, from the deck of an aircraft carrier, George W. Bush declared to the world "Mission accomplished". In effect, after some initial delay and several thousand civilian victims, Baghdad was taken at the cost of 150 allied lives, and even though the declared objectives had not been met. These were not so much the discovery of arms of mass destruction or enriched uranium that the US high-command knew not to exist, but the objectives that had been firmed up during the course of the war: the capture of Saddam, the suppression of terrorism, and the creation of appropriate conditions for a transition to democracy.

Over and above the bellicosity and the statements on "persuasive" force of the White House and the weak autonomy of the media system, what renders this war original in respect of precedents is the extremely high number of journalists that took part, at least 3000, and the range of categories of journalism involved. Considering the dislocation on the battlefield, we can distinguish the reporters as "embedded", "unilateral", on the "battlefield" and "based in Baghdad". The "embedded" journalists can, in the opinion of the vice-secretary of Defense, Victoria Clarke, who, at the time of the First Gulf War worked at Hill and Knowlton, permit an "effective cover" of the conflict. The "war as it is in reality": this is the leitmotif of the most successful public relations campaign success of the Pentagon of the last few years (Rutherford, 2004).

Incorporated into military units, dressed as the military, under the command of the military, guided by the military, the 600 embedded journalists have reported according to the criteria of professionalism that can be maintained in these cases of strong physical and psychological contiguity with one of the parties in conflict. The intention of the Pentagon was no doubt to guarantee maximum coverage of military operations, not to guarantee the fullest and most complete information. The unilateral journalists are those present at the front who are not incorporated into the military unit: they have risked a lot to provide images and news not controlled by the military powers, important documentation that lacks, of necessity, a vision of the ensemble. Finally, a hundred or so journalists remaining in Baghdad: they reported on the war from inside the city both early after the taking of it, controlled by the censorship of the Iraqi regime, and successively with the limitations and risks that all this brings.

From the point of view of the relationship with the newspapers and TV channels it is possible to distinguish between the press or TV and freelance agencies, the the income of which derives from the sale to press agencies of news headlines, photographs, film footage that the official newspapers did not already have. This search for diversity increases the risk run by those journalists. Even greater risks are run by the fixers, a journalistic role not new, but that has grown in recent wars in proportion to the high number of correspondents following them. The fixers are persons who help foreign correspondents, above all in dangerous situations such as in the war zones, resolving problems of a practical type which journalists' activity involves. In the majority of cases they are local journalists who perform various tasks: from contact with sources to the description of the context, from translation to accompanying foreign journalists on the field of conflict. To the risks similar to those run by the foreign correspondent that they accompany are added those deriving from the hostility that their working for the foreign media inspires in the local populations and local governments.

Two other new elements: the first is the mass and significant presence of the Arab news agencies, of both written press and television, whose news reports have been taken up too by other newspapers, definitively legitimating the authoritative role of news in Arabic; the second is the internet blog, written by journalists or by other witnesses, that provide information not subjected to any control, the reliability of which it is however difficult to verify. It is not perhaps accidental that the Second Gulf War has been, at the same time, the war with the greatest number of news sources and with the greatest number of reporters killed in action. The newspapers and TV channels have assumed a role sometimes of mediation, sometimes of true and proper political reporting in reference to single facts, like kidnappings: from media that represent events to subjects that directly promote events. The other characteristic to underline is the fact that journalists witnessing the events – therefore in some way tolerated by different parties in the conflict – have become objects of exchange in the practice of kidnappings (Lynch, 2006; Miles, 2005).

Today more than yesterday news reporting of conflicts is considered strategic by all parties involved who, knowing well the logic of the media, tend to use it to their own ends. It is sufficient to recall how much of an emblematic case the 11 September attack has been constructed as, since with the techniques of media event construction it has attained a high level of trans-national news-worthiness. The eighteen minutes between the collapse of the first Tower and the crashing of the second aeroplane into the other Tower were sufficient for the various TV stations to fix onto the images of the Towers and thus to capture directly the second explosion, as occurred in the TV stations in the taking up of media events programmed in advance. If, for some, there is the wish that the conflict be interpreted as an action to promote and expand democracy, at the same time, for others, it bears messages that tend to interpret this action as a new crusade against the Islamic world. The conflict is also a conflict about the significance to be attributed to events: deciding, for example, which of the concerned parties is "the barbarian", "the oppressed" or "the oppressor", surely influences the sentiments that international public opinion has in confronting the conflict itself. The possibilities offered by the new technologies, amongst which satellite telephones available to correspondents, and the influence of the means of mass communication are relevant in this fight to the death for control of the significance to be attributed to events. And the journalists are torn between the professional duty to report reality and the attempt to achieve the minimal conditions to be able to realise this task with calm, credibility and authority.

These are the themes that we are currently faced with in the transition from wars characterised as a territory to be conquered or defended and from contenders defined and recognisable as being in de-territorialised wars in which the terrain of conflict is everywhere: they are wars with a beginning but for which it is impossible to indicate a certain end, because the final moment is situated in an indeterminate future.

© Translation by Bernard McGuirk

References
Adams, V. (1986) *The Media and the Falklands Campaign*, Basingstoke, Macmillan.
Arlen, M. J. (1982) *Living-room War*, New York, Penguin Books.
Arnett, P. (1994) *Live From The Battlefield: From Vietnam to Baghdad: 35 Years in the World's War Zones*, New York, Simon and Schuster.
Bennett, W. L, and D L. Paletz, editors (1994) *Taken By Storm: The Media, Public Opinion, and US Foreign Policy in the Gulf War*, Chicago: University of Chicago Press.
Berkowitz, B. D. (2003) *The New Face of War: How war will be fought in the 21st century*, New York, The Free Press.
Braestrup, P. (1977) *Big Story: How the American Press and Television Reported and Interpreted the Crisis of Tet 1968 in Vietnam and Washington*, Boulder, Colorado, Westview Press.
Brown, R. (2002) *Clausewitz in the Age of Al-Jazeera: Rethinking the Military-Media Relationship* (paper prepared for the Shorenstein Center/APSA Political Communication Division Workshop, August) Available online at **http: //www.tamilnation.org/media/brown. pdf**.
Carruthers, S. L. (2000) *The media at war*, Basingstoke, Macmillan.
Clark, W. K. (2002) *Waging Modern War: Bosnia, Kosovo, and the Future of Combat*, Public Affairs: New York.
Cumings, B. (1992) *War and Television*, London and New York, Verso.
Dennis, E. E. with others (1991) *The Media at War: The Press and the Persian Gulf Conflict: A Report of The Gannett Foundation*, New York, Gannett Foundation Media Center.
Denton, R. E., Jr., editor (1993) *The Media and the Persian Gulf War*, Westport, Connecticut, Praeger.
Fialka, J. J. (1992) *Hotel Warriors: Covering the Gulf War,* Washington,

D.C., Woodrow Wilson Center Press.

Gilboa, E. (1998) "Media Diplomacy. Conceptual Divergence and Application", *The Harvard International Journal of Press/Politics*, vol. 3, no. 3, pp. 56-75.

Gilboa, E. (2000). "Mass communication and diplomacy: A theoretical framework", *Communication Theory*, 10 (3), pp. 275-309.

Gilboa, E. ed. (2002) *Media and conflict: Framing issues, making policy, shaping opinions*, New York: Transnational Publishers.

Gilboa, E. (2005) "The CNN Effect: The Search for a Communication Theory of International Relations" *Political Communication* 22, pp. 27-44.

Greenber, B. ed. (2002) *Communication and terrorism: Public and Media Responses to 9/11*, Cresskill, Hampton Press.

Halbestram, D. (2001) *War in a Time of Peace, Bush, Clinton and the generals*. New York, Scribner.

Hallin, D. C. (1986) *The "Uncensored War": The Media and Vietnam*, New York, Oxford University Press.

Harris, R. (1983) *Gotcha!: The Media, The Government, and The Falklands Crisis*. London, Faber and Faber.

Hammond, W. M. (1988) *Public Affairs: The Military and the Media, 1962-1968,* Washington, D.C., Center of Military History.

Jamieson, K. and Waldman, P. (2003) *The Press Effect: Politicians, Journalists, and the Stories that Shape the Political World*, Oxford, Oxford University Press.

Jeffords, S. and Rabinovitz, L. (1994) *Seeing Through the Media: The Persian Gulf War,* New Brunswick, New Jersey, Rutgers University Press.

Joxe, A. (2002) *L'empire du chaos*, Paris, La Découverte.

Kellner, D. (1992) *The Persian Gulf TV War*, Boulder, Colorado, Westview Press.

Kennedy, W. V. (1993) *The Military and the Media: Why the Press Cannot Be Trusted to Cover a War,* Westport, Connecticut, Praeger.

Knightley, P. (1975) *The First Casualty: From the Crimea to Vietnam: the war correspondent as hero, propagandist, and myth maker*, San Diego, Harcourt Brace Jovanovich.

Lynch, M. (2006) *Voices of the New Arab Public. Iraq, Al Jazeera, and Middle East Poilitics Today*, New York, Columbia University Press.

Mac Arthur, J. R. (1992) *Second Front: Censorship and Propaganda in the Gulf War,* New York, Hill and Wang.

McLuhan, M. (1968) *War and Peace in the Global Village*, New York, McGraw-Hill.

Miles, H. (2005) *Al Jazeera: . How Arab TV News Challenged the World*, London, Abacus.

Morrison, D. E., and Tumber, H. (1988) *Journalists At War: The Dynamics of News Reporting During The Falklands Conflict*, London, Sage.

Mowlana, H., Gerbner G. and Schiller H.I. (eds.) (1992) *Triumph of the Image: The Media's War in the Persian Gulf: A Global Perspective*, Boulder, Colorado, Westview Press.

O'Shaughnessy, N. (2004) "Weapons of Mass Seduction: Propaganda, Media and the Iraq War", *Journal of Political Marketing* 3, pp. 79-104.

Rutherford, P. (2004) *Weapons of Mass Persuasion: Marketing the War Against Iraq*, Toronto, University of Toronto Press.

Smith, H., editor (1992) *The Media and the Gulf War,* Washington, D.C., Seven Locks Press.

Sontag, S. (2003) *Regarding the Pains of Others*, New York, Farrar, Straus and Giroux.

Taylor, P. M. (1990) *Munitions of the Mind*, Manchester, Manchester University Press.

--------------. (1992) *War and the Media: Propaganda and Persuasion in the Gulf War*, Manchester, Manchester University Press.

Thompson, Mark (1994) *Forging War: The Media in Serbia, Croatia and Bosnia-Hercegovina*, London, Article 19.

Turner, K J. (1985) *Lyndon Johnson's Dual War: Vietnam and the Press*, Chicago, University of Chicago Press.

Van Ginneken, J. (2003) *Collective Behavior and Public Opinion: Rapid Shifts in Opinion and Communication*, Mahwah, N.J., Lawrence Erbaum.

------------------. (2007) "9/11 As a Trigger for Long-Term Shifts in World Public Opinion", *International Communication Gazette* 69 (4), pp. 323-333.

Woods, J. (2007) "What we talk about when we talk about terrorism: elite press coverage of terorism risk from 1997 to 2005", *The Harvard International Journal of Press/Politics*, 12 (3), pp. 3-20.

Wright, C. (2006) "Media representations of 9/11: Constructing the Different Difference", in C. Demaria and C. Wright (eds.), *Post-Conflict Cultures: Rituals of Representation*, London, Zoilus Press.

Zeliter, B. and Allan, S. (2002) *Journalism after September 11*, London, Routledge.

Country Matters?
Denmarked Cartoons: The Terror of the Transcendental

Constance Goh

To address the problematic of fundamentalism, or to explore the conditions that bring about extremism is, importantly, also to express what it means to love and live in a world spurred by power and denunciation. The heart goes out to the moderate Muslims in all parts of the troubled Muslim world who have to deal with the constant fear of harm and death, the economic abjection to which they are subjected and the perpetual confrontation with harsh uncertainties that profoundly unsettle their day-to-day existence. In Michel Foucault's response to the Vietnam War, he says: "The work of an intellectual is not to form the political will of others; it is through the analyses he does in his own domains, to bring assumptions and things taken for granted again into question, to shake habits, ways of acting and thinking, to dispel the familiarity of the accepted, to take the measure of rules and institutions and, starting from the re-problematization (where he plays his specific role as intellectual) to take part in the formation of a political will (where he has his role to play as citizen)" (Foucault, p. xxxiv),. Citing Foucault is a reminder of the value of critical thinking in the rat-race of modernity, a race prompted by the idea of technological progress. Cultural modernity is again at risk because of the emphasis given to practical modernity, a risk manifest in the responses of radical Islam. The fiery eruption of Mount Merapi, a sacred symbol to the Muslims, on 15 May 2006, foreshadows the implosion of the inherent threat of globalisation in contemporary culture (Soetjipto, 2006). And the enormous eruption on 27 May 2006, causing a death toll of four thousand, signals the impending doom that will befall the world because of the mounting strife between the West and the Middle East. Muslim extremism resurges as a manifestation of the dialectics of totality; there is an implicit complicity between the United States' global control and its counterpart, the Muslim fundamentalist resistance. Even if there really is no option between the two locations, radical Islam and the superpower status of the United States, I shall nevertheless, and as a consequence, address the problem from a third location: one that is an in-between position.

With the ever-expanding networks of wireless communication and information access in the global era, political concepts successfully implemented and concretised more rapidly achieve a world influence. If fundamentalist Islam is fascistic, liberal democracy can be said to harbour comparable domineering tendencies. My critique will expose the imbroglios and address the problems arising from economic and political imperialism in postmodernity and taking the different forms of global dominance. The focus on form will show up the contradiction in this power struggle whereby the opposing sides are really not that different from each other, both activating the deceptive ideological support of the big Other. More precisely, the horizontal tropological design of this paper, a swarm-like figure, reflects the contemporary modes of war, advocating the revolutionary possibilities of the displacing act. Displacement, defined synonymously as "fracture", "exclusion", "dynamism", "transfer" and "(r)evolution", is the machinating fulcrum of this mediation, hinging on the disfiguration of the institutional form. The Muslims' staging of violence, read as substitution and simulation, can be addressed, first, by isolating the form in which it appears and, then, with formal manipulation, a tactical intervention on my part, opening up the broader issues of violence and terror. I shall argue that aesthetics, an indicator of what precedes form, provides avenues to the crises of terror in fundamentalism, problems ontologised by the enactment of radical violence. Disclosure, perceived in and through aesthetics as representation, opens up a space for a critical response to the crisis. Islamic terror may be read as a manic attempt to prevent the hijacking of the letter, the power endowed by radical Islamic Law or *sharia*. But aesthetics, when used to interrupt the circular transmission of Islamic extremism, proposes a journey with style and a return of the message to the senders, the terrorists, in subverted forms. Arrivals are always already delayed because of the possibilities given to interventions. Even *sharia* cannot obstruct the interceptions that suspend its auto-affective path. The use of physical violence, in response to the publication of some cartoons, gestures to the pathogenic core of militant Islam, concealed by the fiction of a redemptive future, afflicting the present with gaping wounds of terror.

Violent protests began approximately four months after *Jyllands-Posten*, a conservative Danish newspaper, notorious for its caricatures of religious figures and popular icons, printed controversial cartoons on 30 September 2005, commissioned by its cultural editor, Flemming Rose, after having heard that the Danish writer, Kare Bluitgen, had failed to get illustrators to contribute to his children's book on Prophet Muhammad. The Danish cartoonists refused to participate in Bluitgen's project because they were afraid of attacks from Islamic radicals. Rose contacted forty illustrators, of whom only twelve responded by sending caricatures of the prophet. These were published alongside an article written by him on freedom of expression and self-censorship. The Danish radical Muslims, inflamed by the caricatures, decided to compile a dossier designed to spark off a reaction from the Islamic world. The dossier contained three pieces of misinformation: the first refers to the impropriety of the Danish government in its dealings with the Muslims, citing the difficulties encountered when trying to build mosques in Denmark; the second accuses the Danish of being religiously irresponsible, pointing to their secularised lifestyles; thirdly, the twelve cartoons were said to be used for the promotion of a book that supposedly contained the caricatures (Howden, 2006). In addition to the misinformation, three other pictorials were included, one of which depicts a bearded contestant wearing the mask of a pig intended for a pig-squealing competition (Reynolds, 2006). With the dossier, a Danish Muslim cleric went to the Middle East, hoping to stir up trouble between Muslim nations and the West. The intentional addition of misinformation renders the violent reactions of the Muslim radicals suspect because the portfolio is orchestrated to achieve an end that is other than that of religious dignity.

The Danish-Muslim confrontation is predicated on the clash of ideas. Aiming at the hegemony of the transcendental, the Danish cartoonists were not attacking Islam but the fundamentalism of radical Muslims. The Muslim extremists, fuelled by the satirical representations of the Prophet Muhammad, retaliated by unleashing their fury upon institutions emblematic of Western liberal democracy. The violent occurrences started on 5 February 2006 in Afghanistan and, then, within days, spread to Lebanon, Pakistan, Egypt, Syria, Libya and Nigeria. Not only have did the Muslim fundamentalists vent their wrath at the disregard for their beliefs by rioting in front of European embassies and vandalising them, torching churches in northern Nigeria, demonstrating against Western cultural symbols such as fast-food restaurants, banks, movie-theatres and the offices of a telecommunication company, boycotting Danish and other European products and trampling on European flags, but non-Muslims in these Islamic countries also became targets of aggression (Belien, 2006; Plummer, 2006). The eruptions of violence had, by some estimates, caused the deaths of approximately 285 people and injured 823 by 22 March 2006; the numbers include both the Muslim protestors and bystanders.

Stuart Hall, in an interview, refers to the "revenge of culture" (Taylor, 2006), an appropriate remark on the issue of fundamentalism in postmodernity. Islamic fundamentalism has been problematically labelled a perversion of modernity, which is confluent with my assertion that it arises as a distortion of Western postmodern culture. In a three part documentary called "Reign of Terror", televised by Singapore's *Channel News Asia*, the second part is entitled "Al-Qaeda Calling", a play on the terror group's use of the mobile phone as the detonating device. In view of my argument, the second episode might be re-entitled "Al-Qaeda Returning the Call"; the mobile phone as the symbol of Al-Qaeda's subversive use of Western technology to mobilise its followers to suicide bombings is an example of Derrida's *iterability*, a repetition-in-difference. These vengeful acts have forced the West to reconsider its analytical approach toward the Muslim world. According to Hall, the folly of the West arose from "the failure to deal with race" at the heart of the Western Enlightenment (Taylor, 2006). Islam has never been through Enlightenment. Rationality to most observant Muslims is not and cannot be the same logicality of Western thought by virtue of the fact that they have been guided always by Islamic Law. Second- and Third-World Muslim countries have found adaptation to modern economics difficult and this inability to fit into liberal capitalism, the hallmark of developed democracies, based on principles of logic, is evident with the underdeveloped or still developing status of the Islamic nations. The politicisation of Islam in the 1980s, a consequence of the manipulation of the "language of Islamism" by Middle Eastern dictators to establish themselves, and the rise of Muslim fundamentalism, a new wave of terror that started some time around 1979, are both reactions to the global domination of the United States, making visible the subtle modification to their mental morphology. They have remoulded the lateral axis of their thinking in order to fight Western dominance. Dissatisfied with the western-styled politics that led only to economic stagnation and political subordination, many Muslims turned toward Islamic fundamentalism, which evoked a strong sense of national and racial pride, authenticity and cultural assertiveness. The economic power of the West can be seen in its aspiration to control the oil resources of the Middle East but the western powers have not anticipated the counterattack of the East and the South, in ways which expose all the contradictions in their interaction with the Muslim other.

Hall prefigures his argument by telling us that human agency is circumscribed always by existential conditions and "the agency has to first of all submit itself to the logic of what is there, to the ground it has to operate on. It can't do something until it knows the ground on which it operates. The most original statement has to be made in a language that will always carry the traces of how others have spoken" (Taylor, 2006). Hall's statement attests to the Derridean belief that all "events" are rewritings of the past, reproblematisations of *existing* crises, events that historically reiterate the structural trauma of *existence*, comprehended only with a retrospective narrativisation. The collusion between the West and its fundamentalist antagonist neutralises the polarisation between the good of liberal democracy and the evil of the fundamentalism because the oppositions recreate the same structures. What is the ground of operation here? An answer can be found in Nietzsche's *The Will to Power*. The preface is especially prophetic of the present trauma: "This history can be related even now, for *necessity* itself is at work here. This future speaks even now in a hundred signs, this destiny announces itself everywhere; for the music of the future all ears are cocked even now. For some time now, our whole European culture has been moving as toward a catastrophe, with a tortured tension that is growing from decade to decade: restlessly, violently, headlong, like a river that wants to reach the end, that no longer reflects, that is afraid to reflect" (Nietzsche, 1967, p. 3 [my emphasis]). It is the Nietzschean groundlessness that gives way to the ground of every operation, an apocryphal base achievable only with the abrasive intersections of thought and performance, leading to the creative enactments of power struggles. The embattled interactions between self and other – such as large-scale wars, state terror, insurrections from dissident organisations – are forms of will to power, with the information war as its latest manifestation.

Signifying polyvalence, the chaotic vortex of contesting elements is what makes the self fearful of reflection. A teleological projection as the shield against the Lacanian Real merely reverberates the problem of power clashes. The "tortured tension" between the West and the Muslim world requires an *untimely* meditation, a reflective pause, with reference to "the most fearful and fundamental desire in man, his drive for power – this drive is called 'freedom'" (Nietzsche, 1967, pp. 383-384). The double bind of freedom emerges when we look at its Manichean correlates, power and violence. Institutions are merely mechanisms ordering the play of power, constituting the hierarchical structures of world politics. True democracy cannot and will not materialise because absolute egalitarianism can mean only living death; the failure of Socialism is an obvious instance. For society to function as a whole, the structural necessity inadvertently establishes a hierarchical configuration. Nietzsche's description of the three motivations for power acquisition, happiness, ambition and liberation, reveals to us the driving force of existence: namely the unceasing conflict for supremacy between self and other. For fundamentalist Muslims, as individuals fighting against Western domination, it is the desire to be free from the political and economic subjection to the other, whereas the drive for "freedom" in the United States can be discovered in its will to pursue the course of political and economic colonisation, masked by its espousal of an ethics of democracy, corresponding to the ethics "that disparages the tyrannical individual ... with its glorification of social welfare and patriotism" (Nietzsche, 1968, pp. 383-384). The totalising bent of liberal democracy is unmasked when the United States and its allies provide aid to economically ailing countries with the conditions that the party concerned converts to liberal democracy and inserts itself into the global capitalist economy. Freedom as the drive to power ensures that violence remains the master of our interrelations with the other.

Nietzsche's preface is pertinent to the current crisis because it indicates the oldest riddle in human history: the incommensurability found between representation and reality, the theory of rights and rights in praxis. This postmodern awareness of the contingent in existence has not taken away, however, the desire to master our destiny, evident in the United States' aggressive stand on global control. The following etymological definitions of the word are significant to my assertion that existential fixity is both impossible and counterproductive. "Exist", according to *The Oxford Dictionary of English Etymology*, means "have being" in the Shakespearean context, and "emerge, appear, proceed, be visible or manifest" in Latin. More interestingly, it means "take up a position" and "reduplicate in formation" in French, with attention given to its prefix "*ex-*", explained as "*sense of going out or forth*, sometimes with the notion of *being raised*" (emphasis mine). Dictionary.com provides clear definitions for "ex-": as a prefix, it means "outside, out of, away from" or "not, without" and its derivative, "exed", is defined as "to delete, or cross out". The multifarious meanings support my poststructuralist framing of the historical trauma, a *faux pas* that is diachronically no exception; existential exceptions are raised essentially from the non-exceptional. Existence and exclusion go hand in hand because of the inherent need to master signifying chaos, but the paradox arises when the points of expulsion are also the points of invasion. In *On Female Sexuality, The Limits of Love and Knowledge*, Jacques Lacan plays with the word, "exist", coining a derivative, "*ex-sist*", to denote a state of non-being, a moment of turning away from being.[1] The hyphenated space introduced

---

[1] A comprehensive account of the phantasm as the life support of the individual and the notion of ex-sistence can be found in the chapter "Rings of Strings" (Lacan, 1999, pp. 118-136).

constitutes this ambiguity between life and death: the moment of death as the most energising instant of existence, which I shall appropriate to read the other *jouissance* of the ultimate sacrifice. However, the Derridean notion of the gift of death, being meaning something only when it deviates from being, is not a nihilistic proposal; it is *kairos*, a turning point from which one takes another position. The crossing out of being means that being can be understood only when it is heightened by and through the idea of non-being, the phallic *jouissance* predicated on the other *jouissance*, the Lacanian "not whole" and more. This is a "Catch-22" situation which I shall complicate further by alluding to the space of *différance*, existence as that which oscillates always between being and non-being but this liminality is accompanied always by the consciousness that sacrificial death as the only authentic act of agency is in no way the true act of freedom because subjectivity is fabricated through a visionary response. In bearing witness to the other of being, these thinkers call attention to, besides modes of being, the fearlessness needed to remain open in a world compelled by fear.

Second, Hamlet's vacillation figures the deconstructive hesitation before the decision. According to Jacques Derrida (1992, p. 24), an authentic decision is one always preceded by a moment of quandary, resulting from the recognition that all decisions involve the violence of the incisive act. He recalls the distinction between thought and action by telling us that one does not necessarily preclude the other. A suspension of being as action allows a critical distancing through which the "right" decision is made possible. This does not mean that Derrida privileges pure justice. He tells us that justice in its ideality is impossible; any just action involves an undecidability that may end in disaster. It is only with a leap of faith that the subject decides and it is always marked by an absolutising moment of violence because responsibility to one means irresponsibility to all others. What is crucial to any discussion on the tension between law and justice is the avoidance of bloodshed, which I shall take up by reemphasising the idea of displacement, a dislocation that takes the form of irony, representation as misrepresentation, a sublimation given to reinscription. We may be as free as we are self-limited or bound to the identity that we have fashioned for ourselves. However, irony as distortion gestures to the possibilities of change and it is with the trans*form*ative possibility, a relocation as well as deviation of the traversal, which the desubjectivised can break out of the vicious cycle of dispossession.

Using the iconic and its metonymic, associative displacements, I shall reveal to you both the power and the terror of the simulacrum, the phantasmatic support Lacan speaks of in *On Female Sexuality*. The following wordplays are metaphorical of the possibilities of irruptions in the communicative chain of radical Islam. By calling both the radical Muslims and the cartoonists iconoclasts, one party with actions and the other with aesthetic representations, the signifying slippage becomes obvious when we look at the iconic as representation. In mediaeval times, the Greek version, *eikonoklastes,* signifies "breakers of religious images"[2] but the word has evolved since to denote the destruction of traditional ideas and institutions, favourably signalling my own interceptive reading of the conflict between radical Muslims and the West. Stretching the definitive boundaries of the word, I introduce the term, "iconolatrous", a new coinage, based on the marriage of "iconic" and "idolatrous" to describe those who revere images as means of undermining ideology. My approach to the Muslim-West crisis is predicated on a catachrestic claim that all critical thought and, by extension, political actions are simultaneously iconoclastic and "iconolatrous". The Danish cartoonists are "iconolatrous" and iconoclastic in their use of images as weapons, arrows directed at the bull's-eye of fundamentalism. Their inscriptive assault appropriates a certain language so that they can speak directly to militant Islam. The manifold occasions of violence from radical Islam, gestures disguising representation with *presence*, oscillate between *vertretung* (appearance as political substitution) and *darstellung* (depiction as simulation), supported by the French definition, "be like", for "icon", representations in contradistinction to the very aniconistic practice of Islam. Muslim fundamentalists can be accused of being iconoclastic in their destruction of the Western emblems of liberal democracy and capitalism, the "religious" icons of the modern globalised world, as well as "iconolatrous" in their unquestioning subjection to radical Islamic Law.

My wordplay here is inspired by Nietzsche's in his articulation of the world as appearance, found in his response to Schopenhauer. His play on the word *schein* (from the verb *scheinen*, which means to shine or to glisten) demonstrates its ambiguity as it slides significantly from semblance to illusion to the "being" of that which appears or shines,[3] the golden tropological field of aesthetics, a minefield exploding the illusions of Muslim fundamentalism. Not only is his wordplay a counter to the reification of truth; it also calls attention to the Dionysian nature of existence, existence as will to power, a protean, creative life force appositely inscribed in aesthetics. Aesthetics, with its anarchistic potential, is possibly the best means to uncover the disguise of radical Islam, which explains the acerbity of militant Muslims, and to shatter the phantasmatic ideological support of the United States as the pinnacle of liberal democracy.

The furore of the Muslims had Flemming Rose publish an article in the *Washington Post* on 19 February 2006, entitled "Why I Published Those Cartoons":

The cartoonists treated Islam the same way they treat Christianity, Buddhism, Hinduism and other religions. And by treating Muslims in Denmark as equals they made a point: we are integrating you into

---

[2] Icon is etymologically derived from "L. *īcōn* (Pliny) - Gr. *eikón* likeness, image, similitude, f. *eik-* be like. comb. form icono- ...in the foll.: ico.noclast one who favours the destruction of images XVII. modL. *iconoclastēs* – Gr. *eikonoklasts* (*klân* break)" (*Oxford Dictionary of English Etymology*).

[3] An elaboration of the wordplay can be found in the editors' introduction (Nietzsche, 2006).

the Danish tradition of satire because you are part of our society, not strangers. The cartoons are including, rather than excluding, Muslims ... Angry voices claim the [bomb in the turban] cartoon is saying that the prophet is a terrorist or that every Muslim is a terrorist. I read it differently: some individuals have taken the religion of Islam hostage by committing terrorist acts in the name of the prophet. They are the ones who have given the religion a bad name. (Rose, 2006)

On 26 February 2006, in an interview with *Jyllands-Posten*, the cartoonist responsible for the most controversial of the twelve images, *Bomb in the Turban*, explains:

There are interpretations of it [the drawing] that are incorrect. The general impression among Muslims is that it is about Islam as a whole. It is not. It is about certain fundamentalist aspects that of course are not shared by everyone. But the fuel for the terrorists' acts stem from interpretations of Islam. I think there is no escaping that. That does not mean that all Muslims are responsible for terror. It is about showing a connection, from where the spiritual fuel comes. There are some interpretations of Islam, according to which you become a martyr if you die for Islam, and you can therefore with a calm mind kill the infidels, and you will be rewarded in the beyond. If a religion develops into religious fanaticism we are faced with totalitarian tendencies, as we have been in the past, such as Fascism and Nazism. It is the same situation, where humans have to surrender and do as demanded by the rulers. I think we should fight against that, and the weapon of a cartoonist is this pen or pencil and then a certain degree of *indignation*. *("Jyllands-Posten*: Bomben's Ophavsmand*", 2006)

The comments from Rose and the artist clarify their position *vis-à-vis* Islam: the attack is directed at the repressive violence of Islamic fundamentalism. The cartoonists' public apology on 30 January 2006 did not stop the wave of violence that peaked sometime around 18 February. Anders Fogh Rasmussen, the Danish Prime Minister, in his refusal to bow to the pressure from Muslim ambassadors, issued statements in a letter that upholds the Danish journalistic tradition of free speech:

The freedom of expression has a wide scope and the Danish government has no means of influencing the press. However, Danish legislation prohibits acts or expressions of blasphemous or discriminatory nature. The offended party may bring such acts or expressions to court, and it is for the courts to decide in individual cases. (Rasmussen, 2006)

Given Rasmussen's stance on the controversy, it is clear that the cartoons were taken as an excuse for the protraction of the existing hostilities against the Western "infidels". The cartoonists went into hiding because of the rewards promised for their lives. Osama bin

Laden, in an audio release, was reported, on 24 April 2006, to be unrelenting in his demand for the deaths of the caricaturists. An escaped al-Qaeda militant, Abu Yahya al-Libi, pressed for the continued persecution of the Danish cartoonists. In a video appearance, he tries to provoke Muslims into action with the message: "Believers, don't let your prophet down and don't let our response to this grave insult just be protests and forums ... Muslims, let's not be slack about this ... hone your swords and shake the ground beneath their feet so they can feel our pain, let's send rivers of blood down their streets".[4]

If we refer to the citations above, *Bomb in the Turban* and the other images bounce back the thoughtless violence in the acts of butchery. Life is cheap to radical Muslims since privilege goes to the image of an ideal Islamic world. As revolutionaries countering the terror of the transcendental, the Danish cartoonists performed their law-founding violence on the daedal space of art, problematising the tight control of radical Islamic law. The cartoons can be called khoretic materialisations, Dionysian in the oppositional confrontation between fundamentalism and the freedom of expression, an extraction and a frictional assembling of space-time elements, impelling the other within fundamentalist Islam to being. These caricatures are revolutionary emanations from khora, the doula delivering the birth of exaggerated images, smashing the glasshouse of radical Islam. Aesthetics, interpreted as the arena where inscriptive contests are played out, figures the performances of power in reality. Fifteen hundred students demonstrated in an unannounced rally outside the Punjab University in Lahore and other student demonstrations occurred in front of universities in Cairo and the southern Egyptian city of Assiut. Why the universities? This is because they are sites of learning and the transmission of ideas, proving that it is an ideological war waged by Islamic fundamentalism, an ideological war that achieves its greatest impact with physical violence. Violent outbursts occur before institutions of power because these are khoretic spaces, sites of resistance, arising from the oppositional boundaries of inclusion and exclusion, where clashes are performed between those with power and those without. Within these spaces, power shifts according to the degree of force from the opponents. Derrida speaks of the "game of the world" (Derrida, 1976, p. 50), the empirical ground on which *tekhnē* translates ideas to reality and vice versa with play, a movement that turns a metaphor into a metonym, foregrounding the *position* and the *direction* of the travelling signifier, the conditions permitting the overturning of meaning even as it appears. The ironic twist breaks the circularity of the patriarchal bequest, reality tearing apart the symbolic order of Islamic fundamentalism, unplugging the surplus *jouissance* of its proponents. Lacan's Real, an externality of competing value systems, breaks in to remind the Islamic fundamentalists of the traumatic core of *sharia*. *Bomb in the Turban* exemplifies this invasive penetration, a seismic shake, with its deviant redirection of the message, disclosing the

---

[4] In a Reuter's report (Anonymous, 2006c) dated 12 May 2006 it is reported that the video dates from February 2006.

obscene manipulation of Islamic fundamentalism.

An etymological dismantling of the word "transcendence" demonstrates its always-already contaminated form, requiring the materiality of the aural and visual imprints for the rising above and beyond immanence. Being and writing overlap precisely at the point where the hinge between the structural and the historical reveals the subjection of being to writing with the symptomatic displays of left-handed violence. The cartoonists, by valorising the Dionysian in representation, affirm the cathartic in aesthetics, prompting a critical analysis of the madness in the strategic violence wielded by Muslim extremism. As a demonstration of the potency of art, I cite the reprinting of the Danish cartoons by Mohammed al-Asaadi, editor-in-chief of the pro-government *Yemen Observer*. He was imprisoned even though the reprinted cartoons are largely crossed out and followed by an article condemning the animations. When asked by Rod Nordland, in an interview with *Newsweek* published on 17 February 2006, if he "regrets the decision to run the cartoons, however censored, given the climate", his reply is: "I personally believe these cartoons should be published. If we make it unlawful to look at them, *we give them an importance they don't deserve*, as if there's something holy or special about them. We should be able to discuss them openly, which is what we said" (Nordland, 2006 [my emphasis]). By incarcerating al-Asaadi, the Yemeni government has made him unintentionally a martyr for freedom of expression, indicating the iconoclastic power of the Danish cartoons, an ideological overturning resulting in cataclysmic change. Derrida (1992) reminds us that justice without force is ineffective and force without justice is dictatorial. The power of representation lies with the *force of the word*. Again, the anomaly emerges with the erasure of the inscriptive address of the cartoonists, indicating the "mythical foundation" of Islamic authority.

Institutionally sanctioned violence cannot be divided neatly into legitimate violence and illegitimate violence. Legality backed by institutional power does not necessarily have the right to inflict violence with its judiciary function. If the notion of legitimacy in politics, power and violence is examined from the Derridean reading of the founding and conserving aspects of law (in Derrida, 1992), the law-founding dimension of every political institution encompasses its law-preserving aspect; the law-conserving thread in the State's counter-violence is just an extension of its originary violence, a violence that is concealed so that its autonomy and the monopoly of violence are uncontested. Radical *sharia* law is a sovereign ring dismantled to reveal its violent excesses called power. At some point, this repressive force faces an inevitable onslaught of counter-aggression, an illegitimate violence corresponding to the instituting violence. Somalia is another country in the midst of an ideological war "over whether [it] should be governed by Islamic law" (Anonymous, 2006d). While radical Islamism insists that it will provide the strong leadership Somalia requires, Muslim militants are also the ones pushing the country toward political and economic instability, causing two hundred and eighty deaths within six days. Hoping to become the sole governing body in Somalia, radical

Islamic forces tried to appropriate the strategic route to the city's capital, Mogadishu, an attempt to overtake the interim government backed by the United States. According to an Associated Press report, "Islamic fundamentalists have portrayed themselves as an alternative capable of bringing order and peace to a country that has no effective controlling government since 1991 and have built up their forces as part of a campaign to install an Islamic government in Somalia, something opposed by the warlords and a new interim government that has so far been unable to assert much authority because of infighting and insecurity" (Anonymous, 2006d). This is an instance of radical Islamic law imposing itself on another country, extending its religious colonisation, making it difficult to separate dissidence from tyranny. Having caused disorientation in the country, the insurgents can demonstrate now they are capable of restructuring the fragmented country, imbuing the much-needed national coherence.

The mounting conflicts in Iraq, a failure on the part of the United States to contain the Muslim dissidents, shatter any humanitarian front. Exposed as a paranoiac shield created to maintain its economic and political mastery, it gestures to the excesses of aggression behind the United States' intervention. The Iraq situation is the historical catalyst of the twenty-first century that uncovers a banal barbarity within the United States, mirroring the monstrous trauma with which Iraq has to grapple. To a United States achieving unprecedented political and economic growth in the twentieth century, the Pleasantville of the world, a land whose terror was the apparent lack of terror, the 26 February 1993 bombing of the World Trade Center and the 9/11 incident are slaps from the hand of the Other, rousing the American government from its dreamy sleep of superpower stature, rending its veil of security.

Michael Hirsh's ironic reportage refers to the glossy malformation of the Green Zone at the locus of the Iraqi capital and aptly figured by the comic "Disney-ish" machines:

There's nothing like roaring into Baghdad aboard a Rhino. A Rhino is a giant, heavily-armored bus that can withstand IEDs (small ones), and it is now the favored means of keeping Western visitors from getting blown to bits by these homemade bombs on the dangerous road between Baghdad International Airport and the secure Green Zone at the city's center. "Rhino" is an appropriately Disney-ish name for these wheeled monstrosities, adding to the surreal feeling one gets in moving from the howling chaos outside the Green Zone into the theme-park-like confines within. You drive through several checkpoints, leaving behind tracts of litter and rubble and the desperate, dark faces of ordinary Iraqis trying to earn a few dinars. There, behind high concrete blast walls and razor wire, you find quiet streets and the heart of the American occupation: a double-sized Olympic pool with a palm-fretted patio restaurant, food courts and a giant coffee lounge where lessons in belly dancing and martial arts are offered. (Hirsh, 2006a)

Dispersed because of the heterogeneous insurgencies, Iraq is left with a political void, encroached upon by Western coalition forces, headed by the United States. The latter's control of global politics permits its exception from the same legality and this exceptional state gives rise to a perverse form of violence. The irony manifests itself when Condoleezza Rice, the US Secretary of State, and Jack Straw, the Defence Secretary of the United Kingdom, demand that the paralysed Iraqi government "get governing", realising, at the same time, that the presence of the West in Iraq is the direct cause of the disorder. Hirsh satirises the United States' occupation of the Green Zone, the heavily fortified Disneyland of Iraq, as the ventriloquists talk about transforming the latter into a liberal democratic country. Can one properly draw Iraq's national boundaries now with the Western coalition forces occupying the heart of Baghdad *and in luxury* while the rest of the country falls apart economically because of the political crisis? Later in the report, Hirsh cites Donald Rumsfeld, who was criticising NATO's presence in Bosnia, Kosovo and East Timor. The simile of "a broken bone" he uses to describe the foreign presence in a politically fraught country is ironically prophetic of the American occupation of Iraq: "If it is not set properly at the outset, eventually, the muscles and tendons will grow around the break, and the body will adjust to the abnormal condition" (Hirsh 2006a), leading to the merging of the inside and the outside in the process of national disfiguration. This violent deformation of the Iraqi nation attests to my assertion that the structural possibility of displacement frames the historical; it is only by working through the structural problematic that we gain an understanding of the historical trauma and, hopefully, find a way to repeat the trauma in a different medium, without involving the bloody violence of war and insurgency.

Michael Hardt and Antonio Negri, in *Multitude*, confirm the critique that the West and the East are shadows of each other; one is summoned by the other into existence:

A sovereign power is always two-sided: a dominating power always relies on the consent or submission of the dominated. The power of sovereignty is thus always limited, and this limit can always potentially be transformed into resistance, a point of vulnerability, a threat. The suicide bomber appears here again as a symbol of the inevitable limitation and vulnerability of sovereign power; refusing to accept a life of submission, the suicide bomber turns life itself into a horrible weapon. *This is the ontological limit of biopower in its most tragic and revolting form*. Such destruction only grasps the passive, negative limit of sovereign power. (Hardt and Negri, 2004, p. 54 [original emphasis])

Muslim fundamentalism is now the greatest threat to the sovereign power of the United States, responding to the assumed privilege of the West by overturning the creative and reproductive aspects of biopower, the latest manifestation of the will in its ability to transform itself in accordance to time.[5] Hardt and Negri dexterously capture the philosophical implication of the dialectical rhythms of power relations, but what is not addressed here is the mastery militant Islam has over Muslim individuals. The United States' desire for the monopoly of legal violence is challenged by the sovereign power of radical Islam, which is meeting the West at the limits of its dominance. Violent resistance is perceived by Islamic fundamentalists as the only answer to the economic and political control of the United States. There are multiple cracks in the national image of Iraq because of the intra-sectarian fighting: "The danger in other words is that Iraq's devolution into 'regionalization' doesn't stop there but keeps on going, breaking up slowly like fractured glass" (Hirsh, 2006b). In their revolutionary encounter with the West, radical Muslims activate what was devalorised by the Enlightenment, the "irrational exuberance" so necessary for self-renunciation. If the West, with its biopower, privileges its own people at the expense of others, Muslims, in their opposition, can win only with an absolute erasure of life, a reversal throwing light on the hegemony of the West. Hirsh (2006b) explores this shift from postcolonialism to compassionate colonialism, which has the United States as the unifying force in a fragmented nation: "The logical conclusion is that Iraq may no longer be able to exist, as Iraq, without the glue of American involvement – in politics, in security, in Iraq's very sense of national identity. ... So perhaps this is not going to be a model of democracy after all. Instead it is more likely to be – if it works out – a model for post-colonial imperialism. It is a new kind of colonialism, in other words, one that dare not speak its name. But let us give it one anyway: 'compassionate colonialism'". The juxtaposition of "compassionate" and "colonialism" gives way to the burlesque that marks the casuistry behind which the United States hides.

In the Iraq War, the country becomes a hotbed for revolutionary activities. Launching "Operation Swarmer" against the "insurgents" only brings to the fore the intrinsic contradiction of the technologised assault of the United States, an indiscriminate annihilation backfiring because of the lack of a positive target. The fact that it has taken approximately three years to form an Iraqi government, which has not stopped the violent malcontents, demonstrates the difficulty the United States faces in its attempt to contain the dissidents. Operating in a similar fashion to guerrilla warfare, the insurgents in Iraq have managed to unsettle the control of the Iraqi government, backed by the United States and the Western coalition forces. Hardt and Negri refer to the form war takes in the late twentieth and early twenty-first centuries. According to them, globalisation has transformed the traditional concept of war as large scale face-to-face combats into a highly sophisticated network of low-density confrontations. Converting the verticality of the pyramidical hierarchies of conventional warfare to that of a horizontal web-like linkage, war in the global form undertaken by the United States is a reaction to the way terror organisations spread their influence. With the

---

[5] See Hardt and Negri, 2004, for a full description of the term "biopower", and the United States' advancement of this new form of military tactic.

multiple Islamic factions clashing with each other on a daily basis the Western coalition forces are left to collect human debris instead of actively trying to prevent terror activities.The Americans' problems are compounded by the fact that the same Shiite-led Interior Ministry police forces they are training to protect Iraqis are widely suspected of involvement in the killings – if not as the executioners, then as allies to the Shia militias blamed for much of the bloodshed.

The lack of a clear target for their fight against terror effectively means the failure of the western coalition forces in Iraq. Subsumed by the United States' monopoly of legal violence, the various axes of modern conflicts have become insignificant: "Only one distinction does matter, and it is superimposed over all others: violence that preserves the contemporary hierarchy of global order and violence that threatens that order" (Hardt and Negri, 2004, p. 32). And this is clearly shown in the empty signifier, "insurgents", which sublates differences, used strategically by the United States to justify their attack after the bombing in Samarra. With the United States amassing global power, radical Islam may win by formalistically imploding its legal dominance.

Foucault's *raison d'état*, the rationalised violence of the law, takes the shape of the law-preserving vanguards – the police. Striding between law-preserving violence and the law-founding one, these enforcers are the faceless or ghostly representatives whose omnipotence is defined by an "ignoble, ignominious, disgusting ambiguity" (Derrida, 1992, p. 32), the vile or "evil" substratum of the law. Like the eye in the sky, their gaze can be felt even when they are absent. Occupying the liminal space of the Other, they are the inassimilable. Hardt and Negri explain the difference between traditional warfare and contemporary conflicts: "but war itself had begun to be transformed – less oriented toward defending against a coherent mega-threat and more focused on proliferating mini-threats; less intent on the general destruction of the enemy and more inclined toward the transformation and production of the enemy. War became constrained. Rather than all-out, large scale combat, the great superpowers began to engage in *high-intensity police actions* ... aimed at the construction and reproduction of the social order" (Hardt and Negri, 2004, p. 39 [original emphasis]). Law, for it to be effective, must be enforced but power given to these representatives is marked always by the danger of abuse, the "rottenness" of the state of law, be it Islamic law or Western legality. The terror activities in Iraq unfold, again, the depraved side of the police's aggression. The multiple instances of law enforcers becoming law-makers in Iraq foreground the superficiality of the division between repressive violence and founding violence.

The Askariya bombing on 22 March 2006 ignited a situation in which the distinction between the law enforcers and the insurgents became blurred as the country headed toward a civil war. The mounting sectarian violence in Baghdad has the Sunnis and the Shiites, who were employed as defenders of the law, joining the reprisal attacks. Johnson (2006) reports that insurgents and militiamen are are said to have disguised themselves as soldiers, police and fighters from rival militia groups in order to carry out their terror activities. The Facilities

Protection Services, "a mutant security agency that has grown from a 4000-man group of 'night watchmen' … into a large, amorphous force (of about 146,000) that seems to lack any centralised control", whose duties include guarding the sacred shrines and mosques, is fast becoming a terror force that targets anyone perceived as an enemy of the different factions they represent. Having heterogeneous loyalties, these so-called officers are themselves terrorists "involved in sectarian killings, explosions and mortar attacks". The Facilities Protection Services is known now as "a more problematic force with multiple agendas", a force comprising criminals turned officers, but criminals nonetheless, with their loyalties given to the rival factions funding their operations. By mimicking the police, wearing the same uniforms, carrying the same weapons and driving the same vehicles, the terrorists have found, with their expropriation of the power of the law enforcers, the surest way to demolish security and create a political upheaval. Legal power, simulated by its opponents in their violent actions, is shown to house at its core its illegal trace. Thus, the implicit betrayal of the legitimated violence of law is pushed to the fore, making Derrida's proposal indisputable: "I shall propose the interpretation according to which the very violence of the foundation or position of law (*Rechtsetzende Gewalt*) must envelope the violence of conservation (*Rechtserhaltende Gewalt*) and cannot break with it" (1992, p. 38). The exchange mechanism of the economy is unavoidable, for it gives to the understanding of the irreducible loss in this contraction that is equivocally an expansion noted in the surplus emitted elsewhere, a gaming resulting in a non-zero sum measure with an irretrievable deficit or an unaccountable gain.

Insisting on a permanent contraction is impossible since all efforts at the mastery of being are susceptible to the ravaging of time. The refusal to acknowledge the reciprocity within differences, a doubling encapsulated succinctly by Lacan's subtitle "Encore" to *On Female Sexuality*, is detrimental to many Muslims' survival in the modern world. In fact, the Muslim militants' decision to strive for some pure Islam comes at a great cost: "But naturally, the busier one gets liberating oneself, the more one pays. And the less one pays, the more one pays, such is the trap of speculation" (Derrida, 1991, p. 498). The obsessive compulsion toward freedom draws one back immediately into the binds of power. Islamic fundamentalism is improvident in its law-preservation: the repression in the Name of the Father produces prodigal sons. Instead of reacting instantly to what is before them, leading to deadly actions, affecting their religious brothers and sisters, Muslim extremists must take a step back and reflect on what is *represented* to them as law. They have become merely vehicles, driven by radical Islamic representations, taking it upon themselves to be the preambles of God, walking before God, walking in the shoes of God.

The revolutionary power of inscription throws light on the terror of Islamic radicalism. With the satire of the caricatures, the Danish cartoonists reveal the castration within Muslim fundamentalism. By rendering the yawning hole of the *enfant terrible* obvious, one becomes aware that the attention-grabbing tactics are just counterclaims for the lack of political and economic recognition, what is known now as the "economy of disesteem" (Brennan and Pettit, 2006). The controversy in a Tuscan town over the construction of the largest mosque in Italy exemplifies, first, the difficulties faced by European Muslims because of the lack of cultural integration, which makes them increasingly cling to their traditional ways and religious lifestyles; second, the non-Muslims' fear and unease because of Muslim terror activities; and, third, the problems encountered by those who want to see a greater interaction between Muslims and non-Muslims (Carlile, 2006). Political activists, like the Northern League or *La Lega Nord*, in an atmosphere of protectionism, are fighting now to evict the Muslims instead of just maintaining separatism. The mosque project was approved by the ex-Mayor, Marco Spinelli, in 1999, but after the 9/11 Incident in New York and the July 2005 bombings in London, non-Muslims in Italy are wary of the places reserved for Muslim religious activities. Paolo Brogioni, the current Mayor, faces hostilities from Italians in trying to get the mosque successfully constructed. Controversies related to radical Islam are not found just in Italy; in Germany, the notoriety of fundamentalist Islam is given further publicity with expositions of the maltreatment and betrayal of Muslim women by their family members. The repressed returns as the prurient excesses found in the suffering of Muslims occupying the lowest rungs of militant Islam, those alienated from the European Muslim societies.

Elbaum (2006) provides two accounts of domestic violence and repression. One iterates the abuse resulting from the misogynistic views Islam has of women. Leyla, who is from Turkey, was treated like a slave at home, having to look after her siblings and handle all domestic chores while trying to get an education. Tricked by her parents into returning to Turkey, and almost forced into marriage, she managed to escape with the aid of a social worker in Berlin. She survived her traumatic experience with good counselling and care from a women's shelter, graduated with a degree in early education, and is now doing her bit by helping diasporas in the shelters for female immigrants. The second case refers to an Iranian woman, Shabnam, aged 24, who is still trying to recover from an abusive marriage. Entrapped by Islamic conventions, she married an otiose drunk whose violent behaviour caused her multiple bouts of depression. She eventually had help from the *Interkulturelles Frauenhaus* (Intercultural Women's House) and managed to recreate her life successfully after her husband's departure for the United States. These two examples do not paint the entire portrait of the physical and psychological torture inflicted on Muslim women in Europe:

An editor of the Turkish newspaper *Hurriyet* has estimated that 50 percent of Muslim women in Germany have been victims of domestic violence. In addition, forced marriages often turn into violent homes … In part because of several highly publicized murders of Muslim women by family members for "dishonorable" behaviour – along with the murder of the controversial Dutch filmmaker Theodore Van Gogh, who often spoke out about the abuse of women – there is a new willingness to discuss forced marriage and spousal violence against women taking place in Turkish and other immigrant communities. (Elbaum, 2006)

The economy of disesteem gestures to the dangers inherent in religious and cultural intolerance, giving support to the prevailing perspective that radical Islam is a reaction to Western postmodernity. In order to protect the patriarchal purity of Islam, these women are forced into early marriages to prevent the intrusion of foreign blood. Virginity and marital fidelity are prized only because of patrilineal concerns. The marginalisation of Muslim women and its concomitant abuses are found in all European Muslim communities.

In order to speak against Islamist repression, I am using the Danish caricatures in this paper to make the necessary switch. The asymmetry between the "events" of violence and the ironic representations gestures to the "fustian" quality of the violent revolts, "ridiculously inflated" balloons veiling not only the motivations but also the signifying abyss that underlies the forms of violence. The abyss is an ephemeral site more properly defined as thick absence instead of emptiness. But Islamic fundamentalism prefers to have the void filled only by a univocal and determined principle. Striking with a wooden phallus, a prosthetic projection, only makes the existential vacuum within the actors of violence more pronounced – the more excessive the outward gestures the more hollow the being. Their resistance evokes the aporetic terror at the heart of being, the blinding glare of flux and dissipation, with overkill.[6] Radical Islamic law is a representational fabric woven to mobilise the individual to extreme action in an attempt to purify and rid itself of alien elements. Terror, in order to be effective, must have the element of unpredictability, making it necessary for the performers to exercise a certain level of indiscrimination in the aggressive performances. Complete indiscrimination in their acts of terror proves merely the nihilism behind the Islamist interpretation of Islamic law. A total departure from differential relations spells death, whether physical death or a type of death-in-life, an extreme passivity in activity; the complete submission to the love of the Other makes being an instrument of the Other's satisfaction. This is, paradoxically, the most profound fantasy of man, the rainbow connection with the Supreme Other. But it is a willing existence, an oxymoronic resoluteness and quiescence, which severs one's ties with the rest of the world, resulting in an empty shell of a man whose only function is to act out the will of an Other, falling back into a different sort of co-option.

As the alienated, suicide bombers are the unhomely, whose lack of earthly bounds makes them psychologically open to the *jouissance* of the Other, a vulnerability intuited by radical Muslim leaders. With the fragmentation of the nation, the want of cohesion is used to prime a new master signifier, politics disguised as religion. If radical Islam

---

[6] The full explanation and analysis of Derrida's use of the word "aporia" can be found in Derrida, 1993, pp. 11-13.

prohibits graven images, it has flesh-and-blood ones, suicide bombers whose narcissism reduces God to the image of them. It is not as simple as desiring to be God. By positioning oneself as the lack of the Other, God's object of desire, the being of the Islamic militant manifests itself as the making visible of the ghostly Other, transposing his desire to the desire of the Other; with a compliance through an appellation, he attains the other's satisfaction. His supreme sacrifice gives to a *jouissance* of the Other, the absolute relinquishing of one's fate, which is also the supreme act of agency, a self-love sublimated to the love of the Other. This unspeakable feeling of sublimity points to the signifying emptiness the radical Islamic sub-conscious revolves around, a lacuna elevated to divinity, explaining the individual's willingness to give up the contingent. Therefore, their bodies assume a materiality akin to signifiers, exploding amplifiers of absence, never missing the mark with the impulse from a short circuit, yet completely missing the mark. Giving presence to the Other with the annihilation of self and others means ramming the hole with absent appurtenances, contradictorily rendering the gulf even wider.

Just as the satirical images are iconoclastic in themselves, representations animating the revolutionary in inscription, an insurgency necessary for revaluation, the suicide bombers, in their destruction of human existence, are iconoclasts reacting from resentment and revenge, blasting themselves and others to the smithereens of infinity. If we refer to Schopenhauer's definition of the world as will and representation, the will is being in action and the separation of being and action becomes distinct only with reflection. Knowledge of being is possible by the subject objectifying herself; the subject giving herself to an exterior that returns as a light reflecting the interior. This straddling of the divide between subjectivity and objectivity allows a more comprehensive knowledge; it is a knowledge constituted by the changes of the viewing angle. In their rejection of the iconic, the reflection required in being-in-emergence, the Muslim militants pay profusely by withholding payment. The paradoxical poniard lies with the sacred becoming profane, the religious excesses translating to wastes, human residues whose use value correspond only to tools of destruction. Being as militant action, pure action without consideration, the moment-to-moment reflection, becomes just another baseless appearance. Obliterating the ego results in the erasure of the divide between subject and object, making the individual vulnerable to the imposition of an other's will.

We cannot account completely for the loss in this speculative game between power and freedom, truth and appearance, because one can never anticipate the hand of the Other. An Associated Press report remarks upon the visual absence of Al-Zawahri's left hand in all his video appearances (Anonymous, 2006b). He is shown to be gesturing only with his right hand while his left hand remains hidden from the viewer's gaze. The way he appears is symbolic of the working methods of the leaders of Al-Qaeda, whose operation is deconstruction *par excellence*. They situate themselves as the Other, both in the control over their fellow Muslims and their contentious relations with the West.

This third position, a position of the inaccessible, is a refusal to be objectified, to be known. Identifying with the lack in the Other, the Other as God, using the Other as the mediation between themselves and their subordinates, between themselves and their opponents, executes the potent manoeuvring of the Muslim individual to violent performances and provokes their opposition to reckless actions. Equipped with the profound intuition of the power of the aporia, they can manipulate its dispersive and disruptive potentials in order to give the resistance a vantage point and great scope for terror tactics. Al-Zawahri declares, in the video, "We are in a battle, and more than half of this battle is taking place in the battlefield of the media. And this media battle is *a race for the hearts and minds of our people*" (Anonymous, 2006b [emphasis mine]), thus reinforcing the persuasiveness of my psychoanalytic analysis above.

The globalised form, cyber-terrorism, is an apt metaphor of the unabated recalcitrance against authority, dislocating the analytic dominance of the superpower with a disseminative network of elusive appearances. If the individual Islamic radical has been unreflective, George Bush and his Republican government acted without proper deliberation in their attempts to curb the ever-expanding network of terror. Having to spread their military attention over a vast topography of terror, the United States' army and navy suffer an inevitable dissolution, causing a decline of their military might. Instead of political ineptness, the Muslim militant groups have proven to be astute and agile in "the propaganda war", a war in which even Donald Rumsfeld himself might have acknowledged defeat. Without looking closely at the ground on which it has to operate, whose unevenness does not mean necessarily the lack of technological know-how on the part of its adversary, the United States jumped into the war against terror without thoroughly investigating its enemy. Its failure to deal with the stylistics of terror is most evident in the Muslim militants' recurring successes in targeting the United States' army with IEDs, improvised explosive devices that have become increasingly deadly: the number of explosions reached an all-time high in 2005 with 10,953 attacks, costing the US $3.3 billion in preventive measures (Barry, *et al.*, 2006).

The radical Muslim world speaks to us now in forms that may win the tussle for power. In the warring of wills, the Muslim radicals and the West are synonymous, one calling the other into being. As parallels, they are semblables in the Lacanian sense, rivals in the bid for power. Muslim fundamentalists, "iconolatrous" in the use of God as mediation in their mystification of the future, are beings possessed by a promise, neglecting the earthly demands of the present. When the present, the moment of existential definition, is violently wrenched by an illusory future, dictated by the future, it becomes apocalyptic, a prophetic deception. The Danish cartoons, as counteraction, are an attempt to "remove the shades" of militant Muslims so that they see every moment as a moment of transition. Derrida's *future anterior present*, the decisive moment which is open to reflection and anticipation, is a moment traced always by the other. The movement requires one incessantly to oscillate between the past and the future, an existential journey without a determinate destination. What counts, instead, is the journey itself, a traversal up a non-teleological path, acknowledging and accepting the undecidability that is always already ahead. Hall's dialogue of difference is only effective when differences are seen in a celebratory way. In order to initiate this dialogue in our face-to-face encounter with *the human other*, we must, first, respond to the call of the other without the defensive gesture of encroachment and assimilation.

Derrida's (1992) reading of Walter Benjamin's notion of divine violence indicates, perhaps, the just resistance. All resistances, by laying bare the violence of the legal system in their defiance of the law, uncover the origin of the law as a violent positioning. Looking at the reiteration of the revolutionary makes one aware of the disjuncture between the idea of democracy and its realisation. The historical trauma, a consequence of the assymmetry between representation and reality, ensures the repetition of juridico-political revolutions, and the revolutionary force lies precisely with the unfulfilled desire for democracy. The idea of democracy, depending on the viewing angle of the perceiver, may appear to be the angel or the devil, the messianic or the monstrous. However, radical violence resulting in carnage runs contrary to Benjamin's notion of the messianic, the promise of a democracy that values the sanctity of life. The sovereign injunction to fight for the living, sacrifices made to improve existential conditions *without bloodshed*, is the significant difference between divine violence and ordinary violence. Democracy to come may be a promise forever deferred but that does not mean we stop moving toward that promise. The envisioned, perceived as the horizon of this trajectory, gives us the required measure. Thus, we must recognise the impossibility of democracy as providing the conditions for the possibility of any democratic movement. The opening of doors, to receive the foreign other, is the transfiguring approach to the other as other and the other as self. I propose the deflection of real violence with a re-emphasis on the revolutionary in writing, a proposal that valorises inscriptive violence instead of physical force. If, according to Lacan, knowledge and love are the illusory supports of being, sublimations necessary to survival, then my displacement of radical violence to inscriptive violence here is doubly justified. And this can be realised only by transcending delimitations with an eye on the limitations of remaining wholly bound to traditional or religious conceptions.

References
Anonymous (2006a). "Nigerian Religious Riots Continue", *BBC News*, 24 February, **http://news.bbc.co.uk/2/hi/africa/4749534.stm** (accessed 5 May 2006).
Anonymous (2006b). "Al-Zawahri Says U.S. Hit Hard in Iraq", *MSNBC*, 28 April, **http://www.msnbc.msn.com/id/12536525/** (accessed 28 April 2006).
Anonymous (2006c). "Apparent Al-Qaida Escapee Urges New Attacks", *MSNBC*, 12 May, **http://www.worthynews.com/news/msnbc-**

msn-com-id-12750058-/ (accessed 12 May 2006).

Anonymous (2006d). "Fighting Rages in Somalia's Capital" *MSNBC*, 12 May, **http://www.msnbc.msn.com/id/12742886/** (accessed 12 May 2006).

Barry, J., M. Hastings and E. Thomas. (2006) "WMD: At War with an Insidious Weapon", *Newsweek Online,* 27 March (accessed 27 March 2006).

Belien, P. (2006) "Cartoon War Leads to Role Reversal, Makes First Victim", *The Brussels Journal*, 4 February 2006, **http://www.brussels journal.com/node/756** (accessed 8 February 2006).

Brennan, G. and P. Pettit. (2004) "The Economy of Esteem: An Essay on Civil and Political Society" *Oxford Scholarship Online*, **http://www.oxfordscholarship.com/oso/public/content/econo micsfinance/9780199246489/toc.html** (accessed 27 May 2006).

Carlile, J. (2006) "Mosque Plans bring Controversy to Tuscan Town". *MSNBC*, 25 May, **http://www.msnbc.msn.com/id/12927212/** (accessed 30 May 2006).

-----------. (1976) *Of Grammatology*, trans. G. C. Chakravorty Spivak. London, Johns Hopkins University Press.

-----------. (1992) "Force of Law: The 'Mythical Foundation of Authority'" in D. Cornell *et al.* (eds.), *Deconstruction and the Possibility of Justice*, New York, Routledge.

Derrida, J. (1993) *Aporias*, trans. T. Dutoit, Stanford, CA, Stanford University Press.

Elbaum, R. (2006) "Abuse Plagues Muslim Women in Germany", *MSNBC*, 25 May, **http://www.msnbc.msn.com/id/12812607/** (accessed 26 May 2006).

Foucault, M. (1994) *Power*. trans. R. Hurley *et al.*, New York, New Press.

Hardt, M. and A. Negri. (2004) *Multitude: War and Democracy in the Age of Empire*. London, Hamish Hamilton.

Hirsh, M. (2006a) "Real and Surreal", *Newsweek Online*, 3 April, **http://www.newsweek.com/id/46314** (accessed 3 April 2006).

-----------. (2006b). "Compassionate Colonialism", *Newsweek Online*, 19 April, **http://www.newsweek.com/id/46520** (accessed 23 April 2006).

Howden, D. *et al.* (2006), "How a meeting of leaders in Mecca set off the cartoon wars around the world ", *The Independent*, 10 February, **http://news.independent.co.uk/world/middle_east/article3444 82.ece** (accessed 11 February 2006).

Johnson, S. (2006) "Phantom Force", *Newsweek Online*, 24 April, **http://www.newsweek.com/id/47090** (accessed 19 May 2006).

"Jyllands-Posten: Bomben's Ophavsmand". (2006) *Jyllands–Posten*, 26 February.

Lacan, J. (1999) *On Female Sexuality, The Limits of Love and Knowledge, 1972-1973*, trans. B. Fink. New York, Norton.

Nietzsche, F. (2006) *The Nietzsche Reader*, ed. K. Ansell-Pearson and D. Large. Oxford, Blackwell.

--------------. (1968) *The Will to Power*, trans. W. Kaufmann and R. J. Hollingdale, London, Weidenfeld and Nicolson.

Nordland R. (2006) "Of Course I'm Afraid", *Newsweek Online*, 18 February, **http://www.newsweek.com/id/57143** (accessed 18 February 2006).

Plummer, R. (2006) "Firms feel pain of people power", BBC News, 3 February, **http://news.bbc.co.uk/1/hi/business/4676826.stm** (accessed 3 February 2006).

Rasmussen, A.F. (2006) "Address by Prime Minister Anders Fogh Rasmussen", 3 February, **http://www.stm.dk/Index/dokumenter. asp?o=6&n=0&d=2512&s=2** (accessed 3 February 2006).

Reynolds, P. (2006) "A Clash of Rights and Responsibilities", *BBC News*, 6 February, **http://news.bbc.co.uk/1/hi/world/south_asia/4686 536.stm** (accessed 4 May 2006).

Rose, F. (2006) "Why I Published those Cartoons", *Washington Post*, 19 February, **http://www.washingtonpost.com/wp-dyn/content/ article/2006/02/17/AR2006021702499.html** (accessed 2 April 2006).

Soetjipto, T. (2006) "Indonesia's Merapi Volcano Explodes with Gas". *The Washington Post*, 15 May, **http://www.washingtonpost. com/wp-dyn/content/article/2006/05/14/AR2006051401250_ Technorati.html** (accessed 15 May 2006).

Taylor, L. (2006) "Deeply disillusioned but not without Hope". *The Times Higher Education Supplement,* 3 March.

Žižek, S. (2005) "Against Human Rights". *New Left Review 34* (July/ August) pp. 115-131.

Reconciliation and Forgiving: the Power of Happy Memory

Cristina Demaria

Memory's "identity"

The relationship between identity and memory – or identities and memories – has regained a particular resonance since the 1980s, after the supposed "end" of one conflict (the Cold War), the beginning of many other conflicts – now defined variously as ethnic, post-modern, asymmetrical, and so on – and the consequent collapse and re-moulding of the world's political and cultural boundaries. The intervening years have shown up the limitations and dangers of the "freezing of memories", and have witnessed the re-awakening of a consciousness of History as a restored and surviving collective conscience; history as a fundamental agent of political mobilisation, within which identity operates as an active construction, namely, the interpretation of one's own story mediated by words (Assmann, 1999). The *use* of memory has thus revitalised the *meaning* of memory, not so much as a receptacle or a repetition of the past, but as a source or reservoir of enabling forms with which both to face and to re-structure the present.[1] To re-discover the past means to use it; and to use the past is an act entangled in paradoxes; first of all that of truth. Many national processes of reconciliation do appeal to truth as a value in order to rehabilitate national memories: to demand that the truth of the past must be recognised today has become an almost magical formula, as if to know what really happened could automatically stop, or, at least, curtail its repetition in the future.

Individual memory always represents a particular point of view, a re-focalisation of collective memories which, in their turn, are the result of different strategies of selection of, and from, what is available to be remembered. Memory therefore is not a natural faculty; it is rather a set of representations (verbal, visual, gestural, behavioural) which stems from a constant process of negotiation between different actors and their identities (Mitzsal, 2003). Memory could be contested or even shared, but it is always called upon to justify the present and its meanings. As a discourse, memory is obtained through the preservation – the reconstruction and celebration – of remembrance, but also with forgetting, with oblivion. The *object* and the *agency* of memory are what emerge from the joint operation of forgetting and re-remembering, from both the repression and the re-elaboration of the past; and which are thus a construction and a force always starting from the present, of which it cannot be but a projection.

This is a point on which almost all theorists of cultural memory agree; for example, Marc Augé, who claims that "oblivion is the living force of

---

[1] I am here only very briefly summarising concepts and perspectives on memory that I have developed in Demaria (2006). Literature on memory is vast: for a general overview cf. Pethes and Ruchatz (2001) and, especially, Assmann A. (1999), Lotman and Uspenskij (1975), Ricoeur (2000).

memory, and what is remembered is its result" (Augé 1998, p. 34, my translation). In studying cultures, we need to look at the way they use and re-configure time; to identify the "figures of oblivion" through which individual and collective lives are "rendered fiction" (*mises en fiction*). These are narratives that always bring into play individual stories and references to collective experiences; the discordances of particular times and the concordances of general archives which we hope to find within a multi-vocal telling. They are narratives inscribed in rituals, as Augé emphasises: "no dimension of time can be conceived alone, and the ritual is an exemplary case of that tension between memory and waiting which characterises the present, in as much it organises the passage from a before to an after, of which it is at the same time a transfer and a reference" (*ibid.* p. 79, my translation).

There are three main figures of oblivion: that of *return*, the ambition of which is to find a lost time, eliminating the near past in order to recuperate a remote one; that of *suspension* as opposed to return, in which we seek for the present temporarily splitting it from the past and the future; that of *beginning*, or *re-beginning*, which must not be confused with *repetition*, and which looks for a new future on the basis of a reconstruction of the past. Each of these figures, and the ritual that it underlines, even if it elaborates both social and individual time, does not necessarily maintain a similar meaning for the single person and for the group participating in it: what a community might indeed forget, as, for example, specific episodes or periods of violence might, on the contrary, be not forgotten or, at least, overcome by the subject abused by that violence. Every culture then finds its own ways of remembering, on the bases of its values and its visions of the world. It is thus that a collective memory becomes a culturally determined one, within which identity becomes the objective of a cultural strategy, habitually the function of a power structure.[2]

Do nations have an unconscious? The power of narratives

To re-define an identity always entails building a new and therefore a differently constituted memory and the process applies both to the individual and to the group, to a community, to a nation. But it is precisely the passage from the former, the *private*, to the latter, the *public*, and their specific differences, that constitutes one of the more intractable problems of the politics of reconciliation following both inter- and intra-state conflicts. This politics demands the reconstruction of a collective memory on the bases of violent individual experiences; but it is also a politics founded on the efforts to heal *particular* traumatic pasts on the basis of a collective recognition of the experiences and values inscribed in those very same individual pasts.

How can we extend to cultural memory and to collective social actors

---

[2] There is no space here to deepen the complex debate on social and cultural memory. However, it is important to mention the seminal work of the French sociologist Maurice Halbwachs (1925, 1950) from which all the reflections on the interrelations between individual and collective memories have stemmed. See also Bal, Crewe and Spitzer (1999) and Mitzsal (2003).

the (Freudian) idea of negation and repression, together with that of the necessity of a collective work of mourning lived out, and relived, in order to overcome a moment of horrifying violence, a trauma? The question remains open and is widely debated by psychologists, psychiatrists, philosophers, sociologists, political scientists, and others, including creative writers, critics and journalists. We should perhaps remember, as stressed by Violi (2006), that the term trauma comes from the Greek word of medical origin *titrosko*, meaning to pierce, referring to a "wound with laceration". It designates a concept blending three different semantic components: the laceration of the cutaneous lining, the violence with which the laceration is inflicted, and the consequences on the whole organism of such a piercing. It is established that this concept has been recuperated by psychoanalysis, becoming one of the basic categories of its theory and practice. A trauma is what causes a neurosis, being a violent shock, lacerating the psychic "coating" – the containing structure of an individual – and thus affecting his or her organism.

Individual wounding and traumas can be either repressed or faced through the work of mourning. But for an act of mourning to be successful one needs a reality check, which implies first to accept the loss, and eventually either to enter a phase of a liberating oblivion or to face the past and to integrate it into the present. On the contrary, the work of mourning fails when reality data are repressed, and the past keeps on obsessing the present. The censorship or the manipulation of a collective memory is, for Ricoeur (2002), the perversion of a work of mourning which does not meet and mingle with remembrance: the "patient" does not get active, does not elaborate the trauma, failing to exercise memory as a practice for healing the past. The public space, inhabited by what Freud himself has called psychosocial others, can be interpreted as the equivalent of that intermediate place (a sort of gymnasium) separating, and at the same time uniting, the therapist and the patient. Maybe, as Violi also suggests, this intermediate public space could be seen as the place in which the skin of the social body affected by the trauma is reconstituted. A conflict, the violence of an enemy within, is in fact an event capable of lacerating the social texture of social containment, made by all those rules and norms which allow people to live together. We find this very same idea in Trauma Studies where, it is claimed, a collective trauma is a "blow to the basic tissues of social life that damages the bonds attaching people together and impairs the prevailing sense of communality (...) 'I' continue to exist, though damaged and maybe even permanently changed. 'You' continue to exist, though distant and hard to relate to. But 'We' no longer exist as a connected pair or as linked cells in a larger communal body" (Eikson, 1995, p. 187).

To interrogate a politics of memory, the processes by which it is militarised (or de-militarised), is a complex operation, starting from the fact that it triggers unforeseeable mechanisms. To recognise and, thus, to re-build a past, should in fact imply abandoning one self to the "other" (the distant "You") in the present, yielding to its difference, having welcomed and understood it. Yet this possibility remains more of a project than a practice. It happens, for example, that individual memories refer to a collective memory that does not find any reconciliation in the cultural and historical remembering of a nation, as happened and still happens in Italy in respect of its Fascist past, where memory remains divided. More generally speaking, it happens, as Tzvetan Todorov has suggested, that "in the modern world the 'cult' of memory does not always serve good causes, and we should not be too bewildered by that" (1995, p. 43, my translation). The problem is that of the creation of a public discourse, of the elaboration of what is normally defined as the "official version" of the "facts": "what we blame the perpetrators for is not that they select only specific elements of the past, but that they claim the right to control the choice of the elements to be retained" (ibid.).

It is not by chance that Ricoeur locates the relationship between individual and collective memory in the diverse forms of its manipulation, in its wounds and in its illnesses. But, at the same time, Ricoeur seems to believe in the therapeutic power of recognition, joined with that of a critical history opposing the prejudgments of official collective memories. What is most difficult is not to tell otherwise or to be recounted by others, but to tell otherwise the founding events of our collective identity, mainly national, and to let others tell it: this is the most difficult task. And it is at this level of collective identity that, for Ricoeur, we should raise the notion of "one self as another" (cf. Ricoeur 1998). It is the meaning of what happened that is not fixed once and for all, and not only because there could be different interpretations of what happened, but because, as Ricoeur suggests, the moral charge attached to the sense of guilt for the past can be weighted or lightened, depending either on the accusation imprisoning the guilty one in a painful feeling of the irreversible – or in the forgiving, opening the perspective of a liberation from the debt, which is equal to a conversion of the very sense of the past.

But the reinterpretation of the past can also be seen as a liberating use of memory which operates, at the level of narration, as a retroactive achieving of the future's vision of the apprehension of the past. In simpler words, the past itself can be (narratively) changed in order to build and live a better future. The memory thus resurrected is a model for historical knowledge, informed by an act of forgiving, and by a criticism of the retrospective illusion of fatality. Forgiving is thus a particular kind of oblivion, the final stage of an effective work of mourning. But can we really forgive torture and abuses? Ricoeur cites Derrida's idea of forgiving as one founded on a paradox: if our form of forgiving (based on an essential Abrahamism) forgives only what can be expiated, can we really forgive? Or, better, can we really forgive the unforgivable? And what do we forgive: something or someone? For Derrida (2004, see also Derrida 2005) there are two kinds of forgiving: that which depends on the measurability of the punishment, a conditioned one; and the unconditional one, that which forgives the unforgivable. This is the reason why it will always be impossible to base a politics on acts of forgiving: the law can rely on the conditioned forgiving, but it will always end in a partial reconciliation therapy.

Ricoeur does recognise this paradox, but suggests the possibility of a dis-entangling, a dis-joining of the agent from the action. The agent thus becomes a guilty individual to whom is afforded the capacity to re-commence: he or she is separated from the evil act, an act that remains unforgivable. This split refers to the very core of agency and to its potentiality, which does not limit itself to its inscriptions in "the flows of the world". Of course, it implies an act of trust, even of faith, an act of recognition which could result in the construction of a *happy memory*. Recognition becomes the *minor miracle* of memory:

> Every act of memory (*faire-mémoire*) is thus summed up in recognition. (...) The price to be paid was the conjuction between the work of memory and the work of mourning. But I believe that in certain favourable circumstances, such as the right given by another to remember, or better, the help contributed by others in sharing memories, recollection can be said to be successful and mourning to be checked along the fatal slope of melancholy, that attraction to sorrow. If it were so, happy memory would become memory at peace. (Ricoeur, 2000, p. 494)

Is this miracle possible? Let's now move to one case study where the "miracle" of reconciliation has been at least evoked.

The South African Truth and Reconciliation Commission
The South African Truth and Reconciliation Commission (henceforward TRC)[3] proposed itself as a therapeutics of the social body of the "new" South African nation, working on the edge of immanence and transcendence. It was a ritual aimed at the construction of "shared competences" which, as Luc Boltanski (1992) reminds us, does not always address a social actor's knowledge and beliefs, but rather the capacity to coordinate the temporal dimension of social life. In other words, mobilisation and collective effort aims at the "construction of good causes" in order to justify actions.[4] It seems to me that the testimonies and the confessions that took place in the many halls around the country (in schools, in churches, in theatres) where the TRC organised its hearings, had been, in their turn, an undertaking aimed at the building of good reasons to justify reconciliation by synchronising both different temporalities and diverse memories. Reconciliation appears to be a potentially inter-subjective construction which tries to supplant previous antagonisms and within which, through narratives, different discursive strategies are fused: cognitive and pragmatic strategies, but also emotional ones, based on political and religious

---

[3] For more details on the different TRC bodies and committees, procedures and functioning, see Lollini (2006a and 2006b) and the rich bibliography included; for the role of truth commissions in general see Avruch and Vejarano (2001), Hamber and Wilson (2002).
[4] I am here referring to the Luc Boltanski (1992) theory on the construction of a public opinion and a public space, which, starting from Adam Smith's position, explores the different constructions of a "distant" spectator and his/her mediated relation with the ones who suffer.

beliefs and forms of trust. It has been an immense effort to stimulate a collective sensibility and re-organisation of values, with a view to creating a hypothetical national moral conscience.

Let us now move to some examples of this ritual and, specifically, to key extracts from the transcription of the testimony of Evelyn Zweni, which took place in Cape Town, on 22 April 1996.[5]

DR BORAINE: We invite Nomakula Evelyn Zweni to the witness stand please. Good morning Ms Zweni, you are very welcome, we are delighted to see you. Thank you for coming. Ms Zweni yes first put that on (...) So you have come a very-very long way and we'd like you to tell your story to all of us now, and not only to those in this room, but of course to many – many others who are listening on the radio, or perhaps will watch the television or read about it in the newspapers. You have a story that we all need to hear. And Pumla Gobodo is going to help you as you tell that story.

MS ZWENI: In 1959 we all coveted to get away. We formed an organisation because we were tortured (...) I can still remember what they said to me. Because at that time I was still – I hated apartheid with all my heart (...)

MS GOBODO-MADIKIZELA: Mamma these memories we know are very difficult for you to recall. We understand that they are terrible, we understand. If you want to wait, you can just take your time. You can take your time mamma.

MS ZWENI (...) The citizens were running in front of us. They were just bodies, strewn all over the place in front of us. I am from the ANC, there were just dead bodies all over the place. Some were trying to climb buildings, from Langa, that's where actually everything happened. That was the time I kneeled down and try to pray, that's when – that's when I kneeled down he was bleeding from his head (...) I said God please I am asking you, I am asking you God, we are tired of apartheid, after that I left, I simply left (...) We burned these places up, there was a bar where I use to live, we burnt it – I am telling you we burnt it. Because they use to call us kaffirs how can you call a person kaffir, what is that – what is kaffir, what is that, what is that? I don't want apartheid at all. You will be beaten up – you would be beaten up in your land by the boers. People who came from abroad [intervention].

MS GOBODO-MADIKIZELA: We are sorry mamma – sorry mamma would you like us to continue?

MS ZWENI: Yes we must (...) Nobody – nobody said anything, just shootings. Something said – somebody said it was very full in the room and somebody said we got this from Suvukwe. Bullets were just flying all over, there was a [indistinct] I hid next to a shop, I told – I asked my God, I asked God – God if it is you who has allowed this, if it is you who want us to be killed [intervention](...)

---

[5] All the documents of the TRC, including the transcriptions of the testimonies and the confession, can be found on the South African governmental web site http://www.doj.gov.za/trc

MS ZWENI: Yes I know, I agree we must have reconciliation, now because if you don't – if you don't take the pus out of – out of a wound, that would will never heal. We understand that this pus has to be taken out of this heal – this wound for it to heal. I am grateful that yes this reconciliation must happen. But there is one thing I will never forgive and that's apartheid, apartheid I don't even want to see it anywhere I go.

MS GOBODO-MADIKIZELA: Mamma how do you feel about coming here during these past minutes talking to us, how do you feel now that you have expressed yourself?

MS ZWENI: I feel like that I have vented everything from myself. But now I am worried about my child, God will give me a forgiveness, because I pray to him all the time, yes he will give me peace. I also pray that he gives me peace, a soldier dies in the war. But now how can I – how can I accept the death of somebody else's child if I will not accept my own child's death.

MS GOBODO-MADIKIZELA: Yes.

MS ZWENI: On this date, on the 22nd I do accept reconciliation with both hands.

To the victims, to those who were deprived of an identity, is given not only a voice (*the subaltern can speak*), and thus a recuperated subject position, but also the enormous power of forgiving. Doctor Boraine starts by recognising both the personal suffering of Mamma Zweni and the collective need for her story to be heard, thereby identifying and re-constituting an audience to coincide with that of the nation. A story becomes an object of value that needs to be shared, and that tells us about constant abuses, producing a narrative whereby the main actor is the conflict itself, which sweeps away everything else inexorably and permanently. The reason I choose this testimony is because I consider it to be paradigmatic: there are no direct accusations against specific people or named persons, but rather an individual recounting of a collective condition (very often, in her telling, Mamma Zweni moves from the "I" to the "We"). Here we are not overwhelmed by a scene of torture; we become a spectator of the experience of a tortured life which has already become an individual memory, with its repetitions, with its absence of linearity and cohesion, with its prayers, its rhythm and its unsolved tensions. The testimony of this old woman is imbued with a still vivid and graphic sense of a hounded life lacerated by a conflict that does not allow people to rest.

We are also confronted with the absoluteness of Evil: what the story cannot articulate is precisely the meaning of the past, its sense, the logic of the enemy's deeds, as when Mamma Zweni repeats: "Because they use to call us *kaffirs*, how can you call a person *kaffir*, what is that – what is *kaffir*, what is that, what is that? I don't want apartheid at all. You will be beaten up – you would be beaten up in your land by the *boers*. People who came from abroad… ". To the tiredness, and to the lack of understanding of the past expressed by this old woman, the Commissioner replies with a declaration of empathy: "We are sorry mamma – sorry Mamma, would you like us to continue?", to which mamma replies: "Yes we must". The need to tell is a collective duty, the same one that in the end prompts the victim to say: "I am grateful that yes this reconciliation must happen. But there is one thing I will never forgive and that's apartheid, apartheid. I don't even want to see it anywhere I go".

What is unforgivable is the very past, the past as an ideology which had specific material effects. It is almost as if this woman is performing what Ricoeur has outlined: the criminal act is separated from the agent, the ideas from those who believed in them. The testimony ends with the recognition of the benefits brought by the rituals. "How do you feel now that you have expressed yourself?" asks Mrs Gobodo-Madikizela, and mamma Zweni replies: "I feel like that I have vented everything from myself. But now I am worried about my child, God will give me a forgiveness, because I pray to him all the time, yes he will give me peace. I also pray that he gives me peace, a soldier dies in the war. But now how can I – how can I accept the death of somebody else's child if I will not accept my own child's death". Mrs Gobodo's answer is a simple "yes", followed by the ritual formula of reconciliation which, even if it sounds almost like a performative speech act, leaves us with many doubts about the real efficacy of such a re-beginning (to use Augé's category), about the passage from an obsessive and obsessed memory to a cathartic oblivion. This woman has not yet completed her mourning, therefore how can she identify herself with a healed community and really adhere to a collective subjectivity able to forgive? Mamma Zweni abandons the stage with an unsolved and suspended question: how can I accept other people's suffering, if I am not really at peace? It is not by chance that her last appeal is to God, the only Being who can really concede peace, and to whom Mamma Zweni turns with a prayer, bidding for a perhaps impossible serenity, seeking a probably insufficient justification: her son was a soldier, and soldiers may die fighting. The real enemy, apartheid, is not, however, forgiven. Is it true, then, that we cannot forgive the unforgivable? The performative force of public recognition seems here to surrender to what has been called a weak reconciliation, haunted by a not very happy memory.

I shall now move to the side of the perpetrators, to a case of the so-called *black violence*, to the abuses and the killings committed by the black activists during their fights against apartheid. Here are some extracts from the confession of Mr Peni, a very young man who had murdered an American girl, guilty only of being white. His "confession" takes place in front of the Amnesty Committee, which had the power to concede amnesty if it judged the reported criminal actions a "political act".

MR BRINK: Well now you were a leading light in your organisation, I presume you kept abreast of politics in general?
MR PENI: Are you stating or are you asking a question?
MR BRINK: I am asking you a question. You, according to the information in front of me, you were a leading light in your organisation and you must have had a general awareness of political personalities and political organisations throughout the country.

MR PENI: Yes that is so.

MR BRINK: Yes. So you must have been aware that there were more than just two White people who were members of the African National Congress?

MR PENI: Yes but they are confined to their own areas.

MR BRINK: Yes, but the point is you knew there were White people who were members of organisations with whom you were then in alliance.

MR PENI: Yes.

MR BRINK: Had Mr Joe Slovo been in the township that afternoon would you have also stabbed and stoned and killed him?

MR PENI: No I would not have.

MR BRINK: Why not?

MR PENI: Everybody knew him.

MR BRINK: Yes, but you see I ask that because in answer to your counsel you said that had you known that Amy Biehl was a comrade you probably wouldn't have behaved any differently. In other words notwithstanding the fact that you were aware that she was a comrade you would have taken part in her killing.

MR PENI: Could you please repeat that Sir.

MR BRINK: In answer to your counsel at this inquiry you told the Committee that had you been aware of the fact that Amy Biehl had been a comrade you would nonetheless not have acted any differently. In other words you would have taken part in her murder.

MR PENI: Are you stating or are you asking a question?

MR BRINK: I am asking you a question.

MR PENI: Please repeat it (...)

MR PENI: Nobody knew about Amy Biehl first of all. At the time we were very angry as students as well. The reason why I said that it would not have made a difference if I had known she was a comrade is because of the high spirits of the students at the time.

MR BRINK: Are you then saying that your reason for killing Amy Biehl was because of your high spirits at the time?

MR PENI: I am saying that the reason why I said it would not have made a difference is because it was due to the aims of the organisation (...)

MR BRINK: And your evidence here was that you participated in this murderous attack because the aim of your organisation was to bring back land to the African people, now what I want to know is, how would the killing of an unarmed, defenceless woman possibly help you to achieve that aim?

MR PENI: We believed that the minority White people ruling the country would realise that we wanted our land back. We also believed that they were going to give up this land back to the African people.

MR BRINK: Is it your evidence that by murdering, in the most brutal fashion, Amy Biehl, the African people would get their land back?

MR PENI: Yes it's my evidence.

MR BRINK: The killing of one, single, defenceless woman would effect that?

MR PENI: First of all I would like to rectify something, gender was not significant. Our aim was to attack each White person and go forward.

JUDGE WILSON: But it was not the aim of the PAC at that time to kill every White person they saw, was it?

MR PENI: Please repeat the question.

JUDGE WILSON: It was not the aim of the PAC at that time to kill every White person they saw, was it?

MR PENI: It is true, if it was necessary for the youth to do so it would happen.

JUDGE WILSON: You are not answering my question. Was it the policy of the PAC to kill every White person they saw?

MR PENI: It could not happen that every person be killed, but there was one slogan *"One Settler, one bullet"* (...)

MR BRINK: Mr Peni, isn't it the position that on that dreadful afternoon you were involved in a mindless, savage attack on this young woman, and that it was not politically motivated at all?

MR PENI: Our killing Amy Biehl had everything to do with politics (...)

ADVOCATE DE JAGER: And although you might not have achieved what you politically wanted to achieve by killing one person, one White, but the fact is that if you have killed hundreds of Whites or thousands of them you would have had your land back, or all of them, if you've killed all the Whites?

MR PENI: The land is in the hands of the African people, it is not that the PAC was totally against the White people, all they wanted was their land back.

ADVOCATE DE JAGER: And the struggle, as you understood it, was directed against the Whites, is that correct?

MR PENI: Yes.

ADVOCATE DE JAGER: And I am correct in saying that it was because the Whites had the political power in their hands?

MR PENI: Yes.

ADVOCATE DE JAGER: So if we want to come to the truth, as we try to do, we can't say that it wasn't a racial war that's been fought in this country, it was based on race, isn't that so?

MR PENI: Please repeat your question.

ADVOCATE DE JAGER: Wasn't it in fact a racial war that's been fought in this country and the reason for that was because the Whites had the political power and the Blacks strived to get that power?

MR PENI: Yes it is so.

ADVOCATE DE JAGER: And wasn't that the reason why you would have killed any White you see?

MR PENI: Yes it is so because we wanted our land.

The dialogue between this PAC (the Pan African Congress) militant and the lawyers and judges of the Commission develops through many difficulties and a lot of fatigue. Translation problems, Mr Peni's struggles in understanding not only the whole procedure, but also the linguistic register and the contents of the questions he is asked, produce a fragmented, interrupted, tiring exchange, characterised by the constant need of meta-communication.

I cannot enter all the possible and different ways in which we could analyse this confession. What interests me is that the whole topic of the hearing is not so much what really happened and how, but why: what Peni is called to account for are the reasons and the aims of this terrible murder of an innocent person, who became totally de-humanised and had been reduced to her skin colour. Every white person was in fact an enemy, without any other distinction being relevant. The hatred brought by apartheid as told by Mamma Zweni is directly inscribed (incarnated) in subjects rendered objects. But the perpetrator repeatedly affirms: "Our killing Amy Biehl had everything to do with politics", thus appealing to higher loyalties (Cohen, 2001)[6] which seem not to have been broken. Mr Peni is not repentant: he legitimises himself as an integral, upright subject wholly dedicated to a collective struggle for a re-conquest that justifies a murder as revenge for expropriated land.

The interpretation of what may be judged a political act is rather a forced one. Mr Peni's confession is not a capitulation, neither is it a recognition of the values of the new South African community and the validity of its rules. At the end of this hearing, it is very clear how the Commission itself tries to historicise a practice and to bring Peni's killing back into a frame able to subtract from the violent act its brutality and meaninglessness:

ADVOCATE DE JAGER: So if we want to come to the truth, as we try to do, we can't say that it wasn't a racial war that's been fought in this country, it was based on race, isn't that so?
MR PENI: Please repeat your question.
ADVOCATE DE JAGER: Wasn't it in fact a racial war that's been fought in this country and the reason for that was because the Whites had the political power and the Blacks strived to get that power?
MR PENI: Yes it is so.

Truth is not what happened, but why; and the *why* is because there was a war. Somehow, the very truth which should lead to reconciliation (*revealing is healing* was the TRC's slogan) is based on a denial of responsibility: only conflict – together with a displacement of point of view, and one that traces an individual's action back to an instance of that same conflict – can be guilty; and this in order that the nation and its citizens be freed of guilt. Here is an example of the creation of memory for the present; within which frame is established what has to be remembered.

The TRC is an example of a quasi-juridical procedure which has profoundly changed the concept of evidence, since it does not deal with the establishment of facts, but with beliefs and situations that must be verified in the light of their persuasive strength. The relationship between the *testis contra se* and truth is therefore very problematic. What is at stake is not only how truth is an *effet du discours* [a

---

[6] In *States of Denial*, Stanley Cohen (2001) lists different ways through which perpetrators either deny their wrongs, or justify them assigning the responsibilities to something or somebody else.

discourse effect], always inter-subjectively negotiated, but also which truths are obtained, and how, and what they tell us. When truth is no longer a matter of factual evidence, it multiplies and starts to coincide with the different nuances of the structures of testimonies and confessions, to merge with the effect of the authenticity that it manages to convey: an authenticating of one's own integrity, or of one's own rage, as in Mr Peni's hearing.

The only way to save the South African Nation and to bring it towards some kind of reconciliation seems to be that of a construction of truth that implies a double movement of identification and generalisation of guilt. With the TRC South Africa forces the guilty ones to step out of their anonymity: it isolates them and calls them by their names; but then, in order not to punish them all, it traces back their actions to a disincarnated set of values, to a disembodied manipulating *actant*[7] (not to an *actor*). This kind of ritual somehow de-essentialises truth (accepting the negotiation of evidence), but then needs to re-essentialise reconciliation in the name of a transcendental "Sender". The right of impunity is thus re-defined on the bases of two different strategies: a process of appealing to, and recognition of, the collective in the name of a general Truth (which exists, is there, can be revealed), and an immediate historicising of this truth that in the end is linked to political practices, to conflict. At the same time, forgiving and reconciliation on the one side, and political and ideological causes on the other, transform again this cultural mechanism into something disembodied: the nation. Thus everybody seems to have to participate in the collective construction of truth but, moreover, seems to have to accept the consequences of this construction.

The Chilean *Comisión Nacional sobre Prisión Política y Tortura*

I shall conclude by briefly discussing another example of the rewriting of a national memory, the Valech Report (*Informe Valech*)[8] of the *Comisión Nacional sobre Prisión Política y Tortura*, constituted in August 2003, by the then President of Chile, Don Ricardo Lagos Escobar. Thirty years after another tragic 9/11, that of 1973, when Salvador Allende was assassinated and the dictatorship of Augusto Pinochet began, Chile seemed still to need public and shared recognition of a past. The reconciliation process that followed Pinochet's forced resignation (in the spring of 1990) had in fact been judged by the victims as a way actually to re-create the homogenisation of the political subjectivities of the nation state (Frazier, 1999). The truth of the past had not been revealed, nor had the practice of torture been admitted. The Valech Report (RV) assumes this mandate, and presents to the nation not only a long and detailed analysis of the dictatorship years, but also

---

[7] In narratology an actant is a syntactic unity of the narrative process, who will then, in the course of the narrative, be given a specific role, and be invested by specific values (ideologies). An actant is thus like a character, *a dramatis persona*. The main actants are the subject and the object, the sender and the receiver.

[8] This document is online at http: //www.gobiernodechile.cl/comision_valech

eventually dares to publish the testimonies of the victims of torture. Its aim is therefore as I quote from its Introduction:

> [T]anto por parte del Estado como de la sociedad chilena en su conjunto, de contribuir a reparar el perdurable daño inflingido a miles de personas, cuya condición de victímas de la represión política no había sido admitida en forma explícita hasta ahora. / As much on behalf of the State as on behalf of Chilean society as a whole, to contribute to the reparation of the lasting damage inflicted on thousands of persons, whose condition as victims of political repression had not been explicitly admitted until now.[9]

The healing mechanism underlying this document is very similar to the South African procedure, with the important exception that here the process of recognition is not a public ritual in which truth is revealed, but a public document, a text which denounces a violent past. It is then the practice of the text to function as an act of reparation which

> can lead to some kind of acceptance and reconciliation. Once wrongs are done, they cannot be undone. But I believe that recognition of what actually happened – of the victims' experience and the perpetrators' responsibility, and ultimately of the broader structures of cause and effect, can provide at least a symbolic redress which can allow some healing to take place, and individual societies to move on. (Hoffman, 2003, p. 280)

The Valech Report does not publicise the name of the victims, nor their faces. What is being recognised is a set of events that, thanks to their narration, enter national history by coming out from silence:

> Consciente o inconscientemente, una conspiración de silencio sobre la tortura se fue extendiendo lentamente por el país / Consciously or unconsciously, a conspiracy of silence about the torture has been slowly extended throughout the country. (RV, p. 1)

The report's *Presentación* confides with specific rhetorical strategies in order to obtain its *symbolic redress.* The tone is mainly emotional and the desired effect is a non-rational identification, a premise for a re-formed collective conscience which appears to be the result of a moving transformation. In this way the Report prepares its readers, gives them a competence, an affective readiness to hear and to listen to what happened. But let us see how it does so. What immediately strikes the reader of the Introduction is the absence of specific subjects responsible for a lucid and voluntary conspiracy (they did not want people to know), and a non-voluntary one (people did not want to know, or they were not allowed to know). The Commission points its finger at a condition of literal denial (Cohen, 2001) which is in itself the

---

[9] Since the document is in Spanish, and there is no official English translation, I prefer to include here the original text, followed by my translation.

subject of a slow and inexorable process, without a specific beginning, and with an end that it is the Commission's task to mark.

The image is that of a superior will that, from above, spreads itself – as a liquid, a shadow – contaminating a whole territory. But by recognising this evil, and also the evil of silence, the Commission poses itself as the subject that will operate in contrast to it: the comprehension and the empathy of the present Chilean government are played against the terror and the conspiracies of the past regime. But what is really the sense of denouncing thirty years after the fact a politics which used torture as one of its main tools, the private spectacle of its power, turning fear into the permanent condition of a nation?

¿Qué sentido tiene hacer un informe treinta años después? (...) después de meses de escuchar relatos íntimos, susurrados, relatados con dolor y hasta con llanto (...) de tanto chileno y chilena preso y torturado, no nos asiste la menor duda de que esta parte de la verdad también nos era debida para completar, de la mejor manera posible, la reparación y la justicia que el país le debe a estos hermanos, para avanzar por la senda siempre difícil y necesaria del reencuentro y de la reconciliación entre los chilenos / What sense is there in drawing up a report thirty years on (...) after months of listening to intimate, whispered, accounts, told with pain and even with tears (...) of so many Chilean imprisoned or tortured men and women, we do not have the slightest doubt that this part of the truth was also owed to us to complete, in the best posible way, the reparation and the justice that the country owes to those brothers and sisters, in order to advance on the always difficult and necessary road to the re-encounter and reconciliation of all Chileans. (RV, pp. 1-2)

Intimate stories, painful and whispered accounts, interrupted by sighs: the rhetoric of truth, as we have already seen, demands recognition of the suffering of the other. It is the private and tragic dimension of testimony that transformed the Commission, dispelling its doubts and perplexities, transfiguring it. Moving from a subject "we, the commissioner", to a collective "we, the people", the text further shows the emergence of a new actor with one duty and one need: justice and reparation. The Commission has changed through the reiteration of listening:

Más de treinta mil personas han desfilado frente a nosostros, las hemos visto y las hemos escuchado. Más de treinta mil personas se han atrevido a acercarse a nuestras oficinas (...) Y más de treinta mil veces hemos escuchado el estupor, el temor, la impotencia que aún genera la dignidad violada por agentes del estado (...) Así nos hemos dado cuenta, en primera persona, de que la corrupción del poder es la peor de las corrupciones, pues termina minando las bases de la credibilidad esencial que todo ciudadano guarda de las instituciones del Estado. / More than thirty thousand people have processed before us, we have seen them and listened to them. More than thirty thousand people have dared to approach our offices (...) And more than thirty thousand times have we listened to the stupor, the fear, the impotence still generated by their sense of a dignity violated by agents of the State (...) Thus have we noted, at first hand, that the corruption of power is the worst of corruptions, because it ends up undermining the bases of credibility that for every citizen are held as essential to the institutions of State. (RV, pp. 1-2)

The Report itself becomes a testimony, trying to trigger in its recipient a sort of mimetic desire. But the necessary act of recognition of the past must also involve the victims, and not only "public opinion". The silence which invaded the country had been mirrored by the silence of the victims:

¿Pero por qué el silencio de las víctimas? Se entiende el de los victimarios, que a su vez han sido víctimas de sus acciones? Después de mucho meditar, nos damos cuenta de que es un silencio basado no sólo en el temor, cuanto temor! También hay un aspecto de elemental dignidad (...) descorrer el velo de la tortura, de la humillación, de la violación física y psicológica, es algo muy difícil de hacer (...) Y ese mismo silencio comprensible fue ahondando el daño de los sufrimientos no compartidos, de la confidencia ahogada, de aquello que preferimos poner en la estantería de las pesadillas y arrancar de los archivos de la historia. / But why the silence of the victims? And, needless to say, that of the perpetrators, who in turn have been victims of their own actions? After much meditating, we note that it is a silence based not only on fear, how much fear! There is also an aspect of basic dignity (...) to draw aside the veil of torture, of humiliation, of physical and psychological violation, is something very difficult to do (...) And that same comprehensible silence has deepened the danger of unshared sufferings, of smothered confidence, of whatever we wish to shelve in nightmares and drag from the archives of history. (RV, p. 2).

The apparent denial of the victims is understood after "a long meditation". Comprehending the fear and facing the shame which very often stop the possibility of recounting the past is also a competence slowly, if ever, acquired: to be able to tell what happened encounters the absence of proper words. Victims have to learn to assume a narrative role and a discursive position that refer to an event which annihilated them as subjects, and for which, so far, there has been no frame.

This presentation shows a feature which is proper to the writing of pain and suffering whereby evil emerges as an indexing sign, similar to pronouns, that points to mobile discursive positions that any and every one can inhabit, but also dismiss:

Evil (...) is a movable feast. It has the strange characteristic of being at once an absolute and yet something far closer to what linguistics calls a "shifter". Pronouns (...) are purely indexical signs, which refer only to the moment they are spoken (...) Evil has something of the same aura (...) The surest of terms, invariably invoked with the most passionate if at times desperate conviction, evil also spins on its axis, loses its way. It behaves like that part of language which fatally, if invisibly, undermines the certainty of our speech. (Rose, 2004, p. 115)

But evil is also mobile because it can be diluted and extended, and applied to all sorts of different entities: it is not so much radical as radically unstable.

This introduction reaches its conclusion by moving towards and into the present: in less than two pages not only have thirty thousand people passed by but also thirty years during which the country has already begun to change:

> Treinta años depués en que tenemos un país muy diferente, que nos obliga a reconocer algo que siempre debió ser reconocido como inaceptable. Y, por lo mismo, treinta años depués en que hemos vivido un proceso de enfrentar muchos dolores, en que ha despuntado la justicia en muchos casos y en que miramos con otros ojos el futuro, también se puede esperar una generosidad mayor para acoger e integrar en lo mejor de nuestra vida social a aquellos que han sido víctimas de la descalificación, la injusticia y el silencio. / Thirty years after in which we have a very different country, which obliges us to recognise something that always needed to be recognised as unacceptable. And, therefore, thirty years after in which we have lived through a process of confronting much pain, in which justice has been blunted in many cases and in which we regard the future with different eyes, we can also expect a greater generosity in receiving and integrating into the best of our social life those who have been victims of exclusion, injustice and silence. (RV, p. 3)

Now the subject no longer has to learn and to listen, but to act, and it is his duty to do so in the name of an ethic that extends itself from the present to the future, and to the past, which is then not only recognised, but re-interpreted. A new national identity is therefore stated as a result of a politics of memory that establishes new correspondences between the contents of the past and a belonging to the present, now ready to be charged with that past. The text ends by celebrating the value of fraternity inscribed in yet another subject, which is no longer the people, nor the Commission, but a democratic re-founded Nation:

> Chile quisiera saldar en hermandades tanta deuda pendiente entre hermanos de un mismo pueblo, / Chile would wish to pay in brotherhood and sisterhood so many debts undischarged between brothers and sisters of one and the same people. (RV, p. 3)

In the balance between public recognition of the victims and the retention of memories by those who had denied torture, the people should become one... A happy one?

Can they (we) ever forgive?

What is absent not only from the Valech Report, but from the entire Chilean process of reconciliation is the confession of the perpetrators. The descriptions of the horror, and the few passages in which we witness the victims' feelings, lack their counterpart, the public act of contrition which, on the contrary, characterised the South African TRC. These two commissions are therefore not wholly comparable, at least from a juridical point of view: the TRC's peculiarity was to be invested with the power to give amnesty to those who had bid for it, while the Valech Report displayed a purely symbolic and general accusation for institutions and people with no name. Nevertheless, in the TRC *Final Report* the Commissioners did underline the huge gap that divided the victims' perceptions of the violation of their human rights from that of the perpetrators. For the victims, those violent acts were either simply beyond comprehension, thus entering a dimension of mystery and of the unattainable, or pure sadism, actions deliberately cruel and with an end only in themselves. In both reactions violence is part of a world that nobody would like to acknowledge, or to be part of. For the perpetrators, violence is instead a rational consequence of an historical necessity, hence not only part of this world, but one of its fundamental elements as, for example, an outcome of the war on terrorism. What happened in Chile or in South Africa does not seem to be very different from what happened during Nazism, or from what is still happening in Iraq or in Guantánamo. Always, what is pure horror for the victims, for the perpetrators is a "small thing". Here we face the slippage of evil: "I" am never evil, only "you" are (Rose, 2004, p. 117). Nouns as evil or bad thus mime in a perverse way the functioning of the personal pronouns, turning it upside down: unlike the position expressed by the pronoun "I" – that we are all trying to inhabit – nobody wants to occupy the position of evil. To let the perpetrators speak doesn't automatically mean to prompt forgiving, to overcome impunity and to build reconciliation. It is not by chance that the TRC final report has been criticised for its emphasis on personal responsibilities placed in an historical context, and thus justified, hence for the lack of a deep and serious critique of the state power. As in the Chilean report, evil are the acts, and not the individuals. The perpetrators are thus understood in the light of their social bonding and the consequent identification with the dominant ideology.

True evil is always elsewhere, in a disembodied institution, in the act deprived of its agent. Commenting on the TRC *Final Report*, Rose adds: "Attempting to explain the demonic, the Commissioners find something invisible, unnegotiable, sinister (demonic?) at play. Evil, it seems, is not just an absolute, not just a shifter; it is an empty place" (2004, p. 122). This is what seems to emerge also from the Chilean report. Again: can we be happy with it? Or, instead, can we look for a connection between evil as emptiness and evil as a violent and obscene subject? If evil, as Hannah Arendt suggested, cannot be radical but only banal, because it has no depths, it can but confide in its transcendence. Nevertheless, we are left with the fact that it is almost impossible to find the right distance from another distance, that which allowed the creation of an Other so much alien and un-human that needed to be destroyed, to use Bauman's analysis of the mechanism of the Holocaust. This is shown also by the ritual inscribed in the functioning of all the truth and reconciliation commissions, appealing to the transcendence of acts such as that of recognition, forgiving and confession, or to the *mystique* of the nation, as we have seen in the Valech Report. At the same time this document, along with those produced by the TRC, does represent an example of a politics of memory.

It could now be clearer how both memory and the individual and collective identities resting on it, being narratives, cannot be reproduced automatically: they constantly need to be stated, communicated, adapted and negotiated through ritual repetitions. We have now returned where I started from, to the possibility of healing the traumas of a social body, and to the presumed efficacy of reconciliation as an act of re-weaving the social bonding. Telling and narrating, the very practice of recounting, is meant to recompose broken relations or, at least, as in the Valech Report, to mime the possibility. It is here that lies their symbolic efficacy, in the possibility to express pain in a (more) proper and potentially adequate way.

References

Assmann, A. (1999) *Erinnerungsräume: Formen und Wandlungen des kulturellen Gedächtnisses*, München, Oscar Beck.

Augé, M. (1998) *Les formes de l'oubli*, Paris, Payot et Rivages.

Avruch, K. and Vejarano, B. (2001) "Truth and Reconciliation Commissions: A Review Essay and Annotated Bibliography", *Social Justice: Anthropology, Peace, and Human Rights,* vol. 2, nn. 1-2, pp. 47-108.

Bal, M., Crewe, J., Spitzer, L. (1999) (eds.) *Acts of Memory: Cultural Recall in the Present*, Hanover, University Press of New England.

Boltanski, L. (1992) *La souffrance à distance*, Paris, Éditions Métailié.

Boraine, A. (2001) *A Country Unmasked: Inside South Africa's Truth and Reconciliation Commision*, Oxford, Oxford University Press.

Caruth, C. (1995) (ed.) *Trauma: Explorations in Memory*, Baltimore and London, Johns Hopkins University Press.

-----------. (1996) *Unclaimed Experience: Trauma, Narrative, and History*, Baltimore and London, The Johns Hopkins University Press.

Cohen, S. (2001) *States of Denial: Knowing about Atrocities and Suffering* (trad. it. *Stati di negazione: La rimozione del dolore nella società contemporanea*, Roma, Carocci, 2002).

Demaria, C. and Wright, C. (2006) (eds.), *Post-Conflict Cultures. Rituals of Representation*, London, Zoilus Press.

Demaria, C. (2006) *Semiotica e memoria: Analisi del post-conflictto*, Roma, Carocci.

Derrida, J. (2004) *Pardonner: l'impardonnable et l'imperscriptible*, Paris, Editions de l'Herne.
--------------. (2005) *O perdão, a verdade, a reconciliação*, in E. Nascimento (ed.), *Jacques Derrida: Pensar a desconstrucão*, São Paulo, Estação Liberdade, pp. 45-92.
Halbwachs, M. (1925) *Les cadres sociaux de la mémoire,* Alcan, Paris.
--------------. (1950) *La mémoire collective*, Paris, Albin.
Hamber, B. and R. Wilson, R. (2002) "Symbolic Closure through Memory, Reparation and Revenge in Post-conflict Societies", *Journal of Human Rights* 1, pp. 35-53.
Hoffman, E. (2003) "The Balm of Recognition: Rectifying Wrongs through the Generations", in Nicholas Owen (ed.), *Human Rights, Human Wrongs: Oxford Amnesty Lectures*, Oxford, Oxford University Press.
Lollini, A. (2006a) *Costituzionalismo e giustizia di transizione: il ruolo costituente della Commissione sudafricana verità e riconciliazione*, Bologna, il Mulino.
----------. (2006b) "The South African Truth and Reconciliation Commission Experience: Establishing a New Hypothesis on Post-conflict Culture", in C. Demaria and C. Wright (eds.), above.
Lotman, J. M., Uspenskij, B. A. (1975) *Tipologia della cultura*, Milano, Bompiani.
Mitzsal, B. A. (2003) *Theories of Social Remembering*, Maidenhead and Philadelphia, Open University Press – McGraw-Hill Education,.
Pethes, N., Ruchatz, J., (2001) (eds.), *Gedächtnis und Erinnerung. Ein interdisziplinäres Lexicon*, Verlag, Reinbeck.
Ricoeur, P. (2000) *La mémoire, l'histoire, l'oubli*, Paris, Seuil.
----------- (2004) *Parcours de la reconnaissance*, Paris, Éditions Stock.
Rose, J. (2004) *"The Body of Evil"*, *New Formations*, n. 53, pp. 115-129.
Violi, P. (2006) "Storie di donne in una società post-traumatica. Un case study dai Balcani", in P. Violi and C. Demaria, "Il senso dell'altro", *Versus: Quaderni di studi semiotici*, 100, pp. 133-174.

Part 2
Case Studies

Reconstructions and Memories in the Post-Conflict City

Michelle Pépin

Architecture has always been considered to reflect its political, economic, social and cultural context; arguably nowhere is this more evident than within the city. Equally the discipline also recognises the human being's relationship with their environment. In the 1971 work by Norberg-Schulz on existence, space and architecture he suggests that architectural space provides the environmental context and images which guide our human experiences and the ultimate understanding of the world in which we find ourselves. The 1954 and 1978 texts by Heidegger develop the study of the nature of "being". The nature of "being" is concerned with experiences and the expression of those experiences in defining the human being's comprehension of their "beingness"; the self in manifestation. Notions of memory and truth, as constructions of our experiences and understanding, are conditioned by our environmental images; similarly the image that we perceive is determined through the constructions that we hold. The sense of who we are is revealed as intertwined with our environmental contexts and the memories and truths that we form from those. Identification of the self is created through the lived experience. Consequently the city, and the architectural landscape that it presents, form vital elements in the development of our sense of self. This discussion considers these metaphysical concepts in exploration of the post-conflict city.

Post-conflict city, reconstruction, memory, truth

The city, as it has stood through time, is a place of deep contrast and contradiction. The architectural landscape of its physical articulation provides a built context for its people. Its human inhabitants and visitors give it life rescuing it from spiralling into the desolate anonymity of an abandoned film set. It is at once form and symbol, victim and victor of the experiences and expressions of humankind's greatest failings and achievements. A signification of the kaleidoscopic political, economic, social and cultural images of hope, power, leadership, and wealth, simultaneous manifestation of utter despair, poverty, isolation, hopelessness, crime, corruption and violence; add to this a colliding symphony of odour and sound and the vision of the city becomes whole. The city stands as the harbour to all humanity's strength and weakness, both sanctuary and icon of victory and defeat.

The city, even as it lies in ruins, is reborn in its moments of devastation. Accounts of war and conflict have inevitably involved the cities of their destruction. The seminal International Relations text, *History of the Peloponnesian War* (describing the conflict between the Greek city states of Athens and Sparta 431BC) (Thucydides, n.d., translation by Warner 1954), includes a description of the behaviour of cities. Linking power with self-interest, the acquisition of the city, through an act of war, becomes an extension of dominance and wealth. While the city now may no longer (generally) be the city state, conquering, or control of the city reflects a physical and symbolic political act of superiority in the arena of power politics. The city exposes the political act. The reconstruction of a city, a city of post-conflict, in consequence becomes one of the most visible signs and symbols of either political change or political domination. However, the discourse surrounding the reading of the post-conflict city should include reflection on the nature of memory and truth in addition to that of political act, conflict and reconstruction. The discourse on memory study is rapidly becoming well established as a discipline in its own right exposing how memory is created, manipulated and chosen, forging and forming our human sense of who we are and providing the position from which to explain the understanding that we make of our world. Symbolism is implicitly intertwined within the creation of our spaces and places; the inherent identity of these that is in consequence created impacts on how they are perceived and understood. Constructed from metaphors and symbols, visual images and literary narratives, through to tangible built forms of the environmental landscape, the memories and truths that we come to hold become immersed within interpretation of the representations that surround us. While these concepts are explored in this discussion within the contexts of Berlin and Johannesburg, two very different examples of the post-conflict city, and examples which can be curiously linked in a twist of irony relating to events separated by almost one hundred years, the list of post-conflict cities is extensive. Tragically, almost every country across our planet could justifiably lay claim to such a city and its people.

The Truth and Reconciliation Commission, referred to as the TRC, was a court-like body established in South Africa in 1995 post-apartheid to give victims of human rights abuses, under the apartheid system, the opportunity to tell the story of the horrors and brutality that they had suffered. Anybody who felt they had been a victim of violence, including the perpetrators of violence, could come forward and be heard by the TRC. With some of the haunting testimony broadcast on South African national television at the time, the public atonement and cathartic process fostered by the instruments of the TRC were hailed as crucial components in the transition to democracy within the country. These stories have now become part of public record. However, some 10 years later, the South African process has been criticised by some as a failure. The twinned concepts of memory and truth are brought sharply into focus; the nature of memory and truth are questioned, what has been the creation of the testimony? Within the reconstruction of the post-conflict city these abstract metaphysical qualities become translated into a hard reality, a built form, a concrete representation in every way. However, despite its tangible quality, the reading of the city would seem to remain as abstract as the truth and memory that it at once contains and reflects. Italo Calvino, in his 1997 work *Invisible Cities* creates evocative imagery through the literary narrative demonstrating what his title suggests; he tells us that the "invisible landscape conditions the visible one" (p. 20). The metaphor he develops is of course that even the "visible" city which he creates remains an invisible construct, a double metaphor; "the eye does not see things, but images of things that mean other things" (p. 13), thus entering the dialogue about the nature of memory and truth.

From an architectural perspective the discipline has long recognised the human being's implicit relationship with their built environment created through an architectural language that is rich with metaphor and symbolism contained within its very roots. The architectural landscape contains us as human beings, providing the context for and of our experiences. This sentiment is reflected in the work of Norberg-Schulz (1971) in a discussion about existence, space and architecture, when he contends that space, particularly architectural space, can be understood as a "concretization" of "man's" environmental images that form a necessary part of "his" general orientation in the world (p. 7). While he suggests that the notion of "how we experience something" includes the role of the circumstance and manner in which something is experienced (pp. 37-39), experience is translated within memory. In turn, our memory becomes a powerful signifier for the structure by and through which new experiences and understandings, "truths", will be framed. These, in cyclical consequence, become part of the memory construction continuum; memory and truth, one conditioning the other. For Heidegger (1978) the study of the nature of "being" is concerned with how experiences and the expression of those experiences "shape" the human being's comprehension of their "beingness". This he explains, through his existential notion of "being-in-the-world", is brought about through the individual's experiences and the conception of those experiences; the nature of "being" presents as reflecting a need to experience something in order for "beingness" to exist. The nexus between memory and truth, and the conception and translated understanding of experiences emerge as the act of "being", as the manner in which human beings define and recognise their "beingness". The role played by the environmental image becomes a profound contributor in that process of "beingness". Self-identity, the understanding of sense of the self, is thus created through the lived experience. In this delicately orchestrated synchronicity the objects and events of our lives are elevated to signs and symbols of greater understanding and significance. The architectural landscape emerges as more than merely a built form.

How does this then relate to reconstruction of the post-conflict city? Reconstruction, or re-construction, architecturally, means to rebuild. The term construct can be linked to pile; to pile together. It also has connotations with forge, as in to forge together, to join and to form links, and to build. Construct, in other words, is not merely to pile together, it is also that which creates cohesion between, and arguably builds from that something. Heidegger (in translation from his text *Vortrage und Aufsatze, Bauen Wohnen Denken*, 1954) develops the relationship between the Old German for build, "buan", (also meaning "to dwell"), and "bin", (or "am"), deriving from "to build" thus uniting the conceptions of build and "being" ("am") through the act of dwelling (living), and recognising the outcome, the existence or state of "being", as the process of the performance of being. To construct thus becomes linked with the manner of existence. The process by and through which something is experienced is implicit within the notion of existing and thus construct and experience become inextricably intertwined in a choreography between the human being and their environment.

Constructs, in the philosophical understanding of the term, are the ways in which we as human individuals interpret our experiences of the world, a code of meaning which can be ascribed to the given enabling us to create from the given. These (constructs) guide our behaviour (Kelly, 1955). This would suggest that that which is defined as memory may be an externalised reflection which describes the internalised constructions arising as a consequence of our human experiences. Kelly argues that through that which he refers to as "learning", we are able to alter our human constructs; we can also alter the way in which the constructs relate to one another. Thus re-construction could be considered to be a re-forging or re-joining of something already there, a re-interpretation. Re-forging of our environmental images may be at once both as a response to and a reflection of our human circumstance in simultaneous physical manifestation and metaphoric representation. Re-construction bears reference to the process by which the memories (in this instance of the city) have already been "constructed" and will be contained within the memory of those who have lived through the experience of that city. Kelly argues that human constructs can change. This seems to depend on the understanding of the word. "To construct" suggests "to make from something"; however re-construct, through introduction of the prefix "re-", would suggest that that something is already in existence. In human terms, in terms of memory, to re-construct would mean breaking down the memories which are already there, easily done with trees and stones to quote Calvino: "trees and stones are only what they are". However, he also goes further, "the eye does not see things, but images of things that mean other things" (1997, p. 13). That "other thing" resides within the image, for the image appears not to be that which is given, but that which is created from the given. Thus while it appears that only the links change rather than that about which the links are formed, the result is that that which is created from the given becomes re-created both in image and meaning. The reading of the post-conflict city is thus not merely about physical rebuilding, a reconstruction through architectural manifestation, it is also very much about the human act of being; of experience and existence. Reconstruction of the post-conflict city is about rebuilding human memories and truths through reconstruction of the events and experiences of the city.

Etymology suggests that each word contains within its essence all the meanings that have shaped it and brought it into being. Semiotics describes an interrelationship between language and image through a system of signs and signifiers or signification that leads to a corollary of language and image becoming united in meaning. There is an allusion to this concept within a Socratic dialogue on the institution of the city (Cooper, 1997), asserting that "that which keeps its own form unchangingly, which neither receives into itself anything nor itself enters into anything cannot be perceived by the senses at all" and will in consequence be "apprehended by opinion". This statement has profound implications in the explanation of post-conflict reconstruction within the constructs of truth and memory of the city and supports Calvino's assertion that "the invisible landscape conditions the visible one" (1997, p. 20). However, equally, if the invisible landscape conditions the visible one, it may be at least feasible to suggest that even if the physical image changes, is reconstructed, our truth, our memory, the invisible landscape, remains.

But can the visible landscape condition the invisible, for arguably this is what the reconstructed city is endeavouring to achieve, or will it be merely "apprehended by opinion" and ultimately how will it relate to the reading of the political act that was its architect? On 9 April 2003 the world watched as the twenty foot statue of Saddam Hussein was toppled in Firdos Square in central Baghdad. Footage broadcast by global news networks such as CNN, the BBC and Al Jazeera paint different images of the same event, each providing its own layer upon layer of visually and verbally scripted interpretation to be offered into the experience and subsequent memory of the viewer. An undeniably symbolic act, but which symbol does the viewer perceive? The one of toppling the dictator and joyous celebration presented on the one hand or the more unsettling one of American force in action and a crowd in uncontrolled frenzy hinted on the other; of American action in support of the will of the people or of American action inciting the people? These positions may all appear to reflect a "truth" and, with the aid of state of the art technology, the viewer confidently accepts the authenticity of the unfolding drama as s/he assumes a role of witness within apparently real-time transmission. The witness however merely creates from the given, but the status they have unwittingly been accorded authenticates the scripted memory.

Berlin

Berlin is an obvious example of post-conflict reconstruction. The reconstruction of Berlin has been both revered and criticised on many levels. Architecture has always been considered to reflect its political, economic, social and cultural context and the discourse which supports this is wide and well established. So is the Berlin of today, its re-invention, an architectural manifestation of the twenty first century city, or of the new Europe, or of a city struggling to reconcile its past with its future, or is it merely presenting a fragile and brittle façade to reconstruction, some cruel and obvious irony to be better understood 50 years hence? Certainly the city is being reconstructed, put together differently, but in the memories of those who experience and experienced the city whose truth or what truth is being used? Berlin is however also a city torn apart by war, brutally divided in defeat by a wall which was to survive for almost 30 years, from 1961 to 1989. A wall which was to become, and remains a powerful symbol of simultaneous division and unification is now preserved in sections as a reminder of the unspeakable horror and acts of bravery that it inspired and represents. While sections of the physical form of the wall remain unaltered, the context of the wall has changed and so how it enters into the conscious recollection of those who experienced and experience it will depend on the construct; an expression of creating from the given.

For those who have no experience of the wall it becomes "apprehended by opinion", presented in a new context which strives to dictate the manner of its memory. This type of rhetorical analysis could well be applied to other reconstructed elements of the city.

The architecture of reconstructed Berlin reads like an architectural "Who's Who"; a theme park and architectural playground of signature architects, or the consummate example of architectural democratisation? To name just a few: Sir Norman Foster's dome on the Reichstag, a glass symbol of political transparency allowing the public to look down on the activities of government, a political act on several levels. The public may be able to view the activities of government, however this comes with a powerful but unspoken caveat. Those who visit the building will find that on entry they are herded into a glass box, instructed to move forward until any semblance of personal space is all but obliterated, the box is then sealed shut from both the outside and the inside offering absolutely no option of going either forward or retreating, then the glass door silently slides open for individual processing through security. For that suspended, silent moment the visitor is helplessly reminded that they are totally under the scrutiny and control of others. The symbolism is a chilling metaphor of other familiar images. While security procedures are undeniably essential, is this irony or outrage, accidental or intentional? However, the architectural interpretation of openness and transparency ostensibly portrayed at the Reichstag is a sentiment carried through to the buildings of the Chancellry in which the architecture is again required to reflect the ethos of today's German government. With Helmut Jahn's Sony Centre at Potsdamerplatz, a glittering expanse of glass curtain, Rem Koolhaas's Royal Dutch Embassy, Frank Gehry's Central Bank building – at once gratuitous design intervention and iconic statement of wealth, I.M. Pei's exhibition hall of the German Historical Museum, widely referred to as "Berlin's glass and steel treasure" – the reference to the Pei pyramid hovering over the Louvre is not to be missed, Renzo Piano and Richard Rogers as well as the contrasting memorials created by Daniel Libeskind, and Peter Eisenman, Berlin appears, at least on the surface, to strive to emerge from its dark history.

Reconstructed Berlin gleams, a city of glass, pulsating and resplendent in a seething, glittering cacophony of light and sound that bounces from surface to surface; a never-stationary kaleidoscope of the fractured images of a new Europe, reflecting a city bursting to tell those who enter it how successful it has become; a theme park, a playground for more than just the architects. Politically, economically and socially, the city architecture has become the very essence of inspired transparency but with reference to its past and the memories that its past continue to evoke. Certainly there is even precedent for big names, Mies van der Rohe for example, even the glittering edifice as seen in his Friederichstrasse office building project competition entry (1919-21) and his German Pavilion at the Barcelona Exposition of 1929.

But what other truths can be revealed? The glass curtain wall is taken to the extreme with steel superstructures simply spanning buildings resulting in the building being enclosed in a glass case. The glass façade always reveals three truths: that which lies behind, yet to be revealed – but is it partially revealed or is it partially hidden, on display or entombed? The surface itself – a pristine exemplar of modernity and technology; and finally the reflected sometimes distorted image. The cloaked building becomes a surreal participant, a phantom, as macabre features appear to blur, blend and move viewed through the distorted and refracted images emerging from the glass. The Brandenburg Gate stands as silent witness, its shell-scoured surfaces are "touched up", architectural perfection through the lens of a camera, but stand closer and the scars remain arguably more unsightly because the built form no longer speaks of the history it represents. Libeskind's Jewish Museum, scar on the landscape, achieves its jagged and dissected planes and planar form from the lines drawn on a page linking lost members of Jewish families. The building itself becomes a representation of the scar that Berlin has chosen forever to bear; the Neue Wache, a memorial "commemorating the victims of war and tyranny", would seem to describe a growing ethos of the city. The spaces inside the Libeskind museum inspire emotional response; the visitor becomes a participant in his spatial representation of the disorientation of war. Seldom is the human being's relationship with architecture more profoundly, acutely and intentionally exposed than in this (and indeed other Libeskind buildings). For the thousands of visitors with no experience of war, while it is perhaps comforting to be able to retreat to the argument that understanding of the experience becomes "apprehended by opinion", the emotive response to the architectural intervention that he has created has been widely acclaimed. Because the visitor becomes participant and is not relegated to the status of observer, to an extent the visitor is able to construct his or her own meaning from what has been given.

If observers and visitors are meant to understand this symbolism of memorial and that of the transparency of the new government then let us look more deeply into what may represent the most horrifying of all, the Peter Eisenman Memorial for the Murdered Jews of Europe. First proposed in the late 1980s, but not finally completed until 2005 the 19,000 square-metre tract of undulating land south of the Brandenburg Gate that housed the office of Joseph Goebbels in 1937, not far from Hitler's Chancellery and bunker, is now covered by monolithic concrete blocks. Some lie low on the ground, others impose, towering to a height of almost 5 metres; 2,711 pillars and slabs laid in grid formation represent the 6,000,000 murdered Jews. The site lies alongside the Berlin wall forming part of what was to become known as the German Democratic Republic (GDR) "death strip", the no-man's land separating Communist East from Democratic West. As one of the most tag-ridden cities in the world, the blocks have been given a coating to prevent soiling through tagging. This has resulted in a strange phenomenon; rain water forms droplets on the sides of the stone akin to tears, resulting in "crying stones", adding to the emotion of the overall experience. In a cruel irony the firm which supplied the coating has been linked to the company that supplied Zyklon B, the nerve gas used in the extermination camps. Whilst Eisenman himself contends that graffiti is an expression of the people, the outrage of sanitisation and of condemning those who wish to speak to silence seems to commit outrage upon outrage. A recurring theme of symbolic silencing of voice would seem to become too obvious to ignore and therefore, thankfully, in the final analysis perhaps a voice no longer silenced.

Berlin appears simultaneously to be striving to re-interpret its constructed past through manipulation of the memory of its history and the reconstruction of a new image, a new identity for the city; an endeavour perhaps to reconcile its past with its present and its hopes for the future. As suggested, the concepts of truth and memory are brought into focus; one conditioning the other. However, the reading of the city is not abstract, the city remains the representative of the political act of its architecture, the visible landscape reveals the silenced story; the city consists of the "relationships between the measurement of its space and the events of its past" (Calvino, 1997, p. 10). The invisible landscape, both physically and symbolically, continues to condition the visible one. The notion of post-conflict city is no different from that of the city. Its architectural environment provides the built context for its human inhabitants and visitors. Once silent victim of devastating conflict, the city has taken new form; however, the symbolism of the old Berlin remains indelibly etched into the landscape. Post-conflict Berlin stands as a signification of new political, economic, social and cultural images but will also remain forever an icon to and symbol of some of humanity's greatest tragedies.

Johannesburg

Johannesburg is not a city that has been torn apart in the manner of mass physical destruction but it is a city which represents a country that politically, socially and economically has undergone profound change and does require reconstruction. Johannesburg, a city which architecturally presented the political act of apartheid, should now strive to become a representation of the political act of democracy, if not architecturally then at least within the memory and truth that it tries to reflect. Mention has been made of the relationship between the visual environment and the process through which language and image become united as a signification of ascribed meaning. Additionally those with a common language are more likely to develop a common understanding. Previous discussion has highlighted the role of the environmental image in the process whereby human individuals understand and construct a sense of the self, of who they are. Herein lies one of the conditions of Johannesburg as a post-conflict city.

Due in large part to the apartheid legacy – but not aided by years of drought and generally unfavourable climatic and economic conditions for generating a living within a rural, and sometimes only subsistence economy – millions of "black" South Africans descended on major urban centres across the country post-1990. Cohen and Deng (1998) cite a figure of 500,000 for the "displaced" population in South Africa in both 1995 and 1996 but significantly also suggest that the South African government, whilst recognising those individuals displaced due to violence, fail to recognise the millions of "black" South Africans who are displaced for different reasons. In 1992 the African National Congress (ANC) cited a figure of some five million homeless people as one of the legacies of the apartheid government. By 2002, some ten years later, political rhetoric has redefined this same figure to an informally housed population. This mass of internally displaced people take little solace in the current obfuscation of their status. In 2004 a fire swept through the little-known squatter camp of Imizamo Yethu outside Cape Town (devastating fires that blaze through these cramped living environments with shacks often being built from highly flammable materials, are a common occurrence). Government figures "estimated" approximately five hundred "homes" destroyed and eight hundred people left homeless; community representatives double this figure to over one thousand "shacks" and one thousand six hundred left destitute. Johannesburg, like other major South African cities, has not escaped this lost population. Lindsay Bremner (1998), an eminent South African architectural scholar, describes how those "who were confined by apartheid (...) converged on the streets of Johannesburg to claim its promise of a better life" (p. B2). Whilst the mass population displacement had begun long before (images of military-led forced removal of "squatters" during the 1980s, a period when apartheid faced some of its most powerful challenges, remain stark and brutal reminders of the time), the instruments of the apartheid government largely contained these individuals in "squatter camps" and townships on the outskirts of cities. However, by natural process, these individuals gradually sought to take their place within an economy previously denied to them. South Africa is a country of eleven "official" languages and countless others not "officially" recognised. For those entering the city at that time familiar experiences, images and language failed to provide adequate or appropriate points of reference for individuals to decode the new set of experiences and subsequently form understanding of the new environment. The environment was challenging their very "being", the understanding and sense of who they were; the emergent threat in Johannesburg was that of an environment in conflict with its new inhabitants. Due to a failing economy, left partly by the legacy of international sanctions and a plummeting currency compounded by the "brain drain" phenomenon in which tens of thousands of "white" South Africans anxious about the country's future fled the country, employment opportunities were scarce. Where opportunities did exist rural people largely lacked the skills required within an urban market economy. Perceptions, expectations and beliefs were being challenged by an environment unable to respond to the demands placed on it. Environmentally the city has been slow to respond; architecturally, Johannesburg in its role as a post-conflict city still fails to project a democracy to its people.

A brief internet search on Johannesburg brings forward a host of images relating to a perceived global cast of "the city" extolling it visually as a tourist destination and commercial hub of South Africa. On closer inspection most of these images are rather alike; the Johannesburg skyline either ablaze by night or against the much vaunted notion of the "African sunset", imagery of the cityscape which defies detail. The virtual traveller is content to accept these images because they are what s/he expects to find; these are images which even for the first-time "visitor" are familiar. The observer is not required to become participant in any way. The global city often holds its identity within the image of its skyline, the arrangement of and manner in which its buildings meet the sky; for example, the New York skyline forever recognisable and now irrevocably changed post 9/11. Johannesburg appears to be trying to retain a certain image of credibility for itself. But there is another view of the city as well. This view is where the buildings meet the street, of the dirt and grime in the cracks and crevices of broken pavements. Here hungry and homeless black people live side by side during the day on pavements congested with litter and informal market traders, but that by night, in contrast to that which the image of the night skyline would suggest, remains a largely no-go zone for issues of safety. The new inhabitant becomes a forced participant in an environment which is hostile and unfamiliar. The dour grey concrete brutalist architecture of the 1960s, seemingly favoured by the apartheid fathers of the city at the time, ironically, now offers shelter in the day but a forebodingly sinister backdrop by night. These are totally contradictory and conflicting visions of Johannesburg; however all contain a truth and since the city becomes representative of the political act, the political truth that this city, Johannesburg, reflects remains unclear.

> The city is home to the tallest building in Africa (and at the time of construction the tallest building in the southern hemisphere), The Carlton Centre at 223 metres, and the Hillbrow Tower at 270 metres, both 1970s constructions. Post 1970s very little development of significance took place in the city. A notable exception to this was the 1984 construction of the building housing the Johannesburg Stock Exchange designed by Helmut Jahn. Lacking the grace of some of his other architectural works, and appearing almost like brutalism in glass, which in itself becomes a disconcerting metaphor in consideration of architecture as representation of political, economic and social context, the building was ultimately abandoned by the Stock Exchange with a move to a new address outside of the city. The inner city [of Johannesburg] … is cluttered, intensely overcrowded and unkempt. It is owned by no-one. Abandoned gradually from the mid-1980s onwards by property owners fleeing its foreseen demise, its economic and social base is now substantially outside the law. People simply take over buildings; foreign nationals produce and sell goods for export markets; health and safety standards are widely infringed; buildings are dilapidated and overcrowded. People cram streets and pavements with makeshift structures, cheap commodities and litter; taxis line pavements and fill open spaces. Crime is fast, armed, anonymous, unexpected and invisible. (Bremner, 1998, p. 82)

The escalating levels of inner-city crime and violence which began to emerge through the decade of the 1980s and exploded in the 1990s resulted in corporations abandoning the city to decay and rediscovery of new purposes arguably adequately and ironically now reflected in the dichotomy of images which post-apartheid Johannesburg projects. Johannesburg consists of a built environment still joined irrevocably to its pre-democracy history which, while it may be prudent and expedient to retain within the image, becomes a reflection of a political act and a political process that is struggling to come to terms with the post-apartheid aspirations and expectations of its people. The images associated with this do the city no favours and thus it remains caught between the images and memories of its history, the truth of its present and the yet-to-be defined vision of its future.

Post-conflict South Africa in a political sense is not post-conflict in a human sense due, not solely but at least in part, to the changing environmental context. The environmental context or, in the words of Norberg-Schulz (1971), our "space", provides the "concretization" of the images that form and guide our general orientation in the world. These images that we create from what is given form the construct by and through which we interpret who we are. Conflict theory establishes that the likely and probable outcome of a threat to our human identity is conflict. The scale of this can vary ranging from minor resistance to physically violent confrontation. The human need to establish an identity, a sense of who we are, is so profound that it is the one single human need that is not negotiable. Human needs for recognition and security become subsumed within a greater need for the establishment of our identity, both as an individual and as part of a community. Any threat or challenge to identity will be defended. In the South African position, reflected within the political act that is the architect of the images of Johannesburg, the environmental context that allows people the sense of who they are remains undefined and contradictory, in a process of transformation and yet to be determined reconstruction. From necessity, a new city will emerge, but until this is in some way established, the country, its people, reflected within the context that is Johannesburg, remain in a state of conflict. This reality poses an interesting question and one which would appear to lie at the heart of truth and reconciliation and perhaps even reflect on a reason for comments relating to the "failure" of the TRC process. Can post-conflict – the "after" of the conflict – only truly come about after the process of reconstruction? Conflict becomes thus aligned to reconstruction and an integrated component of the reconstruction process. Notions of reconstruction, if they can be argued to be reflected within conceptions of the post-conflict city, within the context of the city being representative of the political act that was its architect, would appear to be unfulfilled within a post-conflict Johannesburg.

There are however some signs of progress. The country's new Constitutional Court, opened in 2004, is housed (along with the Human Rights Commission) in what would seem to be a fitting regeneration of the old Johannesburg Fort. Architecturally the building has a rich symbolic heritage which it has strived to retain. For example, a dry-stack wall to the rear of the constitutional chamber is constructed from bricks salvaged from the waiting trial block. The fabric of the building becomes imbued with a meaning more eloquent than an act of architectural restoration would achieve; the conceptual act of breaking down and rebuilding, reconstructing with new meaning retains a poignant reminder of past events; creating a new image from the given emerges in literal manifestation. Originally designed in 1895 by the Dutch architect Sytze Wierda, The Fort was to become one of the most feared and hated buildings of the apartheid era; a building in which many eminent anti-apartheid activists, including Nelson Mandela, had been incarcerated. In an ironic twist, the building was commissioned by the then president, Paul Kruger, following a visit to Berlin. Kruger had been impressed by the city and realised that the way to build national spirit and identity was through architecture, something that he sought to instil in South Africa. Wierda subsequently became the government architect designing many of the Kruger government's buildings, several examples of which still remain. The façade of the central Johannesburg Post Office (also designed by Wierda) is acknowledged to have been inspired by the Reichstag, and certainly visual reference points would seem to provide the evidence to confirm this connection.

The Johannesburg Apartheid Museum is perhaps one of the first endeavours to acknowledge the scarred history of the country through physical built articulation. The philosophy behind the museum is not unlike that of the Libeskind museum in Berlin, but is not as successful in achieving its emotional impact through an engagement with the built form. While the architects have tried to achieve this, at times the interpretation becomes too literal; the visitor is relegated to the role of observer rather than participant. This is not meant to suggest that emotional impact is not present, because it is and ultimately it may be argued that the result will have greater significance in fostering an environment conducive to reconciliation than the TRC although it is intended that the history of the TRC will become part of the record of the museum. Installations and images offer sad insight into and reminders of the tragic history of apartheid, but again one is conscious of an alternative position, that visitors' observations may be manipulated and ultimately their experiences become "apprehended by opinion". Visitors are at no stage left to construct their own experience, the visual image is fed to them, and whilst offering insight, the visitor becomes neither participant nor witness. Records guide the experience, the observer creates from the given, but the memory becomes likened to a symbolic photograph, a metaphor of the events, what the images omit cannot be known.

Neither the Constitutional Court at The Fort nor the Apartheid Museum is however located within the inner city of Johannesburg and while both presume to be described as public spaces for the people of Johannesburg, neither is truly widely geographically accessible to the mass population. The Apartheid Museum is located on the south of the city adjoining a tourist attraction of the recreation of an old gold-mining village and thus the intentions of the museum may be somewhat cynically questioned. The inner city today still remains largely as it was described by Bremner in the 1998 text although the government would argue that commercial enterprise is moving back to the city. This is debatable and, regardless of the argument, essential evidence is not provided by some quoted isolated examples; fifteen years after the dismantlement of apartheid any position that does not provide comprehensive supporting evidence cannot seriously be considered. The central services of the city remain woefully inadequate although recently the government has apparently made available a sum of one and a half billion rand to upgrade essential services to the city such as sewerage, electricity and water supply. How this sum of money ultimately translates into service provision only time will tell.

Reconstructions, reconciliation and the 21st century post-conflict city

In reflection on the nature of memory and truth, these are always only as we perceive them to be, and even then they may not be our memory, or our truth, they may be the memory and truth of expediency or simply that which we want others to have. In order to understand we need to deconstruct. Reconciliation is about finding a way to reconcile the memories and the truths, to reconstruct from the deconstruction process that has revealed the different faces or facets of these shadow images. The TRC process in South Africa fails perhaps because it does not yet find a way to reconstruct that which it has revealed. The city comes to represent the political act and one of the most visible signs of political change. Through a complex interrelationship between memory, truth, human experience, and codes of construct and behaviour in which we as individuals create from the given, guided in part by our environmental circumstance, arguably a post-conflict city which does not reflect the images of reconstruction, cannot yet guide notions of reconciliation. As in Berlin, the reading of the city is not abstract. Johannesburg remains representative of the political act of its architecture. The visible landscape of the city conditions, but it also always contains within, and is conditioned by, the invisible created within the memories and truths of those who continue to experience it. In an extension of the ironical connection between events which resulted in the commissioning of The Fort in 1895 and the establishment of the TRC one hundred years later, Johannesburg is again in need of presenting a national spirit and sense of identity for itself and its people. The city could do well once again to look to Berlin for architectural direction, not in physical manifestation, but in the response that Berlin has made toward memory and reconciliation which, while not without fault and widely criticised on many levels, has much to commend it.

The post-conflict city continues to offer the contrasts and contradictions of the city but with the added responsibility to reconstruct and provide both reconciliation with the past and direction for the future. The architectural landscape provides the context from which the new city, born out of necessity, can emerge. It remains form and symbol, victim and victor of the experiences and expressions of the failings and achievements of its humanity. The post-conflict city stands as icon to the tragedy of its time but must also act as a reminder of the human endeavour to rise above and to move beyond the conflict. The post-conflict city must also represent the victory of post-conflict, but it must choose carefully, through the representations that it makes, how these shadowed images emerge in its eventual identity and that which it will give to those who pass through it. The post-conflict city of the twenty first century must also take note of global political changes taking place and the need to democratise our environments in line with the new political ethos. Our human identities become increasingly fragile and while the role of cities previously was to create and drive a sense of national identity, in the increasingly globalised world, our identity can no longer, if it ever was, be geographically contained. The cities of the twenty first century need to reflect this reality.

References
Bremner, L. (1998) in "Crime and the emerging landscape of post-apartheid Johannesburg", in H. Judin and I. Vladislafic, I. (1998) (eds.), *Architecture, apartheid and after,* Rotterdam, NAi Publishers, p. 82.
Calvino, I. (1997) *Invisible cities,* trans. W. Weaver, London, Vintage.
Cohen, R. and F. M. Deng (1998) *Masses in Flight: The Global Crisis of Internal Displacement*, Washington, D.C., The Brookings Institution.
Commission on Human Rights. (1992) *Analytical Report of the Secretary-General on Internally Displaced Persons*, E/CN.4/1992/23, United Nations.
Cooper, J. M. (ed.) (1997) *Plato: Complete Works,* Cambridge, Hackett.
Heidegger, M. (1954) *Vortrage und Aufsatze (Bauen Wohnen Denken)*, Pfullingen, Verlag Gunther Neske.
---------------. (1978) *Basic Writings from Being and Time (1927) to The Task of Thinking (1964),* London, Routledge and Kegan Paul.
Judin, H. and I. Vladislafic. (eds.) (1998) *Architecture, apartheid and after,* Rotterdam, NAi Publishers.
Kelly, G.A. (1955) *The Psychology of Personal Constructs, vol. I, A Theory of Personality*, New York, Norton.
Norberg-Schulz, C. (1971) *Existence, Space and Architecture*, London, Studio Vista.
Thucydides, (n.d.) (1954) *History of the Peloponnesian War*, trans. R. Warner, Baltimore, Penguin.
Tuan, Yi-Fu. (1974) *Topophilia: A Study of Environmental Perceptions, Attitudes, and Values*, New York.

Towards a Poetics of Rubble in the Twentieth Century
Ruins and Reconstructions of the Post-Conflict City[1]

Elena Pirazzoli

> With bombs we are expressing ourselves;
> we are writing our history in shattered blocks of stone.
> Gustav Hasford, *The Short-Timers*

The time of rubble

In the last part of the twentieth century, an obsessive preoccupation with memory has come to define identity. It has become necessary to preserve all that is related to the past. Not only masterpieces, works of art or objects of great scientific or cultural significance, but also even objects belonging to everyday life are now worthy of preservation. All these objects, in fact, are like "traces" – human traces – left to testify to past times, which in the twentieth century – an accelerated century – follow each other at high speed. This change in velocity creates a sense of displacement and the desire to hold on to these marks or traces.[2]

The necessity to preserve regards above all the fragment, that which remains of the past and of past life. This is true both for individual memory and for our collective memory. The most important remains of the twentieth century are the ruins of buildings and the rubble of cities, in which we find the clearest signs of the passages of recent history, not least the two iconic catastrophes of the Second World War, that is, the Shoah and Hiroshima. But are we talking about ruins or rubble? These two terms are often confused, and connote two different conditions of what remains of a building. Rubble is the early phase of destruction, that is, the return to the original material. With a cyclical movement, through destruction, what is constructed becomes the material of composition. The ruin, however, is a form of "elaborated" rubble. This rubble has great significance for a group, community, city or nation, and is preserved for its value vis-à-vis historical-cultural identity. What is interesting to note in reference to these two terms is the fact that in many European languages the words for the English term "ruin" (French: *ruine;* Italian: *rovina;* German: *Ruine*) originate from the same Latin root (*ruĕre*) which means to rush, to fall violently or to collapse, meanings which all point to the notion of a swift falling movement. The French, Italian and German words for "rubble", on the other hand, derive from different roots and thus generate different terms: *débris* (or *décombres*)[3], *macerie, Trümmer*. Whilst the words for

[1] The author wishes to acknowledge the precious advice offered to her by Jennifer Varney in the preparation of this essay.

[2] This term also relates to the emotion felt by the displaced persons returning from the concentration and death camps.

[3] In French we have two terms for "rubble": "débris", that has a more general meaning of "fragment, detritus", and "décombres", that indicates more precisely

ruin seem to derive from the discourse of high culture, the words for rubble seem to be inscribed in the sphere of popular usage in their respective countries. Rubble, *débris/décombres*, *macerie*, *Trümmer*: what is designated by all of these terms is a sort of "raw material", something which triggers new construction. And also the removal of rubble can be considered a starting point. After the huge destruction caused by the massive bombings of the two World Wars, what remains of cities are not "ruins" as such, but, more precisely, "rubble". The transformation or elaboration of this rubble, that is the form of reconstruction, reflects the political needs of a group or community.

In German, the language of the cities examined in this paper, the word *Trumm*, whose plural is *Trümmer*, dates back to the fifteenth century (Maj, 2003, p. 15). But in contemporary language what we find is a clear and strong association with the landscape of destruction after the bombing campaigns of World War II. After the passage of bombers, the cities were reduced to *Trümmer*, like Pompei after the Vesuvian eruption, when the city was *"ein Trümmerfeld"*, a field of rubble. To indicate several phenomena developed around the rubble of the Second World War, many compounds have been created, like *Trümmerfrau*, to underline the female role in post-war reconstruction, or *Trümmerliteratur*, that is, the intense post-war moment in German literature. One of the strangest compounds is *Trümmermadonna*, that is, "Madonna in den Trümmern"; this expression has been created to indicate a Gothic sculpture recovered from the rubble of the Kolumba church in Cologne. The *Trümmermadonna* was welcomed as a sign of hope in the destroyed town. In the early post-war period, a chapel was built to preserve the holy image, and took the shape of a concrete shelter. Now the chapel will be incorporated in the Kolumba Diocesan Museum, a project designed by the Swiss architect Peter Zumthor.[4]

In his 1911 essay entitled *Die Ruine,* Georg Simmel gathers some reflections on architecture and in particular on the ruin; today's readers of this work will immediately perceive a certain difference between Simmel's ruins and our "new" ruins. In Simmel's essay, architecture fulfils itself in the balance between spirit and matter, while the ruin is generated by the prevalence of matter, that is, nature. So, the ruin is a "new form", a natural form and a re/conciliated one, surrounded by an atmosphere of peace. The twentieth century has completely altered this romantic vision: [5] the new ruins are more human than natural, and are

---

the fragments of a building.

[4] See http: //www.kolumba.de, and the catalogue of *Next. 8 Mostra internazionale di architettura* (2002), edited by Sudjic D., Marsilio, La Biennale, Venezia, pp. 112-113.

[5] Cultural history, from the Renaissance through the Enlightenment to Romanticism, gives different readings to the concept of ruins. Having always created a sense of fascination for the ancient world, the image of ruins became a subject in their own right for eighteenth century painters, according to Diderot's "Poetics of ruins" that presented a more meditative or melancholic vision of ruins as vestiges of lost civilisations which signal the unavoidable collapse of all human undertaking. Amongst the many books written on this theme, see especially Michel Makarius, *Ruines*, Flammarion, Paris 2004.

rarely surrounded by a peaceful atmosphere; rather, they are often places of memory and fields of identity battles.

In wartime, and as a result of technological progress, the human being became capable of wielding a form of destruction that only nature could produce before the dawn of the twentieth century. This destruction was immediate and resembled the effects of natural disasters, such as earthquakes, eruptions and so on, and what we find is a sort of *crescendo*, from the Great War to the Second World War, from trench warfare to the war in the cities. Necessarily, what remains is a landscape of rubble, a "degree zero", from which reconstruction begins:

> à partir de 1945, les ruines ne renvoient plus au passé, mais au présent – un présent qui voit le pouvoir de destruction changer d'echelle. Cette table rase trouve sa juste expression dans le titre que Roberto Rossellini donne à son film tourné en 1947 dans le ruines de Berlin: *Allemagne, année zéro Germania anno zero*. /from 1945, ruins no longer refer back to the past but the present – a present which sees the power of destruction change scale (...) This *tabula rasa* finds its rightful expression in the title give by Roberto Rossillini to his film shot in 1947 amidst the ruins of Berlin, *Germany Year Zero*.[6]

If the ruin is a new form, rubble is "formless". Rubble is raw material, without a proper form, thus it is malleable and moves towards urban reconstruction and the reconstruction of identity. This new kind of war dissolves form: both the form of the human body – the missing soldier, for example – and the urban form, reduced to signs on the ground, perceptible only from the skies and which resemble archaeological sections.

We shall now examine several cases in which the form of reconstruction reflects a particular use of memory and which creates different feelings of identity. All these cases come from Germany, because this land bears the signs of several important moments in twentieth century history: Nazism, the Shoah, the massive bombing of many cities, the division, the wall, and so on.

Nuremberg and the embarrassing ruins of the Third Reich

In the early thirties, Nuremberg was chosen as the site of the *Reichsparteitag*, the annual NSDAP (*Nationalsozialistische Deutsche Arbeiterpartei*[7]) party convention. In 1933 the *Stadt der Reichsparteitage* was built in the suburbs to hold masses of members and to give the annual event a monumental setting. The project, designed by Albert Speer with several collaborators, planned a "city" composed of two main areas for the rallies, that is the *Zeppelinfeld* and the *Luitpold Arena*, the *Kongresshalle* – a building similar to the Colosseum – the *Grosse Strasse*, paved with granite to emphasise the link between the centre of Nuremberg, the ancient seat of the Imperial

---

[6] Michel Makarius, *Ruines*, Flammarion, Paris 2004, p. 208.
[7] National Socialist German Workers Party, the Nazi Party.

Diets, and the new site of National Socialist conventions. The project also included the construction of a *Märzfeld*, or drill ground, and the imposing and immense *Deutsche Stadium*, but the outbreak of war blocked construction.

Here, in 1934, Leni Riefensthal shot *Triumph des Willens*, the famous film that helped to create and diffuse the image of order, perfection and exalting triumph for the Third Reich. To free the chosen site, it was necessary to pull down the bus station, built only a few years previously; the vision of its ruins, a tangle of concrete, brought Speer to elaborate his *Theorie vom Ruinenwert*, the theory of the value that a building can hold, when seen as a ruin. Those *rostende Trümmerhaufen*, or "dusty heaps of rubble", as Speer writes in his memoirs (1970), prevent all sense of power or greatness. So, his new buildings, created to immortalise the millenarian Reich, had to be made with noble materials, like granite, which, once gone to ruin, would testify to the powerful magnificence of the Reich. This theory of ruins convinced Hitler, and became one of the planning policies of Nazi architecture, and the rebuilding plans required plenty of granite and brick, as well as manual labour. Thus, after 1937 many of the Nazi concentration camps (Mauthausen, Flossenbürg, Sachsenhausen, Gross-Rosen and others) were located near marble quarries, clayey ground or gravel pits so that prison labour, the labour of masses of *Zwangarbeiter*, could be used for the production of building materials (Dwork and van Pelt, 1996, pp. 171-173).

In the post-war period these imposing buildings became embarrassing remains of the megalomaniac project of Hitler, Speer and Himmler; while the perishable barracks of *Konzentrationslager* and *Vernichtungslager* – the concentration and death camps – survive as signs of the plan of annihilation directed towards the Nazi eugenic project. The preservation of these structures has become increasingly difficult over time, and each conservation project has altered these structures in a different way, generally improving or "sweetening" them, for want of a better word. This situation is most evident in Auschwitz, that final product of a process of optimisation of extermination, which now resembles a park, with lawns and restored barracks (Rose, 1993).

The main buildings of the Third Reich were demolished after the end of the war. In Berlin, for example, the enormous *Neue Kanzlei*, the new Chancellery designed by Speer, was razed and its marbles were re-utilised to build the *Sowjetisches Ehrenmal Treptower Park*, which was the monument to the Soviet Army erected in Treptower Park in 1946-49, and part of its rubble was probably used to put up the Wall in 1961.

In Nuremberg, on the other hand, after the war, the buildings of the *Parteitag* were fundamentally undamaged. In the sixties, the columns of the Zeppelinfeld's tribune were demolished because they were not stable. Afterwards every attempt to re-utilise those buildings, either as a site to house trade fairs or sporting events, caused feelings of embarrassment, even provoking a sense of revenge or rejection. Only in 2001, thanks to the light architectural intervention of Günther Domenig, work on the *Kongresshalle* began with an explicitly conscious approach: an arrow in glass and metal – modern materials refused by the Reich – passes through the building, which now houses a documentation and research centre, with a permanent exhibition on Nazism in Nuremberg.

Dresden and the impossible reconstruction of a symbol

During the Cold War, reconstruction in the two spheres of influence was marked by significant differences, both in terms of time-scales and methods, and after 1989 this became evident. In the western part, reconstruction was quick and often involved the removal of the rubble that signalled an awkward or cumbersome past. Berlin is the place where many contemporary and famous architects have planned and redesigned whole areas and monumental buildings, and in this regard we can cite the various editions of IBA – *Internationale Bauaustellung* and the projects of *Kulturforum* (for example the *Neue Nationalgalerie* of Mies van der Rohe, the *Staatsbibliothek* and the *Berliner Philharmonie* of Hans Scharoun).

In the DDR, on the contrary, the economic situation did not allow complete reconstruction and, in many cases, the past was archived or abandoned in heaps of rubble and only after 1989 was this rubble dug up and used for reconstruction. The case of Dresden is emblematic; this was the target of the most famous Allied bombings, and was part of a strategy of "morale bombing" carried out to topple popular consent for Nazism. At the end of the war, all that remained of the wonderful capital of Saxony was blackened rubble. Even though in the 1960s great efforts were made to rebuild some of Dresden's former landmarks, such as the *Zwinger* (where the famous picture-gallery is located) and the *Semperoper*, only a few buildings were brought back to their former splendour.

Conversely, the *Frauenkirche*, an evangelical-Lutheran baroque church remained an enormous heap of rubble until 1990. This religious building was a sort of symbol of the city, its most beautiful Protestant church, and a sign of religious tolerance. With the firebombing, the building vanished from Dresden's skyline, and the blackened stones lay in a heap in the centre of the city for the next 45 years. If popular sentiment discouraged the authorities from clearing the ruins away to make a parking lot, the Communist administration itself used the ruins of the *Frauenkirche* as a memorial to the war. On 14 February 1990, the forty-fifth anniversary of the bombing was celebrated just a few months after the fall of the Wall, and a Citizens' Initiative (*Ruf aus Dresden*, the call of Dresden) was formed to promote the whole reconstruction of the *Frauenkirche*, and began a private fundraising campaign. At the same time, architects, art historians and engineers sorted the thousands of blackened stones, identifying and labelling each for re-use in the new structure, rebuilding the church according to the original project, old prints and pictures. The blackened stones have been put in the new light-coloured sandstone structure and the visual impact is reminiscent of an enormous puzzle. The funds raised were turned over to the "*Frauenkirche* Foundation Dresden", the actual rebuilder, backed by the State of Saxony, the City of Dresden and the

Evangelical Lutheran Church of Saxony. The reconstruction of its exterior was completed in 2004, its interior in 2005, and after 13 years of rebuilding the church was re-consecrated on 30 October 2005. Whilst it can be defined as an architectural "horror, insofar as it conforms neither to current architectural trends nor to norms of restoration, it nevertheless has an important symbolic and identitary value.

Berlin and the stratifications of the recent past

In Berlin, reconstruction has seen several different important moments, influenced by historico-political events. What we now see are the many signs, or rather remains, of the several historical lives of the city, including its various incarnations as capital of Imperial Prussia, capital of the Third Reich, destroyed city, divided city, and then, finally, the capital of reunification: the city bears all the signs of these "stratifications of History".

After a long and difficult experience of mourning connected to Nazism and the Shoah, this would appear to be East Germany's time of memory, a time to remember the Wall and so on. But this memory is still difficult and embarrassing. For example, in February 2006 the authorities decided to demolish the *Palast der Republik*, the parliament building of the German Democratic Republic (DDR). This building was constructed in the 1970s in the prevailing style of East Germany, with characteristic bronze mirrored windows. The building stands on the site of the former *Berliner Stadtschloss*, which was partially destroyed by World War II bombings. In the 1950s, the reconstruction of the Hohenzollern Castle was turned down, because the building was seen as a symbol of Prussian militarism and imperialism and its ruins were thus removed. After the demolition, the area was used as a park and for national celebrations and, in 1976, the *Volkskammer* was opened. Its spaces were also used for cultural purposes, as a community building where public rituals and social events such as exhibitions, balls, weddings, and concerts were held and which were important symbols for a modern communist society. The building stands on the bank of the River Spree, between the actual Schlossplatz and Lustgarten (together called Marx-Engels-Platz from 1951 to 1994), near Alexanderplatz, in the heart of East Berlin.

After German reunification, in 1990 the *Palast der Republik* was found to be contaminated with asbestos and so considered dangerous. By 2003, all the asbestos had been removed along with internal and external fittings. In November 2003, the German parliament decided to demolish the building and leave the area as a green space until funding for the reconstruction of the *Stadtschloss* could be found. Demolition started on 6 February 2006 and was scheduled to last about 15 months. The demolition needed to be carried out as a careful and slow disassembly in order not to endanger neighbouring historical buildings such as the Berliner Dom.

But in the period of uncertainty in which the parliament and public opinion debated the destiny of the Palace, many artists dedicated much attention to the building, seeking to raise public awareness. In particular, in January 2005 the Norwegian artist Lars Ramberg installed enormous neon letters (6 metres high) on the roof of the building, which spelt *Zweifel*, or "doubt". On the artist's website we find the following:

> The project «Palast des Zweifels» (Palace of Doubt) engages in both a local discourse and a larger one; the global contemporary discourse addressing lost utopia, the urge for perspectives and new identities. Part of the project, is a site-specific installation located on Palast der Republik, in the heart of Berlin. Sculptural neon letters installed on the roof of the building "Palast der Republik" are forming logo: ZWEIFEL for a virtual institution, Palace of doubt. Palast des Zweifels connects to the local discourse generated since the German reunion. The project is unwilling to submit to any political dualism or consensus regarding demolition or not. Taking place on historical ground the project becomes an aggregate for politics itself, performing a new debate, connected to the current one. With no intention to take sides in the political parties the project can be seen as a dedication to 15 years of highly sophisticated German doubt, and transparency regarding identity. (**http: //www.larsramberg.com**).

In the reunified Germany, one of the most important political topics has been that of the value of communist icons, buildings, monuments and public spaces. The heated discussions have been rather emotional and have been dominated by one-sided rhetoric. Symbols from the former DDR have been marked and most parts of the modernist architecture that was built between 1961 and 1989 have already been torn down.

Now, the debate regarding the future of the *Palast der Republik* is one of the best examples of this political dilemma: if the reconstruction of the *Stadtschloss* can be seen as an attempt to recapture German history, then this questions the priority placed on Prussian history over the more recent past of East German communism. At a level of identity, both are important, but the second is more pressing. Several artists have sensed this importance, and the *Palast* has become a sort of "artistic public laboratory". Along with Ramberg, we should also mention Tacita Dean, an English artist attentive and sensitive to Berliner life, who has lived in Berlin since 2000. In exploring Berlin, she captures in her films the complex histories imbued in the architecture, in the "memorial stratigraphy". Evocative, melancholic and precise, her work suggests a personal experience wrapped up in the larger rhythms of history. With *Fernsehturm* (2001), she shoots a film in the revolving restaurant of former East Berlin's Television Tower, capturing the changing atmosphere of this landmark place as day turns to night, the mutation of light, and the different sounds of the restaurant, revealing shifting perspectives of locality, social history and politics. The stronger sensation is one of suspension, maybe a suspended happiness (and also an impossible one), as a utopian place over the city, indifferent to the great changes in Berlin.

In 2004, Tacita Dean shot a film about the *Palast der Republik*, in which she registers the change in the light of the orange-brown windows as they gradually gain golden reflections. Each expanse of glass is a screen on which is projected a separate scene from the city's transformation. Gradually, other buildings and objects are reflected on the Palast's surface: the Berliner Dom, the Fernsehturm, graffiti, with a melancholic feeling. About this project, Tacita Dean said:

> I just filmed the Palast der Republik which a lot of people want to keep, but it has been decided to destroy it because Honnecker was in there and a lot of bad things obviously happened in there. And a lot of people think it is an ugly building, but I do not think it is ugly, I think it is fantastic. But it is definitely a Soviet building (...) What I like about it is that it is right in the centre of Berlin, on Museum Island, with the dome right opposite. It is clad with this orange mirrored glass, which has of course a whole lot of connotation attached to it in terms of surveillance. But what it does, which is so beautiful, is it traps the sunlight, the setting sun, in the most majestic way in the centre of the city (...) What is so beautiful about Berlin is that it has two cultures in it, these two architectural situations, side by side. But they are going to make it homogeneous (...) Anyway, I am nostalgic. That is what I do, I guess, that is what all my work is in a way, trying to hold on to something before it disappears. (Dean in De Cecco, 2004, pp. 62-63)

These are only two cases of artistic intervention in contemporary Berlin, and in the urban texture of the city. Artists suggest that demolition is not the answer: the presence of the building is a sort of "memento" and the building itself is a landmark to memory and remembering. These artistic interventions release a myriad of emotions connected with memorial reflections, and they present new ways of remembering the tragedies of the twentieth century.

References
Capezzuto, R. (2002) "Confronting the architecture of evil: Günther Domenig's interventions in Nuremberg's Kongresshalle go right to the heart of its Nazi past", *Domus* 847, pp. 80-91.
Dean, T. (2005) *Tacita Dean: Berlin works*, London, Tate St. Ives.
De Cecco, E. (2004) *Tacita Dean,* Milan, Postmedia Books.
Dwork, D. and R. J. van Pelt. (1996) *Auschwitz: 1270 to the Present*, New York, Norton.
Makarius, M. (2004) *Ruines*, Paris, Flammarion.
Maj, B. (2003) *Idea del tragico e coscienza storica nelle "fratture" del Moderno*, Macerata, Quodlibet.
Rose, G. (1993) *Judaism and modernity: philosophical essays*, Oxford, Blackwell.
Scarrocchia, S. (1999) *Albert Speer e Marcello Piacentini: L'architettura del Totalitarismo negli anni '30*, Milan, Skira.
Sebald, W.G. (2003) *On the natural history of destruction: with essays on Alfred Andersch, Jean Améry and Peter Weiss*, London, Hamish Hamilton.
Simmel, G. (1911) *Die Ruine*, in *Philosophische Kultur: Gesammelte*

Essays, Leipzig, Klinkhardt.
Speer, A. (1970) *Inside the Third Reich: memoirs*, London, Weidenfeld and Nicolson.
Sudjic, D. (ed.) *(2002) Next. 8 Mostra internazionale di architettura* (2002), Venezia, Marsilio.

Bombs and Poems
The Representation of Conflict through Performance Art

María José Contreras

The aim of this discussion is to situate and analyse the construction and communication of a representation of cultural trauma by means of the performance *Poem Bombing* carried out by a group of Chilean artists called *Casagrande*.[1]

Santiago, Dubrovnik, Guernika, Dresdren and Nagasaki: five cities that have been bombed during the twentieth century without being military objectives. In Santiago, on 11 September 1973, the military forces of Chile under the command of Augusto Pinochet bombed the government palace, in what was the starting point of a long-lasting dictatorship. On 6 December 1991 Dubrovnik was bombed by the Serbian military forces, with a tragic outcome for civil victims. Guernika in Spain, on 26 April 1937, became the first city that suffered an air-bombardment in history; this bombardment was cruelly planned by the Nazi military, suffered one of the most barbaric military actions during the Second World War. Last but not least, the atomic bombardment of Hiroshima and Nagasaki on 5 August 1945, where, apart from the hundreds of thousands of direct victims, many people from the following generations have suffered the costs of the attack.

The *Poem Bombing* project's aim is to bomb again these five cities, replacing bombs with poems.[2] The first time the performance was presented was in 2001, when a helicopter dropped more than one hundred thousand poems written in bookmarks over the Chilean government building *La Moneda* in Santiago. The project continued in 2002 with the release of more than three thousand kilos of poems over the city of Dubrovnik and in 2004 with a poem rainfall in Guernika. Next, *Casagrande* was preparing poem bombings in Dresden and Nagasaki. I shall analyse the *Poem Bombing* as a cultural embodied practice that renegotiates the representations of conflict, recomposes cultural memory and collaborates in the construction of an alternative

---

[1] *Casagrande* was founded in 1996, by a group of Chilean visual artists and writers (Cristóbal Bianchi, José Joaquín Prieto and Julio Carrasco). The group has three main projects: 1. Publication of a journal that changes its format in every number (for example: Transitable edition (2002), giant posters attached to the walls of some metro stations in Santiago, Space edition (2006) a DVD sent to the International Space Library). 2. Cinematographic projects. 3. Public performances such as *Poem Bombing*. www.revistacasagrande.cl

[2] The idea of releasing pamphlets from the sky has been used both with artistic and propaganda aims. One of the most remarkable launches of political literature from the sky was that of the founder of the Futurism movement Filippo Marinetti (1910) with the launch of the *Contro Venzia Passantista* manifesto from the San Marco Campanile in Venice, and Lauro de Bosis (1931) with the dropping of anti-Mussolini fliers over Rome. The dropping of massive quantities of leaflets is a propaganda practice that has been used in war since World War II.

cultural identity. I shall show how the *Poem Bombing* catalyses new discursive configurations that transform and organise cultural values in innovative narrative and emotional articulations. It will become clear that the *Poem Bombing* performance, as a representation of a past traumatic event, allows the effective elaboration of painful memory.

Poem Bombing in Guernika (photo by Casagrande), 2004.

Conflict as an essential characteristic of culture
The relationship between culture and conflict may be described from different points of view. I shall use as a theoretical frame the model of the cultural semiotician Jurji Lotman who establishes, in *Culture and Explosion* (1992), that culture is a semiotic dynamic device that changes by means of a constant transformation of meaning. Lotman considers culture as the sum result of the individual texts that relate to each other constructing the *semiosphere*, a metaphor he uses in order to illustrate, by a spatial model, the complex relations between different kinds of texts.

Lotman claims that culture changes in two different but complementary ways: by continual development and by explosion. They are interdependent aspects of the same process, continually replacing each other in the unity of dynamic development. Lotman imagines a *semiosphere* built as a whole containing layers at different stages of development. In fact, any synchronic cut of a given culture could reveal such stages. From this point of view, culture works as a tri-dimensional multilayered organism where explosion at a certain layer may coexist with continual development in another. Continuity is a type of predictability whilst explosion brings sudden and unpredictable changes. A balanced condition of culture is characterised by a predominance of continual development, the movements of which are relatively unsurprising. On the contrary, at the moment of explosion, or we could say of crisis, the outcome is unpredictable, and the system loses definition.

Lotman's semiotic model of culture is of interest primarily because it emphasises that culture is a dynamic system that will never be absolutely stable, and that conflict is an essential characteristic in the definition of culture. From this point of view, culture is in everlasting metamorphosis: change occurs at the same time in multiple ways from subtle mutations to drastic transformations, from agreed modulation to breaking conflict, but in any case, conflict is inscribed in culture as culture in conflict. In this particular context, the notion of "post-conflict culture" is problematic, because culture may not be considered "pre-" or "post-" conflict, but rather essentially "in conflict". The notion of "post-conflict cultures" may be applied to cases were there is a specific type of conflict, a "delimited conflict" that takes place within a definite space and time. In these cases, it should be possible to distinguish clearly a starting and a final event, and the territory where the conflict takes place. The paradigmatic example (but not the only one) of this kind of conflict is war. Only in this definite panorama is it possible to employ the term "post-conflict" in a specific and useful way.

Trauma as a conflict marker

As mentioned, conflict in culture may assume different characteristics, for instance long perpetual wars that continue to exist in different shapes and forms throughout history, "interventions" where a country or organisation attacks a territory in the name of democracy or freedom, sudden terrorist actions, etc. Here, I wish to concentrate on one specific kind of conflict, the cultural trauma. Many authors have used the concept of trauma when referring to a specific sort of cultural conflict (among which *cf.* Caruth (ed.) 1995, 1996; Alexander, 2004; Smelser, 2004; Sztompka, 2004). Here, I shall draw mainly on Jeffrey Alexander's model of cultural trauma:

> Cultural trauma occurs when members of a collectivity feel they have been subject to a horrendous event that leaves indelible marks upon their group consciousness, marking their memories forever and changing their future identity in fundamental and irrevocable ways. (Alexander, 2004, p. 1)

A traumatised culture is then a culture the articulation of which has been destroyed, where the basic tissues of social life are damaged, threatening the collective identity. In these cases, communities are no longer able to think together as a "we" about what happened, but each individual or reduced group is isolated trying, probably without success, to interpret the traumatic event. If we think of culture as a system where values, norms, ideologies, beliefs, knowledge and practices bond together in a meaning system (Lotman, 1992), then a cultural trauma may be considered a specific kind of conflict where chaos irrupts into organisation, breaking through the textual articulation of culture and thus affecting the meaning system.

The relation of trauma to conflict is that trauma installs itself as a "marker of conflict", occupying a particularly significant place in its representation. For example, in the case of Chile's dictatorship, political and social conflict lasted for many years, but the representations of the conflict usually recall the bombing of *La Moneda*, of course, because it was the beginning of the totalitarian regime, but also because it was experienced as traumatic and, as a result, this particular moment strongly determines historical memory and identity.

Trauma summarises in a particular concrete experience the broader conflict, becoming a paradigmatic example of the whole. Collective traumatic experiences take a specific position in the construction of cultural memory because of their particular quality in terms of an intense emotional arousal of which is difficult to think. After a bombing, the collective subject of culture remains perplexed, paralysed, incapable of any understanding. Cathy Caruth (1995) describes these "limit" circumstances as characterised by collective silence and by the impossibility of talking about what happened, of telling of the traumatic event.

As in psychological trauma, trauma marks conflict by narcoticising the past and constantly returning as the most prominent remembrance, defining the diachronic perspective of the system. From an individual psychoanalytical point of view, Freud (1899, 1920, 1929) gave reasons for this ever-returning behaviour through the fact that in a traumatic experience there is neither a motor reaction nor a thought-association able to represent the experience. So the unelaborated memory is always ready to re-emerge as the most important and immediate aspect, haunting persistently conscious life. According to Freud, in order to position the traumatic experience as a past event, it is necessary for the remembrance to be associated to thinking. In a parallel way, we may think that the cultural trauma comes back to cultural memory because it lacks a collective representation, shared by the whole community and stable in time. Until a cultural representation of the traumatic experience is constructed, the major reaction to cultural trauma will continue to be shock that, instead of provoking representations, usually blocks them.

In semiotic terms, we may say that one consequence of cultural trauma is the loss of competence with regard to providing a stable meaning to the experience. In the face of a high intensity stimulus, culture remains in a state of perplexity, of diffuse emotional arousal, that is not attached to any narrative meaning. In this status, culture is not able to situate the traumatic experience within a cognitive frame that could in the first instance represent the violent event and could then endow it with a cognitive description and explanation. So, from a semiotic point of view, the consequence of trauma is the impossibility of giving a narrative closure to the event that remains in the meaning system as an ever-circulating experience disjointed from a stable meaning.

Bombardment as cultural trauma
The bombardments of the cities listed before may be considered

cultural traumas, in the sense that the bombs not only destroy human lives and infrastructure but also the meaning system of the community. In the case of bombing, the community itself is threatened, the survival of its people is at risk, and the circle of the "we" is reduced to the minimum members. The abruptness of war bombardments facilitates the experience of trauma: in a short period of time, radical unexpected changes at various levels take place, people die, institutions are not able to function anymore, the urban landscape changes radically, the whole daily routine is broken, and intersubjective bonds are broken.

A bombardment is a catastrophe that irrupts into the city's territoriality, breaking the key distinction between city and sky as non-city and, in doing so, somehow destroys the nature of the city itself. As Juan Pastro Mellado (2005) claims, the bombardment breaks down with violence the territory of the city and, in doing so, injures its symbolic composition. War bombardment perverts the symbolic boundary of the city, in the sense that it distorts articulation in a freakish way. The sky, which usually belongs to the ambit of nature, becomes a space used by the enemy. Aggression comes from a non-anthropoid space, but nonetheless is a cultural aggression. The enemy is not nature any more (as it usually is when the destructiveness comes "from the sky", as in the case of natural catastrophes), but it clearly comes from a "cultural other". The consequence of this perversion is confusion and the inability to trust the most fundamental distinctions such as: nature-culture, city-sky, safety-danger, etc. A semiotic result of this symbolic perversion is that sense loses its definition so that the socially agreed conventions are debilitated. After a bombardment, culture is damaged in an analogous way as human bodies are injured: sense is mutilated, lacerated, becomes anaemic, a fragile sense that is not efficient in provoking a stable interpretation of what happened.

Poem Bombing as isotopy
One of the strategies to deal with trauma is the artistic manifestation that may produce and communicate alternative representations of the catastrophic event. In this context, the performance *Poem Bombing* is an attempt to cope with trauma, by offering a way to represent it.

The *Poem Bombing* recalls the traumatic event not as a perfect double of it, but by selecting and emphasising certain elements that are similar to the original bombing and narcoticising other aspects. This performance may be interpreted as an *isotopy* of the original bombing because it possesses elements common to that of the original traumatic bombing. In Umberto Eco's words an *isotopy* is a "constancy in going in a direction that a text exhibits when submitted to rules of interpretative coherence" (1984, p. 201).

In the case of the *Poem Bombing* the interpretation of the *isotopy* is possible because some similarities recall the past bombardments in a direct way. The *isotopy* of bombing functions on several levels, in the first place, both events (the traumatic event and the performance) are cases of "bombing", that is of "massive dropping of objects from the sky". Independently from the type of objects that are dropped in each case (bombs and poems), there is a semantic constancy that allows the interpretative linking of both events. But the *isotopy* is sustained as well by other kinds of constancies, for instance from the common gesture of throwing things from the sky. Other than the semantic constancy, at the level of gesture, the performance repeats the gesture of the bombing. As in the case of war bombardments, the artists of *Casagrande* did not alert the population about the performance in order to recapture the original surprise effect. So both events were unexpected even if the emotional quality of the surprise is radically different and this similarity supports and strengthens the construction of the *Poem Bombing* as an *isotopy*.

Furthermore, from the point of view of the corporeal experience of the participants, at one level the body relates to both bombings in a similar way. It is not usual to observe objects falling down from the sky into the city, so this rare perception constructs a constancy at the level of perception and of body related to space. At least at one moment, the perception of things falling down from the sky implies a certain physical action in order to perceive what is happening. This initial constancy runs parallel to a significant difference in the behaviour of the body, that in the case of the war attack closes and folds into itself looking for protection, but in the case of the performance opens in a receptive gesture.

Another constancy that contributes to the generation of the *isotopy* is the coincidence of the geographical area where the *Poem Bombing* occurs with the area that suffered the war bombing. If the performance could have been presented in a city where no original bombing has occurred, then of course it could have been difficult for participants to associate, from a narrative point of view, both events. But the performance actually occurs *in situ*, becoming then a comparable event that commemorates the exact space of the original bombing. In the case of Santiago the space is quite reduced, it is the square and surroundings of the government palace of *La Moneda* bombed during the *coup d'état* in 1973. In Dubrovnik the *Poem Bombing* takes place over the centre of the city, where the attack was strongest during the bombardment in December 1991. Also in Guernika the *Poem Bombing* occurs in exactly the same place as the original bombing in 1937. The fact that the performance happens in the same city, or in the case of Santiago, in the same single spot of the city, facilitates the construction of a link with the original bombing.

The construction of a ritual space: a scenario to render visible the traumatic event

The unexpected bombardments, both with bombs and poems, allowed the conversion of the daily space in a particular special *place*. As a result of the war bombardment, an unsafe, dangerous, unknown, unpredictable space is generated. Instead, in the case of the poem bombing, the space became the place of ritual, where reflection about the past and the present identity is authorised and animated.

According to Richard Schechner, ordinary spaces can be transformed temporarily especially by means of ritual action (2002). The *Poem Bombing* may not be considered a proper rite, but a sort of ritual action or, in the words of Schechner, "memory in action" (*ibid.*, p. 214), in fact it presents at least five of the ten characteristics that Schechner (*ibid.*) describes as essential characteristics of ritual. In the first place, the performance is inscribed in a symbolic time of repetition, of the timeless eternal present, where tenses are not linearly ordered. On the other hand, participants actively take part in what is going on (even if they do not really know what is going on), they are not mere spectators but they participate in the event. People collect the bookmarks while they are floating in the air, or they pick them up from the ground, they exchange the bookmarks with one another, and they talk about what is going on. In this sense, creativity is in the hands of the collectivity, all the participants in the performance, without distinction between artists and spectators, take part in the carnivalesque event that is happening at that particular moment, they all participate and believe. And, as we shall see, the performance, as a true rite, has its efficacy in provoking results and transformations.

The surprise effect of the *Poem Bombing* performance inaugurates a new quality of space, transforming it into something different from the everyday space: streets, squares, the historical centre, suddenly become spaces where something unusual takes place. The ritualisation of the space is possible where a public space shared by all participants is yet to be constructed. In fact, on the three occasions when the performance was presented, the public space had been constructed previously by other kinds of events: in Santiago, the poem bombing occurred during the *Festival Internacional Chile Poesía*, and thus people were gathered in the square before the performance started, in Dubrovnik the performance took place in the context of a Dubrovnik Festival and in Guernika during a popular feast. So even before the performance takes place, the space is already a public space.

What the *Poem Bombing* adds is the fact that the public space becomes a place of and for ritual: it transforms into a new cultural environment signed by symbolic value capable of hosting a self-reflexive event. The constitution of a ritual place allows the individual trauma to be staged in public and by doing so to become an experience to share, to talk of, to tell, in few words, a representable experience.

The construction of a representation of trauma in a public ritualistic place helps the elaboration of trauma, for the reason that it then becomes a collective task that must be assumed by the whole community. The *Poem Bombing* performance, allows the creation of a spontaneous *communitas* that in Victor Turner's (1982) description corresponds to the experience of camaraderie, the sense that "we are altogether in this", that emerges spontaneously thanks to certain procedures of ritualisation of space and time. When the experience of *communitas* happens, then the communal sense is reinforced and empowered and people may feel that their problems can be resolved with the help of the group which is felt (in the first person) as "essentially us" (Turner, 1983, p. 48). In this ephemeral but powerful state the elaboration of trauma is the responsibility of a communal effort, and is thus more affordable for individuals who are no longer alone.

Novelty of repetition: a healing temporality
In order better to comprehend the temporality that cultural trauma inaugurates, I shall take inspiration from the vast psychoanalytic literature on individual trauma and then discuss in what measure it generates insights about the cultural trauma. In this context the exemplary point of view is that of Freud's theories of psychic trauma. From the beginning of his theory Freud studies trauma and its relevance in psychic life. Even though he develops and changes his understanding about trauma throughout the theory, some theses however remain constant. In particular, I am interested in his description of traumatic experience as an indelible imprint producing permanent effects in the conscious life. To Freud, the psyche remains fixed on trauma, and the memories of the traumatic event, as Charcot describes it, become "parasites of mind" that come back persistently as nightmares or re-enactments. In this sense, the traumatic experience turns into a foreign body which long after its entry must continue to be regarded as an agent that is still at work (Freud and Breuer, 1893-95). Even when repressed, trauma somehow manages to remain vital, coming over and over again to conscious life, insisting on presenting itself as an enigma (Freud, 1905). In Freud's successive conceptions of trauma (1926), he reiterated the fact that trauma constantly re-emerges, intruding into the mind of the patient as repetitive nightmares, unexpected thoughts related to trauma, and compulsive preoccupation with the event.

It is not until "Beyond the Pleasure Principle" (1920), that Freud offers a metapsychological explanation about this drive to repeat the traumatic experience that cannot be stopped. According to Freud, the repetition of traumatic experiences in nightmares and re-enactments responds to the *thanatos* principle, that is a natural tendency to death and *status quo, an instinct "inherent in organic life to restore an earlier state of things"* (ibid., p. 36).

Freud's theories of trauma change their etiological explanations throughout time but, nevertheless, particularly interesting is the persistence of noting a paradoxical movement between the unconscious resurfacing of the memory of trauma and the psychic effort to forget it. He notes that people that have a traumatic neurosis are not necessarily completely engaged with thinking about their own trauma but, on the contrary, spend a lot of psychic effort in order to forget and repress the memory of trauma. This particular relation between memory and forgetfulness relates to a rather steady conception of trauma's temporality. To my mind, this precise postulation may be very useful to the comprehension of cultural trauma where one can also observe this ever-returning of traumatic experiences that culture cannot simply leave behind.

Cathy Caruth (1995), from a psychoanalytic point of view that also wants to explain social processes, states that trauma is actually not about the "objective" event itself, nor about the instant reaction to it, but rather what becomes pathological is the remembering of trauma. As a pathology of memory, trauma is not healable at all, it remains between memory and amnesia, it will never be completely remembered or completely forgotten. Trauma is condemned to remain in a transitional dimension as an unassimilable memory and at the same time as a memory that is impossible to forget.

To my mind, rather than the complex relation between trauma and memory that Caruth explains, what is more crucial is the *impossibility of positioning trauma as a past experience*, the ever-coming-back of a plain rustic repetition of the original experience. After a traumatic experience, the system (whether it is the psychic apparatus or the meaning system of culture) is unable to elaborate the experience, the brusqueness of the event prevents the functioning of a cognising strategy and as a result it remains as an outright experience that is not connected to a specific meaning and thus does not have a narrative closure. The experience comes back in a never-ending re-presentation but without achieving the status of a stable representation. In this sense, trauma would be described as a hole in meaning (Caruth, 1995), an inability to associate the plain experience with a representation or meaning.

The inability to give a representation and thus a meaning to the traumatic experience relates to the fact that the traumatic event does not belong to the quotidian parameters of reality. In Shoshana Felman and Dori Laub's words:

> The traumatic event, although real, took place outside the parameters of 'normal' reality, such as causality, sequence, place and time. The trauma is thus an event that has no beginning, no ending, no before, no during and no after. This absence of categories that define it lends it a quality of 'otherness', a salience, a timelessness and ubiquity outside the range of associatively linked experiences, outside the range of comprehension, of recounting and of mastery. (Felman and Laub, 1992, p. 69)

The difficulty in giving a stable cognitive meaning can be explained by the temporality that trauma inaugurates, a temporality that is not linear but is similar to the temporality of unconsciousness where no before or after is possible. This particular type of temporality is what I call the *trauma's temporality*, signed by the double effort of *ever-returning* and at the same time *never becoming* a memory.

Performance art may also fit into the same genre of temporality, a conception of time as *repetition and eternal present*. I have shown before how trauma is characterised by the ever coming back of the traumatic experience, in the same way one of the crucial characteristics of performance is that it is inscribed by the total lack of spontaneity, in Shechner's words, performance is "never for the first time, always for the second to the nth time; twice-behaved behaviour" (2002, p. 29). As Taylor (2006) asserts, both trauma and performance are characterised by their "repeats": the ever-coming back of something that cannot be left in the past, that cannot acquire the status of a memory.

The equivalence of trauma and performance exceeds the nature of its "repeats". Both cases are not only simple "repeats" but also "unique repeats". Traumatic cultural symptoms like, for example, the constant recalling of the horrors of the wars and ethnic conflict in the former Yugoslavia in theatre that Munk (2001) remembers are a repetition from two points of view: in the first place because they repeat the traumatic experience, for instance, in a performance that directly reproduces a war situation; but these performances are also a repetition of other performances: the last recall to war in theatre is a repetition of the preceding performance and of all the others that came before. So every event is not just a repetition, it is also a unique event that has its own singularity. On the other hand, the status of performance may not only be described by repetition. Performance and all kinds of living arts (theatre, dance, etc) are marked by the ephemeral nature of each presentation. Even if a theatre company repeats the same performance for twenty years, each time it performs the spectacle is different.

Jaime Coloma (1999) claims that there is always a novelty in repetition that makes the quality of each repeat unique. So repetition is never a simple double of the preceding event, but it defines itself in the dialectic dynamic between repetition and uniqueness. The fact that trauma and performance are both constituted by this paradoxical status of being both a repetition and at the same time a unique event allow them to match in a structural way, and thus empowers performance to cope efficiently with trauma. The performance, more than any other artistic manifestation, as a live event is able to weave multiple temporalities: through the alive present happening (here and now) past can be represented and thus appraised, and simultaneously future can be imagined in novel ways and somehow rehearsed.

The ambiguous way in which performance and trauma relate to reality may turn out to be therapeutic in the sense that even if it cannot "solve" the traumatic experience (what may?) it does produce important effects and transformations in the view of the past traumatic event and also in the perception of time and of how history is constructed. The *Poem Bombing* produces emotional, somatic, cognitive and narrative effects that transform the way culture produces meaning and understands the world. The novelty in repetition implies a whole new manner of interpreting history and time, instead of promoting an ideology of the ever-returning it animates an ideology of time as a spiral where transit on the same point is never equivalent to preceding transits, where what happened before may never be repeated in the same way, and it implies that a new passage implies a growth in knowledge; for instance, to represent representing of history not as an eternal repetition of painful events but as a fluid collective marching through time, where healing is achievable, where an optimistic elaboration of the traumatic past is possible. The performance as an embodied practice engages different temporalities advancing a conception of time and history as more manageable cultural devices.

The embodied experience and transmission of traumatic memory – the interactions among people in the here and now – make a difference in the way that knowledge is transmitted and incorporated. (Taylor, 2006, p. 155)

So the effect of performances such as the *Poem Bombing* is not exclusive to the theme it broaches, it also influences the way culture understands and signifies the past in general. This broader effect has to do with accepting other kinds of history management that go beyond the official archive. As Taylor (2003) suggests, history is constructed both by the archive and the repertoire where the embodied memories rest as live knowledge. And live performances, even in their ephemeral status, may construct the ruins of what may become in the future part of the collective memory.

Multiplication of enunciation: the transmission of trauma

The live performance implies the co-presence of artists and spectators in the same space and time, and this produces an important semiotic effect: enunciation takes place at multiple complex levels. The fact that the *Poem Bombing* is a live performance creates the multiplication of the enunciators and also the enunciataries. Whenever a live event takes place, one can distinguish two simultaneous levels of enunciation: the first level that we could call *presentation* and that is of the material co-presence of the performer and the participant. At this level, the performer is not representing anything different from its own psychophysical presence, the operation is mainly that of self-reflexivity and self-referentiality. Another successive level is the *representational* where the representation of something other than the mere presence of the performer prevails, as in the case of traditional theatre where the actor represents a character. As Marco de Marinis (1982) notes, the live performative event is always in between these two dimensions of *presentation* and *representation*, as if these were two poles of a continuum between which it is possible to position any kind of performative event. The double dimension of performative events results in a sort of multiplication of the enunciators and encunciataries, constructing a kaleidoscopic dynamic of enunciation.

When artists from *Casagrande* drop from a helicopter or a plane hundreds of thousands of bookmarks with poems they are performing a concrete action from the site of their individual subjectivity, in the role of artists, and in the case of Chile in the role of young people who were born during the dictatorship. The effect is even more complicated when *Casagrande* performs the artistic gesture of bombing with poems the cities of Guernika and Dubrovnik. This gesture is enunciated from their individual position, but also from their national identity. What does it mean that a group of Chilean young men are releasing poems over Guernika to commemorate a bombing that occurred more than 60 years ago? Who is performing the action: the single artist, the group of artists, the person, a young man who, as many other young men, rejects war and violence?

A multiplication also takes place on the side of those that participate in the performance, when people attending the social events in each of the three cities discover themselves being bombed by poems. At one level, those who are actually present when the performance takes place are there physically but, at the same time, they are somehow "acting" several roles, for instance, the role of those who years ago were in the same place during the original bombardments or the role of the sons and daughters of the traumatised generation who have been vicariously traumatised by the telling, or the silence, of the older generation.

According to the time that has passed since the original bombing, we may distinguish important differences in the enunciative strategies and in the pragmatic relation that is established each time the performance is presented. In Santiago, some of the population who were present when the performance took place lived the original traumatic event, except for those who were under twenty-eight years old who could probably interpret the performance in a different way. In Dubrovnik, the situation was radically different because we may assume that almost everybody who participated in the performance (except for children under eleven years) had a personal memory related to the bombardment of 1991. In this case, it may be supposed that the efficacy of the *Poem Bombing*, at least at an emotional level, was stronger. In Guernika, the performance is done after sixty-seven years. At this time, probably few of the people who survived the 1937 bombardment participated in the *Poem Bombing*. The effect of the performance is then less emotive and more symbolic, in the sense of a historical repair or commemoration of the bombardment.

This multiplication of the enunciation characteristic of the live artistic events allows the transmission of the traumatic experience to younger generations and thus the construction of a collective memory. The performance not only works for those who experienced the original trauma, but it also produces effects in the whole community. The *Poem Bombing* allows the elder to remember and evoke the past and, at the same time, to tell and communicate it to the younger generations. The performance distributes the knowing of the traumatic event, permitting all of the community via the witnessing of the re-enactment, symbolically to witness the traumatic event. Something similar to what Felman and Laub (1992) explain about the traumatic experience that, until it is actually told, remains as non-existent:

> While historical evidence of the event which constitutes the trauma may be abundant and documents in vast supply the trauma – as a known event and not simply as an overwhelming shock – has not been truly witnessed yet, not taken cognizance of. The emergence of the narrative which is being listened to – and heard – is, therefore, the process and the place wherein the cognizance, the "knowing" of the event is given birth to. The listener, therefore, is a party to the creation of knowledge *de novo*. The testimony to the trauma thus includes its hearer, who is, so to speak, the blank screen on which the event comes to be inscribed for the first time. (Felman and Laub, 1992, p. 57)

In the case of a public performance the co-participation of the hearer in the construction of the representation of the traumatic event is amplified, the hearer becomes a multitude of hearers who are also viewers and participants. The blank screen that Felman and Laub describe becomes then a cultural screen where the inscription of the event responds to a collective effort. The horrible original experience cannot be told, there is no possible frame that may explain what happened, but the performance at least in some measure distributes the perception of a bombing that isotopically recalls the original bombing and by doing so offers visibility to the past traumatic event. Even if the bombardment is presented in a modified modality, it is still capable of offering visibility to the past, to render somehow perceptible to the community the past traumatic event. In this sense, the performance becomes a vehicle that transmits the memory of the traumatic event from the affected generation to younger generations. Young people in some way witness the traumatic event during the performance and thus become part of the future memory of the community. Elaboration is possible only by sharing the experience with those who were not present in the traumatic event, and these non-present "available" people are the younger generations.

By re-externalising the traumatic event, the performance places it again into the public domain, giving by these means the possibility of cultural and historical repair. Projecting the personal traumatic experience into the public space functions as a metaphor of the restitution of trauma to its source: to the *other*. But what maybe helps healing and elaborating trauma is that at the same time, another *other* emerges that is no longer the enemy, but their own community that is now capable of coping with the memory of the past. As an *isotopy*, the *Poem Bombing* recalls the traumatic event, allowing the association of trauma with an experience where the creativity is in the hands, again, of the collectivity. As a result, there is a restitution or reinforcement of the "we" that the cultural trauma drastically damaged. Even after sixty-seven years, these kinds of actions strengthen the community identity by giving a space and a time to represent the past altogether in a creative way.

History is transmitted to the younger generations not by means of an archive, but by means of a practice that creates an embodied, singular memory. So in the case of traumatic experiences, as Felman and Laub (1992) emphasise, it is not enough to tell and hear the testimony, but to live the experience of *living through* testimony and, I could add in the case of cultural trauma, of *living through testimony altogether in the community and for the community*.

Embodiment of the memory of cultural trauma
The *Poem Bombing* performance provides the community an opportunity to react to the overwhelming past traumatic event. As a delayed re-action, this collective performance helps the coping with the traumatic event in particular ways but mainly it allows the *embodiment* of the memory of the cultural trauma. The re-interpretation of the original traumatic event is an operation that happens in the first place in the body of individuals and the body of the community. Then, from this embodied practice, in a second moment, some verbal narratives may emerge, but these are supported by the physical experience of participating in the performance of *being here and now recalling a here and then*.

112

From this point of view one cannot agree completely with Juan Pastor Mellado who affirms:

> Causing to rain printed words in precarious backups implies, in this framework, the desire for filling a hole. The word appears like a matter that fills the empty one of sense. It is then, that the act of repair is produced. (2005, p. 3)

The *Poem Bombing* actually responds to the desire to fill the hole of meaning, but it does so not by means of the word, but by means of performance, by means of an embodied practice. The *Poem Bombing* inscribes the memory of the past event by means that go far beyond the verbal strategies.

On an individual scale, living through the re-enactment of the past provokes the construction of corporeal isotopies that, rather than semantic links, are associations that work at the level of the memory of each individual. Those who in Santiago, Dubrovnik and Guernika had the experience of the original bombing, from a certain viewpoint, live an analogous, perceptive, stot, and gestural action with different emotional reactions. The original perception of bombs falling from the sky is attached to emotional reactions such as terror and panic. In the case of the performance, the perception is somehow the same (still objects dropped massively from a flying device) and thus, by a corporeal memory, it recalls the original emotions but that are no longer pertinent or coherent to the context. By re-experiencing a gesture that recalls the trauma but that is no longer marked by vital danger (in the performance there is nothing to fear) the effect may be liberated, cancelling the strictly firm fixation that characterises the experience of trauma.

In this way, the *Poem Bombing*, drawn from physical memory, connects to affective, cognitive and collective memory. An embodied practice that thus recalls a physical individual experience is able to link with emotions and then with a narrative memory. We could think of the *Poem Bombing* as an operation that works from the bottom to the top, it constructs sense and memory from the most immediate levels to more rational and sophisticated organisations. The sense- making from an embodied level executes an efficient *re-semanticisation* of the trauma, thanks to the fact that the performance is an embodied practice, the traumatic experience may acquire a more complex meaning that is rooted deeply (as the traumatic event) in the body knowledge of the individuals. Simultaneously, from this individual bodily constructed sense, the community may start attempting a *re-semanticisation* of trauma that may include not only a horrifying view of the past but simultaneously the perception of a community that is capable of constructing a collective meaning of the past.

Laub and Felman (1992), among other authors, insist that trauma is impossible to tell and that only a live performative and participatory process of telling and listening to the traumatic memory may transmit it to others. As said before, the specific feature of a performance art event such as the *Poem Bombing* is that it encourages the re-elaboration of trauma by means of an *embodied collective practice*, spreading the witnessing process to other generations. Accepting the impossibility of telling, the *Poem Bombing* proceeds from being silence privileged as action. There is no voice, no narrator, no verbal discourse, just a collective *living through* the experience of a delayed re-action to the catastrophe. I do not mean here that this performance may be enough to heal trauma, but rather that it is an efficient attempt to elaborate the lack of meaning that a traumatic experience leaves behind.

The *Poem Bombing*, even as a public event, is focused on the embodied (re)action and thus reaches the collectiveness by soliciting the individual singular experience. The notion of the body as an archive proposed by Nicholson (2003) is useful to understand the effects of performance. Nicholson affirms that by live performance, by participating in the telling of others' stories, the memory becomes part of the participant's own experience. Those who did not suffer the original bombardment, through the performative re-enactment may acquire a bodily knowledge both of the present performance and of the past event. The elaboration of trauma is then anchored in individual body experience and from there projected to the cultural space. Schechner (1985, 2002), in his famous thesis about restored behaviour typical of performance, insists that behaviour is separate from those who are behaving:

> Restored behavior is living behavior treated as a film director treats a strip of film. These strips of behavior can be rearranged or reconstructed; they are independent of the casual systems (personal, social, political, technological, etc.) that brought them into existence. They have a life of their own. The original 'truth' or 'source' of the behavior may not be known, or may be lost, ignored, or contradicted – even while that truth or source is being honored [...] Restored behavior is 'out there', separate from 'me'. To put it into personal terms, restored behavior is 'me behaving as if I were something else', or 'as I am told to do', or 'as I have learned'. (Schechner 2002, p. 28)

By means of performance then, what was individual is no longer property of the individual but is transmitted, and distributed in the community. The strategy of acting through singular bodies to social bodies is efficient as a way of re-externalising the trauma and thus allowing a public elaboration of it, resituating it to a public and political dimension. So what initially came from the external sphere and that tragically irrupted into the individual's system, finally returns to the external social dimension where it may find, in collaboration with a cultural embodied system, a meaning that may come back into the individual to help the elaboration of trauma.

The capacity of these kinds of embodied practices to cope with collective trauma responds to the fact that performance art works on several levels simultaneously: from the individual physical experience to the collective body of culture, from the lack of semantic meaning to a bodily meaning, from the impossibility of remembering and forgetting to the transmission of memory. As Diana Taylor affirms: "Embodied practices make the 'past' available as political resource in the present by simultaneously enabling several complicated, multilayered processes" (Taylor, 2006, p. 68). The restitution of the traumatic experience to the public space renders available the past experience to the community not only to elaborate the trauma, but also to manage and manipulate the political representation of the past. In the case of the *Poem Bombing,* the political aspect is of course present, but I could say in a more general way, the political message is unspecific, promoting the need to evoke and reconstruct historical memory rather than to propose a particular connotation of the past event.

From fiction to reality and backwards

Is it possible that a fictional event such as the *Poem Bombing* may in any way have real effects and provoke cultural transformations? What I maintain here is that the *Poem Bombing* performance rather than transmitting and representing the cultural trauma, retroactively collaborates in the historical reconstruction of it. In this sense, the efficacy of the performance goes beyond the elaboration of trauma, even sixty years after, as in the case of Guernika, it still affects and transforms the *way in which the original event is conceived.*

As said before, the performance reproduces some constancies of the original bombing, and by dong so it creates the sense effect of an *iconic* relation to the original traumatic experience, being therefore interpreted as in direct relation to the traumatic experience. This semiotic operation gives reality to both the fictional performance and also to the original traumatic event.

On the one hand, the representation of the conflict by means of performance art produces a truth effect, collaborating and constructing the real of discourse and representation. As Peggy Phelan (1993), from a cultural psychoanalytic perspective, claims:

> The visible itself is woven into each of these discourses as an unmarked conspirator in the maintenance of each discursive real. I want to expose the ways in which the visible real is employed as a truth effect for the establishment of these discursive and representational notions of the real. Moreover, I want to suggest that by seeing the blind spot within the visible real we might see a way to redesign the representational real. (Phelan, 1993, p. 3)

From this point of view, the representation of the traumatic experience acquires the status of a real event that somehow leaves the original experience behind an obscure screen that makes the traumatic experience unintelligible. When the representation is established then it is somehow impossible to go back to a clean unpolluted vision of the original historical event. But, in the same way, by rendering visible the past event, the performance allows consideration of the past event itself as a real and undeniable event. In finally giving the traumatic experience some kind of representation it heightens it to the status of a *real* past event. Even if the original event may always remain in the shadow of the representation, the fact that it really happened remains as an uncontestable evidence.

In this dialectic movement, the real and its representation construct each other at the same time. As Judith Butler says, "the real is positioned both before and after its representation, and representation becomes a moment of the reproduction and consolidation of the real" (1990, p. 106). In this sense, the movement is double and mutual: the real is interpreted through representation and at the same time representation is interpreted through the real. Therefore, the reality effect influences the status of the original event, in this case the war bombing, and it collaborates (together with other representations) in producing the reality effect for the past event.

In this sense, we may think of the *Poem Bombing* as a true *liminoid* manifestation. In the words of Victor Turner, liminal entities "are neither here nor there; they are betwixt and between the positions assigned and arrayed by law, custom, conventions and ceremonial" (1969, p. 95). Liminality describes this status of transition, a passageway that is often inaugurated by traditional rites that allow people to play with familiar cultural aspects and render them unfamiliar. According to Turner (1982), in complex societies liminality is presented in the form of the liminoid, mostly signed by play and individual initiative, where an artist or a group of artists plays by recomposing in experimental organisations conventional cultural elements. For Turner, the existence of such entities is fundamental to maintain the elasticity of society, the continued transformations of social life. The consideration of performance art as a *liminoid* phenomenon is relevant to underline the fact that the efficacy of the representation of conflict depends on its ambiguity towards the event that it is representing. I believe that the greater the tolerance to ambiguity of the representation the more the representation embraces with efficacy the complexity of the historical conflict and events.

(In)conclusions: some questions about happiness

In this discussion we have examined the complex relation that in this case emerges between conflict, trauma, and the representation of trauma and memory. Trauma relates to conflict because it "marks" a certain precise space and time, and thus it has much more radical effects on individual and collective memory. Bombings, such as the ones in Santiago, Dubrovnik, Guernika, Dresdren and Hiroshima are powerful signals that crystallise memory, that become specific and intense marks that people identify and remember clearly.

Because of this particular characteristic trauma is an excellent core for strategies that have the objective of coping with trauma. In fact it is not accidental that cultural therapeutic strategies of representation of conflict usually concentrate on traumatic events rather than on the general conflict. Trauma, as said before, is easy to recall because it is still present in people's minds, and so also the cultural strategies of representation of conflict take advantage of this quality of trauma. Once the traumatic experience is represented then it may be associated with a more stable meaning, and from there move to the understanding, reconstructing and meaning making of the broader conflict.

As an embodied practice, the *Poem Bombing* used certain specific strategies in order to cope with the cultural trauma such as the installation of a ritual space that permits a collective witnessing of the re-enactment (and by these means also a symbolic witnessing of the experience of trauma), the weaving of several temporalities that are in-between repetition and uniqueness and the multiplication of enunciation as a way of transmitting the memory of trauma.

The case of the *Poem Bombing* has been useful in discussing the relationship between conflict, trauma and memory, but we have not reflected deeply on its relation to happiness. The first obvious assertion is that we are dealing with a complex, not direct nor unidirectional, relation. In one way, the *Poem Bombing*'s purpose is to install the exact opposite values from those of war, if war is about violence and breaking through the social organisation, the performance promotes values such as peace, a creative way of life, and community participation. In this sense, I could say, with polemic intent, the *Poem Bombing* is a "happy representation" of a tragic event. But, then, some important questions emerge: is it possible to represent conflict by a "happy representation"? How much of the original conflict is left out of the "happiness" and "optimism" that the performance encourages?

Performances and artistic events that deal with conflict use two alternative strategies: either they represent the event in a tragic way or, as in the case we are studying, they represent it by a "happy representation". In the first strategy, the representation is loyal to the pain and destruction that the original conflict situation generated, whereas the second obscures the painful aspects of the original event and masks them behind a joyful appearance. I suppose that the happy representation does not mean necessarily that the traumatic event had any positive aspects, but it prefers to recall it from the present time by happy means. In this sense, the happy representation is oriented (optimistically) towards the construction of a happier future and the painful representation is oriented towards the recalling of the tragic past. Whether one strategy is better or more effective than the other does not seem important to me. What is crucial is to maintain the complexity of the original traumatic event in the representation of it. I am not maintaining that the representation should be realistic, but I think it is necessary that it support a degree of indeterminacy, that it allow and contain an open question about the past.

References
A'ness, F. (2004) "Resisting Amnesia: Yuyachkani, Performance, and the Postwar Reconstruction of Peru", *Theatre Journal* 56 (3), pp. 395–414.
Butler, J. (1990) "The Force of Fantasy: Feminism, Mapplethorpe and Discursive Excess", *Differences* 2 (2), pp. 105-125.
Caruth, C. (ed.) (1995) *Trauma: Explorations in Memory,* Baltimore, Johns Hopkins University Press.
------------. (1996) *Unclaimed Experience: Trauma, Narrative, and History*, Baltimore, Johns Hopkins University Press.

Coloma, J. (1999) *Lessons in Psychoanalytic Theory*, Santiago, Universidad Catolica de Chile .

De Marinis, M. (1982) *Semotica del Teatro: L'analisi testuale dello spettacolo*, Milan, Bompiani.

Eco, U. (1977) "Semiotics of Theatrical Performance", *The Drama Review* 21, pp. 107–117.

---------. (1984) *Semiotica e Filosofia del Linguaggio*, Turin, Einaudi.

Felman, S. and D. Laub. (1992) *Testimony: Crises of Witnessing in Literature, Psychoanalysis, and History*, New York, Routledge.

Freud, S. (1986) "The Aetiology of Hysteria", *The Standard Edition of the Complete Psychological Works of Sigmund Freud.* trans. James Strachey *et. al.*, London, Hogarth Press, vol. 3, pp. 189-221.

---------. (1905) "Fragment of an Analysis of a Case of Hysteria", *The Standard Edition of the Complete Psychological Works of Sigmund Freud.* trans. James Strachey *et. al.*, London, Hogarth Press, vol. 7, pp. 3-122.

---------. (1920) "Beyond the Pleasure Principle", *The Standard Edition of the Complete Psychological Works of Sigmund Freud.* trans. James Strachey *et. al.*, London, Hogarth Press, vol. 18, pp. 3-64.

---------. (1926) "Inhibitions, Symptoms and Anxiety"", *The Standard Edition of the Complete Psychological Works of Sigmund Freud.* trans. James Strachey *et. al.*, London, Hogarth Press, vol. 20, pp. 77-124.

Freud, S., and J. Breuer. (1893-5) "Studies on Hysteria" ", *The Standard Edition of the Complete Psychological Works of Sigmund Freud.* trans. James Strachey *et. al.*, London, Hogarth Press, vol. 3, vol. 2, pp. 1-151.

Lotman, J. (1992) *Kul'tura i vzryv*, Gnozis, Moskva (trad, it. *La cultura e l'esplosione : prevedibilità e imprevedibilità, Milan,* Feltrinelli, Milano, 1993.)

Mellado, J.P. (2005) "Palabras de Reparación", *Bombardeo de Poemas sobre Guernika*, not published.

Munk, E. (2001) "Before the fall: Yugoslav Theatres of Opposition". *Theatre* 31 (1), pp. 5-25.

H. Nicholson, (2003) "The Performance of Memory" *Drama Australia* 27 (2), pp. 79-92.

Phelan, P. (1993) *Unmarked: The politics of Performance*. London, Routledge .

Schechner, R. (1985) *Between Theatre and Anthropology*, Philadelphia, University of Pennsylvania Press.

---------------. (2002) *Performance Studies: An introduction*, London, Routledge.

Smelser, N.J. (2004) "Psychological Trauma and Cultural Trauma", in *Cultural Trauma and Collective Identity*, ed. Jeffrey C. Alexander *et al.*, Berkeley, University of California Press.

Sztompka, P. (2004) "The Trauma of Social Change: A Case of Postcommunist Societies" , in *Cultural Trauma and Collective Identity*, ed. Jeffrey C. Alexander *et al.*, Berkeley, University of California Press.

Taylor, D. (2002) "You are here: The DNA of Performance", *The Drama Review* 46 (1).

---------. (2003) *The Archive and the Repertoire: Performing Cultural*

Memory in the Americas. Durham, N.C., Duke University Press.
---------. (2006) "Performance and/as history" *The Drama Review* 50 (1), pp. 67-86.
Turner, V. (1969) *The Ritual Process: Structure and Anti-Structure*, Chicago, Aldine.
------------. (1982) *From ritual to theatre*: *The human seriousness of play,* New York, Performing Arts Journal.
Zatzman, B. (2005) "Staging History: Aesthetics and the Performance of Memory", *Journal of Aesthetic Education* 39 (4), pp. 95-103.

Post-Communist Block Estates: Are We Happy There?
The Case of Przymorze District in the City of Gdańsk

Stanislaw Rzyski

In this article I shall outline the ideological context and circumstances which have accompanied the development of estates of blocks of flats in Poland in the time of socialism. Special attention will be paid to the rift between ideology, planning, and the actual completion of these estates of blocks of flats. The issue of perceiving the block estates as heritage from the former system and the role of the word "blokowisko" – block estate, in the forming of this perception, will be raised. The example of Przymorze, an estate of blocks of flats which exists in Gdańsk, shows the conditions in which its dwellers live and their attitudes towards this kind of housing, which was in effect imposed upon them. Following on from this, the present situation on the estate will be described, fifteen years after the fall of socialism. In the final part of the paper, which is based on qualitative research carried out in the spring of 2006, I shall try to answer the question whether or not the estate dwellers are happy today, and if living on a "blokowisko" estate has any influence upon their happiness and well-being.

Estates of blocks of flats represent the most dominant and popular kind of residential housing in the city landscape of the post-socialist countries. At the same time, it is estimated that these estates are inhabited by about 50% of the cities' population, hence the role of the estates of blocks of flats in the shaping of all social and economic phenomena in the urban regions should not be underestimated. This heritage of "blokowiska"– block estates, left by the former system, constitutes an unwanted and troublesome one, which still plays a key role in the shaping of the city dweller's living conditions. Therefore examination of this phenomenon is of particular interest.

Ideology and Reality

The form of government imposed on Poland by the Soviet Union brought about changes which affected all spheres of life in the country. After World War II the new communist authorities immediately launched a fierce attack on the remains of the old system as they set about laying the foundations for a new communist state. One of the most significant factors in establishing the dominance of the new ideology was architecture and spatial planning. Thanks to these the authorities got the opportunity to shape space and build cities in a way that allowed them to provide society with clear information concerning the new ideology and to create individual and collective standards of behaviour of the new, socialist citizen (Bańka, 1985). Central planning and state land-ownership let the authorities control the development of the city and the distribution of flats (Smith, 1996).

In the planning of new socialist cities postulates of equality, modernisation, urbanisation and industry were also being realised. It needs to be emphasised that social policy, and the housing policy that was connected with it in those days, were subordinated to economic

120

goals, namely the greater industrialisation of the country. The housing industry had to provide the employees of the newly-set-up industrial plants with accommodation. However, this situation caused a delay in the urbanisation process in relation to the priority given to the process of industrialisation, which resulted in a chronic shortage of flats (Węcławowicz, 2003).

Housing policy was to realise the egalitarian principles of social policy concerning mainly equal access to flats of a uniform standard, to housing estates of similar appearance and to services of the same approximate level. The estates were supposed to be socially diversified. The postulate of modernisation was to be realised by improving the living conditions of the working class, which the newly-built modern housing estates were expected to do (Demko and Regulska, 1987; Smith, 1996). Housing estates were an ideal manifestation of the ideological and economic postulates of the socialist era.

Over time the ideological attitudes influencing the manner in which the housing estates were designed and built gave way to real factors, the most important of them being the huge demand for flats caused by war damage, the industrialisation of the country and demographic changes. In order to achieve a positive result in the form of a large number of the newly-built flats, they began to design bigger estates and bigger blocks with smaller flats. In this way the standards of the flats and blocks of flats were lowered. Among other things, so called "dark kitchens", meaning small and without windows, became common. In addition to this, there were lifts which only stopped at every second floor (Basista, 2001).

The quality of workmanship considerably influenced the quality of the flats. The decisive factors here were the new technologies that brought in prefabricated components, which made it possible to construct buildings quickly and cheaply. The poor quality of materials resulted in the fact that flats were relatively cold and required high costs of maintenance, while the paper-thin walls allowed residents to hear what the neighbours were doing. Another vital factor which influenced the poor living conditions was the very poor quality of workmanship of the buildings. As a result, the lucky ones who obtained their own flats after years of waiting moved into buildings of very poor quality. Besides, the state expenses minimisation rule led to a lack of infrastructure such as shops, schools, cultural institutions or recreational amenities, on the newly-built housing estates.

Because of all these factors housing estates built in socialist countries considerably differed from those constructed in western countries. They were substantially less diverse in respect of their architecture, they were bigger, of a lower standard, of poorer quality and lacked infrastructure. In contrast to western countries, big estates of blocks of flats were built until as late 1989, which directly influenced the scale of the whole phenomenon in the post-socialist countries (Basista, 2001; Węcławowicz, 2003).

Heritage
1989 brought a change in the political system, which rejected the

former ideology for the benefit of a new democratic and liberal one. Changes in the ideological and economic sphere were taking place very quickly, but heritage in the form of more durable buildings, infrastructure, social-spatial structures and the mentality of the people remained, with changes taking place only much more slowly (Sykora, 2000).

It seems that the most common durable heritage, which is easily noticeable in the landscape and still influences the quality of life and attitudes of its inhabitants, are the estates of blocks of flats. These estates of blocks of flats were built throughout the whole period of the People's Republics and so exist nearly everywhere. Small blocks of flats were even built in the countryside. Due to the universal character of this phenomenon a large percentage of the Polish population live on an estate of blocks of flats. According to Basista (2001) during socialism the public sector built no fewer than 4,000,000 flats, which means that at least from seven to eight million Polish people, about 20% of the population, live on such estates. In the big cities such as Warsaw, Krakow, Poznań, Gdańsk and Łódź, this percentage is even higher and often exceeds 50%.

Following the changes to the system in 1989 the estates have become something unwanted or at the very least troublesome. They are synonymous with the old system, of mediocrity, poverty, lack of prospects, and deprivation. The notion of the "blokowisko" has taken on a pejorative meaning which has become an inherent part of Polish mentality. Films about block estates have been made, for example *"Blokersi"* (*The Blockers*) by Sylwester Latkowski of 2001, *"Cześć Tereska" (Hi, Little Teresa)* directed by Robert Gliński of 2001, or *"Dzień Świra"* (*The Day of the Freak*) directed by Marek Koterski in 2002. All these films portray the traumas connected with living in blocks on these large estates of blocks of flats and strengthen the image of the "blokowisko" as a pathological space which is unattractive and dirty, and which is, furthermore, inhabited by people who live on the fringes of society without any prospects.

In spite of this, the universal character of "blokowiska", millions of average Poles still live on these unwanted estates and have to face up to their negative image which dominates the consciousness of Polish society today. Some people fight effectively against this stereotype of the estates by continuous space adaptation and normalisation of the social conditions. Others, because they cannot cope with the pressure, try to move to more people-friendly districts.

Block Estates Close Up
According to Sagan (1997), the cities of today in which the estates of blocks of flats prevail have become anonymous, impersonal spaces of mass structures, which are dehumanised and with which the inhabitants do not identify. Rykiel (1999) mentions a number of factors which in his opinion play a key role in the weakening of social bonds and influence the poor quality of living standards on estates of blocks of flats including:

- the atomisation of society caused by the ban on free association with others and lack of local authorities
- a considerable percentage of new village immigrants in the population of the new estates
- the alienation of the local community resulting from a lack of opportunity to shape the local space
- the dilution of responsibility for the place of residence due to lack of actual owners for the blocks of flats
- the anonymity of social relationships due to the scale of the flats and blocks, as well as the estates themselves
- the social heterogeneity of the estates
- lack of possibility to choose the place of residence
- the underdevelopment of the social infrastructure on the estates
- the underdevelopment of transport infrastructure in the city.

However, for many years people have lived in these dehumanised spaces trying to individualise their own fragment of the space, in other words, to create their own place. These aspirations manifested themselves in a variety of ways. The most popular activity was the furnishing of their own flat because it was the only space where they had the freedom for individual creativity. Flats in blocks were often furnished luxuriously, which stood in stark contrast to the dullness and mediocrity of the stairwells. At the same time the expressions of individualism noticeable outside were, among others, the entrance doors, which in the course of time became an indicator of the inhabitants' financial status. Balconies were often decorated and walled up as well. Besides this, a further sign of individualism was the sectioning off of parts of the stairwell for private use, by fitting in grills, as well as by establishing "by-the-house gardens", on the lawns near the blocks (Sagan, 1997; Basista, 2001).

It was different in the case of public space where the inhabitants' potential for development was limited or not possible at all. This concerns the space in the blocks of flats such as stairwells, corridors, lifts or the space inbetween the blocks including car parks, lawns, playgrounds etc. These places were neglected for a long time and the inhabitants on their way back from work or the shops sneaked quickly past these hostile spaces to their luxuriously furnished flats.

The block estates were especially poor in shopping centres and recreational facilities. Every housing estate plan secured an adequate area in which to build a service centre often located in the centre of the block estate. However, a shortage of funds and the policies of the state made it impossible to put up these buildings and the terrain allotted to these investments sometimes remained empty and neglected for years (Basista, 2001).

Because of the problems cited above, so common on the block estates, at the beginning of the 1990s numerous questions concerning the future of these block estates were brought up. Many authors, seeing the negative image of the estates, expected and still keep expecting that the social degradation will escalate and that the "blokowiska" will turn into big city slums.

Przymorze Yesterday and Today

Przymorze district estate is located in Gdańsk in the direct vicinity of the seaside. It is a neighbour to other districts made up of block estates such as Zaspa, Żabianka and also Oliwa, where tenement houses and houses from the beginning of the twentieth century predominate.

The plan to build Przymorze district estate in a 200 hectre area, earmarked for fifty thousand inhabitants, won first prize in the Polish Architects Association (SARP) competition in 1959. Public buildings were planned to cover 70% of the area and were expected to take up 25% of the buildings' cubic capacity. The average flat area was supposed to be 40 square metres with 12.2 square metres earmarked for each inhabitant. The plan also comprised 30 garages and 10 parking spaces per 1000 inhabitants and the construction of one primary school for 960 children, a 700-seat cinema-theatre, as well as the creation of green areas. Furthermore, a number of 11-storey high-rise blocks with outside galleries running along them, commonly called "falowce" (wave-buildings) and considerably smaller, 5-storey buildings, were to be built in the spaces between them. Primarily, the district estate was intended to provide flats for the employees of the rapidly developing harbour sector (Czepczyński, 1998). The Gdańsk Housing Construction Company undertook the realisation of the project. The actual building works in Przymorze district began in 1964 and finished in 1975.

Until 1989, Przymorze, and likewise scores of similar districts estates in Poland, was an unattractive, neglected quarter lacking sufficient infrastructure. After the collapse of the socialist system, the spectre of an uncertain future hung over Przymorze as well. According to Grabowski (2000), the Mayor of Gdańsk, Paweł Adamowicz, gave up on Przymorze having realised that the only future for the district was its social and material degradation. However, the processes taking place in the district at present do not confirm the nightmarish scenario outlined by the panel of experts a few years ago. A number of positive processes have made Przymorze an attractive place to live in.

One of the major factors delaying the social degradation of the estate is its class diversity resulting from the former socialist policy. Thanks to this great social diversity the pathological phenomena are still marginal in nature. Despite the fact that the flats in the blocks in Przymorze are not very big and not very functional, they have been modernised and their standard improved for many years by their users. Because of this, many of the inhabitants do not want to move out of them because, among others things, they have invested substantial amounts of money in their modernisation. The flats are now comfortable and their residents have grown used to them. Quite important also is the fact that some of the inhabitants have lived in the blocks since their birth and simply do not know a different housing standard.

The blocks themselves, like the flats, are not very functional and their size is rather overwhelming. Nevertheless, modernisation work has brought numerous positive results. In the first place their elevations have been painted and insulated. Thanks to this the block estates' image is no longer so grey and monotonous as it was in socialist days. The insulation and replacement of old windows has meant the up-keep on the flats, especially in winter time, is lower. In many blocks the lifts have been modernised and the access of unwelcome visitors limited thanks to the installation of intercoms, as well as cameras to monitor people entering the building.

During the past few years the surroundings of the blocks have been improved as well. Wastelands covered with weeds have been replaced with playgrounds and green areas in relatively good condition. The social degradation, for example, in the form of beer drinking by youngsters, has been driven away from the neighbourhood of the blocks, which in turn has increased the inhabitants' sense of security. In addition to this, a very important element for the improvement of living conditions has been the modernisation of the strip of green separating the district from the beach. This once totally neglected terrain, changed into a very attractive recreational area, is now visited with pleasure not only by the inhabitants of Przymorze but also by visitors from other districts of Gdańsk. The shortage of car parks still remains an unsolved problem however. This affects not only drivers who waste time looking for somewhere to park, but pedestrians who have to squeeze between cars parked on pavements and grass verges.

After 1989 thanks to market liberalisation, shops and services were opened in the poorly equipped commercial centres of the block estates, a large number of which have been responsible for considerably improving the living conditions of the whole estate. A significant role in providing better access to shops, other services and cultural outlets has been played by the building of the "Alfa Centre" shopping centre nearby Przymorze itself. At present a considerable number of the inhabitants do their shopping there and take advantage of the different entertainment on offer.

In the case of Przymorze, a very significant factor in its revitalisation is its attractive location. Thanks to its nearness to the main communication routes and the proximity of retail service centres Przymorze still remains an attractive place to live. The inhabitants of Przymorze, unlike the inhabitants of the newly-built housing estates on the outskirts of the city, spend less time on their daily journey to work, to school or to meet friends on social occasions. The district also has well-developed bus and tram links with other parts of the city.

Contrary to many authors' opinions, for example, Rylka (1999), in spite of the unfavourable conditions due to the size of the blocks and block estates as such, its inhabitants have been able to build strong and satisfying social bonds, so that today they do not want to move to the more attractive parts of the city, because they do not want to break off these relationships. This issue especially concerns middle-aged people. Usually it is the young people who start their own families and want to live in their own flats who move out of the block estates. The outcome of this process is the ageing of Przymorze's community which has resulted in lower crime rates and better public safety in the district.

Are we happy?

The findings presented in this part of the study are the result of pilot research carried out in the spring 2006 which are preparatory proceedings for a survey which is planned for autumn of 2006. The findings are based on interviews conducted with the inhabitants of "falowiec" ("a wave block of flats") – the longest block of flats in Poland which is located in Przymorze. It also includes findings from interviews with other block inhabitants, as well as with students living in Przymorze. It is worth mentioning that most of Gdańsk's inhabitants perceive the "falowiec" as a building providing very poor living conditions, and associated with a number of different social problems. The findings are surprising and dismiss the initial assumption that the "blokowiska" are places where severe pathologies develop, places which are socially and physically degrading.

The interviews and conversations proved that the district's inhabitants are happy, and the fact itself that they live in Przymorze does not influence their sense of happiness or well-being very much. This means that the living conditions on the estate are sufficiently good for its inhabitants to realise their aspirations and life plans. Although the inhabitants do not identify themselves with their district, still most of them would be likely to recommend it as a place to live.

Among the advantages of living in Przymorze the inhabitants mention such factors as its good location, good access to service centres and attractive recreational areas, as well as well-developed transport. In addition to this, the inhabitants feel safe in the district and find neighbourly bonds satisfying. The most frequently mentioned drawbacks of living there continue to be the neglected staircases and lifts, the shortage of parking places and flats which are not very functional.

It seems that a very important factor for a sense of happiness and well-being, and identification with the place, is the pernicious myth of the "blokowisko", which is slowly being debunked. Przymorze's inhabitants do not feel that their district is a place where sociological problems are nurtured. However, they admit that their district is a block estate, but only in regard to the buildings, not social degradation.

Another factor which the inhabitants are appreciative of is the fact that they no longer feel forgotten and abandoned. Good care is being taken of them at last! This was initially manifested through the blocks' modernisation undertaken by the housing cooperative. Then they set about developing the space between the blocks and over the past two years they have established an attractive recreational park separating the district from the beach.

The inhabitants also feel good thanks to the new investments made in the housing industry sector in the district, especially because of the high prices for the flats on offer there. The old inhabitants of Przymorze are aware of the fact that many people are ready to pay a high price to live there. Even though the standard of the newly-built flats is considerably higher than the old ones, their location within the city is the same.

All in all however, the relatively good living conditions in Przymorze do not eliminate, among Przymorze's inhabitants, the desire to move to different places. The majority of the respondents declared that ultimately they would like to move to a detached house with a garden which is unattainable because of financial restrictions. Those who do not dream of a detached house would most like to move to Przymorze or near it, but to a flat of a higher standard than the one they live in today. This fact supports the thesis regarding the poor standard of flats built in socialist times, as well as regarding the good location of the district within the city.

The interviews proved that decisively negative attitudes towards the district are rare. One interview included a statement that all "blokowiska" should be demolished. Unfortunately the young author of this statement was not able to provide arguments for her beliefs. Further conversation revealed that it was the negative myth of the block estate created by the media that had influenced her opinion the most. The young respondent was not able to point out any real disadvantage of the district that she lived in, besides the oppressive landscape. This example illustrates how much the negative myth created by the media is able to influence the feeling of satisfaction with the district where one lives and identification with it.

Conclusions

The findings of the initial research show Przymorze's inhabitants feel happy, and that their place of residence is not the main factor which determines their sense of happiness and well-being. For a long time the inhabitants have been aware of the downsides of living in a "blokowisko" – block estate, but today more and more of them appreciate the features of their district, especially in the context of the constantly improving living conditions.

It seems that the process of the successive adaptation of the estates by inhabitants and the identification the inhabitants have built up is of fundamental significance for the future of such estates. At the same time it is vitally important to fight against the myth that has been created around the "blokowisko" and which, to a large degree, is incompatible with the reality of the estates. In this process a key role should be played by the local authorities, which can modernise public areas in such a way that they become inhabitant-friendly.

References

Bańka, A. (1985) *Psychologiczna struktura projektowania środowiska. Studium przestrzeni architektonicznej*, Poznań, PP.

Basista, A. (2001) *Betonowe dziedzictwo. Architektura w Polsce czasów komunizmu*, Warszawa–Kraków, PWN.

Czepczyński, M. (1998) "Wybrane elementy warunków życia mieszkańców dużych osiedli mieszkaniowych Gdańska – na przykładzie Przymorza i Zaspy i ich przemiany", in *IX Konwersatorium Wiedzy o Mieście*, Łódź, UŁ, pp. 49-68.

------------------. (1999) "Rozwój i upadek koncepcji osiedli blokowych", *Budownictwo mieszkaniowe w latach 90.- zróżnicowanie przestrzenne i kierunki rozwoju, Biuletyn KPZK PAN*, z 190, pp. 49-67.

Demko, G. J. and J. Regulska. (1987) "Socialism and its impact on urban processes and the city", *Urban Geography* 8 (4), pp. 289-292.

Grabowski, K. (2000) "Biedabloki", *Wprost,* nr 914, pp. 38-40.

Rykiel, Z. (1999) *Przemiany struktury społeczno-przestrzennej miasta polskiego a świadomość terytorialna jego mieszkańców, Prace Geograficzne IGiPZ PAN,* nr 170.

Sagan, I. (1997) "Wielkie zespoły mieszkaniowe – niczyja przestrzeń czy nasze miejsce?", *Kwartalnik Geograficzny,* nr. 2/3, pp. 15-21.

Smith, M. D. (1996) "The socialist city", in G. Andrusz *et al.* (eds.), *Cities after socialism: urban and regional changes and conflict in post-socialist societies,* Oxford, Blackwell, pp. 70-99.

Sykora, L. (2000) "Post-communist city", in *XIII Konwersatorium wiedzy o mieście. Miasto postsocjalistyczne – organizacja przestrzeni miejskiej i jej przemiany,* Łudź, WUŁ, pp. 41-45.

Szczepański, M. A. (1991) *"Miasto socjalistyczne" i świat społeczny jego mieszkańców,* Rozwój lokalny, Samorząd Terytorialny t. 32, Warszaw, Uniwersytet Warszawski.

Węcławowicz, G. (2000) "Kształtowanie się nowego modelu zróżnicowań społeczno-przestrzennych miasta w europie środkowej – wybrane elementy przejścia od miasta socjalistycznego do miasta postsocjalistycznego", in *XIII Konwersatorium wiedzy o mieście. Miasto postsocjalistyczne – organizacja przestrzeni miejskiej i jej przemiany,* Łudź, WUŁ, pp. 25-30.

-------------------. (2003), *Geografia społeczne miast. Zróżnicowanie społeczno-przestrzenne,* Warszawa, PWN.

Part 3
Histories

Constructed Happiness
On the Seductions of Messianism:
Portugal with or without Sebastian

Rui Gonçalves Miranda

> The Thing is neither dead nor alive, it is dead
> and alive at the same time. It survives.
>
> Jacques Derrida

A false beginning... 1578 and all that

After the battle not much was left of the proud Portuguese army that planned to invade Africa... and maybe move on to take Jerusalem: dead bodies, some artillery pieces and weapons, a surprising amount of guitars (or is that part of the legend? Where to draw the line?), and a reasonable number of noblemen who could be ransomed for a no less reasonable sum of money.

After paying for a war it could not afford, the country now had to pay for the return of the few of those belonging to the Portuguese elite of the time who were left alive. Of the three kings involved in the battle of 4 August 1578 none was to be found living. One would not be found at all (at least with valid witnesses willing to give their testimony): King Sebastian, the "Desired One", aged 24, who was living the moment for which he had waited during the whole of his short existence. No one saw his corpse. Apparently. It is known he fought very bravely, as he was said to be an exceptional soldier, although a mediocre military commander who even failed to give an adequate order of attack: "Morrer sim, mas devagar" were, allegedly, his last words. "To die, yes, but slowly". Assertively deferent; deferring... A young king, with a very specific background in terms of national history, projecting his mantle as a martyr for his religion and for his nation. Messianism in the making.

After the conflict, it became obvious that not much would be left the same in Portugal (if things were to be left at all). How could the Portuguese Empire survive, how could national identity, uprooted so tragically, be clung onto? How could the Portuguese be at peace with themselves again, how could they remedy this failed strategy, how could they live with it, make amends for it? Who was to blame? The King? An obvious answer, and one that has been proffered through time. But in the speech at the burial of his alleged body, Fr. Luís Álvares proclaimed that the guilt was not on the King's side: It was "ours": *we* failed you, for not stopping you, as others have stopped kings before in this country (Loureiro, 1989, p. 244).

Alleged body, as no one saw the King's corpse. Of course not. The King was not killed. The King was not dead. How could it be possible that this king, the hope and sustenance of the Portuguese Empire and the Christian faith, be dead? He was most certainly not. There would be a body, one which the nation could bury and forget (even if not

131

forgive... either the King or itself). Or remember, which would amount to the same. But there was no body, only rumours. Rumours that mentioned that the gates of a Portuguese fortress had been opened after the battle to someone who had claimed to be the King. Who would do so if not the King? Some claimed that the King, embarrassed by his defeat, did not want to appear publicly, but indeed had returned in one of the ships that brought the news of the disaster home. He was just waiting for the time to be right for him to resurface. Those were sad times: an Empire without a head to run it, a King without heirs (despite the requests and the warnings), Castile so close, so powerful; but times would be set right again and all would end well (why is one so hasty when it comes to ending things?).

Strange that the King should not appear in times of such great distress. Something, someone must be delaying him. But the King did not return in 1580 either, when Philip II of Spain became the King of Portugal (the game of intermarriage finally had a winner).[1] The King did not make himself visible either before or even after the risk of losing his throne. But he would come back. Of course. How could he not? On a misty morning, riding a white horse, he would not only redeem himself and save the country from occupation, but also provide the world with harmony and unity. He would become what he had always been meant to become, ever since he had been a small child: God's Captain. But maybe even much more... maybe what prophecies had referred to. Surely they meant the King. How could *we* not have seen it? And the many prodigies before birth, after the battle (someone told someone who told someone who had seen, who had heard)? Certainly these had happened for a reason. The King will come back. He will come back. He must, it is only natural that he should. How could he not? In some way or another he will, and *we* shall be waiting.

After all, and in spite of everything, happiness is still (t)here. It will come to Portugal once again (when was it here before?). It is always to come, everywhere. There are good years to come. Happy years... Sebastianism in the making.

Sebastian

After a succession of misfortunes and disasters, the day came in 1554 when the country's desire was fulfilled. Only one out of the several royal offspring had been able to live long enough to leave a successor to the throne. The dangerous gap in the line of succession had been filled. As a matter of fact, Dom João, the Prince, having died some days before the birth of his son, had no public ceremonies held in his honour so as not to disturb the womb where the "desired one" lay. The people rejoiced. After so many processions and pilgrimages, the country had a King, maybe one who would escape the terrible fate of his father and siblings, condemned to premature death. Sebastian's mother left him

---

[1] There were several attempts at unifying the crowns of Castile and Portugal through marriage, including some in which the king and heir to the two kingdoms would reign from Lisbon (Miguel da Paz, who died in 1500, is an example of that).

as a baby, never to return to Portugal.

Raised by the Jesuits (on whom much of the blame for Sebastian's fanaticism and misogyny is usually deposited), whose task, like that of others responsible for the upbringing of the king, was that of "reaportuguesar" the King, to return him to the ways of the Portuguese of old and to implement the interrupted policy (of conquest) on Africa. The Queen was not Portuguese enough (that was the opinion of the Council) and her closeness to Castile had caused enough damage already.[2] One should make sure that the country remained independent, autonomous, remained itself, its own self; that it would not lose the very substance of which it was composed... whatever that might be. One must purge one's self of that which, though within, remains yet somewhat exterior, and therefore is a weakening agent.

He was not the healthiest of kings. A disease without a clear diagnosis to this day (there is still considerable dispute on the matter), influential or not on his behaviour, caused fits with symptoms that worsened due to the king's relentless physical and military exercise. These same feats, simultaneously courageous and disregarding of their consequences, whether in bullfighting, during hunting or at sea, were but visible signs of the King's insistence on being more of a warrior than his grandfather, who had abandoned several Portuguese possessions in Africa. The ancestors Sebastian was proud of were warriors (he let everyone know that when he opened their tombs). He took with him to battle in Africa the sword of the first king of Portugal and the helmet that his grandfather, Charles V, the Holy Roman Emperor, had worn during the conquest of Tunis. The king's fervent religiosity and his impetuous spirit of Crusade manifested themselves very early on. Ever since he was a boy, his desire had been that of becoming God's Captain in the conquest of Africa. Anachronistic? Idealistic?

The poets had a part to play in this. Camões (in the celebrated poem of the Portuguese nation, *The Lusiads*) and many more had made him believe that he was God's chosen one and had encouraged him to go to war, not exclusively, but especially, in Africa. "North-Africanism" was a strong current of opinion in the kingdom, and had been so for a number of years (expansion into Africa had first occurred in 1415). The country was poorer, the Indies did not represent a substantial profit, and no profit at all to the noblemen who were not involved in trade. From where would they get more land and titles if there were no more battles to fight? And then there were the threats of the Turk, the constant attacks of pirates on Portuguese ships. Maybe Africa was a safer option than the "fumes of India"; maybe Africa could bring strategic and commercial benefits that the East could not. An empire "at our doorstep", a place where Portugal could expand, where Christian faith could reign supreme and Sebastian could be held as the no less supreme King, as a Holy Emperor, as a unifying and redeeming

---

[2] The Queen played an important role in the marriage of her son with a Princess of Castile, thus endangering the independence of the Portuguese kingdom in the case of the death of the heirs. The Council of 1562 with all its anti-Castillian measures is a response to this same influence (Baños-Garcia, 2006).

presence that could maybe annihilate the Turk and assure the political and religious safety of Europe. And, of course, it could bring glory, immense glory such as the poets had foretold. A feat worthy of the "desired one", of a true Christian warrior, of a Virgin King.

Sebastian's impetuous character along with his youth, his dreams of glory and his desire to prove himself worthy of the position he held, his belief in his victory, in God's plans for him and his kingdom made the battle for Africa the most natural of paths to follow. He is reputed to have told the Council, used to being at least listened to, that he had just come to inform them of the journey to Africa so that the arrangements could be made, not to ask for any sort of advice. The many military errors that followed (made either by the King himself or by the military commanders who accompanied him), starting with the disgraceful constitution of the army and ending in the wrong and even non-existent orders in combat, not forgetting the disastrous location of and route to the battle, resulted in an astounding defeat.

History is unkind, one might hear some say: it only judges by results. If success had befallen Sebastian, what would have happened then? The only answer which is (almost) certain is that there would be no Sebastianism. Great victories make better legends than myths, heroes rather than messiahs. And no other event, military or other, defeat or victory, had quite such a marked effect as this one (although kings as reckless as Sebastian are not uncommon). The country (and the world, of course, given the special plan in which God held the Portuguese and their sacred mission in the world) was not at one with itself any more. As Barradas de Carvalho described this century, Portugal was never the same again (Calafate, 2006).

But the King was expected to come back. There was still hope. How could he not come? Had he not come to *us* before, when he was desired as the guarantor of independence of the kingdom? How could he fail to come back when his actions had caused such turmoil, such sadness, such conflict? The country believed, during the twenty-four years of existence of the King, that the successive crises and conflicts could be resolved. After all, there was a King. But now the throne was empty, and though others occupied it after Sebastian, the throne never ceased to be unoccupied. Although others were sitting on it, it was inhabited by the ever-present absence of Sebastian. What was to be done with such a place, with such a gap?

Sebastianism(s)

The King is dead, long live the King!

There are, of course, several Sebastianisms which may have nothing in common except a name. Clearly they are not manifestations of the same underlying phenomenon, nor do they share the same intents, or apply in the same manner, nor are they even understood and interpreted similarly. At least, nothing could link them directly. Except this name, this figure, and what it entails, accordingly different: messianism. To fill a gap, to find a centre, to project a *to-come*, to construct happiness (and happiness is *always-to-come*).

Sebastianism started as a political movement. It involved political connections in order to legitimate, for instance, the figures of the false "Sebastians", especially the one known as the "Sebastian of Venice", so as to guarantee Portuguese independence at all costs. Dom João de Castro, known as the Saint Paul of Sebastianism, played an important role in this process by printing the "Trovas of Bandarra" (in 1603). Gonçalo Anes Bandarra was a Jewish cobbler, persecuted by the Inquisition for his unorthodox readings of the Bible and his messianic prophecies.[3] The "Rei Encoberto", the "Hidden King", of which he spoke became identified with Sebastian, although it is likely that, in practical terms, the *trovas* referred to either the particular situation of the Jewish community in the national context or to a conflict of interests between the people and the local nobility (Serrão, 1983).

With the passage of time, it clearly became obvious, at least to the *intelligentsia*, that the King himself was not to return. Here Sebastianism transcends not yet altogether the facts, but it identifies the "Hidden King" not with Sebastian (Sebastian who?), but with the Duke of Bragança, later King João IV, in 1640. This shift played an important role as a myth in support of the legitimacy of the new King, given that the interpretations of the *trovas* of Bandarra by the Jesuit António Vieira (not without some degree of flexibility) "clearly" indicated, at least to whomsoever wanted to believe in it, a new Hidden King.[4]

Vieira's sermons explained the disaster of Alcácer-Quibir and justified it through his readings of diverse parts of the scripture in his sermons, attributing it to God's mysterious plan and even more mysterious ways of fulfilling it. This "Hidden King", now unveiled before all, would establish the Fifth Empire, as described in Daniel's prophecy of the statue with the feet of clay. Portugal, again, regained a purpose, a *raison d'être*, had a sense and a mission. But since this King did not achieve it, Vieira *naturally* assumed he had made his mistake and attributed that destiny to the heir (even to the one who was already dead when Vieira attributed to him this messianic role, unaware of his death).

A hundred years after the restoration of the Portuguese crown, 162 years after the disappearance of Dom Sebastian, another Sebastian was in power, the Marquis of Pombal, and Sebastianism still had to be fought.[5] Rationalism and progress were concepts embedded in the minds of the elites (known to be "foreign-like") and the Jesuits were persecuted and expelled from the country. This movement of

---

[3] These *trovas* were very much a set of prophecies in a very simple and popular verse form, although in no way clear as to what concerns their content. It implied the use of symbols and ambiguity as part of their resources.

[4] António Vieira (1608-1697) was a leading figure in the fight for the rights of the natives in Brazil and one of the most distinguished preachers and experts in the holy texts of his time.

[5] Sebastião José de Carvalho e Melo (1699-1782) was the actual ruler of the Kingdom during the reign of Dom José. He introduced enlightenment into Portugal not without some degree of authoritarianism, being a very controversial figure in terms of the judgment of History.

polarization towards central Europe as symbol of progress and source of admiration and solutions for the country's problems represents the other "ism(s)" that guided the country's ideals, structured exactly in the same way as Sebastianism but with other names (Serrão, 1983): liberalism, socialism, we can add Europeanism. One shall talk only of those who share a name, a figure, a metonymy.

Inevitably, conflicts still emerged, and how could the country want to become like France, for instance, when France invaded Portugal during the Napoleonic Wars? One can accept that people might actually have missed having a more belligerent king, one that would not set sail to govern the kingdom from the colony of Brazil. Maybe the figure of Sebastian, even if just a figure, could resist the French, restore the kingdom to its old self. The "guerra sebástica", propelled by the writings, among others, of José Agostinho de Macedo in 1810 was indeed a public war of accusations and insults between sebastianists and anti-sebastianists (Hermann, 2002).

Sebastianism becomes part of the canon not much later, primarily with Romanticism. Almeida Garrett, the leading figure of the first generation of Romantic artists, himself an ex-soldier, actually exposed the superstitions of popular sebastianism in his play *As Profecias do Bandarra* (1875). But in his tragedy *Frei Luís de Sousa* (1843), Sebastianism was a spectre. A happy family (very happy indeed), and a patriotic one, is destroyed by the return of the woman's first husband, taken captive in Alcácer-Quibir, returned after 21 years, although his presence had always haunted them. His absence (although illusory) was the small flaw in the painting that allowed everyone to realise how happy they were. His faithful manservant expected his return, but refuses the destruction it implies – amongst other things, the death of the daughter of the couple, now illegitimate, in love with the image of Sebastian.

The myth definitively became part of Portuguese History. Oliveira Martins, in his book *História de Portugal* (first published in 1882) stressed its importance in the understanding of the history of the nation. It was "the posthumous proof of the existence of our nationality" (Martins, 1882, p. 79). The Portuguese had decided to "exchange life for a myth", "died for History" and entered into the "sepulchre" of "messianic hope" (ibid., p. 82). By this time, the descriptions of the nation as being a corpse in a tomb were abundant. The idea of decadence had by then been completely installed (and there were hints about resurrection).

The republican movement knew how to take advantage of this. The nation "had to be resurrected (and writers such as Guerra Junqueiro urged that), saved from its subservience to the English (England had issued a famous "Ultimatum" to Portugal considering the latter's intent to establish a land passage between Angola and Mozambique) and from that foreign, naturally unnatural, dynasty of Bragança that had betrayed Portugal. Portugal had to become its own self again, now through Republicanism (implemented in 1910).

But others still preferred to see Sebastian as the redeemer of the nation instead in these times of crisis. António Nobre's tender description of this King, very close to the popular and naive conception of Jesus as "El-Rei Menino" (Nobre, 2000, p. 456), the Infant King (put together and published in 1900 under the name of *O Desejado / The Desired One*) was followed by the statement that Sebastian embodied the qualities of the Portuguese race (or did the qualities of this race now embody him?). His thirst for more, his dreams, even if with sad results in this case, were what had allowed the Portuguese to go so far, to be what they were. And more than Sebastian, Sebastianism was a manifestation of the messianic characteristics of the race and of its essence. Such was the view of authors such as Teixeira de Pascoaes, Lopes Vieira and others who were part of the movement of "Renascença Portuguesa" ("Portuguese Renaissance"). Sampaio Bruno, in 1905, had identified Sebastianism as a particular trait of Messianism, respectable for that and for nothing else. The *Hidden One* discussed Sebastianism now on philosophical grounds.

The "Polémica Sebastianista" (1924) was the public discussion of the subject with the most immediately visible impact on Portuguese cultural life in the twentieth century. It consisted of a series of attacks between the Sebastianist Carlos Malheiro Dias and the rationalist António Sérgio. The King was referred to both as a Virgin King and a martyr, as well as an idiot and a fool. But Fernando Pessoa, if nothing else because he is the country's most respected poet, did more than anyone else for the myth. He has no illusions as to the necessity for the myth to be (re-)constructed. It is a lie, of course. One must lie in order to raise the name of the nation, one must believe the lie one is telling. And one needs not go any further: in Portugal, the myth to propel the nation onwards is Sebastianism. It must only be "renewed" (Pessoa, 1986b, p. 165).

The return of Sebastian is symbolic. Sebastian would return from within each Portuguese, being a national and an individual myth at the same time. Thus, it will not be the return of someone. It will be an event, of which there are avatars, different forms. It was reconfigured (more explicitly) as a process of ongoing, never-ending change, of constant movement and dislocation. Its end is not to end. After all, Fernando Pessoa says it about Ulysses (and Ulysses is the classic hero of return): "O mito é o nada que é tudo"/ "The myth is the nothing which is everything" (Pessoa, 1986a, p. 100).

But what was Sebastianism for Pessoa? It was seen as a "national religion", "in the sense of a myth" (Pessoa, 1986b, p. 151). The notion of Fifth Empire was recovered and reconfigured: it was then understood as a cultural empire, one of civilisation, one of language, one of culture, an immaterial one. Can we conclude that Sebastian is a national Jesus? It suffices to say that the world needed to become Portuguese in essence. And the essence of the Portuguese is to be simultaneously themselves and everyone else. The "spiritual discoveries" that Pessoa foretold were the *raison d'être* of the Portuguese (Pessoa, 1986b).

The myth of Sebastianism kept on being reshaped in novels and plays by the likes of Jorge de Sena (*O Indesejado*, written in 1944-45), José Régio (*El-Rei Dom Sebastião* in 1949), (Natália Correia *O Encoberto* in 1969) and other canonical writers, in allusions to questions such as political exile, analysis of the man behind the myth and resistance to an oppressive dictatorship. Cinema has also not been immune to it, whether in the examination of the process of the closure of the Discoveries and the thirteen-year colonial conflict in Africa (*Os Demónios de Alcácer-Quibir* by José Fonseca e Costa (1975) and *Non ou a Vã Glória de Mandar*, by Manoel de Oliveira (1990), supplemented by the novel *Jornada de África* by Manuel Alegre (1989)); in the portrayal of the country's quest for a national identity (*Quem és tu? / Who are you?* João Botelho, 2002); or even in a reflection on terrorism and dreams of hegemony in the world of today (*O Quinto Império, Ontem como Hoje / The Fifth Empire, Yesterday as Today*, Manoel de Oliveira, 2004).

With the revolution of 25 April 1974, ending a 48-year-old right-wing dictatorship, it was written and performed that Sebastian needed to be buried (Manuel Alegre's poems repeatedly reinforced this need). But a new reinterpretation of the figure of Sebastian took place, based on Pessoa and on the disenchantment with the rationalist and outward-looking model that the revolution had embodied. This event, influenced by a much earlier movement named *Filosofia Portuguesa* (*Portuguese Philosophy*), affirmatively engaged the figure of Sebastian as one of hope and desire in a reflection embracing Portuguese history and tradition and moving towards a better understanding of the national roots and identity. And Sebastianisms move on as one speaks.

Messianism
It would not be difficult to explain Sebastian (causes, consequences, and so forth, or even draw lessons from the events) and one would perhaps feel quite capable of understanding the desire, perhaps even the necessity for the people that the King be alive. The disappearance of a desired, young, brave King and the consequent submission to foreigners, loss of independence, financial ruin, and above all the loss of an aura of invincibility and predestination that previous failures and defeats had nevertheless left unspoiled would explain that same feeling of hope and desire. The enemies against which the Portuguese, by opposition, had created a national identity (Castillian and Moors), had forced to their knees a people who were proud of what they thought was a fierce, untameable character that had allowed them to achieve what others could only dream of.

And yet none of this would prove to be substantial in explaining Sebastianism. Indeed, there is nothing substantial except for the existence of a process. Sebastianism is independent of Sebastian, on the grounds that myths are not concerned with or restrained by mere facts. They are configured and reconfigured by facts, but these facts relate to the emergence of the myth. Historical and biographical facts may explain some features (metonymically), and they can provide an instance and a pretext for resurgence. One deals with the "desired one" or the "hidden one", not with Sebastian. One deals with a representation, both in the sense of a modelling and of a play, of an act.

A relatively well-known remark of a British official in Portugal in the nineteenth century held that not much could be expected from a country of which half the population were waiting for the Messiah, and the other half for a dead king. But the fact is that no one waits for a dead king. No one expects anything from a dead king. One only expects what can come back. And, in Portugal, the identification between Sebastian and Christ has been made in books, films and paintings.

Sebastianism (let us pretend it is singular for the sake of grammar) is a Messianism, and it is itself a transfiguration of many other forms of mysticism and Messianism that had penetrated the culture of the Iberian Peninsula. The teleological view of Portuguese history and destiny is expressed in the founding myth of Ourique, in which Christ announced the intent of establishing his empire in the world through the Portuguese kingdom to the first King, Dom Afonso Henriques, in 1139. Later on, before the rise of the new Avis dynasty (in 1385), Fernão Lopes would claim that the world (he actually meant Portugal) was entering its "Seventh Age", one of peace and prosperity for all. But this teleological view, indebted as it was to Jewish-Christian thought in general, was also indebted to Jewish Messianism, in particular, that was still present despite the many attempts to destroy it by the Inquisition. The presence of many prophets (Simão, o Sapateiro Santo; o Bastião and many others) only emphasize the importance of this movement, whose most prominent figure, Bandarra, was to become so important that an image of him was placed on an altar during the coronation ceremony of the Duke of Bragança as the new King of Portugal in 1640.

Besides all of that, the influence of Joachim di Fiore is reputed to have been brought into the country through the Franciscans. The age of the "Holy Ghost" (following those of the "Father" and the "Son" in Fiori's view) was clearly interpreted in Portugal, by some sectors at least, as a reasserting of the Portuguese mission in the world, distributed in caravels across the seas. The tales of King Arthur were also widespread at the time (the dynasty of Avis is known to be influenced by tales of this sort), and certainly the analogy with a disappearing king struck a chord in desperate times. Other myths flowed into Sebastianism as well. The prophecy of the "hidden one" was established in the Islamic world, and concerned the twelfth Iman who would return and establish peace and concord among all the peoples. It resurfaced in Valencia during the conflicts between the "comuneros" and Charles V. "El Encubierto" would restore justice and take on the usurpers from the House of Austria. The figure persisted through the usage and appropriation of the image of the grandson of Charles V.

Messianism is more about appearance than apparitions (configurations, projections). But it is as frequently an appearance of apparition as it is an apparition of appearance. And disappearance. As a system, it includes the Messianic figure as its centre. Or the demand for it, the search for it. The centre is not empty. It is pregnant with Messianism. It appears empty but it appears as being filled. It is filled by a promise, a desire, a will, a *telos* (that could bear the appearance of an idealised origin). And yet this centre holds the system together because it is filled with nothing but the expectancy of being filled in. To accomplish this system, to make it total, to close and enclose it, one would be forced to include in it the Messiah. But the Messiah excludes everything around it, because the Messiah is everything and all, the Messiah is a unifier. The "desired one" aspired and desired to be a Messiah. But the "hidden one" is not a Messiah. It does not have a name, by definition it does not have a visible face. It is no one and anyone at the same time. Or it can be… which amounts to the same thing.

Sebastian was a symbol, but that symbol perished (even if not in the desert of Alcácer-Quibir in 1578). Symbols entail a code, and codes present more difficulties of translation (and by translation one can evoke the physical dimension of the word). But surely Sebastian is a symbol, how can he not be a symbol? He *must* be. He was a martyr, sacrificed in the name of a higher deed (his death allowed for the establishment of a kingdom strong enough to keep the Turks at bay, actually). There were phenomena before his birth, there were comets before the battle, there were visions, there were prophecies, there were bells that rang untouched, there was a coat of arms of Portugal made in rock that cracked in Lisbon at the time of the Prince's death.

Was there all of this? Yes. But did they happen? Probably not, and it does not matter. All of this was constructed, staged, formulated and adapted. The centre would not hold if Sebastian were to be but a symbol, be it of resistance or backwardness, fanaticism or religiosity, treason or martyrdom, cause or consequence of national decadence, past or future, passivity or appeal to action. Sebastian has been configured and reconfigured, used and abused in times of crisis, to different purposes, in connection with different needs: dealing with the end of colonies, resisting invading armies and dictatorships, acting as a scapegoat in times for revolution, *et caetera ad infinitum*.

The different configurations of Sebastian are as fleeting as they are fluid, amorphous, establishing immediate and contiguous relationships to that which they appear to represent and appear as the representation of. Messianism is a question of *will*, not *must.* Sebastian became an agency, a disembodied instance of manipulation, a projection: present in and through its absence, an illusion of present existence, although every projection is past; both in its conceptualisation and in its practice. It appears to exist now, and it appears as existing now. And it appears to show the future. But there is no projection of the future; by definition, any projection is past. What there is, is representation, construction and act. A presence is constructed, one which bases its existence on absence. And it is due to and through the existence (presence) of this absence that it persists.

"Portugal is yet to be accomplished", "It is time.", says Fernando Pessoa in a poem titled "Nevoeiro" / "Mist", with which he ends his book *Mensagem* (Pessoa, 1986a, p. 123). Time for what? Since we are left in the mist, we can only wait for what is to come. The Messiah with all its metonymies, always delayed, never possessed, never tangible, always inaccessible although ever represented as present, accessible. Oh, if only He were? Maybe He can be… Maybe He will come back. That would make us all happy indeed.

Happiness: un fait inaccompli

Why Messianism? Why not? Should the Portuguese not have expected that the country (the world) would become once again what it had been *before* (the spatial-temporal location of this is matter of dispute, of course). Even better, it could become what it never was: paradise, utopia. Something else, bigger, better, happier (how could it not?). Messianism is about hope, and to hope is to expect what is *to come*. Hope means that there is a future. And a future must always be better, happier. The concept of happiness, surely of Happiness, possesses (and is possessed by) something of a messianic quality. No Messiah brings misery and dissatisfaction, disharmony and disarray (could that be an anti-Messiah?). Happiness, as a governing idea, is a *telos*. Not where it might happen, not even that it must happen, but most importantly and most precisely, that it *will* happen, it is *to come*. And *will* is the key word, if one wishes to use this metaphor. *Will* is operative. *Will* for a *to come*, expectancy (one can call it hope, or desire) for a *will* become. *Where there's a will, there's a way*. One also expects that there is an end, one expects that there is one, if there is a way. But that might not be the case. Happiness is to expect, is to be in waiting. Once the waiting is over, happiness is no more. The unaccomplished and absented character of happiness must never be absent, for *there to be* happiness. And happiness will never be present otherwise it ceases.

Messianism, and the happiness it promises (Happiness itself is a promise), depends absolutely (one could say almost solely) on the absence of the Messiah, if it is to exist. The Messiah is never a presence, but not an absence either. He is absent in his presence and present in his absence. He is already (t)here even though he can never be, could never be, at the risk of losing precisely that which allows him to be a Messiah. One *will / is to* reach Happiness because and through the presence of such absence, the presence of a messianic figure for refiguring, configuring and even disfiguring. A messianic figure which is bodiless, flexible; which is not a "who", but a "what", a certain something, beyond reasoning but within understanding, within the grasp of the mind but yet never without fundamental characteristics that will stand out and stand away from the spheres of reasoning and the reasonable.

Sebastianism, Messianism, Happiness... in inaccomplishment.

References

Anes, J. M. (2004) *Fernando Pessoa e os Mundos Esotéricos*, Lisboa, Ésquilo.

Azevedo, J. L. de. (1984) *A Evolução do Sebastianismo*, Lisboa, Editorial Presença.

Bandarra, G. A. (2001) *Profecias do Bandarra*, Lisboa, Moderna Editorial Lavores.

Baños-Garcia, A. V. (2006) *D. Sebastião, Rei de Portugal*, Lisboa, A Esfera dos Livros.

Bruno, S. (1983) *O Encoberto*, Porto, Lello and Irmão.

Camões, L. V. de. (1980) *Os Lusíadas*, Lisboa, Círculo de Leitores.

Campos, F. (1986) *A Casa do Pó*, Lisboa, Difel.

Happiness and Post-Conflict

Calafate, P. (ed.). (2006) *Portugal como Problema (Vols. I - IV)*, Lisboa, Público/Fundação Luso-Americana.
Centeno, Y. K. (ed.). (1993) *Portugal - Mitos Revisitados*, Lisboa, Edições Salamandra.
Correia, N. (1977) *O Encoberto*, Alfragide, *Galeria* Panorama.
Derrida, J. (1994) *Specters of Marx: the State of the Debt, the Work of Mourning and the New International*, New York, Routledge.
Franco, A. C. (1986) *Vida de D. Sebastiâo, Rei de Portugal*, Lisboa, Europa-América.
Gandra, M. (1999) *Joaquim de Fiore, Joaquimismo e Esperança Sebástica*, Lisboa, Fundação Lusíada.
Garrett, J. B. Da S. L. de Almeida (1997) *Frei Luís de Sousa*, Porto, Porto Editora.
Hermann, J. (2002) "Dom Sebastião contra Napoleão: a guerra sebástica contra as tropas francesas", *Topoi*, dezembro, pp. 108-133.
Leão, F. da C. (1998) *O Enigma Português*, Lisboa, Guimarães Editores.
Loureiro, F. S. (1989) *D. Sebastião e Alcácer Quibir*, Lisboa, Publicações Alfa.
Marinho, J. (2003) *Nova Interpretação do Sebastianismo*, Lisboa, Imprensa Nacional Casa da Moeda.
Martins, J. P. O. (1882) *História de Portugal, Tomo I*, Lisboa, Livraria Bertrand.
Nobre, A. (2000) *Poesia Completa 1867-1900*, Lisboa, Publicações Dom Quixote.
Pascoaes, T. de (1998) *A Arte de Ser Português*, Lisboa, Assírio e Alvim.
----------. (1987) *Os Poetas Lusíadas*, Lisboa, Assírio e Alvim.
Pessoa, F. (1986a) *Mensagem e Outros Poemas Afins*, Lisboa, Europa-América.
----------. (1986b) *Portugal, Sebastianismo e Quinto Império*, Lisboa, Europa-América.
----------.(1986c) *Textos de Intervenção Social e Cultural; A Ficção dos Heterónimos*, Lisboa, Europa-América.
Pires, A. M. (1982) *D. Sebastião e o Encoberto*, Lisboa, Fundação Calouste Gulbenkian.
Quadros, A. (1989) *A Ideia de Portugal na Literatura Portuguesa dos Últimos Cem Anos*, Lisboa, Fundação Lusíada.
-------------. (1984) *Fernando Pessoa, Vida, Personalidade e Génio*, Lisboa, Publicações Dom Quixote.
-------------. (1982) *Poesia e Filosofia do Mito Sebastianista*, Lisboa, Guimarães Editores.
Régio, J. (1949) *El-Rei Dom Sebastião. Poema Espectacular em Três Actos*, Coimbra, Atlântida.
Ribeiro, A. (1936) *Aventura Maravilhosa de Dom Sebastião*, Lisboa, Livraria Bertrand.
Saraiva, A. J. (1980), *Para a História da Cultura em Portugal, Volume I*, Lisboa, Livraria Bertrand.
Sena, J. de (1986) *O Indesejado (António, Rei)*, Lisboa, Edições 70.
Sérgio, A. (1924) *O Desejado*, Paris-Lisboa, Livrarias Aillaud e Bertrand, Paris-Lisboa.
Serrão, J. (1983) *Do Sebastianismo ao Socialismo*, Lisboa, Livros

Horizonte.

----------. (1981), *Fernando Pessoa, Cidadão do Imaginário*, Lisboa, Livros Horizonte.

Silva, A. da (1994) *Ir à Índia sem Abandonar Portugal; Considerações; Outros Textos*, Lisboa, Assírio and Alvim.

----------. (2003) *Textos Vários/ Dispersos*, Lisboa, Âncora.

Silva, J. P. P. da (2005) "Entrevista a António Machado Pires", *E-Topia: Revista Electrónica de Estudos sobre a Utopia* no. 3.

Telmo, A. (2004) *O Mistério de Portugal na História e n' 'Os Lusíadas'*, Lisboa, Ésquilo.

Valensi, L. (1996) *Fábulas da Memória. A Gloriosa Batalha dos Três Reis*, Lisboa, Edições Asa.

Veloso, J. M. de Q. (1935) *D. Sebastião: 1554-1578*, Empresa Nacional de Publicidade, Lisboa.

Vieira, A. (1982) *História do Futuro*, Lisboa, Imprensa Nacional Casa da Moeda.

----------. (1935) *Sermões e Lugares Selectos*, Porto, Educação Nacional.

The Dialectic of Conflict and Culture
Leon Trotsky and Less Fortunate Statesmen

Macdonald Daly

It is well known that the phase following the October Revolution in Russia in 1917 (of which Trotsky, my eponymous protagonist, was one of the principal agents), Russia's exit from the Great War at the Treaty of Brest-Litovsk in 1918 (at which Trotsky was the Soviet Union's chief negotiator), and the eventual Soviet victory in the Civil War which ended in 1921 (throughout which Trotsky was the leader of the Red Army), was one of extreme cultural ferment in the new-born USSR. My interest at the time I first engaged with this period was rather narrow: I was concerned with how it affected the future course of Marxist literary and cultural criticism in Western Europe, particularly, such of it as there was, in England. Today I remain interested in what another look at this period can tell us about the way we negotiate the issues of culture and conflict here and now, in an England that is certainly different, but one that, like almost everywhere else, has even less interest in Marxism than was the case in the nineteen-twenties and 'thirties.

The two decades or so after the October Revolution are commonly characterised as a period which began with notable artistic experimentation. There is no need to go into any great detail about these developments here. Let the image reproduced as Figure 1 stand synecdochically for them.

Figure 1. Wassily Kandinsky, "Composition VIII" (1923)

144

After the death of Lenin in January 1924 and his supersession by Stalin, this phase of modernist efflorescence gradually turned into its opposite, the rigid, sterile, ideologically slavish practice known, and understandably universally reviled, as Socialist Realism. Let the image reproduced in Figure 2 stand for that.

Figure 2. Arkady Shaikhet, "A Komsomol Youth at the Wheel" (1936)

I do not dislike this photograph or consider it particularly comparable to the painting, excepting the fact that the obviously experimental painting renders any particular reading of meaning or representation ambivalent while the photograph proclaims its own (no doubt) prescribed obviousness: here we have Soviet youth literally turning the wheel (through a revolution). This perceived shift away from relatively unhindered experimentalism towards enforced ideological dogmatism typifies the received view of Soviet post-conflict culture of the nineteen-twenties and 'thirties, and it is not my intention to challenge that view here, but to indicate what cultural (as opposed to political or military) part Trotsky played in the period. But I also want to articulate, to join up, what I have to say about Trotsky with attention to something closer to home in both place and time.

Whenever one contemplates the dramatic and varied life of someone like Trotsky one cannot help but reflect that contemporary times throw up hardly any examples of his seeming combination of man of action with man of aesthetic inclination and intellectual ability – certainly not in Britain. Here, politicians don't even write their own memoirs, which are ghosted for them (compare Trotsky's *My Life*); at best they produce pulp novels (one thinks of Jeffrey Archer, Douglas Hurd, or Edwina Currie); Gordon Brown, the current Prime Minister, has a little advertised Ph.D from the University of Edinburgh,[1] and wrote a semi-respectable biography of James Maxton, the Scottish Socialist labour leader,[2] but it hardly ranks with Trotsky's three-volume *The History of the Russian Revolution*, which was published in English in 1932-33. You have to go back to Churchill before you get anything like that from a British statesman but, although Churchill wrote a noted multi-volume history (*The Second World War*), he did not also have a lot to say about the state of contemporary literature, art and criticism. Trotsky did: and in what follows I shall compare him in this regard to some typical contemporary British Parliamentarians. But before I adjust to these twin foci, I wish to air some more general thoughts, to which I shall return finally, on the relation between conflict and culture.

Trotsky is a proponent of post-conflict culture proper: for him, the culture which might be made possible by the cessation of the conflicts he participated in would be the ultimate triumph of those conflicts. To quote from the introduction to *Literature and Revolution*:

> [...] even a successful solution of the elementary problems of food, clothing, shelter, and even of literacy, would in no way signify a complete victory of the new historic principle, that is, of Socialism. Only a movement of scientific thought on a national scale and the development of a new art would signify that the historic seed has not only grown into a plant, but has even flowered. In this sense, the development of art is the highest test of the vitality and significance of each epoch (Trotsky, p. 9).

Coming as it does from the Soviet Commissar of War, that statement seems a refreshingly congenial endorsement of art and its social importance. It is harder to find a name for what contemporary British Parliamentarians see as the relation between conflict and culture. As we shall find out, they largely envisage "culture" (or a certain kind of "culture") as a means of preventing conflict. It would be nicely

[1] Brown, Gordon. (1982) *The Labour Party and Political Change in Scotland, 1918-1929*, Ph.D thesis, University of Edinburgh.
[2] Brown, Gordon. (1986) *Maxton*, Edinburgh, Mainstream.

symmetrical if we could call this "pre-conflict culture", but as, ideally, culture in this view prevents conflict from occurring, there is no "pre-", there is only an "instead of". However, both positions share a certain structural notion of conflict and culture, in which there is a very obvious culture/good, conflict/bad binary opposition.

Thus, neither party would entertain the extremism of the notorious adage, "When I hear the word 'culture' I reach for my gun." Such a statement entirely reverses the terms of the opposition I have just described (it is now culture/bad, conflict/good), and it will come as no surprise that the statement has a Nazi provenance.[3] I flag up the quotation here because we shall hear an echo of it, in significantly modified form, from the mouth of a British noble, a little later. What can we call this attitude except "anti-culture conflict"? It is not uncommon. When certain Islamic groups hear the words "American culture" they may indeed reach for their firearms or their *fatwahs*. Others may harbour a less militant but otherwise similar antipathy. But, again, this is in the realm of the specific. It is very rare to find antipathy to culture *as such* in the abstract, and even philistinism is not quite that (it is simply a failure to see the point of culture in general or specific manifestations of culture in particular: it is not necessarily principled opposition to culture). Likewise, hostility to American culture is hardly ever opposition to that culture *per se*, but it indicates a conflict between cultures – what used to be called "culture clash" – in which formulation, I would point out, the opposition between conflict and culture is in fact dissolved: here, culture is the arena of contestation, or it is what you have conflict over. Thus, for example, you are not meant to be able to procure Coca Cola in Cuba or Havana cigars in the USA. Of course, one opposition is here abandoned only for another to be instated, *viz*: our culture is good; theirs is bad, let's fight it out, by the pen or the sword or, in the case of my last example, by resort to economic sanctions. But "clash of cultures" is a phrase that seems largely to have dropped out of contemporary parlance, replaced by "cultural difference", a term which attempts to restore all cultures to an equivalence (i.e. non-opposed, non-conflictual), *viz*: we have our culture; they have theirs; they are different, but equal or incommensurable.

The other body of thought I can identify as contributing to this constellation is the Marxist one. It argues that culture, in a capitalist economy, does not deliver us from conflict. We are *always* in conflict, and there will be no true culture until we are beyond conflict. It does not matter what you think of this position. My point is that, logically, it renders the term "post-conflict culture" tautologous. Culture is the reward we shall enjoy only after the cessation of conflict, and conflict is virtually coextensive with capitalism. Not surprisingly, this Marxist note signals the true entry of Trotsky into my discussion.

---

[3] "Wenn ich 'Kultur' höre, entsichere ich meinen Browning!" is a remark usually attributed to Hermann Goering, but in fact it is a quotation from Hanns Johst's *Schlageter*, a play first performed in celebration of Adolf Hitler's forty-fourth birthday: see Johst, Hanns (1933), *Schlageter, Schauspiel*, Munich, A. Langen/G. Müller.

Literature and Revolution is seen by many as a bizarre and indeed politically irresponsible aberration of Trotsky's. Why? Isaac Deutscher, Trotsky's most famous biographer, sets the scene:

> In the summer of 1922, when he refused to accept the office of Vice-Premier under Lenin and, incurring the Politbureau's censure, went on leave, he devoted the better part of his holiday to literary criticism. The State Publishers had collected his pre-revolutionary essays on literature for republication in a special volume of his *Works*; and he intended to write a preface surveying the condition of Russian letters since the revolution. The "preface" grew in size and became an independent work. He gave to it nearly all his leisure but failed to conclude it. He resumed writing during his next summer holiday, in 1923, when his conflict with the triumvirs, complicated by the expectation of revolution in Germany, was mounting to a climax; and this time he returned to Moscow with the manuscript of a new book, *Literature and Revolution*, ready for the printer (Deutscher, p. 164)

In other words, Trotsky failed to seize the political position which might have enabled him to achieve the official adoption of the cultural policies implied by *Literature and Revolution* (had he become Vice-Premier it would have been automatically easier for him to succeed Lenin) and instead absented himself from the intense political fray so that he could adumbrate those very policies. As a political miscalculation, this is second in notoriety only to his later weekend wild duck-shooting trip, taken in November 1923, when Stalin's machinations against him were at their height. The adventure laid him up with a malarial infection that rendered him largely *hors de combat* during the crucial following months, leaving the field virtually clear for Stalin to assume the succession.

Nonetheless, the implied cultural policies of *Literature and Revolution* remain on record. One must remember that a great deal of thinking about literature and criticism in Bolshevik circles was influenced by Lenin's articles on Tolstoy (published between 1908 and 1911), in which, in a manner reminiscent of Marx and Engels on Balzac and Goethe, Lenin argued that Tolstoy overcame the limitations of his own class ideology by transferring his loyalty to the Russian peasantry in the revolution of 1905. The sharp contemporaneousness of Lenin's focus is a feature that Trotsky's book shares; but where he differs from Lenin is in his refusal strictly to align aesthetic judgments with fairly immediate political purposes. The dangers of this Leninist position come to the fore most strongly in Lenin's essay, "Party Organisation and Party Literature" (1905), which with apparent liberality admits that "everyone is free to write and say whatever he likes, without any restrictions", but reserves the quite illiberal right to expel from the Bolshevik Party those whose exercise of this freedom brings them into conflict with the party line. It is clear in the essay that Lenin's strictures may be applied to creative writers as well as political commentators and interventionists (Lenin, 1965, pp. 44-49). Lenin justified such a policy because the Bolshevik Party was a "voluntary association" whose ideological integrity needed to be protected if it was to achieve its historical aims. Once it had achieved those aims, however, and actually become the governing party in 1917, a little later making itself indissociable from the state, such a policy applied to literature was indisputably potentially repressive.

Yet it is perfectly clear that the evaluation of literature according to its political tendency was never originally intended by culture-inclined Bolsheviks to preclude other kinds of evaluation or to necessitate what eventually took place under Stalin – intensifying censorship, rigid prescriptivism for writers prepared to toe the line, and systematic liquidation or geographical banishment of those who were not. In Trotsky's *Literature and Revolution* all the best possibilities of artistic tolerance were promoted alongside the recognition that "it is silly, absurd, stupid to the highest degree, to pretend that art will remain indifferent to the convulsions of our epoch" (Trotsky, p. 12). Unreservedly suspicious of philistine attempts to reject the achievements of bourgeois art, to impose a "proletarian culture" in its place, and to exercise widespread repression in the cultural field, Trotsky undertook a vigorous and trenchant survey of the contemporary state of Russian literature from his undeniably partisan position as one of the architects of the revolution. Insofar as government was concerned, he stated:

> Our policy in art, during a transitional period, can and must be to help the various groups and schools of art which have come over to the Revolution to grasp correctly the historic meaning of the Revolution, and to allow them complete freedom of self-determination in the field of art, after putting before them the categorical standard of being for or against the Revolution (Trotsky, p. 14)

The position may seem characteristically contradictory. Once writers have "come over to the revolution", and once they have been helped to "grasp correctly" its historic meaning, they will be allowed "complete freedom of self-determination". But what if they do not "come over", or what if they do but fail to "grasp correctly" the revolution's "historic meaning", or, even if they do both, what if their allegiance to and "correct" understanding of the revolution later flags or is otherwise found wanting by those who consider themselves empowered to judge? The implications are obviously anxiety-provoking to liberal democratic sentiment. Yet Trotsky's position goes to the heart of the debate about literature and politics. If literature has no political effectivity, but is merely a concern of hobbyists, then it can be left well alone by the state. But if it does indeed have an appreciable role in shaping a society, it would be a foolish government that did not keep an eye on and attempt to control its workings – and, indeed, many liberal democratic governments have imposed censorship and repression precisely out of a recognition of literature's perceived social effectivity. If it happens that the best known cases in the "free world" are to do with the sexual rather than political content of literary texts – from the bowdlerisation of Shakespeare to the banning of *Lady Chatterley's*

Lover – all that is demonstrated thereby is that liberal governments have considered public discussion or dramatisation of sexual mores to be a powerful social force requiring their vigilant control in much the same way as the Soviets came to consider expressions of political "deviance" a threat to October. Inimical as all writers and most readers understandably are to such control, where it is present it is clear that literature is not politically underestimated.

It is simply not true in any case that democratic governments do not prohibit literary texts which depart from what one might call the "party bottom line". How many are aware that Joseph Goebbels, that other notable statesman who was a man of action and a man of aesthetic inclination and intellectual ability, wrote a novel called *Michael*?[4] The answer is probably not many, because in present day democratic Germany it is still on the prohibited list along with Hitler's *Mein Kampf*. It doesn't toe the "democratic bottom line" and none of us is losing any sleep over its state-sanctioned repression. Closer to home, and closer in time, Edward Bond's anarchic play *Early Morning* was refused a public performance licence as recently as 1968 because, among other things, it depicted Queen Victoria as a lesbian, a murderer and a cannibal.

If these comments enable us to put the somewhat bothersome problem of potential textual censorship and repression on political grounds in brackets, then Trotsky strikes me as the only twentieth century politician of major historical importance who has shown anything like a grasp of the indispensability and potency of cultural production and a willingness, given those propensities and capacities, to encourage it to flourish as freely as possible. One has to remember the tremulous fragility of the October Revolution almost up to the eve of his writing the book, as well as the stormy political environment in which he moved (note his qualification that his remarks applied only to the "transitional period" of the revolution: they were not meant to apply to an established and consolidated state of affairs). It is somewhat easier, in times of peace and plenty, for ruling liberal bourgeois politicians to let artists say whatever they like, not least because, under examination, they ironically turn out, in my view, to be more thoroughgoing materialists than Trotsky ever was. That is to say, whereas the Trotsky who wrote *Literature and Revolution* was the one who argued that the acid test of an economic revolution was whether or not it ultimately delivered in the realm of culture (which in my view, contrary to all popular conception, is the classic Marxist position), the acid test of culture, for liberal bourgeois politicians, is whether or not it delivers in the realm of economics. This latter conclusion I hope to demonstrate in the remainder of this essay, and so I now turn, as promised, to what I have called those "less fortunate" statesmen.

*

[2] Goebbels, Joseph (1936). *Michael: ein deutsches Schicksal in Tagebuchblättern*, Munich, F. Eber nachf.

Late one evening in the January of 1989, I learned that the familiar and time-honoured term "Cultural Relations" had been replaced in official British political discourse by the phrase "Cultural Diplomacy". I was listening to the BBC radio programme *Today in Parliament*, which reported that the House of Lords had debated a motion calling for increased government funding for the British Council and the BBC's external services (particularly the World Service, which broadcasts to foreign territories worldwide). These are two main agencies of Britain's overseas cultural representation, and both had recently suffered financial cuts in real terms under the Thatcher government. The entire (and entirely astonishing) debate can be found in the official Parliamentary record.[5]

To be fair, some of the noble Lords expressed dislike for the new designation – Lord St. John of Fawsley (then better known as the Rt. Hon. Norman St. John Stevas, Conservative ex-Minister for the Arts) thought that "Cultural Diplomacy" had a "forbidding ring" – but they grudgingly took it up. Lord Bonham-Carter, the Liberal peer proposing the motion, wasted no time in launching a strategic military metaphor, referring within five minutes to the external services of the BBC as "an essential weapon in our armoury". He gave a stirring example of how, shortly before the Falklands War, the BBC's broadcasts to Spain had been cut, with the result that Spain's coverage of the War came almost entirely from Argentinian sources. The amount saved by this cut had been £230,000 – "rather less," he ventured, "than the cost of a single Exocet missile". All around Lord Bonham-Carter, parliamentary minds started to whirr into characteristic British warspeakmode. The Earl of Stockton, Harold Macmillan, ex-Prime Minister and then Director of the Macmillan Publishing Group, which has always profited greatly from the British Council's promotion of British books overseas, said that in supporting calls for increased government funding he was "speaking from the sharp end of the publishing salient" (a salient is a military fortification or line of defences which points outwards). Lord Weidenfeld (another publisher, of Weidenfeld and Nicolson fame) piped up with the idea that cultural diplomacy was "an excellent conduit for reconciliation and peace" in the hostilities he seemed convinced Britain was involved in: "it heals wounds and builds bridges". He ardently hoped that, by the nineties, assuming increased funding for the British Council, Britain's involvement in belligerence around the globe would be at an end and that our motto would be, "If I hear the word 'gun', I reach for my culture" (a quaint inversion of the Nazi *bon mot* we encountered earlier, although the noble lord wrongly attributed it to Goering because he dredged it up from the *Penguin Dictionary of Quotations*). Lord Moore of Wolvercote also hit the target when he repeated what nearly every other peer had said, namely that the universality of the English language gave Britain a ready-made market: "from that base we have various weapons with which to press our cultural offensive".

In this fashion, the Lords harangued the government for two-and-a-

---

[3] *House of Lords Weekly Hansard*, no. 2379, cols. 209-46. Unless otherwise indicated, all quotations in this section are taken from this text.

half hours, like Generals come back from the field to sort out the bureaucrats who were holding up supplies. It became clear that there was indeed a foreign war of sorts going on, which had to be fought on two fronts. There was the Influence Front, on which a Britain sadly dispossessed of Empire must scramble anew for cultural colonies, in the teeth of fierce competition from the other Western capitalist nations and from the "unfree" world (which then meant Communist countries). The Influence Front had to be secured if Britain was to be successful on the Trade Front, where there was (and no doubt still is and for any foreseeable future always will be) a frenzied struggle going on to flog everything from aeroplanes to zoom lenses in foreign markets.

An obvious instance raised in the debate of how the Trade Front cannot neglect the Influence Front is in the markets created abroad when foreign students educated in Britain return to take up influential positions in their countries of origin. But how can you get people to come and study here when they haven't learned English because the British Council hasn't enough resources to teach them; when they can't hear BBC broadcasts demonstrating how marvellous Britain's culture is, because of poor signals, outdated relay equipment, or sheer absence of a service; when the number of scholarships offered to overseas students is inadequate, and their tuition fees are going through the roof? And so on. This is where the "civilising" quality of "British culture" is usually deployed, because, naturally, it would not do to advertise straight out what a commercial coup you stand to effect on foreign nations who allow themselves to fall under your influence. At this point in the debate was heard a tactically evangelical maiden speech by the said Conservative ex-Minister for the Arts. Cultural diplomacy, he averred, is simply "the increase of British influence in the wider world", and yet:

> This increase is not pursued principally for commercial or economic reasons, but because we believe the long, continuous, extraordinarily rich and varied experience of this nation constitutes a unique contribution to the welfare of mankind, and we are therefore under a duty to make it as widely available as possible.
>
> If I were asked what had been this country's three greatest contributions to world civilisation I should reply unhesitatingly: the common law, parliamentary government, English language and literature, and at the heart of all three lies the idea of liberty. I do not believe that we can export our institutions indiscriminately, but by informing people of how they work and flourish, by imparting thoughts about them, we can enhance the chances for freedom elsewhere.

Listening to this on radio – so boundlessly confident was the delivery – one was almost tempted to disregard the strangeness of the argument. Our legal, political and cultural institutions are all about liberty, so we have a duty to press them on everybody else. To force people to be free Britain cannot use gunboats as it used to, so it has to resort to convenient arks such as "English language and literature". We should count ourselves lucky, because we invented English, and know how to use it:

> The benefits of the universality of that language are truly incalculable. I often reflect on the extraordinary disposition of Divine Providence that a language spoken originally by a few thousand savages trapped on a fog-encrusted island on the edge of the North Sea should, in the fullness of time, and in the era of communications, become the common language for the entire world [...]
>
> Culture may seem a frail boat to embark on the tempestuous waters of great power and international diplomacy. What has that quiet, nuanced voice to say in the world of telegrams and anger? – I think rather more than one might suppose [...]
>
> Let me say this in conclusion: worldly powers, dynasties, empires rise and fall, culture and learning abide. They are the achievements by which future ages looking back assess the value of previous generations. Power in the 19th century sense has passed from us, never to return. But it has been replaced by something perhaps even more important – influence. Through the dissemination of our culture that influence can be exercised for the good.

This was a hybrid tale of the fertile Noah (the frail boat), delivered in the cadences of Ecclesiastes ("empires rise and fall, culture and learning abide"), told by St. John the Divine. Whatever one's political persuasion, it would be difficult not to admit that the sentence, "What has that quiet, nuanced voice to say in the world of telegrams and anger?" approaches the condition of the poetic. It is arguably two lines of iambic pentameter blank verse. Most of the noble assembly no doubt attended in hypnotised wonderment.

But the proposing Lord (Bonham-Carter) had not asked for poetry: he only wanted cash for the British Council and the BBC. Perhaps he was aware (unlike St. John) that God, actually, was responsible for the confusion of the tongues in the first place (Genesis, xi). At any rate, the only bibliolatry he was interested in was the kind that would profit the Earl of Stockton and Lord Weidenfeld. Sadly, English will not reach foreigners along the effortless route of Divine Providence any more. We have to teach them it. And if we do not, there are American cowboys who will: their Lordships were reminded by Lord Bonham-Carter that "there is a battle going on about the teaching of English English and American English" because, "believe it or not, the Americans claim to be able to speak English".

If you are taught English English you are likely to buy books and other goods from this country: if you are taught American English you are likely to buy books and other goods from the United States of America. Cultural diplomacy is therefore an important commercial consideration and one which should not be forgotten.

This was a blunt and belated formulation of a sense of demise. We may have invented English, but the patent ran out years ago, and we perhaps need to remind ourselves that Britain builds very few boats these days. So, alas, the plea was to no avail. Naturally, in that straitened post-credit-boom heading-towards-the-Thatcher-sunset year of 1989, the cash just was not on the table for Lord Bonham-Carter's cause, no matter how ardently he argued the case for overseas cultural representation being part of the diplomatic service.

It seemed to me at the time, and it still does, that it was a sign of the increasingly frank recognition of the inescapably political nature of cultural work that Whitehall should have accepted the re-designation of "Cultural Relations" to "Cultural Diplomacy". Of course, it always was starkly political, even when it was called "Cultural Relations". But the new term caught on very rapidly in the immediately ensuing years. Perform a search today on Google for "cultural diplomacy" and you will come up with an appreciable number of Masters programmes offered by British and American higher education institutions. Its other recurrent surfacing is in the pages of *Hansard*, the publication of the proceedings of the two chambers of the UK Parliament. For example, as recently as 19 March 2001, there is an exchange like this:

> *Lord Puttnam*: My Lords, is the Minister aware of the fact that in 1995 a conference was held in London under the title "Britain and the World", at which the Foreign Secretary, Mr Cook, the then Foreign Secretary, the noble Lord, Lord Hurd, and the then Prime Minister, Mr John Major, all confirmed unequivocally that cultural diplomacy represented the best value for money in presenting Britain to the rest of the world? Has anything happened in the past six years that would allow Mr Cook to think that that is no longer true?
>
> *Baroness Scotland of Asthal*: My Lords, absolutely not. It is incredibly good value. Britain's creative sector, including music, design and advertising, generates more than £112.5 billion each year and employs more than 3.3 million people. It is growing faster than the economy as a whole: in 1997-98 it was growing at 16 per cent a year. Exports total £10.3 billion. It is a very vibrant sector, of which we are rightly and justly proud.

This exchange not only demonstrates that British Parliamentarians are impressively telepathic (Baroness Scotland was able to read Robin Cook's mind, despite the fact that he was not even a member of the House of Lords, and thus was not present during this debate): more sinisterly, note how Puttnam's "cultural diplomacy" is simply equated by Baroness Scotland to "Britain's creative sector" and that the only terms in which it is lauded are economic.

Ultimately, such overseas culture-mongering has always been directed towards the process of consolidating the already powerful economic position of Britain in the global economy. Even before the 1989 Parliamentary debate as I have summarised it, the late Sir Anthony Parsons (former Foreign Policy adviser to Margaret Thatcher), had stated this without disguise, and had been quoted with approval by the British Council, in terms which can conclude any case for the thoroughgoing materialism at the heart of the British political establishment:

Leon Trotsky and Less Fortunate Statesmen

It is really dazzlingly obvious. If you are thoroughly familiar with someone else's language and literature, if you know and love the country, the arts, the people, you will be instinctively disposed to buy goods from them rather than a less well-known source, to support them actively when you consider them to be right and to avoid criticizing them too fiercely when you regard them as being in the wrong. (British Council, p. 7)

*

The juxtaposition of an individual of world renown and his capacious views on literature and culture and their potential for human liberation with a comparatively indifferently talented bunch of unelected politicians and quango-masters mouthing pious nationalist banalities on the relations between trade and commodifiable cultural artefacts is, no doubt, the throw of a loaded dice. Can anyone who truly believes in the social value of culture consider Trotsky the loser from this comparison? This we can ask even before we draw attention to the ironies which result from the contrast, such as the spectacle of Trotsky, the thoroughgoing communist, recommending what one might call a "regulated free market" approach to culture, while apparently liberal bourgeois lords try desperately to pressgang cultural endeavour into the narrow service of enhanced balance of trade figures, a manoeuvre that makes them seem a little Stalinist, in the sense that Stalin also attempted – much more successfully than they – to extend state patronage to culture as long as it knelt at the feet of narrow economic and ideological dictates.

However, such observations are far from my main purpose in here co-locating these ostensibly disparate attempts to construct and project cultural policies. To juxtapose them may raise questions and prompt conclusions about the general relations between conflict and culture. I suggest that a predictable dialectic of supply and demand is at work between them. Conflicts of the kind that Trotsky and the nascent Soviet Union had survived at the time he was writing were deeply privative. Russia in the years before the Great War was already a materially poor peasant society, whose culture (in the sense of high or artistic culture) was accessible only to a very restricted élite. The War, the February and October Revolutions, and the subsequent Civil War all put culture (in this specific sense) into a suspension even more extreme – who can engage in artistic pursuits or pleasures or enjoy their potentially edifying consequences amidst an absolutely shattered material infrastructure and within a mercurial polity (from which the culturally inclined classes understandably, if they could, tried to escape)? What may explain Trotsky's apparent irresponsibility in turning to literary debates in 1922 was his sense that only with reference to cultural practices and their potential benefits did the privations suffered in the immediately preceding years seem worthwhile: *Literature and Revolution* may have been intended as a timely clarion call (from someone to whom everyone, friend or foe, would certainly have to pay attention) to see the point of it all.

One might feel, by comparison, rather sorry for well-fed-and-feathered politicians plying their trade in times of apparent relative material plenty and peace. Few grand gestures seem possible in such un-Renaissance-like circumstances, when there is an uninhibited plethora of cultural choices and practices to choose from. At best, all that seems possible then to the official political mind is petty calculation. If anything, such a situation seems to lead politicians implicitly or explicitly to turn the important question on its head, to ask what the point of culture is, and to come up with justifications for it which are stultifyingly pragmatic (it wins us friends abroad) or banally economic ("an important commercial consideration and one which should not be forgotten"; "the best value for money in representing Britain to the rest of the world"; "growing faster than the economy as a whole"). Culture is at such a moment even susceptible, as we have seen, to redesignation in econospeak as the "creative sector" to which one can apply income generation figures and with reference to which one can calculate a national contribution to gainful employment.

If this supply-and-demand thesis seems justified, it may tell us why the notion of post-conflict cultures is so important – because it is perhaps when cultural practices are allowed to come back into the light after enforced benightedness that they are most valued and understood, and have their greatest capacity to make people happy.

References

British Council. (1988) *The British Council Overseas Career Service* [British Council staff recruitment brochure], London, The British Council.

Deutscher, Isaac (1959) *The Prophet Unarmed: Trotsky: 1921-1929,* Oxford, Oxford University Press.

Lenin, V. I. (1965) "Party Organisation and Party Literature", *Collected Works*, vol. 10, Moscow, Progress Publishers.

Lenin, V. I. (2005) *Articles on Tolstoy*, Amsterdam, Fredonia Books.

Trotsky, L. (1960) *Literature and Revolution,* Ann Arbor, University of Michigan Press.

Out of the Ashes: Unamuno and Hispanicity Post-1898[1]

Stephen Roberts

The Spanish "Día de la Hispanidad" [Day of *Hispanicity*], which for nearly thirty years, from 1958 until 1987, celebrated each 12 October the historical, cultural and linguistic ties between Spain and her former colonies, grew out of an earlier commemoration known as the "Fiesta de la Raza" [Festival of the Race], which had been officially set up in 1918 by the Unión Ibero-Americana with the express purpose of celebrating Columbus' "discovery" of the Americas. This festival took place, coincidentally, on the same day as the festival of the Virgen del Pilar, who has consequently become known as the Virgin Patroness of *Hispanidad*. This complex history of the festival which has been known since 1987 as the "Fiesta Nacional de España" [National Festival of Spain] reveals clearly that, beneath the desire for closer links between the different nations that make up the Hispanic world, there are obvious vestiges of the old religious and colonialist spirit which characterised Spain's long relationship with her overseas possessions.

The term *Hispanidad* itself was first popularised by Ramiro de Maeztu, one of the foremost ideologues of authoritarianism in 1920s and 1930s Spain. In his *Defensa de la Hispanidad* [*Defence of Hispanicity*] (1934), Maeztu provided a justification of Spain's influence on the New World and explained that the historical mission of the Hispanic nations was to continue "la obra incomparable de ir incorporando las razas aborígenes a la civilización cristiana" [the incomparable work of incorporating the aboriginal races into Christian civilization] [2] (Maeztu, 1952, p. 151).[3] In a talk given in Buenos Aires, also in 1934, Dr Isidro Gomá y Tomás, the Archbishop of Toledo, developed Maeztu's thesis and claimed that "América es la obra de España. Esta obra de España es esencialmente de catolicismo. Luego hay relación de igualdad entre hispanidad y catolicismo, y es locura todo intento de hispanización que lo repudie" [(Spanish) America is the work of Spain. This work of Spain's has essentially to do with Catholicism. For that reason there is a relationship of equality between Hispanicity and Catholicism, and any attempt at Hispanization that repudiates this is madness] (Maeztu, 1952, p. 246). With these words, Gomá provided a direct link between Maeztu and the ideology which would form the basis of the Francoist régime for, as Paul Preston has pointed out,

> the more or less racist vision which linked the Civil War to the crusading spirit of the wars between Christians and Moors and to the evangelical imperialism of the conquest of America was to be inflicted on Spanish society with varying intensity for more than twenty years

---

[1] A modified version of this article appeared, in Spanish, in the *Cuadernos de la Cátedra Miguel de Unamuno*, vol. 39 (2004); see Roberts, 2004.

[2] This and the other translations that feature in this chapter are the author's own.

[3] On Maeztu's notion of *Hispanidad*, see Hennessy (2000).

under the banner of *Hispanidad* (Preston, 1990, p. 32).[4]

There is no denying, therefore, the imperialist and orthodox Catholic overtones in Maeztu's and Franco's notion of *Hispanidad*. Despite this fact, the concept has a longer and more complex history, especially in the works of Miguel de Unamuno (1864-1936), the most important and prolific Spanish writer to deal with Spanish America in the first third of the twentieth century. Unamuno in fact used the term relatively infrequently, and mainly in the 1920s and 1930s, but all of his writings on Spanish America can be seen as an exploration of the relationship between the different elements in the Hispanic world or, more exactly, as an attempt to create a new relationship between Spain and her former possessions in the aftermath of the colonial disaster of 1898. An examination of these writings can therefore provide us with an understanding of the genealogy of the concept of *Hispanidad* in Unamuno's work.

Before this, however, it is essential to spend some time forming an idea of both the Spanish and Spanish American contexts within which Unamuno came to be interested in, and develop his ideas on, the Hispanic world. In Spain, that context was the Spanish-American War of the 1890s and the aftermath of the defeat of 1898. The events leading up to the loss of Cuba, Puerto Rico and the Philippines, Spain's final major colonies, gave rise to an atmosphere of rupture, insecurity and disorientation in the country, above all amongst the political and intellectual classes.[5] Many leading figures started to seek ways of regenerating the nation and espoused projects as diverse as the modernisation of the country's economic, political and social structures and the reaffirmation of those traditional values which, supposedly, had guided Spain during the years of her imperial splendour.[6] Unamuno's position on this debate is well known. In *En torno al casticismo* [*On Authentic Tradition*] (1895), he trod a middle path between modernisers and traditionalists, rejecting the potentially abstract programmes of the former and the reactionary nostalgia of the latter and calling instead for a progressive policy which took into account the latent potential of the Spanish people: "tenemos que europeizarnos y chapuzarnos en pueblo" [we have to Europeanise and immerse ourselves in the people] (Unamuno, 1966, I: p. 867).[7] From 1897, and especially 1900, onwards, however, he gradually shed his modernising and Europeanising zeal and concentrated more on teasing out those characteristics which set Spain apart from her neighbours in Europe. In this process, Unamuno's writings on Spanish America were to play an essential role.

Between 1901 and 1906, Unamuno looked after the "De literatura

---

[4] On Franco's appropriation of the notion of *Hispanidad*, see Payne (1987, pp. 360-62).
[5] For a vivid description of this atmosphere, see Balfour (1997, pp. 49-131).
[6] For an excellent study of the traditionalist and modernising strands in regenerationism, see Pike (1971, pp. 73-102 and 103-27 respectively).
[7] The most detailed study of *En torno al casticismo* is still Ramsden (1974).

hispanoamericana" [On Spanish American Literature] section of *La Lectura* (Madrid), an activity which brought him into contact with the latest literary and historical works emerging from Spanish America. Even before this, however, and thanks to the offices of Rubén Darío (Unamuno, 1966, IV: p. 998), he had been invited to write for *La Nación* (Buenos Aires) and assiduously sent out hundreds of articles to this newspaper, and consequently to other Spanish American papers and journals, between 1899 and 1935. This collaboration was of great importance for the young Unamuno, as his *Epistolario americano* reveals. For one thing, it allowed him to establish his international reputation as a writer, as he wrote gleefully to his friend Pedro Jiménez Ilundain in May 1899: "Empiezo, pues, a tener nombre y mercado en América y a sonar por allí" [I'm starting, therefore, to have a name and a market in Spanish America and to make some noise out there] (Unamuno, 1996, p. 64). More importantly, however, his contact with the Spanish American world and its readers enabled him to escape from the confines of his grieving nation and to create a wider perspective for his evolving thoughts on the state of Spain. He genuinely believed that Spanish American history and culture provided himself and indeed all Spaniards with what he called in 1904 "un reflejo de nuestro estado y de nuestros vicios" [a reflection of the state we're in and of our vices] (Unamuno, 1966, IV, p. 837).

It is not surprising, therefore, that Unamuno should use his writings on Spanish American themes in order to identify and castigate the vestiges of the old Spanish colonial and imperialist spirit which was still haunting Spain and affecting her relationship with the other Hispanic nations. As early as 1899, he railed against the new Spanish obsession with "la gran raza hispano-americana" [the great Spanish American race], which he put down to a simple knee-jerk reaction to the disaster of 1898 (Unamuno, 1966, IV: p. 723). For that reason he was a firm opponent of any official talk of "fraternidad iberoamericana" [Ibero-American fraternity], which, he claimed, served only to hide a profound ignorance of, and even feelings of superiority towards, the nations of the New World (Unamuno, 1966, IV: pp. 899-90). He warned his Argentine readers in 1907 that the Spanish were still, "en el fondo, apegados a la estimación colonial" [deep down, attached to the colonial way of seeing things] (Unamuno, 1966, IV: p. 908) and added in 1916 that many in the Peninsula still dreamed of re-establishing their hegemony over the Spanish-speaking world (Unamuno, 1966, IV: pp. 992-93). But Unamuno's fury with such attitudes reached new heights when, in 1918, the Spanish Government officially established the "Fiesta de la Raza", the forerunner first of the "Día de la Hispanidad" and then of the present-day "Fiesta Nacional de España". In 1919, he wrote the first of many articles in which he bitterly attacked the festival, denouncing the inappropriateness of the reference to a "Hispanic race" and claiming that such events were simply an imperialist manoeuvre on the part of "official Spain" and therefore "huelen a colonia" [smell of colonialism/cologne] (Unamuno, 1966, IV: pp. 1044-47). By this date, he had embarked on a crusade against the new authoritarian strain that had entered Spanish politics, a crusade which would lead him in 1927, when in exile from the dictatorship of General Primo de Rivera, to claim rather hyperbolically that King Alfonso XIII was "una especie de patrono de la catolicidad hispanoamericana" [a sort of patron of Spanish American Catholicism] who was actively planning "la reconquista de América" [the reconquest of America] (Unamuno, 1996, pp. 510-11).

But Unamuno's writings on Spanish America helped him not only to recognise and denounce the ills which were eating away at his country but also to define his own position on the best way to regenerate Spain. The articles that he published between 1899 and 1912 reveal how the shift from his early Europeanising fervour to his later espousal of what he took to be native Spanish values was influenced by his reading of Spanish American literature. A key text in this sense is "Algunas consideraciones sobre la literatura hispano-americana" ["Some Considerations on Spanish American Literature"], of November 1905 (Unamuno, 1966, III: pp. 900-24), where he openly attacks not only Spanish traditionalism but also, and more centrally, the European materialism which he believed was destroying the essentially spiritual nature of the Hispanic nations (p. 923). In a passage which could have come straight out of the pages of *Vida de Don Quijote y Sancho* [*Life of Don Quixote and Sancho*] (1905) or *Del sentimiento trágico de la vida* [*On the Tragic Sense of Life*] (1912), the works in which Unamuno finally expressed his Spanish philosophy of life, he claims that both Spaniards and Spanish Americans need to reject the "mamonismo" [Mammonism] that comes from a blind belief in Science and Progress and to espouse instead "un ideal que nos dé originalidad; [un] sentimiento religioso de la vida" [an ideal that can give us originality; a religious sense of life] (Unamuno, 1966, III: p. 917).

Given the important role that Spanish America played in the formation of his Spanish philosophy, it seems ironic that the years that led up to and followed the publication of *Del sentimiento trágico...* should also have witnessed a cooling of Unamuno's interest in the Hispanic world beyond the Atlantic. And yet the Conclusion to that work reveals how he pits the Spanish, Quixotic, conception of life against the whole of modern European civilisation, which he characterises as superficially progressive and materialistic (Unamuno, 1966, VII: pp. 283-302). The logical next step for Unamuno would therefore be to carry out his mission, which he had long announced, to "españolizar a Europa" [to make Europe Spanish].[8] It must be noted that there was a selfish motive behind this shift in Unamuno's interests. As he said in a letter to his Spanish confidant Jiménez Ilundain in November 1913, "[l]o de España y los países de lengua española no me interesa apenas. Ahora mi intención está en ser traducido [...] tengo fe en mi buen éxito en Europa así que se me traduzca" [Spain and the Spanish-speaking countries hardly hold any interest for me. My aim now is to get translated (...) I'm confident that I'll be successful in Europe as soon as I've been translated] (Unamuno, 1996, p. 411). In early 1914, he felt no qualms about making the same point to the Chilean writer Ernesto

[8] He was already talking of this mission in a letter to Jiménez Ilundain from May 1905 (Unamuno, 1996, p. 212).

Guzmán: "Cuando buscaba difusión y eco en los países americanos de lengua española me interesaba por sus cosas y sus hombres; ahora que empieza a traducírseme a lenguas europeas, la cosa varía algo" [When I was after being read and creating an echo in the Spanish-speaking American countries, I took an interest in their things and their people; now that I'm beginning to be translated into the European languages, things have changed somewhat] (Unamuno, 1996, p. 415). Despite this, Unamuno's desire to conquer Europe had a serious side: he seemed genuinely to believe that his quasi-Christian and essentially Spanish message could save the Old Continent from herself, and this belief became even more rooted in the writer as he witnessed the carnage of the Great War and the crisis in European values in the 1920s and 30s.

This change in attitude did not, however, signal a final rupture in Unamuno's relationship with Spanish America. In the early 1920s, during his campaigns against the anti-democratic activities of Alfonso XIII and some of his ministers, he received the support of many Spanish American intellectuals and readers and soon realised that such support could act as a powerful weapon. He therefore wrote a series of articles in the Argentine press, such as an open letter "A la juventud argentina" ["To the Youth of Argentina"], in which he called for all good-minded Spanish Americans to join him in his struggle to free Spain from tyranny (Unamuno, 1996, pp. 468-69). Unamuno knew exactly what he was doing, as he revealed in a 1922 talk in which he claimed that the King was finally reconsidering his autocratic stance "merced, sin duda, a la que nosotros armamos, sobre todo en América, que es donde el golpe duele" [thanks, without doubt, to the ruckus we are causing, above all in (Spanish) America, which is where the blow really hits home] (Unamuno, 1966, IX: p. 368). The truth of Unamuno's words is borne out by the fact that it was a letter of his which was published in *Nosotros* (Buenos Aires) that led the Dictator Miguel Primo de Rivera to banish him in February 1924 (Unamuno, 1966, IX: pp. 1181-82). In exile, Unamuno made full use of his Spanish American connections, writing many private and open letters such as the one entitled "Un llamado a los liberales de América" ["An Appeal to the (Spanish) American Liberals"], which he finished with the words: "yo, en nombre de mis hermanos los españoles liberales, os pido que nos ayudéis a recobrar aquí patria y tierra, libertad y trabajo" [in the name of my brothers the Spanish liberals, I beseech you to help us here to recover country and homeland, freedom and work] (Unamuno, 1996, p. 475). Indeed, it was during his time in exile that Unamuno developed a theory which he had first formulated in the 1910s and early 1920s: that the same spirit had animated both the successful Spanish American wars of independence and the Spanish liberals' frustrated resistance to the tyranny of Fernando VII (see, for example, Unamuno, 1966, IV: pp. 1065-68). As a result, he claimed in 1925 that "España tendrá que reconquistarse desde América" [Spain will have to reconquer herself from (Spanish) America], since only that old liberal spirit which had been kept alive overseas could lead to the restoration of freedom in Spain (Unamuno, 1966, VIII: p. 1114). In short, throughout the 1920s and, to a lesser degree, the 1930s, we find Unamuno playing up the specifically political dimension of his understanding of the relationship between Spain and Spanish America.

Such is the shifting Spanish context in which Unamuno worked out his position on the relationships and tensions within the Hispanic world. Before going on to look at what he actually had to say about the literature and culture of the New World, however, we need also briefly to consider the Spanish American context.

Unamuno started collaborating in *La Lectura* and *La Nación* at a moment when Spanish America, like Spain, was going through a period of change and turmoil. After independence and throughout the nineteenth century, many Spanish American intellectuals had looked away from Spain and sought new philosophical and cultural guides in the rest of Europe. At first, as Davis (1972, pp. 63-134) has pointed out, they drew on French Enlightenment thought and British utilitarianism, but then, after the 1850s, they absorbed the sociological and positivist ideas of Comte and others.[9] Then, from the 1880s onwards, there was a backlash against positivism in the form of *modernismo*, a movement which imported the attitudes and styles of French Parnassianism and Symbolism and combated the growing materialism of the age through the deification of art.[10] Both positivism and *modernismo* continued to hold sway over Spanish American intellectuals well into the twentieth century. But Spanish America, like Spain, was to experience the Cuban War and the 1898 Spanish defeat as a trauma, so much so that critics such as Lago Carballo (1997) have recently claimed that many writers, including Rodó, Ugarte and Santos Chocano, should be seen collectively as members of a so-called "generación hispanoamericana del 98" [Spanish American Generation of 1898]. One of the commonly-held assumptions of this generation of writers was that the Cuban War had proved once and for all that the greatest imperialist and colonialist threat to Spanish America now came not so much from Spain as from the new economic superpower, the United States.

The key moment in this change of attitude was without doubt 1900, the year in which José Enrique Rodó published his highly influential *Ariel*. As is well known, Rodó did not set out in this work simply to denounce the United States or her utilitarian and, as he saw it, essentially Protestant conception of life, which he believed had proved successful in providing material welfare for so many (Rodó, 1967, p. 51). His aim was rather to write a passionate defence of the other America, the Latin America which had a long history of links with Mediterranean Europe and nurtured what he referred to as "un ideal desinteresado del espíritu" [a disinterested ideal of the spirit] (Rodó, 1967, p. 96). Playing the role of a modern-day Virgil, he concluded the work not by expounding a particular regenerationist project but by

[9] The classic study of Latin American positivism is Zea (1966)
[10] For a bibliography on *modernismo*, see Wainwright, 1993. Viñas (1995) is especially relevant here because he traces the links between Argentina and Europe throughout the ages of positivism and *modernismo*.

announcing a new dawn for the Latin American world. And yet, despite, or perhaps because of, the fact that it did not recommend a specific course of action, *Ariel* became a blank page on which many Latin American intellectuals, of very different political tendencies, could write their own cultural programmes. For some, such as Manuel Gálvez and Leopoldo Lugones in Argentina, it acted as a confirmation of the need for an intensified cultural nationalism, for an exploration of those values that allowed each Latin American nation to stand out from the rest.[11] For others, it was a call for a new brand of *Americanismo* which would lead to a deeper understanding and therefore exaltation of the common indigenous and, above all, European traits which bound together the whole of Latin America.[12] Yet others, however, believed that the new *Americanismo* should bring with it a renewed respect for, and understanding of, the specifically Spanish influence on the New World. As Jean Franco has said: "With the concept of a united 'Latin' America, many writers came to look more kindly on the former 'mother country', Spain, no longer a threat since its defeat in 1898" (Franco, 1967, p. 53). One such writer was Rubén Darío who, in his final years, seemed to move towards a position which could perhaps be called *Hispanismo*, that is, a Hispanic rather than a Latin conception of America which laid more emphasis on her Spanish than on her more generally European heritage and led him in *Cantos de vida y esperanza* [*Songs of Life and Hope*] (1905), which he dedicated to Rodó, to sing hymns of praise to "Hispania fecunda" [fecund Hispania] and "la América española" [Spanish America] (Darío, 1983, pp. 31 and 50). These three positions – cultural nationalism, *Americanismo* and *Hispanismo* – were somewhat modified after 1914-18. As Franco (1967, p. 69) says, the general disaffection with Europe which resulted from an awareness of the horrors of the Great War served to reinforce Spanish Americans' interests in their own autochthonous traditions and therefore intensified the tendency towards either cultural nationalism or self-sufficient *Americanismo*. In some cases, though, as with the Mexicans Alfonso Reyes and José Vasconcelos, the European conflagration encouraged still further the belief in a common Hispanic destiny, a belief which would become even more rooted in the work of certain intellectuals and poets during and after the Spanish Civil War.[13]

Unamuno's work on Spanish America, therefore, must also be seen in this context, not simply because of the influence that he may or may not have had on these different tendencies (an influence which has not, as yet, been studied) but also because his own views on Spain and Spanish America necessarily had to enter into a dialogue with the cultural developments on the other side of the Atlantic. With this in mind, it is now possible to consider in more detail Unamuno's ideas on

[11] On the cultural nationalists, or traditionalists, see Davis (1972, pp. 135-81) and Franco (1967, pp. 40-102) and, in the Argentinian context, Shumway (1991, pp. 214-96).
[12] Franco (1967, p. 44) identifies Carlos Bunge's *Nuestra América* (1903) as one of the first modern works to deal with Latin American reality as a discrete whole.
[13] On this latter point, see Franco (1967, p. 136).

Spanish American culture, on the relationship between the Old and New Worlds, and on the existence of a common Hispanic identity and destiny. In order to do this, I intend, first, to look at what he had to say about Spanish American literature, culture and history and then, secondly, to consider his thoughts on the role and function of the Spanish language.

Apart from his correspondence and his personal friendships, Unamuno's most important contact with the Spanish American world came through his reading of her literary and historical works. One thing that becomes clear from his letters and also his literary criticism in *La Lectura* is that Unamuno believed that he had a duty to combat Spain's ignorance of the Hispanic world beyond her borders, which he saw as yet more proof of the cultural isolation that had followed upon the 1898 disaster. His precept seems to be summed up in a reply to Ricardo Rojas' 1907 "Encuesta" [Survey] on the teaching of history in Spain and Spanish America in which, after once again castigating Spain's self-absorption, he writes: "Y como el conocerse a sí mismo tiene que ser algo comparativo, pues nadie se conoce sino en cuanto conoce a los demás, todo pueblo que quiera conocerse debe estudiar a los demás pueblos" [And as self-knowledge has to be a comparative matter, since one only knows oneself insofar as one knows others, any people that wishes to know itself should study other peoples] (Unamuno, 1996, p. 290). But Unamuno's writings in *La Nación* and other newspapers and journals on the American continent reveal that his aim was in fact to open up lines of communication not only between Spanish America and Spain but also between Spain and Spanish America: as he wrote in 1922, "[m]i empeño ha sido dar a conocer aquí las modalidades espirituales de esos países, sus maneras de sentir y de pensar, y ahí las de aquí" [I have striven to make Spain aware of the spiritual outlooks of those countries over there, the way they feel and think, and to make those countries aware of Spain's spiritual outlook] (Unamuno, 1966, IV: p. 1077). On one occasion, he even implied that his reviews could foment greater understanding between all Hispanic nations, since "no es sólo que en España se conozca poco y mal a la América latina, y que en ésta se conozca no mucho ni muy bien a España, sino que sospecho que las repúblicas hispanoamericanas, desde Méjico a la Argentina, se conocen muy superficialmente entre sí" [it is not just that Latin America is little and badly known in Spain and that Spain is little and badly known in Latin America, but, I suspect, that the Spanish American Republics themselves, from Mexico to Argentina, only know each other in a very superficial way] (Unamuno, 1966, III: p. 499).

It was this desire for knowledge and self-knowledge that led Unamuno to read and comment on as many Spanish American books as he could lay his hands on. There is no doubt that he was the most important Spanish critic of the continent's literature since Juan Valera and *Clarín* but, unlike his illustrious predecessors, he made a concerted effort to form an idea of the different characteristics of each Republic's cultural output as well as to seek out common aims and concerns.[14]

---

[14] On Valera's, *Clarín*'s and also Marcelino Menéndez Pelayo's Spanish American

Indeed, he announced to Ernesto Guzmán in 1907 that he was working on a book (which he never actually wrote) "sobre la literatura hispanoamericana contemporánea, o sea un estudio de conjunto sobre ella desde los que la cultivan en Méjico hasta Chile y las repúblicas del Plata" [about contemporary Spanish American literature, that is, a survey of this literature from those who produce it in Mexico to Chile and the Republics of the River Plate] (Unamuno, 1996, p. 283). And yet Unamuno was by no means an undiscriminating reader and critic. He told the Venezuelan writer Rufino Blanco-Fombona in 1901 that, as far as the Spanish American books he received were concerned, he was finding it necessary to "cerner y separar el trigo de la paja" [sift and separate the wheat from the chaff] (Unamuno, 1996, p. 115), and he added to Rodó in 1902 that "[p]or lo que a América hace, me esfuerzo por llamar aquí la atención acerca de lo que ahí se hace de serio, sustancioso y conceptual, y desvanecer la leyenda del sinsontismo y de que no hay apenas más que poetas chirles que cantan a las manos pricipescas [sic] de esta o la otra beldad u otra lilaila por el estilo" [as far as (Spanish) America is concerned, I go out of my way to draw attention here in Spain to all the serious, substantial and conceptual work that is being written over there, and to dispel the legend that Spanish American literature is all superficial birdsong and that there are hardly any other writers apart from the chirping and insubstantial poets who sing of the princessly hands of some beauty or other or some other nonsense of the sort] (Unamuno, 1996, p. 137). It is here that one starts to notice that Unamuno was in reality a reader and a critic with a more or less secret agenda. In fact, a closer reading of his reviews and letters reveals that he allotted to himself the role of a literary policeman who would sort the wheat from the chaff according to criteria which were more ideological than aesthetic in nature.

As the aforementioned letter to Rodó implies, Unamuno's greatest enemy, especially in the first decade of the century, was in fact Spanish American *modernismo*. It was not simply that he objected to the *modernistas'* subject-matter and style, although his reference in a letter from 1900 to the fact that Spanish American poetry "[a]búsase de sátiros, ninfas, driadas, orientalidades, *mignardises* franceses del tiempo y mundo de Watteau, etc, etc" [makes excessive use of satyrs, nymphs, dryads, orientalisms, French *mignardises* from the time and world of Watteau, etc., etc.] certainly shows that he did (Unamuno, 1996, p. 92), but, more importantly, that he took the movement as proof that Spanish American writers continued to be unhealthily obsessed with France and French literature.[15] Many of his reviews in *La Lectura* take the form of bitter denunciations of collections of *modernista* poetry, such as Leopoldo Díaz's *Las sombras de Hellas* [*The Shadows of Hellas*] (Unamuno, 1966, IV: pp. 824-26), or, more commonly, of laments for the fact that perfectly good writers, like Enrique Gómez Carrillo in *El alma encantadora de París* [*The Enchanting Soul of Paris*] (Unamuno, 1966, IV: pp. 786-90) or Amado Nervo in *El*

---

criticism, see Pike (1971, pp. 32-42 and 67-69).
[15] On this point, see Roberts (2000).

Éxodo y las flores del camino [*Exodus and the Wayside Flowers*] (Unamuno, 1966, IV: pp. 815-20), have been seduced by the decadent charms of *fin-de-siècle* Paris. These articles are therefore peppered with attacks on the Spanish American mania for what Unamuno variously calls "París, Cosmópolis" (Unamuno, 1966, IV: p. 750), "decadentismo" (Unamuno 1966, IV: p. 792) or "los artificios bulevarderos" [boulevard affectations] (Unamuno, 1966, IV: p. 866), although nowhere is Unamuno more petulant than in his review of B. Vicuña Subercaseaux's *La ciudad de las ciudades* [*The City of Cities*] (Unamuno, 1966, IV: pp. 872-84), which he concludes by saying rather condescendingly that "[e]s, por lo demás, muy natural la fascinación que la literatura francesa ejerce sobre sociedades en formación cultural, pues ofrece papilla espiritual para espíritus tiernos" [the fascination that French literature exerts on societies that are still developing culturally is, in all other respects, quite natural, since that literature provides spiritual pap for young and tender spirits] (p. 883).

Gradually one realises that what Unamuno is objecting to is the fact that France continues to exert a sort of cultural imperialism over Spanish America, encouraging her to carry on turning her back on Spain and the Spanish literary traditions. He often refers to this situation in terms of a French "invasion" of Spanish American letters (Unamuno, 1996, p. 76) and complains bitterly of the tendency to "hacer a la literatura francesa sinónimo de la literatura universal" [make French literature a synonym for universal literature] (Unamuno, 1966, IV: p. 880). He also associates this Gallophilism with "la leyenda del *latinismo*" [the legend of *Latinism*] that dominates Spanish American cultural life (Unamuno, 1966, IV: p. 874). He goes some way to explaining this idea in his first letter to Rodó, from 1900, which provides us with the most complete review that he would ever write of *Ariel* (Unamuno, 1996, pp. 88-90). Unamuno warmly welcomes the work because of its defence of spiritual values, but complains that Rodó, perhaps influenced by French culture, has been unable to appreciate Protestant religiosity, which, at that stage in his career, he considered to be superior to the Catholic strain. "[C]atolicismo y latinismo son una misma cosa" [Catholicism and *Latinism* are one and the same thing], he goes on to say (Unamuno, 1996, p. 89), adding in his second letter to Rodó (also of 1900) that the Catholic, Latin conception of religion, which he associates with the non-Spanish Mediterranean nations, is too aesthetic and too insufficiently mystical to bring about the necessary spiritual revolution in the Hispanic world (Unamuno, 1996, pp. 104-05).[16] In later writings, however, he associates *Latinismo* with Spanish America's general admiration for things European and for this reason rejects what he calls the pedantic term "América latina" [Latin America] in favour of the more traditional "América española" [Spanish America] (Unamuno, 1966, IV: p. 611). The implication is clear: he wishes to combat the Spanish American tendency to seek out models in Europe because that tendency

[16] On the relationship between Rodó and Unamuno and on Unamuno's reading of *Ariel*, see Roberts (2001).

undermines the influence of Spain in the New World. As he put it in a 1909 letter to a Colombian journal: "cuando un americano, sea argentino, chileno, colombiano, mejicano, etc., da en hispanófobo, más que por amor a su propia patria, más que por argentinismo, chilenismo, colombianismo, mejicanismo, etc., lo es por deslumbramiento de Francia, Inglaterra o Estados Unidos; lo es por afrancesado, anglómano o ayanquizado" [when a (Spanish) American, be he Argentine, Chilean, Colombian, Mexican, etc., takes to disliking Spain, he does so not so much because of his love for his own homeland, his Argentinism, Chileanism, Colombianism, Mexicanism, etc., as because he has become dazzled by France, England or the United States; he does so because he has become Frenchified, England-obsessed or Yankeefied] (Unamuno, 1996, pp. 314-15).

An awareness of this anti-French and increasingly anti-European attitude helps to clarify Unamuno's central mission in his Spanish American articles. He wishes to combat what he calls the growing cult of cosmopolitanism, which he believes is becoming confused with the notion of "universality" (Unamuno, 1966, IV: p. 938), and to prove that "cuanto más de su tiempo y de su país es uno, más es de los tiempos y de los países todos" [the more one belongs to one's own time and country, the more one belongs to all times and all countries] (Unamuno, 1966, III: pp. 538-39). For that reason, he praises those books that speak of the realities of the Spanish American world, such as Francisco Grandmontagne's *La Maldonada*, a novel "que nos cuenta cosas de la Argentina, que nos descubre algo de aquella vida americana y no enrevesados quintaesenciamientos y exquisiteces mal vertidos del francés" [that tells us things about Argentina, that reveals to us something of that (Spanish) American life and not convoluted quintessentialisms and refinements that have been badly translated from the French] (Unamuno, 1966, IV: p. 720). For that reason too, he talks of Spanish American literature in terms of "incipientismo" [incipientism] rather than "decadentismo" [decadentism], because her writers "se están buscando, mas sin haberse encontrado aún" [are searching for themselves, but without having found themselves yet] (Unamuno, 1966, IV: p. 730). Spanish America, he adds, is still a young continent and therefore needs to create her own traditions (Unamuno 1966, IV: p. 731); indeed, until she does so, she will not be able to create "un arte definitivo, clásico en el mejor sentido" [an art that is definitive, classic in the best sense of the word] (Unamuno, 1966, IV: p. 729). This is why he ends up reading more works of sociology and history than of literature. His favourite authors are without doubt Domingo Faustino Sarmiento and Bartolomé Mitre (Unamuno, 1966, IV: pp. 903-06 and 1065-68), although he also speaks highly of his contemporaries Carlos Octavio Bunge and Francisco Bulnes (Unamuno, 1966, IV: pp. 808-14 and 834-42). All of these men have helped to lay the historical foundations on which "la fábrica de [su] cultura nacional" [the fabric of (their) national culture] can be built (Unamuno, 1966, IV: p. 859).

In all of this, it is obvious that Unamuno is rejecting the Europeanising *Americanismo* in Spanish American letters and siding instead with the cultural nationalists: "cuando sólo me interesan de verdad los escritores americanos [...] es cuando me hablan de sus propias cosas" [(Spanish) American writers only really interest me when they speak to me about their own things] (Unamuno, 1966, IV: p. 970). But he is one step ahead of the latter too because he does not espouse and encourage just any type of cultural nationalism. For one thing, he believes that the incipient *indigenista* literature, which he refers to as "americanismo histórico" [historical *Americanism*], is a failure because "los americanos son poco menos extraños que nosotros a las civilizaciones quechua, azteca o guaraní" [the (Spanish) Americans are only a little less unfamiliar than we are with the Quechua, Aztec or Guarani civilizations] (Unamuno, 1966, III: p. 916). For another, he rejects the notion of, for example, *Argentinismo*, pouring scorn on "la ridícula pretensión de que *Martín Fierro* pertenezca a una literatura *primitivamente argentina*, brote de un espíritu nuevo que diferencia a los argentinos de los demás españoles" [the ridiculous pretension that *Martín Fierro* belongs to a *primitive Argentine* literature, offshoot of a new spirit that distinguishes the Argentines from the rest of the Spanish] (Unamuno, 1966, IV: p. 714). Rather, as this final quotation attests, he goes out of his way to play up the Spanishness of Spanish American literature, at least of that literature which was supposedly uncontaminated by other European influences. His theory here is that Spanish and Spanish American literature belong to the same tradition when they tap into popular, rather than highbrow, sources (Unamuno, 1966, IV: pp. 781-82). For that reason, he is constantly pointing out the Spanish antecedents of his favourite Spanish American works, such as *Martín Fierro* (Unamuno, 1966, IV: pp. 709-19), and the most effusive praise in his reviews is reserved for those writers like José Santos Chocano (Unamuno, 1966, IV: pp. 766-68), Manuel Díaz Rodríguez (Unamuno, 1966, IV: pp. 797-801) and Amado Nervo (Unamuno, 1966, IV: pp. 1057-59) who recognise and cherish their links with Spain. This leads Unamuno to claim that "las literaturas hispano-americanas no se distinguen sustancialmente ni forman, en el fondo, nada diferente y aparte de la literatura española" [the Spanish American literatures are not substantially distinct nor, deep down, do they constitute anything that is different and separate from Spanish literature], although he does add that this means that Spanish literature too cannot be distinguished from its Spanish American counterpart (Unamuno, 1966, III: p. 916). Similarly, when talking of historical works, he continually points out that Spanish Americans cannot divorce their history from that of Spain. Indeed, they can only understand their past and even their present through reference to what went on and continues to go on in the Peninsula (Unamuno, 1996, p. 290), just as Spain can learn from Spanish America many basic lessons about her own history (Unamuno, 1966, IV: p. 930). As a result, Unamuno can confidently proclaim that "cuando se quiera ver la historia en argentino, en nativo, se acabará por verla en español" [when one wishes to see history from an Argentine, that is, a native perspective, one will end up seeing it in Spanish] (Unamuno, 1966, III: p. 546).

All this gives some idea of the complexity of Unamuno's position on

Spanish and Spanish American culture. On the one hand, he plays up the differences between Spain and Spanish America and between each Republic in the New World, writing that "mi batalla es que cada cual, hombre o pueblo, sea él y no otro" [my battle is to ensure that everyone, man or people, is himself rather than someone else] (Unamuno, 1966, III: p. 545). In this vein, he can applaud Ricardo Rojas' attempt to define *Argentinidad* [*Argentinicity*] (Unamuno, 1966, III: p. 543) and can even exhort the intellectuals across the Atlantic to "americanizarse" [Americanise themselves] (Unamuno, 1966, IV: p. 834), although elsewhere he shows opposition to the term *Americanidad* [*Americanicity*] because it seems to negate the differences between the Spanish American nations (Unamuno, 1966, IV: p. 1008). On the other hand, he works hard to forge a sense of unity between the different elements in the Hispanic world, to make clear that all her writers are working within an essentially Spanish tradition, although he points out that this does not confer on Spain any special status or privilege (Unamuno, 1966, III: p. 916). He therefore places cultural unity and cultural difference in a dialectical relationship which he explains in a 1908 article in the following terms: "si los españoles que a la vez que queremos a nuestra patria sabemos algo de esos pueblos americanos, hacemos votos porque defiendan y corroboren y acentúen sus caracteres privativos y propios, porque se hagan una cultura indígena y peculiar a ellos mismos, es porque estamos convencidos de que es así como más han de acercarse a nosotros" [if those of us Spaniards who both love our homeland and know something about the (Spanish) American peoples over there hope and pray that those peoples defend and corroborate and emphasise their own and exclusive characters, that they create a culture that is indigenous and peculiar to them, it is because we are convinced that it is in this way that they will move closest to us] (Unamuno, 1966, IV: pp. 936-37). Or, as he put it as early as 1899, in words that clearly show the influence of Herbert Spencer, "[s]in diferenciación no hay integración posible, y a la vez es el fondo último de homogeneidad, lo que hace posibles las diferenciaciones y la integración de ellas" [there is no integration possible without differentiation, and, at the same time, it is the ultimate and underlying fact of homogeneity that makes both differentiations and their integration possible] (Unamuno, 1966, IV: p. 735).[17] Differentiation and integration, divergence and convergence: these are the keys to Unamuno's understanding of the cultural ties between Spain and Spanish America. But it would be in his discussions on language that he would finally manage to define his mature position on these matters and also to clarify his notion of *Hispanidad*.

Unamuno's starting-point here was his overall philosophy of language. He consistently defined language as "la sangre del espíritu" [the blood of the spirit] and explained this in 1910 by claiming that "[p]ensamos con palabras, esto es evidente; no pensamos en álgebra, con fórmulas. Pero creo aún más, y es que con palabras también

---

[17] On the influence of the Spencerian notion of progress on the young Unamuno, see Storm (2001, p. 184).

sentimos. Una lengua lleva consigo, no ya una manera especial de concebir la realidad, sino hasta una manera de sentirla" [we think with words, that is obvious; we do not think in algebra, with formulae. But I believe something more than this, that we also feel with words. A language brings with it not just a special way of conceiving reality but even a way of feeling it] (Unamuno, 1966, IV: p. 380). Each of us, therefore, on learning our native language, inherits a whole worldview, since, as he wrote in 1935, "un idioma de habla es una raíz, más que depósito, de tradiciones, y lleva en sí una visión y una audición del universo mundo, una concepción de la vida y del destino humano, un arte, una filosofía y hasta una religión" [a spoken language is a root, more than a deposit, of traditions, and carries within it a way of seeing and of hearing the universe that is our world, a conception of life and of human destiny, an art, a philosophy and even a religion] (Unamuno, 1966, IV: pp. 652-53). For that reason, "todo aquel que piense desde niño en español, pensará a la española, créalo o no, sépalo o no, y aunque no corra ni una sola gota de sangre española en sus venas" [everyone who has thought in Spanish since they were a child will think in the Spanish way, whether they believe it or not, whether they know it or not, and even if not a single drop of Spanish blood flows through their veins] (Unamuno, 1966, III: p. 911).

It was with this view in mind that Unamuno had turned his attention at the beginning of the century to the question of the different languages of the Iberian Peninsula. Caught up perhaps in the general atmosphere of insecurity which had invaded the country after 1898, he became a fierce opponent of the cultivation of the regional languages of Spain, especially Basque and Catalan, which, he believed, signalled a return to the Medieval cantonalist spirit that had always posed a threat to the unity of the nation (Unamuno, 1966, IX: p. 249). He saw in the cultivation of these languages both a cause and a symptom of the "enfermedad de íntima desintegración nacional" [sickness of inner national disintegration] that was undermining Spain's role and mission in the world (Unamuno, 1966, IV: p. 521), and proclaimed his belief that, "abandonadas a sí mismas, acabarán por perecer" [left to themselves, they will end up perishing] (Unamuno, 1966, IV: p. 1013). His duty, therefore, was to encourage his regional compatriots to use Castilian, "la única lengua nacional de España" [the only national language of Spain] (Unamuno, 1966, IV: p. 377) and the only language in Spain which was "internacional" and "mundial" [worldwide] (Unamuno, 1966, IV: p. 375). At the same time, however, he invited them to view the Castilian language as a battlefield on which they should join in the "lucha por la personalidad" [struggle for personality] (Unamuno, 1966, IX: p. 318): using Castilian, "cada región debe esforzarse por expansionar el espíritu que tenga, por dárselo a los demás, [...] por sellar a las demás regiones con su sello" [each region must strive to expand its spirit, to give it to the others, (...) to stamp its seal on the other regions] (Unamuno, 1966, IV: p. 375). Only in this way, according to Unamuno, could they participate in the creation of the "conciencia patria colectiva" [collective national consciousness] (Unamuno, 1966, III: p. 496) and also help to ensure that the Castilian language played its universal role in the world. Unamuno even on one occasion applied these thoughts to the whole of the Peninsula, foreseeing the day when Castilian and Portuguese would fuse to create an even more universal language (Unamuno, 1966, IV: p. 528).

Unamuno was to apply a similar perspective in his writings on Spanish America. He viewed the autochthonous languages of the continent in the same way that he viewed Basque and Catalan, although he added erroneously that "[a]hí, en general, no tuvo el castellano que sustituir a idiomas indígenas, pues los que los hablaban, o se extinguieron, o se fundieron en la población de las colonias" [over there, on the whole, the Castilian language didn't have to replace indigenous languages, since those who spoke them either died out or merged into the population of the colonies] (Unamuno, 1966, IV: p. 592). In general, he treats these languages with disdain, pointing out that Mexican laws are written in Castilian and not in Aztec (Unamuno, 1966, IV: p. 383) and laughing at the very thought that Guaraní could be made the official language of one of the Argentine provinces (Unamuno, 1966, IV: p. 1013). He did, however, celebrate the fact that certain writers such as Rubén Darío had managed to express part of their Indian nature in their work, although he quickly added that they had achieved this by writing in Castilian (Unamuno, 1966, IV: pp. 1027-28).

As far as the Castilian language which was spoken and written in the Spanish American nations was concerned, it is true to say that Unamuno was sensitive to, and often appreciative of, difference, albeit *within* a hegemonic model. He once wrote that each nation should speak its own Castilian and not "sujetarse en el uso de ella a prescripciones de ninguno de esos pueblos" [submit in the way they use it to the laws laid down by any of those peoples] (Unamuno, 1966, IV: p. 577). Indeed he seems to have seen such linguistic diversity as some sort of defence against the influence of the French language in Spanish America, as he implied in the review of a work by Manuel Bernárdez (Unamuno, 1966, IV: pp. 855-56), and also as a means to appropriate the *modernista* desire to "enriquecer, movilizar y flexibilizar el castellano" [enrich Castilian and make it more dynamic and flexible] (Unamuno, 1966, IV: p. 804). And yet he was firmly opposed to the idea that each nation was forging its own language or that there was any language that could be called Argentine, Mexican or Peruvian. In this, Unamuno was deliberately striking a blow against the cultural nationalists, especially those in Argentina who had been told by the linguistician Lucien Abeille and the politician and former President Carlos Pellegrini that there really was such a thing as an Argentine language and that, within a few centuries, Castilian would have spawned a whole series of new languages in Spanish America. Abeille was a Frenchman and Pellegrini "un argentino de origen italiano" [an Argentine of Italian ancestry], he said petulantly, and neither of them had any idea of how the Castilian language was spoken and developing in Spain herself (Unamuno, 1966, IV: p. 636). For this reason, Unamuno constantly berated his Spanish American readers for their ignorance of Peninsula Castilian, claiming that "el lenguaje hablado en los distintos pueblos americanos se diferencia del lenguaje hablado en España mucho menos de lo que creen los que allí lo oyen hablar sin oírlo hablar aquí" [there is much less difference between the language spoken by the different (Spanish) American peoples and the language spoken in Spain than those who hear it spoken over there but not over here actually believe] (Unamuno, 1966, III: p. 911). There may be differences in the Castilian used in "la espuma literaria, escrita y en cierto modo muerta" [the literary and written froth that is, in a way, dead], but in the all-important spoken and popular language, the language used by the noble *pueblo*, there was no real difference between the Castilian used on both sides of the Atlantic (Unamuno, 1966, IV: pp. 587-88).[18]

It is at this point, however, that he takes his argument a step further, just as he had done in his writings on Basque and Catalan. Once he has established that all the Hispanic nations are in fact speaking the same language (Unamuno, 1966, IV: p. 635), he can then exhort them to infuse it with their own spirit: "La cuestión hay que ponerla, a mi juicio, en otro terreno, y es que los argentinos y todos los demás pueblos de habla española reivindiquen su derecho a influir en el progreso de la común lengua española" [In my opinion, the issue should be looked at in a different way, that is, that the Argentines and all the other Spanish-speaking peoples should demand the right to influence the progress of the common Spanish language] (Unamuno, 1966, IV: p. 576). In a sense, he is putting them on the same footing not only as his regional compatriots in Spain but as all Spaniards, because every country and region in the Hispanic world, by using Castilian in its own way, is contributing to the creation of a new language, which Unamuno variously refers to as "la lengua española o hispanoamericana" [the Spanish or Spanish American language] (Unamuno, 1966, IV: pp. 242 and 570; IX, p. 229) or "la lengua hispánica" [the Hispanic language] (Unamuno, 1966, III: p. 915). In this process, as Unamuno is very careful to make clear, no one country, not even Spain, should be seen as the leader. He continually and even obsessively reiterates this point. When it comes to the question of language, he denounces any exclusivism (Unamuno, 1996, p. 157) and opposes all "monopolios puristas" [purist monopolies] (Unamuno, 1966, IX: p. 229) such as that of the Real Academia Española which encourages "un casticismo trasnochado" [an outdated and inauthentic traditionalism] (Unamuno, 1966, IV: p. 373). Such attitudes can only hurt the relationship between Spain and her former colonies, since "[l]a necia y torpe política metropolitana nos hizo perder las colonias, y una no menos necia ni menos torpe conducta en cuestión de lengua y de literatura podría hacernos perder [...] la hermandad espiritual" [foolish and clumsy metropolitan policies made us lose the colonies, and a no less foolish and clumsy conduct in matters to do with language and literature could well make us lose (...) our spiritual brotherhood] (Unamuno, 1966, III:

---

[18] By saying this, Unamuno is deliberately inverting the more commonly-held belief (see Lapesa Melgar, 1997, p. 526) that the Castilian used in *intellectual* texts is the same throughout the Hispanic world.

p. 915). In this creation of the new Hispanic language, Spain must not see herself as "la metrópoli" or the "madre patria" [mother country] (Unamuno, 1996, p. 174) but as the spiritual sister of all the Spanish-speaking countries (Unamuno, 1966, IV: p. 1020).

This Hispanic language is therefore "una y varia, flexible y rica, dilatada como sus dominios" [single and various, flexible and rich, spread out like its dominions] (Unamuno, 1966, IV: p. 242) and can only gain strength from its variations because, "[p]or fuerte que pueda llegar a ser la tendencia a la diferenciación, la tendencia a la integración será mayor" [however strong the tendency towards differentiation may become, the tendency towards integration will be stronger] (Unamuno, 1996, p. 154). It is also, however, more of a project than a reality, "una creación continua" [a continuous creation] (Unamuno, 1966, IV: p. 628) that is "de continuo naciendo, haciéndose – y deshaciéndose y rehaciéndose -, en perpetuo proceso constituyente y reconstituyente" [continually being born, making itself – and unmaking and remaking itself – in a perpetual process of construction and reconstruction] (Unamuno, 1966, IV: p. 461). And, in the light of his belief that "la lengua es la sangre del espíritu" [language is the blood of the spirit], it is obvious that what Unamuno is saying about language he is also saying about the spiritual outlook and mission of the Hispanic peoples: by forging a common language, he says, our diverse peoples are also forging a "visión común" [common vision] (Unamuno, 1966, IV: p. 499). Here we reach the very nub of Unamuno's understanding of the "común destino histórico" [common historic destiny] of all Hispanic nations (Unamuno, 1966, IV: p. 499). In 1935, he wrote that "ya se anuncia [...] una interpretación, una conceptuación del universo, y de su vida y de su destino, hispánica, una filosofía brotada de nuestro verbo universal" [there is already on the horizon an interpretation, a conceptualisation of the universe, and of its life and destiny, that is Hispanic in nature, a philosophy that has sprung from our universal Word] (Unamuno, 1966, IV: p. 653). That interpretation, that philosophy, that "verbo" [word], he called our "*hispanidad* común" [common *hispanicity*] (Unamuno, 1966, IV: p. 654).

We can now see that Unamuno's notion of *Hispanidad* is predicated on the belief that all the Hispanic nations are, through the process of differentiation and integration, engaged in the task of creating a new spirit which is "en perpetua formación" [perpetually in the process of being formed] (Unamuno, 1966, IV: p. 975).[19] And yet, when one places this belief in the context of Unamuno's whole literary and philosophical output, it can be seen to contain a fundamental inconsistency. Much of Unamuno's mature work can be read in terms of an attempt to identify and define the Quixotic philosophy that he had spoken about in *Vida de Don Quijote y Sancho* (1905) and the Conclusion to *Del sentimiento trágico de la vida* (1912). Although he had actually formulated this philosophy, at least in part, through his dialogue with Spanish America, it remained an essentially Spanish

---

[19] For a Hegelian analysis of Unamuno's belief that the Hispanic nations were involved in the process of creating a common spirit, see Pérez Prendes (1989).

conception of life which he often referred to as his "Verbo castellano" [Castilian Word] (Unamuno, 1966, IX: p. 451) or as "un Evangelio traducido a la española" [a Gospel translated in the Spanish way] (Unamuno, 1996, p. 176). Behind his call for the creation of a Hispanic language and spirit, therefore, one can perhaps identify the signs of a new and more subtle form of Spanish imperialism.

It would seem that Unamuno was well aware of this fact. For one thing, alongside his talk of the need to respect difference, one also finds many references in his work to the *union* of all Hispanic nations. As early as 1894, he wrote that the independence of the Spanish American nations "nos ha separado para unirnos en unión más alta y más profunda" [has separated us in order to unite us in a higher and deeper union] (Unamuno, 1966, IV: p. 715); in 1912, he claimed that he had done more than anyone to ensure "la unión espiritual de los pueblos de lengua española" [the spiritual union of the Spanish-speaking peoples] (Unamuno, 1966, IV: p. 967); and in 1927 he actually referred to this unified Hispanic world as "mi grande España" [my great Spain] (Unamuno, 1996, p. 508). But Unamuno could never be absolutely sure of this union: "Tal vez hemos perdido América para mejor ganarla" [Perhaps we have lost America so as to be better able to win her], he wrote in 1904 (Unamuno, 1996, p. 201), adding two years later that only Spain's Quixotic philosophy could protect Spanish America against the threat of "el horrendo mamonismo" [horrendous Mammonism] (Unamuno, 1996, p. 234). Spain, or at least Quixotic Spain, still had a lot to do, therefore, in order to save the New World from itself: she needed, in a sense, to repossess Spanish America, to recolonise her with her language and her spirit. By the 1930s, Unamuno was fully prepared to concede that such a position came close to imperialism, albeit a linguistic or spiritual imperialism. Recognising that "[s]e conquista con la palabra" [one conquers with the word] (Unamuno, 1966, IX: p. 451), he openly admitted that he was involved in the project to make the Spanish language "ecuménica, universal, imperial" [ecumenical, universal, imperial] (Unamuno, 1966, IV: p. 460 and IX: p. 460) and was therefore able to condone what he called "un imperialismo espiritual o cultural [...] a base de la lengua" [a spiritual or cultural imperialism (...) based on language] (Unamuno, 1966, IV: p. 1124). And it is with this in mind that we can best understand the only article which Unamuno ever entitled "Hispanidad", written while he was in exile in 1927 (Unamuno, 1966, IV: pp. 1081-84). He starts by saying that he uses the term *Hispanidad* in order to refer to "todas las razas espirituales" [all the spiritual races], including Portugal, which, through both union and discord, have helped to create the soul of the Peninsula (p. 1081). During the conquest and colonisation of the Americas, this soul came in contact with another soul, with *Americanidad*, and entered into dialogue with it (p. 1084). However, the implication is that *Hispanidad* – which, by this point in the article, seems to have been shorn of any reference to Portugal – remained untouched by *Americanidad* or, at the very least, tamed and dominated the American spirit. Unamuno's point seems crystal clear: the *Hispanidad* which he both searches for and proclaims is in fact the ever-evolving soul of

Spain, the "eterna y universal hispanidad quijotesca" [eternal and universal Quixotic *Hispanicity*], as he put it in a letter from 1928 (Unamuno, 1996, p. 522).

All of which returns us to our starting-point. Can Unamuno's notion of *Hispanidad* be equated with that of Maeztu in his reactionary and even proto-fascist *Defensa de la Hispanidad*? The answer to this has to be no, firstly because Unamuno always rejected the idea of a Hispanic "race" and secondly because, even at his most "imperialistic", he remained a firm opponent of any vestige of the old traditionalist and *casticista* Spanish spirit (see, for example, Unamuno, 1966, IV: pp. 648-50). But, more importantly, Unamuno's *Hispanidad*, unlike Maeztu's, was not based on the defence of orthodox Catholic values but rather on the unorthodox, agonic Christianity that he had attempted to define in *Del sentimiento trágico de la vida* and which he referred to in 1935 as "una común concepción paganocristiana" [a common pagan-Christian conception] (Unamuno, 1966, IV: p. 654). In a sense, therefore, it was Unamuno's liberal and undogmatic Christianity, as well as his view that the Hispanic spirit was more of a project than a reality, that saved him from being an ideologue of traditionalist authoritarianism. And it was also the same liberal open-mindedness that made him such an influential figure for a younger generation of Spanish writers who continued to tussle with the question of the relationship between Spain and Spanish America. In the wake of the Spanish Civil War, another moment in Spanish history which led to a sense of rupture and insecurity, Spanish writers like Américo Castro and Salvador de Madariaga, living in exile, returned to the notion of *Hispanidad*. Both distanced themselves openly from Maeztu's and Franco's use of the term – Madariaga actually called it an "enfermedad" [sickness] and a "cursilería" [pathetic affectation] (Madariaga, 1959, p. 14) – but both also defended the very Unamunian idea of a Hispanic federation based on the spiritual, anti-European and anti-materialist legacy that they believed Spain had left behind her in the New World (Castro, 1954, p. 633 and 1976, p. 26). More recently, Julián Marías, a disciple of Unamuno and of Ortega y Gasset and a survivor of the Francoist régime, called for a "recomposición de las Españas" [new coming together of the Spains] that could counteract both Spain's post-transition Europeanism and the Spanish American "myth" of a self-sufficient identity and destiny (Marías, 1995, p. 414) and could thereby take forward and develop the Hispanic religio-existentialist philosophy of life (ibid., 1995, pp. 416-21). Even in an age of global communications and ever-shifting national identities, therefore, it seems that *Hispanidad* continues to be a living as well as a polemical concept.

References

Balfour, S. (1997) *The End of the Spanish Empire, 1898-1923*, Oxford, Clarendon Press.

Castro, A. (1954) *La realidad histórica de España*, México, Ed. Porrúa.

-----------. (1976) "The Meaning of Spanish Civilization", in José Rubia

Barcia (ed.), *Américo Castro and the Meaning of Spanish Civilization*, Berkeley, University of California Press, pp. 23-40.

Darío, R. (1983) *Cantos de vida y esperanza*, Madrid, Austral.

Davis, H. E. (1972) *Latin American Thought: A Historical Introduction*, New York, The Free Press.

Franco, J. (1967) *The Modern Culture of Latin America: Society and the Artist*, London, Pall Mall Press.

Hennessy, A. (2000) "Ramiro de Maeztu: *Hispanidad* and the Search for a Surrogate Imperialism", in J. Harrison and A. Hoyle (eds.), *Spain's 1898 Crisis: Regenerationism, Modernism, Post-colonialism*, Manchester, Manchester University Press, pp. 105-17.

Lago Carballo, A. (1997) "La generación hispanoamericana del 98", in Juan Velarde Fuertes (ed.), *Perspectivas del 98: Un siglo después*, Junta de Castilla y León, Consejería de Educación y Cultura, pp. 49-59.

Lapesa Melgar, R. (1997) "España, creadora de una lengua universal", in Eloy Benito Ruano, *et al.*, *España. Reflexiones sobre el ser de España*, Madrid, Real Academia de la Historia, pp. 499-533.

Madariaga, S. de. (1959) *Presente y porvenir de Hispanoamérica y otros ensayos*, Buenos Aires, Ed. Sudamericana.

Maeztu, R. de. (1952) *Defensa de la Hispanidad*, Madrid, Ediciones Fax.

Marías, J. (1995) *España intelligible*, Madrid, Alianza Universidad.

Payne, S. (1987) *The Franco Régime 1936-1975*, Milwaukee, University of Wisconsin Press.

Pérez Prendes, J. M. (1989) "La proyección iberoamericana de Unamuno", in D. Gómez Molleda (ed.), *Actas del Congreso Internacional Cincuentenario de Unamuno*, Salamanca, Ediciones Universidad de Salamanca, pp. 81-90.

Pike, F. B. (1971) *Hispanismo, 1898-1936: Spanish Conservatives and Liberals and Their Relations with Spanish America*, Notre Dame, University of Notre Dame Press.

Preston, P. (1990) *The Politics of Revenge*, London, Unwin Hyman.

Ramsden, H. (1974) *The 1898 Movement in Spain*, Manchester, Manchester University Press.

Roberts, S. G. H. (2000) "El nacimiento de un prejuicio: 1898, América Latina y la galofobia de Unamuno", in Cirilo Flórez Miguel (ed.), *Tu mano es mi destino: Actas del Congreso Internacional Miguel de Unamuno*, Salamanca, Ediciones Universidad de Salamanca, pp. 417-23.

------------------. (2001) "The Reception of *Ariel* in Spain: Rodó, Unamuno and the Emergence of the Modern Intellectual", in Gustavo San Román (ed.), *This America We Dream Of: Rodó and Ariel One Hundred Years On*, London, Institute of Latin American Studies, pp. 68-91.

------------------. (2004) "'Hispanidad': El desarrollo de una polémica noción en la obra de Miguel de Unamuno", *Cuadernos de la Cátedra Miguel de Unamuno* 39, pp. 61-80.

Rodó, J. E. (1967) *Ariel*, ed. Gordon Brotherston, Cambridge, Cambridge University Press.

Shumway, N. (1991) *The Invention of Argentina*, Berkeley, University of California Press.

Storm, E. (2001) *La perspectiva del progreso: Pensamiento político en la España del cambio de siglo (1890-1914)*, Madrid, Biblioteca Nueva.

Unamuno, M. de. (1966) *Obras completas*, Vols. I-IX, ed. Manuel García Blanco, Madrid, Escelicer.

--------. (1996) *Epistolario americano (1890-1936)*, ed. Laureano Robles, Salamanca, Ediciones Universidad de Salamanca.

Viñas, D. (1995) "La mirada a Europa: Del viaje colonial al viaje estético", in D. Viñas (ed.), *Literatura argentina y política* Buenos Aires, Editorial Sudamericana, pp. 13-59.

Wainwright, J. (1993) "Bibliografía selecta de la crítica sobre el modernismo hispánico", in R. A. Cardwell and B. McGuirk (eds.), *¿Qué es el modernismo? Nueva encuesta, nuevas lecturas*, Boulder, Society of Spanish and Spanish-American Studies, pp. 379-456.

Zea, L. (1966) *The Latin-American Mind*, University of Oklahoma Press.

"Le poids des mots, le choc des photos": Conflict and the News Magazines *Picture Post* and *Paris-Match*

Nicholas Hewitt

In a retrospective article on news coverage of the Second World War in 1989, the former editor of the photo-journal *Picture Post* from 1940 to 1950, Tom Hopkinson, wrote:

> For about three decades towards the middle of the 20th century, picture magazines were the most popular journalistic source of information and entertainment throughout most of the Western world. This brief spell lasted only from about 1928 to 1960, but during that time their circulation ran into millions; journalists and cameramen were as eager to work for them as they are today for prestigious television programmes. (Hopkinson, 1989, p. 12)

This comment highlights not merely the intrinsic historical importance of the photo-journalism magazines in the decades of the 1930s, 1940s and 1950s, and which in the case of *Paris-Match* continued until the present, but also the crucial impact upon the entire production of news media: the allusion to television signifies not only an interchange of journalistic staff from the print media to the broadcast media, but also, more broadly, the way in which the news magazines of the inter-war years and beyond established a format for news presentation which influenced profoundly subsequent audio-visual coverage of news and the images which that news utilised. In other words, the way in which the news magazines dealt with news and, especially, conflict, came rapidly to determine our ways of perceiving news events, what we consider as news, the news agenda, and the filters through which the viewer perceives conflict. In this context, they are a vital ingredient to our understanding of the news agenda of conflict and its subsequent portrayal.

The history of the news magazines, and of modern journalism itself, begins, as Hopkinson recognises, with a major and permanent technological invention, namely the development in the 1920s of the miniature hand-held camera, the Leica 35mm, invented by Oskar Barnack in 1913, and launched on the market by the new company Leica in 1925.[1] As Hopkinson records, "This transformed the nature of photo-journalism from 'photography by consent' to 'photography by enterprise', or at times 'photography by theft'" (Hopkinson, 1989, p. 12), which paved the way, inter alia, for the paparazzi in their search for candid shots of the rich and famous, but also for hitherto unprecedented images of conflict and violence, as illustrated by the early career of Robert Capa (see McCabe, 1989, p. 4). It was no coincidence, therefore, that the heyday of photo-journalism in the West should have been the late 1930s, when the West was coming to terms

---

[1] See **http: //www.photoxels.com/history_leica.html**.

with wars in Abyssinia and Spain, and when the threat of a global war was a virtual certainty. Apart from the daily newspapers, which tended to rely upon textual reports from specialist correspondents, the major source of information, and, especially, visual images of conflict, which had a defining impact on the way in which ordinary people saw conflict, should have been the news magazines: *Berliner Illustrierte*, in Germany, *Life Magazine*, founded by Henry Luce in the United States in 1936, and which established itself as an international model for the genre, *Picture Post*, founded in London in 1938, and *Paris-Match*, which started life as the more humble *Match* in Paris in 1938.

All these magazines, and their numerous stable-mates, adopted a common format, remarkably similar in their content: articles on, and pictures of, popular film stars, testifying to a recurrent symbiotic relationship between the print media and the audio-visual industry; domestic and general-interest stories, often centred on the lives of ordinary people; science, technology and visions of the future; and, above all, wars and rumours of wars: the staple of the news magazines for the rest of their career. In fact, it is very doubtful if any of these magazines could have survived for as long as they did, and in the case of *Paris-Match*, right up to the present day, without the public's interest in conflict and the threat of conflict. As such, the new magazines relied upon a complex reciprocal relationship between editorial concerns and the expectations of the readership, based upon a prurient interest in conflict and fear of its consequences. As such, they laid down a template for news coverage, particularly in its visual form, which influenced indelibly the way in which we perceive and react to conflict through the mass-media.

This paper proposes to analyse two such news magazines, *Picture Post*, published in London from 1938 to 1959, and *Paris-Match*, founded in 1949 and which is still a highly successful, albeit rare, example of the survival of the genre. In both cases, two issues dominate: the role and power of the photographic image of conflict, but also its ability or inability to adapt; also the way in which the potentially contestatory power of the images, together with their attendant written texts, can be acceptable to, or assimilated by, mainstream commercial media publishing. As such, they raise important questions regarding subsequent ways of seeing conflict, together with issues of control and censorship, both overt and covert.

Picture Post

Picture Post was founded in October 1938 by the liberal, but by no means left-leaning publisher Edward Hulton, and its launch coincided with the Munich Agreement, marking a relationship between the magazine and conflict which was to last until its demise thirty years later. Indeed, such was the interest of the public in the threatening international situation, that, against all the expectations of its staff, it immediately sold out its print run of 750,000 in the South-East alone (see Hopkinson, 1989, p. 12; Hopkinson, 1948, p. 47). In fact, as Tom Hopkinson later recorded, it also owed its astonishing success to a combination of a revolution in news photography and an unusually democratic attitude towards its subject matter and its readers. To the question from a distinguished visitor as to what kind of paper *Picture Post* would be, he replied:

> It would be a shock. It would use photographs as they'd never been used before. It would show the lives of ordinary people as they were. It would treat all human beings as of equal dignity and importance. It would show the life of a charlady and the life of a big business boss, without laughing at the charlady or touching its cap at the big boss, the duke, the bishop. It would treat its own method as important – the method of the photograph. If a photograph were good, we'd print it big. We wouldn't mess about with it, write headings over it, or paint plush easels round it – which was the pleasant fancy of the day…..
> "Would the paper be political?" the visitor asked. Of course it would. All life was political – and would become a lot more so, if we were going to go on at all. (Hopkinson, 1948, p. 13)

It is interesting, incidentally, that Hopkins uses the work "shock" in his description of *Picture Post*, thus anticipating the slogan of *Paris-Match* a year later, "le poids des mots, le choc des photos" ["the weight of words, the shock of photos"].

Good photographers were essential to the success of any news magazine, and *Picture Post* was exceptionally fortunate in recruiting one of the finest news photographers of his day, Bert Hardy, who was one of the first to use a Leica 35mm camera. He subsequently went on to become a distinguished war photographer, covering the bombing of London in 1940, the Normandy invasion in 1944, the Korean War and the French war in Indochina.[2] It was essentially the high quality and dramatic impact of the photographs in Picture Post, taken by Hardy and others, which made it a newspaper of record; but it was also an unusual ambition to use photography, not merely to record events, but to shape their future course. As Hopkinson notes:

> It was with the war, and particularly after the fall of France in May-June 1940, that *Picture Post* took photo-journalism into a new element, using photographs not just to record events – at that time there were only disasters – but also to try to influence them. Photo-journalism was to become a weapon. (Hopkinson, 1989, p. 12)

Thus:

> for its first issue of 1941, at the very lowest point of Britain's fortunes, *Picture Post* devoted the whole magazine to "A Plan for Britain", virtually a blueprint for the programme which the Attlee government would carry through. (Hopkinson, 1989, p. 12)

---

[2] See "Bert Hardy", **http: //www.spartacus.schoolnet.co.uk/USAPhardy. htm**.

In this respect, the edition of the beginning of January 1944 was typical of the magazine's format and concerns. War coverage was very much to the fore, with photographs of a new phosphorus hand grenade and of Russian snipers on the Eastern Front. There was a more analytical report on the London meeting of the Council of Christians and Jews, at which the Archbishop of Canterbury "expressed his horror at the extermination of Jews in Europe" (Edelman, 1944, p. 11). At the same time, *Picture Post* willingly exploited its readership's interest in the cinema and its female film stars with a cover photograph of Betty Grable, and looked towards the post-war future with an enthusiastic project for the urban regeneration of an area of the city of Swansea. Nor was the magazine reluctant to pull its punches in criticism of certain aspects of the conduct of the war, even if, in this case, it used the indirect device of a reader's letter. Under the title "A Czech Girl says 'Amgot' Has Failed", a refugee Czech schoolgirl attacked the military occupation of Italy, in terms which would serve for Iraq 60 years later:

> There has been much discussion lately about the advantages and disadvantages of "Amgot" – the government of occupied territories. The British public has failed to realise that it is not their feelings which should be primarily considered, but the feelings of the peoples living under the yoke of Nazism, who are waiting expectantly for the day of liberation. What do they think of "Amgot"? We believe that they will clamour for the immediate setting up of a democratic government and will turn away with as much contempt from an Allied dictatorship, of however temporary nature this may be, as they did from the Nazi "herrenvolk". "Amgot" is failing: it has not succeeded in gaining the confidence of the conquered peoples, and it is high time we set about finding its successor. (*Picture Post*, 1944a, p. 26)

Further disquiet was expressed over what has become known more recently as "embedded reporting", in this case with reference to British military restrictions on the supply of photographs of the June 1944 D-Day landings. Although the landings had taken place on 6 June 1944, it was not until its issue of 24 June, over two weeks later, that *Picture Post* was able to print photographs of the event. The reason became apparent in an acerbic editorial in the July 15 number, entitled "Where are the Pictures?":

> The British Army in the past few weeks has performed some of the most terrific achievements of its long career. Where are the pictures showing what it has done? Rome fell on June 4. Since then the Allied armies under General Alexander have raced through Italy in a campaign of extraordinary brilliance. Where are the pictures? Cherbourg fell June 26-27. The dailies printed many excellent pictures of this great American victory. The pictures we should have liked to publish were those of the great tank battles fought by the British and Canadians around Caen and Tilly which had helped to make possible this success. The battle has been raging since June 11. At the moment of going to press we ask again – Where are the pictures?

They may come later. They will still have been too late. (*Picture Post*, 1944b, p. 3)

For *Picture Post*, the fault lay squarely with the British military authorities, who, unlike their American counterparts, effectively conscripted news photographers like Bert Hardy into the Army Film and Photographic Unit and had sole power over the release of their work, overruling even the Ministry of Information.

If *Picture Post* owed its phenomenal success and unique relationship with its readership to its photographic coverage of conflict, the post-war period was to prove more troublesome, with a greater reliance on glamour photographs of film stars, coverage of social issues and articles on scientific discoveries and the way of life of the future. When conflict did appear, it was gratefully seized on, as in extensive reporting on the Berlin blockade and airlift and an in-depth series of articles by the proprietor Edward Hulton on the South African Prime Minister Dr Malan and his nascent apartheid regime, concluding "Dr Malan's real fight, it seems, is with the realities of 20th-century life" (see Hulton, 1948, p. 24). This measured, but critical, approach was met with a seven-day delay in distribution of the previous issue on the orders of South African customs.

The liberal image of *Picture Post*, and that of its proprietor, however, was terminally damaged by its coverage of the Korean War in 1950. It shipped out the by now veteran war photographer Bert Hardy, together with the finest foreign reporter of his generation, James Cameron, who had recently joined *Picture Post* from the *Daily Express*. In the South Korean town of Pusan, Cameron came across a "terrible crowd of men", a "grisly mob", starving, beaten and degraded, and about to be led away to mass execution (see Cameron, 1969, pp. 132-5). As Cameron soon realised:

These prisoners were of course not convicts, nor prisoners of war; they were political hostages of the South Korean administration for whose integrity the United States and Britain and the United Nations were at the moment fighting. They were not North Koreans, but South Koreans in South Korea, whose crime – or alleged crime, since few of them had been accorded the formality of a trial – was that they had been named as opponents of the Synghman Rhee regime, the one-man oligarchy called with Asian irony the Liberal Party (*Picture Post*, 1944b, p. 133).

Accordingly, Cameron filed a dispassionate article, fully documented by Hardy's photographs, entitled "An Appeal to the United Nations": "All things considered, it was a journalistic essay of elaborate moderation" (*ibid.*, p. 146), "which could not possibly be opposed by anyone of goodwill, least of all by a journal of the liberal and humane pretensions of *Picture Post*" (*ibid.*, p. 145). Someone in a position of considerable influence, however, saw to it that the proprietor, Edward Hulton, was informed of this implicit attack on the Americans, and, in circumstances not unlike the removal of the *Daily Mirror* editor Piers Morgan in 2004 over, as it transpired, bogus photographs of British atrocities in Iraq, Tom Hopkinson was unceremoniously sacked as editor, with the terse announcement: "Tom Hopkinson has been instructed to relinquish the position of editor of *Picture Post*, following a dispute over the handling of material about the Korean War and other matters" (*ibid.*, p. 147). James Cameron resigned later, but noted that the crisis marked a watershed in the history of the magazine:

> Its proprietor issued yet another statement around which there already clung the scent of defeat: "There is no intention to change the tradition of *Picture Post*", he said, "whereby the staff have full freedom to develop their creative abilities and rely on their own judgement. It is my intention to maintain the political independence of *Picture Post*". In fact, *Picture Post* soon painlessly surrendered all the values and purposes that made it a journal of consideration, before the eyes of its diminishing public it drifted into the market of arch cheesecake and commonplace decoration, and by and by it died, as by then it deserved to do. (*Picture Post*, 1944b, p. 149)

In fact, there were other factors to the magazine's terminal decline, not least the transfer to television of most of the journalists who had made its reputation in the post-war years, but the episode of the Korean War was undoubtedly crucial.

Paris-Match

If *Picture Post* came to grief because it had raised expectations of integrity in its coverage of conflict which it could no longer sustain, *Paris-Match* has perhaps owed its survival to a more conservative approach, both politically and editorially. Initially, it came into being the same year as *Picture Post*, 1938, when the press baron Jean Prouvost, who owned the phenomenally successful daily paper *Paris-Soir*, decided to produce a news magazine on the model of *Life*. In one of the press empires which his group had absorbed, there was a weekly sports magazine called *Match*. Prouvost took control of the magazine and immediately changed its format and direction: on 5 July 1938, the new proprietor announced his intentions:

> A partir du jeudi prochain 7 juillet votre hebdomadaire sportif *Match* se transforme, élargit sa formule et devient le grand magazine du sport, des loisirs, de la vie au grand air, de la jeunesse, de l'aventure, de l'héroisme. Il vous donnera chaque semaine une puissante sélection des images de la vie moderne. *Match*, libre, indépendant, dira tout ce qu'il pense... [From Thursday 7 July next your sporting weekly *Match* is changed, has a bigger format and becomes the great magazine, of sport, leisure, outdoor life, youth, adventure, heroism. It will give you every week a powerful selection of images of modern life. *Match*, free, independent, will say what it thinks...] (*Match*, 1938, p. 2; Hewitt, 1991, pp. 111-128)

As with *Picture Post*, the new format was immediately successful, taking *Match* to a pre-war circulation of 1,400,000 by October 1939, a feat which owed much to "les événements et la tension internationale" ["events and international tension"] (Boegner, 1969, p. 55). The defeat of France in 1940 and the subsequent occupation put an end to this glittering career, although Prouvost, based in Lyon, was able to launch a replica, called *7 Jours*, which sold 700,000 copies in the Southern Zone alone (*ibid.*, p. 8). After the Liberation, this success looked rather more ambiguous and Prouvost, who had also served as Pétain's Haut Commissaire de la Presse at Vichy, was tainted with the whiff of collaboration, which seriously delayed his return to mainstream press actvity. In fact, it was not until 1949 that he was in a position to relaunch *Match*, but with the modified title of *Paris-Match*.

The delay in re-launching *Paris-Match* was in many ways providential. In the immediate aftermath of the Liberation, the market-place was crowded with photo magazines, some of which, like the Communist-oriented *Regards*, dated from the pre-war period, and others of which, like *Le Monde illustré*, *France-Illustration*, *Noir et Blanc*, *Point de vue*, *Images du monde*, *Nuit et Jour*, *Ambiance* and *Radar*, were new (Bellanger *et al.*, 1975, p. 310). In fact, the market-place was not merely crowded, but over-crowded, and most of these titles were unable to withstand the crippling "grève du livre" of 1947 and the major crisis which affected the entire French press from 1949 to 1953 and which led to the disappearance of 137 weekly publications (Faucher and Jacquemart, 1968, p. 220). With its later launch date, its professional experience derived from the pre-war period and the Occupation, and the compelling model of *Life* magazine, *Paris-Match* was able to dominate the market over its more fragile and decidedly more old-fashioned rivals. In the 1950s, one of its major competitors, André Beyler's *Radar*, still used engraved line-drawings for its front covers, with the consequence that, whereas the circulation of *Paris-Match* continued to rise, that of *Radar* declined from 500,000 to 300,000 between 1952 and 1957, and, despite a belated attempt at a new format, Radar disappeared from the screen in 1962 (*ibid.*, pp. 220, 234).

Not, however, that *Paris-Match* had things all its own way in the first years of its career: Philippe Boegner recalls that at the end of 1949, circulation was static at 200,000 copies, advertising was proving difficult to attract, and the entire operation was running at a deficit of 250 million francs (Boegner, 1969, pp. 41-2). What saved the magazine was effectively war and death: its coverage of the Korean War and, most importantly, its reporting of famous deaths: Marshall Pétain in 1951, Marshall de Lattre de Tassigny, and King George VI of England, to which *Paris-Match* devoted two special numbers, each selling more than a million copies (*ibid.*, p. 57). Most important of all was its coverage of the final phase of the Indochina War, culminating in the Battle of Dien Bien Phu, in which it raised one of the nurses on the battlefield to the iconic status of "l'Ange de Dien Bien Phu" and established itself as the major source of information, over the cinema newsreels and the still-primitive and embryonic French television.

From the very beginning, *Paris-Match* had adopted a formula, essentially derived from *Life* and shared with *Picture Post*, which it later expressed in the slogan "Le poids des mots, le choc des photos": a clever blend of textual reportage and analysis with dramatic photography. Within this format, its content ranged from the trivial to the portentous, with a marked preference for coverage of war and conflict. The very first number, on 29 March 1949, carried news stories on changes in the Soviet leadership, Winston Churchill's speech to the European Assembly, but led with extensive photographic coverage of the Chinese revolution: "Panique à Shanghai, ruée vers le riz, ruée vers l'or" ["Panic in Shanghai, rice rush, gold rush"]. At the same time, there was a full-page photograph of General Giroud's body lying in state in the Invalides, together with four pages devoted to French domestic politics. Later articles introduced a lighter tone, with stories on French technological advances in the realm of defence, the painter Raoul Dufy, the world-wide impact of Paris fashion, and reviews of films and theatre.

This powerful formula, which has remained broadly unchanged since 1949, was, of course, highly conservative, both explicitly, particularly through the articles of the magazine's political editor Raymond Cartier, and implicitly, in the way in which the "choc des photos" was always effectively neutralised by the mixture of drama and trivia in the format itself and in the perspective offered. *Paris-Match* was often compared to a middle-aged Frenchman in slippers looking out of the window of his comfortable apartment at events which might be harrowing in themselves, but which remain safely at one remove. Or, as Roland Barthes comments famously in *Mythologies*, looking at the outside world,

> Voilà le lecteur de *Match* confirmé dans sa vision infantile, installé un peu plus dans cette impuissance à imaginer autrui que j'ai déjà signalée à propos des mythes petits-bourgeois. [Here we have the reader of *Match* confirmed in his or her infantile view of the world, a little more stuck in that impotence to imagine anyone else that I have already referred to in respect of *petits-bourgeois* myths.] (Barthes, 1970, p. 66).

It is no coincidence, therefore, that, if *Paris-Match* owed its early success and, indeed, survival, to René Coty's Fourth Republic, it should have been able to accommodate itself superbly with De Gaulle's Fifth Republic, in which the "impossibility of imagining anyone else" was reinforced by a celebration of apparent enhanced national pride and international prestige.

In this context, the year 1967 was a good one for *Paris-Match*. Not merely did it cover urban riots in the United States, the Cultural Revolution in China, anti-French rioting in Djibouti and revolutionary movements in South America (in which, characteristically, the magazine employed the veteran journalist and adventure-novelist Jean Lartéguy to track down Che Guevara), it also had two major wars: the Six-Day War in the Middle East and the ongoing war in Vietnam, the scene of its previous triumph. In all of these, but particularly in the Middle East and Vietnam, *Paris-Match* was able to call upon unprecedented resources, both from its own photographers and journalists and from news agencies. Also, in both wars, the magazine was apparently able to break away from some of the controls of embedded journalism which had restricted the operations of *Picture Post* in World War II and which was to become such an issue in the first, but especially the second, Gulf War.

Thus, during the Six Day War, *Paris-Match* could proudly announce that it could put ten correspondents in the field, covering each of the warring camps, reflecting, incidentally, the ambiguous attitude of the French government to the combatants. Nevertheless, the war narrative depends upon a result and, in the same way that *Picture Post* dwelt upon the pathos of the vanquished in World War II, *Paris-Match* emphasised scenes of defeat and flight. In Vietnam, at the same time, the coverage is both similar and more nuanced. Again, *Paris-Match* prides itself in reporting the war from both sides. Thus, in its number of 25 February 1967, it carries pictures from the photographer Pic with the North Vietnamese in Nam-Dinh and from Marc Riboud on board the USS Enterprise. Similarly, it published pictures by the American photographer Lee Lockwood from Hanoi and stills from a film by Joris Ivens, again in Hanoi. On 28 October, it carried a report on the Vietcong themselves. At the same time, *Paris-Match*'s coverage of Vietnam exploits the same narrative of suffering and defeat, but this time exclusively on the American side. Here, the symbolism is clear: the North Vietnamese are depicted either as resilient victims and survivors or as powerful adversaries; the Americans, in contrast, are bogged down in Con-Thien, their very own Verdun, and carried away wounded from the battle of Hill 881. The American predicament is summed up in the photograph of an exhausted and terrified marine at Con-Thien by the American photographer David Douglas Duncan.

Interestingly, in 1967, Paris-Match was at pains to highlight the role of women reporters in situations of conflict, although often in a curiously subordinate role: the photographer and heroine of the article on the Cultural Revolution, "Une Française chez les Gardes Rouges" ["French woman amidst the Red Guards"], is identified as Suzanne Vincent, "femme du correspondant de l'A.F.P." ["wife of the A.F.P. correspondent"] (*Paris-Match*, 1967b, p. 28), whilst one of the main stories from Vietnam concerns the war correspondent Michèle Ray, taken prisoner by the Vietcong, but better known as the former model for Chanel under the name of "Moune" (*Paris-Match*, 1967a, p. 45).

In contrast, whilst the work of women reporters is no longer a story, the coverage of the 2003 Gulf War is considerably more limited in its scope. *Paris-Match* is at pains to emphasise the suffering wrought on the civilian population of Iraq, but also careful to avoid attributing blame. At the same time, unlike its coverage of the Six Day War and Vietnam, *Paris-Match*'s photographs of the American army have a staged appearance which, in group shots, is reminiscent of the earliest days of war photography.

Conclusion

This issue, in its turn, raises an important point regarding the photographic depiction of conflict in general: namely its effectiveness and its ability to evolve. Tom Hopkinson makes a powerful case for the former, and asserts the photograph's superiority over the moving image:

> Think back to the Vietnam War, and two pictures come to every mind: the street execution of a Vietcong guerrilla by a South Vietnam police chief; and the little girl running down the road, naked and screaming, her clothes burned off by napalm. Both sequences have been shown many times on television, but it is the still version which makes the lasting impact. The reason is plain. In the filmed version the bullet is fired, and all is over. But in the still photograph his face, distorted by fear of death, is for ever distorted; and the girl, twenty years later, is still running down the road. (Hopkinson, 1989, p. 12)

It is also true that the news photograph, consciously or unconsciously, appeals to experiences derived from our collective visual culture in art history: the celebrated photograph by Robert Capa of the death of a militia-man in the Spanish Civil War, so celebrated that it has been accused of being staged, owes its effect, not merely to the drama and pathos of the incident, but also to the allusion to crucifixion. Similarly, the picture of the shocked and grieving student at Kent State University over the body of a fellow-student shot in 1970 by the Ohio National Guard, is both the record of an event and a *pietà*.

However, if this is a powerful source for the news photograph's impact, it also raises questions regarding its adaptability. War reporting, and war photography, began in the Crimean War, where, as in the American Civil War, cumbersome equipment and slow film speeds ruled out anything but static, or staged, set-piece shots. In spite of Hopkinson's undoubtedly correct assessment of the technological impact of the Leica, however, even during the World War I, stills from undeniably clumsy movie cameras could achieve the same effect as action photography a generation later. In other words, the aesthetic format was created before the technological means to implement it. It is difficult, indeed almost impossible, to distinguish between frames of advances of troops in World War I and the photographs of similar advances in World War II, just as it is almost impossible to identify photographs of defeat or misery. And, if war photography is curiously impervious to chronology, it is also remarkably non-partisan: the captured British Tommy at Dunquerque, photographed for the German magazine *Signal*, stares at the camera with the same exhaustion and resignation as his American counterpart at Con-Thien in 1967. In other words, in the same way that there are alleged to be only seven basic plots for novels, of which others are merely variants, and only six core jokes, it may well be that photography in conflict follows a similarly restricted pattern, which endows the images with the enhanced power of accumulated memory, but which also contains our perception of conflict within a more limited field than we might normally accept. The line between originality and cliché, or visual shorthand, thus becomes more blurred. However, the role of the news magazines and the invention of photo-journalism in defining the way in which we perceive conflict, and which spills over into all areas of visual culture, becomes more important.

This also, finally, raises questions regarding the relationship between the viewer and the object, and here the issues are complex. On the one hand, the editorial concern of the news magazines must be to disquiet, disturb and galvanise their readers in the wake of the issues raised and portrayed. On the other, as Barthes indicates, there is a more ambiguous process at work: the Western reader, often likened in the case of *Paris-Match* to a comfortable bourgeois clad in slippers and looking out from the comfort of his window to the mayhem below, is both challenged and reassured by the images and texts contained in the magazine he is holding. The anguish is compensated by happiness and for every image of pain and misery, there is a picture of a reassuringly comfortable lifestyle. The news magazines, like their successors in the broadcast media, wove a complicated menu of concern and happiness which constituted a winning formula.

References

Barthes, R. (1970) *Mythologies*, Paris, Seuil, coll. "Points".

Bellanger, C., *et al.* (1975) *Histoire générale de la presse française, IV: De 1830 à 1958*, Paris, Presses Universitaires de France.

Boegner, P. (1969) *Presse, argent, liberté*, Paris, Fayard.

Cameron, J. (1969) *Point of Departure*, London, Panther.

Edelman, M. (1944) "A Good Augury for 1944", *Picture Post,* 8 January.

Faucher, J.-A. and N. Jacquemart. (1968) *Le Quatrième pouvoir: la presse française de 1830 à 1960*, Paris, Special Number of *L'Echo de la Presse et de la Publicité*.

Hewitt, N. (1991) "The Birth of the Glossy Magazines: the Case of *Paris-Match*", in B. Rigby and N. Hewitt (eds.), *France and the Mass Media*, Basingstoke, Macmillan.

Hopkinson, T. (1948) "How *Picture Post* began", *Picture Post*, 2 October.

----------------. (1989) "When Britain armed itself with a Camera", *The Weekend Guardian*, Saturday-Sunday 11-12 February.

Hulton, E. (1948) "Where is South Africa Going? I talk to Dr Malan", *Picture Post*, 11 December.

McCabe, E. (1989) "Image Makers", *The Weekend Guardian*, Saturday-Sunday 11-12 February.

Paris-Match. (1967a), "Notre consoeur Moune ex mannequin de Chanel", 28 January.

------------. (1967b), "Une Française chez les Gardes Rouges", 18 February.

Picture Post. (1944a), "A Czech Girl says 'Amgot' has failed", 8 January.

-------------. (1944b), "Where are the Pictures?", 15 July.

Remembering the Future: the Construction of Gendered Identity and Diversity in the Balkans

Patrizia Violi

Memories for the future

In recent years memory has become the object of increasing interest in domains of the human sciences far exceeding the focus of traditional historic research.[1] History has always been, obviously, the discipline that, *par excellence*, deals with the reconstruction and conservation of memories. Today however, on the geographical map of the academic disciplines, research on memory has multiplied to such a degree that there is even a specific domain recognised as "Memory Studies". Memory seems to have become an object of study in itself, in accordance with a move towards the "objectification" of various topics that is currently quite popular in our contemporary research landscape. So now we have, besides the well established field of Cultural Studies, also Tourism Studies, Memory Studies, and even Holocaust Studies.

In this vein, a large number of corpora with memories, life stories, interviews and similar documents have been collected, especially regarding conflict and post-conflict situations, and these are often available on the web. The web is an ideal place to keep trace of a virtually unlimited memory that might well extend to thousands and thousands of individual records, becoming factually, and not only metaphorically, the cultural encyclopaedia of our own civilisation.

There is however a risk in such an operation, the illusion that the more data, testimonies, or life stories we collect, the more we will be able to "reproduce" the past and thus capture it as an objective, "complete" reality. This of course cannot but be an illusion. It is not through a multiplication of records that we will manage to obtain a more precise reconstruction of the past, but rather through an interrogation that, from our present time, is projected into the past, questioning our data from a specific point of view.

In this sense we could say that memories do not represent the past, unless they are put into perspective by a specific hypothesis regarding our own present time, and especially our future. To read the past, and to make sense of it, we need to examine it from the present, while bearing in mind the future. Memories and history can tell us something about our present only with a view towards the future. This is the stance I shall take in the present analysis of a particular collection of memories, an electronic archive of interviews with Kosovan women with different ethnic and religious backgrounds. The analysis of such a corpus will enable us to formulate hypotheses about the construction of gendered identity and difference, and to put forward some ideas on reconciliation practices. In this sense the reading of the past will be, in my perspective, a tool to imagine the future, and how possibly to start imagining a (difficult) future coexistence.

Two hypotheses form the basis for my work: first of all that

---

[1] See, for example, Demaria (2006).

subjectivity, our own, but also that of the other, is not an ontological entity, defined once and for all, but always the result of a complex net of relations, a place of continuous transformations and reconfigurations, of conflicts and tensions, but also of possible renegotiations. In this perspective *The Other*, in capital letters, is another metaphysical pitfall, that should be dissolved in a multiplicity of different individuals. The second hypothesis, directly connected with semiotic methodology, is that subjectivity can never be captured through an abstract definition, beyond its inscription in some specific form of manifestation, which is always a discursive practice, i.e. one of several textual *genres* in a larger sense, and socially regulated. Not only is every description of subjectivity and otherness partial but, more relevantly from a semiotic point of view, it is also constructed in discourse.

Even more complex is the case of gendered subjectivity, which is the object of the present analysis. Gender is indeed a complex semiotic construction, the result of a social sense-production that, starting from a "natural" attribution of functions based on division by sex, designs a full system of values, competences, life forms, profiling some possible narrative developments for our experience and preventing others.

The Archive "Memory and Culture of Women in Kosovo"
The electronic archive I analysed includes 34 life stories of Kosovar women of different origins – Albanian, Serbian, Roma – collected in the period 1999-2000 in Kosovo and Italy. The project was promoted by the international organisation "Women's World", in collaboration with the Women's Centre of Bologna, which at the time was running a number of projects in Kosovo, and the Schuman Center at the European University Institute in Florence. It is officially "signed" by Luisa Passerini, Enrica Capussoti and Liliana Ellena, but many more women took part in it, as interviewers, translators, web designers and so on.[2]

The archive includes a description of the original project, a framework and guide used for the interviews, transcripts of the 34 original interviews, the biographical data of the women interviewed, three "itineraries" signed by the women who took part in the project regarding the three groups of interviews in Italy: Kosovaro-Albanians, Kosovaro-Serbs, Kosovaro-Roma. In my analysis I will focus mainly on the two groups of interviews of Kosovaro-Albanians and Serbs, but some brief comments are in order here, too, on the three "itineraries". These indeed represent three autonomous texts, with an obvious framing function relative to the interviews, but at the same time they show the complex, divergent relationship between the subjective voices of the interviewers and those of the interviewees. Interestingly, the two texts devoted to the Albanian and Serb women adopt quite different strategies. While the first, by Silvia Salvatici, is in the first person, centred on the subjective and pathemic experiences of the interviewer, and foregrounding her emotional and even somatic reactions, the itinerary framing the Serb interviews, by Liliana Ellena, is, on the

---

[2] The archive is hosted today by the web site of the Women's Centre of Bologna, at **http: //www.women.it/bibliotecadelledonne/donne_kossovo**.

contrary, fairly objective – a kind of historical reportage packed with data. Seen from this point of view, these itineraries play an important role in the construction of the overall sense of the archive: indeed it would be a mistake to think of the archive as merely a container for interviews. On the contrary, the archive is a complex textual object, whose entire sense emerges from the interaction of its various components. In particular, the speaking voices and their different subjectivities have a crucial role here: if the whole site can be seen as a generalised, impersonal enunciator, the singular voices of the interviewers become more specific forms of "delegated enunciators".[3]

Gender and *genre*: women's life stories

The aim of the project – as described by Luisa Passerini on the archive website– is to save and transmit personal and community memories related to cultural traditions in historical periods of emergency, such as the Kosovo war. In this perspective it is worth noting that women are taken as the "natural" keepers of community memory, and they are therefore seen as competent subjects endowed with specific knowledge about traditions and everyday life, a kind of "gender competence", so to speak. The interview guide is particularly enlightening in this respect.

In this process, gender competence is both presupposed and simultaneously constructed by the discourse of the archive, in such a way that we could say that the role and function of women in preserving and transmitting cultural tradition – that to which I refer as gender competence – is in part a *genre* construction. More specifically, in the case we are examining, gender representation is the result of a particular textual *genre* in which it is embedded, i.e. the autobiographical life story interview. The life story interview is a highly specific *genre* often used in women's history because it can voice what is generally hidden in official histories, especially everyday knowledge and experiences forgotten by "official" histories of international relations, wars and treaties.

In such a choice we can see the sign of a double valorisation: on the one hand the valorisation of the "residual" aspects of life, more related to everyday experience, which are generally left at the margins of historical research; on the other hand the valorisation of the singular individuals who are part of a collective history, to whom the life story interviews give voice. In our case, "to give voice" is certainly not a metaphorical expression, since life stories were first used in oral history, starting in the fifties and sixties. In the web site of the archive we can only find the transcripts of the interviews, and this is of course an inevitable reduction and flattening of the original richness of the rhythm, intonation and physical substance of real voices. The transcription also loses much of the intrinsically dialogical form of the interview, especially when other people were present during the interview.

Life story is a textual *genre* endowed with specific features. At the level of discourse structure it is characterizsed by the form of an

---

[3] On this issue see Lorusso and Violi (2004)

ongoing discourse, similar to a conversation. In this sense it is a kind of non-planned or incompletely planned form of discourse. Certainly there is a pre-existing script to guide the development of the interview. The guideline does not however represent a rigid structure, and each interview has, so to speak, its own life, depending on the situation, the different foci of attention, the attitudes and inclinations of the interviewees and, last but not least, the specific relationship established during the interview. From the very same script, very different discursive elements can emerge. At the level of enunciation, a life story is always a dialogical text, built up around the interaction of at least two voices. Quite often in our corpus, other people are present, having the role of what Goffman (1981) defined as Overhearers.

As far as thematic content is concerned, life stories are mainly focused on everyday life and personal experience, but they are not rigidly structured, and allow a lot of potential for alternative developments, varying considerably depending on the interviewer and the relationship between interviewer and interviewee. As we saw, life story interviews are embedded in a more complex text, the computer archive itself, producing a kind of hierarchy of textual levels and genres. From this point of view, the archive is a complex multi-layered text type that includes different sub-texts: the project, the schema, the itineraries, the interviews, all functioning together as a complex frame for life stories. In a way we could consider the whole archive, with its textual complexity, as a new textual *genre*. My decision to concentrate mainly on life stories depended on the focus of the present analysis: the construction of gendered identity and difference within a highly specific discursive *genre*. While not believing that gendered subjectivity is *only* a discourse strategy, an effect of meaning inscribed into texts, it is certainly *also* a process, a construction that takes place within discursive practices. In particular the schematic script that guides interviews is quite enlightening on this matter: it is completely focused on personal life, family traditions, domestic habits. In a way, we could say that the script shapes and prefigures at one and the same time a given idea of gender, focusing on some specific aspects of it and predetermining the modalities of expression of gendered subjectivity. This is not a criticism of the interview schema, which will prove to be quite productive, but a way to remind us how discourse form is never "innocent".

Yet life stories are not only the report of individual lives, they cannot but be read upon the background of a particular socio-historical conflict. Life stories, as a *genre*, include and intertwine both the private experience dimension and the socio-historical dimension of a whole culture and a collectivity. This is what makes them extraordinarily interesting texts from a semiotic point of view, since we can see at work, as in a kind of virtual laboratory, meaning dynamics that belong to a psycho-semiotics of personal experience together with a socio-semiotics of culture. Or, more precisely, a semiotics of *cultures*, since a plurality of many and different cultures inhabit the voices of these women. Gender too can be seen, in this perspective, as a multidimensional category constructed at the same time by personal, individual experience and socio-historical elements. To read these texts one constantly needs to keep in mind how culture affects the construction of that which we are used to calling "subjectivity", and also how individuals may develop very different responses to the same cultural environment. Two general issues are involved in this double movement. The first refers to what I would call the "subjectivisation" process: subjectivity should not be seen as something given and organied once and for all, but rather as an ongoing process of construction and transformation. And sometimes a process of deconstruction, as tragically testified in some of our interviews. The second issue is the very complex question of individuality, not often taken into consideration in semiotic research, which is more oriented toward generalisation. Life stories reframe the historical dimension at the level of individuals, reading generality explicitly though individual experience. Semiotics has always been concerned with general forms and, in that particular approach, subjectivity has always been taken into account only as a particular textual effect, i.e. as long as it appears as textually inscribed. It was probably only Julia Kristeva who claimed the relevance of individual and unconscious subjectivity as an essential component of the meaning of texts.[4] While Kristeva's work is centred on "feminine genius", materials such as the ones we are considering here suggest a less exceptional reading of women's subjectivity, which is captured in the normality of common, everyday lives.

Individual and collective identities: identification and distance

The identity construction of the individual self emerges in the interviews on the background of two main thematic dimensions: the construction of a collective "us", i.e. the construction of ethnic and religious identities in the two groups of Albanian and Serb women; and the image of the "other", the enemy – the collective "them" – and the representation of the conflict.

Identity and conflict appear to be the two semantic isotopies that frame the form of subjectivity in discourse. First of all the individual "I" is profiled in a complex relation with a group – the "us" – that represents the culture of belonging. Such a collective actor is not however a homogeneous entity, but a highly stratified reality, where different subcultures and positions coexist with different types of relevance: traditional *vs* innovative, religious *vs* lay, nationalist *vs* more cosmopolitan.

The culture to which the individual belongs is never a singular one, but is the locus of interaction for different forces that place the subject at the centre of a complex, multidimensional network. Consequently, the relations between the "I" and the collective "us" are not univocal or

---

[4] See Kristeva 2001, 2002, 2004, on, respectively, Hanna Arendt, Melanie Klein, and Colette.

definable once and for all, but appear to be a consequence of a process of mediation between identification and distance. In some cases the "I" becomes completely collapsed into the group, so that each singular identity assumes the full array of collective values of the ethnic identity. In other cases, on the contrary, each singular woman defines herself by her opposition towards her community, and in this case the relation between "I" and "us" becomes one of contrariety.

The second axis of identification (often more powerful than the collective "us" in defining one's own identity) is the relation of the opposition between one community and the "other", the enemy. This is the polemical dimension of the conflict that opposes, as contrary terms, "us" to "them". In the semiotic square these two terms imply two other positions as their logical contradictions, the "not them" and the "not us". In the corpus of our interviews these positions are variously occupied by different actors, for example the European community or international public opinion, NATO troops, the UN representatives, and so on.

Us   Them

Not them   Not us

Different strategies can be found in the construction of the enemy: sometimes it is seen as an indistinguishable whole, sometimes it may present individually differentiated faces, names, biographies. Furthermore, it will be interesting to see the temporal and aspectual dimension of the textual construction of the enemy: sometimes there is a sudden and punctual transformation of the neighbour into the enemy; sometimes the process has a longer more gradual growth; sometimes the enemy is seen as historically given since ancient times, according to a durative aspectual perspective. The forms of representation of the Other are numerous and variable, concealed behind their apparent univocality, as well as ethnic identity.

Albanian-Kosovan women between archaism and innovation

The interviews from the Albanian-Kosovan group sketch an image of a very archaic society, deeply entrenched within a patriarchal culture, centred on a highly traditional family life. Marriages are arranged by families, and before puberty girls are promised to young boys that they might not meet or even see before the day of marriage. The level of education is quite poor, especially for girls, who generally stop going to school before high school level, and very rarely go to university. Albanian society in Kosovo is characterised by a very strong gender-based division of work; everyday life, too, is organised according to a strict separation of space and time between men and women, who have their different rituals, meeting places and communal activities strictly regulated by gender division. As a result, a fairly strong women's community and women's life parallel men's community and life, often producing a certain degree of freedom within this separated group.

The majority of the women belonging to the Albanian-Kosovan group seem to accept and share the system of values of their traditional culture: they assume without question the authority of the father and the family which are taken as "natural". Women's subjectivity seems to be inscribed in a non-problematic way in that culture. Notice that this position is also shared by some quite young women, in their forties, and even in their twenties. For this group singular subjectivity (the "I") appears to be syntonic, and in continuity with the "us" of cultural identity of the community, which is not only the extended family, but also the larger Albanian culture whose traditions and habits are widely practised. At the same time, the strong separation of the sexes offers an alternative space for feminine identification, allowing the construction of a "feminine us" within the community. Women have their own separate life, rich in relations and communal activities, from which men are excluded.

The identification with the women's group, however, is always a way of declining a general belonging to a collective identity, more than a claim of feminine autonomy. In other words, among the group of more traditional Albanian-Kosovan women, individual subjectivity seems to disappear in a larger feeling of belonging. We could make the hypothesis that the stronger the agreement with collective traditional values, the more each singular individual inscribes her own subjectivity in a collective form, whether that of Albanian culture as a whole, or that of the more restricted traditional women's community.

Within the Albanian-Kosovan group there is however a small minority with a different story. They are women between 30 and 45, with a much higher level of education and in two cases with a university degree. Their position is characterised by an explicit distance from, if not an open rebellion towards, the traditions and the values of their community, especially as far as family life is concerned. None of them accepted an arranged marriage, and all chose their husbands outside the traditional community, unknown to, and in some cases too, not accepted by, the family. Interestingly enough in these cases a quite different picture of the family appears: we are not facing an extended family, but a nuclear entity, very close to our modern western families, where the couple plays the dominant role. The role that was occupied by the father and the traditional community is covered here by the couple itself, the identity is found in the new family style, in opposition to both the traditional family and the community of women, which no longer plays a role for emancipated Albanian-Kosovans.

We could synthesise in the following way the different identity structures of the two groups: where traditional culture is still very strong, subjectivity is inscribed in a collectively regulated belonging; more emancipated, more educated women are more defined within a nuclear couple.

Albanian "us"   Nuclear couple "us"

Dependency   *Autonomy*
Tradition   *Innovation*

          Feminine collectiveness   Individual "I"

As far as representation of the enemy is concerned, we can notice an interesting difference between traditional and emancipated women in the Albanian-Kosovan group. The more emancipated women are definitely the most radical in their opposition toward Serbs, as if only in the polemic dimension are they able to retrace a sense of belonging to their community that is otherwise lost at the personal identity level. For example, one and the same woman, Manduha, while claiming her own non-traditional choice of a marriage in order to be free from family conditioning, asserts at the same time the absolute impossibility of interethnic marriage because of "psychic impossibility". The conflict here appears to be naturalised, in the sense that it is not attributed to cultural or historical reasons, but to a deeper, more archaic psychic ground, where no possible solutions are available.

Paradoxically, the position of traditional women on this topic is more open: most of them seem to assume that religion is the main reason that prevents mixed marriages. In general this group does not express their hostile feelings with the same radical negativity as the emancipated women do. This becomes particularly noticeable in recall of the traumatic experiences that almost all the Albanian-Kosovan women have suffered during the war, where most of them lost relatives, even very close ones, and material goods. Remembering these tragic facts the group of traditional women do not emphasise the pathemic, emotional side of the experience, neither do they insist on the cruelty of the enemy. Quite the opposite: in some cases even some sporadic episodes of humanity are registered, as in the interview with Zijaver, whose husband and older son were killed by Serbs, but whose younger child was saved because the soldiers were moved by the crying of this little girl.

We could say that, in a way, both the expression of pain and of rage are emotionally "neutralised", and that in general, feelings of hostility towards Serbs are less predominant. It is as if the more these women have a strong feeling of belonging to their own community, the less they seem to contraposition themselves relative to the other community. On the other hand, the more women are emancipated and the less they identify with their original culture, and thus have an identity that is more individually than collectively based, the more they emphasise the difference of the Other as Enemy.

How can we interpret such data? We might hypothesise that traditional culture functions as an "emotional container" for individual feelings and reactions: the more people feel they belong to a community that shares the same culture and value systems that they do, the more they are emotionally "contained". Traditional culture operates, so to speak, as an emotional conflict regulator; this is not to say that traditional culture weakens emotional valence, only that it gives it a less individual, more collective, form of expression, inscribing emotions within a common pathemic frame. Whenever such a containing frame is weakened, the more direct and violent becomes the expression of hate and contraposition with the Other.

Serbian women A fragmented culture:
A quite different picture emerges from the interviews with Serbian-Kosovan women. First of all, while the Albanian group is a well defined and univocal one, Serbian women do not belong to a unique common culture, and do not share the same sense of ethnic belonging. Rather, we are in the presence of a fragmented constellation of different identities: Kosovan Serbs, Montenegran Serbs, Montenegran non-Serbs, Christian Serbs and even Muslim Serbs. The lack of any univocal communal "we" explains the very weak feeling of belonging to any given community. But another element should also be considered. All the women in this group come from a much more emancipated situation than the Albanian women: the influence of patriarchal structure is much less relevant, women have always been used to a very high level of freedom, where girls have the same access to education as boys and where arranged marriages would not be conceivable. Almost all the women in this group have a university degree, and some among them work for "the internationals", as the KFOR troops are called, as interpreters. A strong awareness of, and possibly pride in, their emancipation is probably the key identity element unifying the group in the face of all other differences: more than an ethnic belonging they acknowledge a common culture of feminine emancipation that is often asserted as an element that marks a relevant difference with respect to the Albanian community. In a way, although within a very different socio-ethnic context, we find a parallelism here too between emancipation and a weaker feeling of community belonging that we have already observed in the case of the emancipated Albanians. In the case of Serbians, however, in contrast to that of the Albanians, the culture of reference was already highly fragmented and multifaceted.

Perceptions of the conflict
The transformation of relations between the two communities and the starting point of the crisis is perceived in quite different and non-univocal ways. Among the Albanian group there is no common agreement on "when" the conflict started, or in accordance with which temporal sequence it proceeded. In particular it is noticeable how the aspectual dimension of the beginning of the conflict is differently perceived. For some women, the conflict situation has always been so ("since I was a child", says Nushe), in a continual, a-temporal opposition in relation to which the actual situation is nothing more than a natural consequence.

On the other hand, many women remember a past of good and reasonably peaceable life together, for some, even excellent and without particular problems, up until 1989 or 1990, but they differ on the modality of the change. While for some women this was a sudden and in some way non-understandable transformation, others describe a more gradual transition and a progressive deterioration of relations between the two communities.

If the latter is probably the more realistic account of the effective factual reality, it is interesting to notice how widespread and diffused is the subjective perception of a sudden, sharp change. It seems that subjective memory reconfigures continuous processes in the form of discontinuities, with sudden punctual changes instead of progressive transformations. Maybe this is a realistic description of what we subjectively perceive, more than the reality of facts: often we realise all of a sudden that which *has already happened,* and that became real for us only whenever we became conscious of it. According to this hypothesis we would tend to fix, in the reconstruction of gradual events, moments of precise discontinuity, catastrophic points more than durative processes.

Within the Serbian group the most striking feature is certainly the total lack of reflection on the causes of the conflict, or on the concatenation of events and their causal links. They all describe themselves as victims of a discriminating situation, objects of an unfair disparity, both economical and political. Albanians are always represented as more powerful and rich, and are considered totally responsible for the conflict. None acknowledge any responsibility on the part of the Serbian side, nor any form of discrimination against the other community.

There is a high level of agreement on the starting point of the conflict, which is generally localised in 1980, coinciding with the Albanian protests against discrimination and lack of power. Curiously enough, nobody seems to realise the contradiction between those manifestations and the supposed privileged situation of Albanians, and nobody tries to understand the reasons for it. The lack of any analysis of the causes of the conflict, as well as the repression of a possible role on the part of the Serbian side, makes impossible and opaque any reading of the past.

Distant and close enemies
In the Serbian group, as we saw, a curious paradox seems to characterise the perception of the "other" as enemy: while the description of Albanians collectively considered is extremely conflictual and lacking any understanding, when everyday life is taken into account a very different situation emerges. Most women describe an almost friendly "community life" among the different ethnic groups before the start of the conflict, characterised by good neighbourhood relationships and the absence of tensions. In some cases two almost contradictory descriptions coexist in the same life story, without a solution or continuity. But, at least to some extent, the same shift is present also in the interviews with Albanian-Kosovan women: here too the conflict emerges when women talk in more general and political terms, while in recalling individual, everyday experience a quite different picture appears, more open to a possibility of dialogue.

What appears to be an almost schizophrenic description reveals, at a closer look, less contradictoriness than one would assume. Indeed, the two situations, the conflictual and the friendly, do not refer to *the same contexts*, but to two very different spheres: a public sphere of political and impersonal relations, where there is no direct and immediate personal knowledge, and a private sphere of neighbours and people who are personally known. While the public sphere is dominated by the conflict dimension, the private one, the one of direct interpersonal relations, seems to be more open to a possible, although difficult, contractual dimension. Notice that this not to say that neighbours *did* actually behave in a friendly way, or were any better than the unknown enemies. We know very well that unfortunately this was not the case, and awful crimes were actually committed by people who were very close. Here we are analyzing a discourse world, not the "real" one; in the realm of discourse all these women seem to make a distincton when they refer to the enemy within a dimension of direct personal knowledge, or in a more public, distant form. The latter is dominated by conflict, while the former seems more open to contact. We can summarise the difference in the following square:

Public sphere	**Private sphere**
(political space)	(family)

conflict   *contract*

Non-private sphere	**Non-public sphere**
(school, church)	(neighbours)

We could say that in these interviews, the more the women refer to everyday personal life and individual relationships, the more they seem able to shift from a conflictual to a contractual dimension and to acknowledge the humanity of the other.

If, as I suggested at the beginning, the reading of the past and its memory is meaningful insofar it can help us in (re)constructing the future, what help could such a conclusion offer us in view of a possible future? When directly addressed on this matter, both groups, and in particular the Albanian-Kosovans are very sceptical, when not openly negative, towards the possibility of a common future of peaceable cohabitation. However, if my suggestion is correct, we can hypothesise that, when people move from a more public dimension to a more interpersonally grounded one, they might change their perceptions of the other. It is at the macro level of general political discourse that we found a stronger, more irreducible opposition, while at the micro level of everyday experience and personal knowledge, a community life is still remembered. This seems an important suggestion for any practical reconciliation work in post-conflict situations, where the trauma has lacerated the most constitutive structures of social life. In such a perspective, work on life stories may acquire a value that is something more than just a collection of testimonies of collective memory. If subjectivity is also textually and discursively constructed, then a textual *genre* that focuses on individual and personal dimensions of experience may help the emergence of a freer and less homologated subject than the one inscribed in other discourse forms, from traditional media to historical discourse. And in doing so it may become at least one small contribution to the difficult path of coexistence.

References

Demaria, C. (2006) *Semiotica e memoria: Analisi del post-conflitto*, Rome, Carocci.

Goffman, E. (1981) *Forms of Talk*, Philadelphia, University of Pennsylvania Press.

Kristeva, J. (2001) *Hannah Arendt*, New York, Columbia University Press.

-----------. (2002) *Melanie Klein*, New York, Columbia University Press.

-----------. (2004) *Colette*, New York, Columbia University Press.

Lorusso, A.M. and P. Violi. (2004) *Semiotica del testo giornalistico*, Bari, Laterza.

Part 4
Literatures

"It's just what they called themselves"
The Restitution of Indigenous Identity in South African Fiction

Elizabeth Taylor

In November 1497, the Portuguese explorer Vasco da Gama entered in his diary one of the earliest descriptions, in a European language, of the inhabitants of Southern Africa:

> The inhabitants of this country are tawny-coloured [...] Their food is confined to the flesh of seals, whales, and gazelles and the roots of herbs. They are dressed in skins, and wear sheaths over their virile members. Their numerous dogs resemble those of Portugal and bark like them. (Ley, 1947, p. 5)

Da Gama had anchored in a bay on the west coast of Africa which he named St Helena. The day after he made this entry he ordered the capture of a man, "small of stature", who was gathering honey among the bushes above the shore line. The Portuguese, anxious to make a good impression, sat their captive down to dinner where he "ate of all we ate".

The sailors dressed the honey-gatherer in European clothes and rowed him back to land. This paternalistic behaviour had the desired effect for when, some weeks later, da Gama anchored off São Bras, Saint Blaize (the modern Mossel Bay, a small port east of Cape Town) the Portuguese were greeted by "a large group of natives [who] came down to the shore, bringing with them oxen, cows and sheep", for the news had apparently reached them that these white strangers even gave away what was their own. Reassured that the natives were friendly, da Gama and his crew went ashore to be welcomed by the local orchestra:

> They forthwith began to play four or five flutes,[1] some producing high notes and others low ones, thus making a pretty harmony for negroes who are not expected to be musicians; and they danced in the style of negroes. The captain-major then ordered the trumpets to be sounded, and we, in the boats, danced, and the captain-major did so likewise. (Ley, 1947, p. 5)

On this occasion the Portuguese traded three bracelets for a black ox whose meat they found "as toothsome as the beef of Portugal".

People have lived in southern Africa from very ancient times, perhaps as long ago as the 8th millennium BC. The KhoiSan, as they are now generally described, were hunter-gatherers; the San (*Boesman* in Afrikaans, Bushmen later on in English) small of stature, light-skinned, great hunters and story tellers, were genetically related to Khoikhoi who were the agro-pastoralists described by da Gama (Moisert, 1992). The

---

[1] The *gora*, a reed flute played only by men, the favourite musical instrument of the Khoi.

Khoikhoi (whose name means "man of men") were taller than the San, probably because of the meat and milk in their diet, but still light-boned and brown, rather than black complexioned (Ross, 1999).

It was not long before da Gama's romantic picture of this early encounter between Europeans and the Khoikhoi was replaced by accounts of more frightening incidents. The Portuguese fleets which soon began regular sailings on the *Carreira da India*, sought the south-east trade winds to sweep them round the dangerous Cape up the east coast of Africa where they established fortified ports. However in 1510, three East Indiamen returning home were given permission by Dom Francisco de Almeida, the first Portuguese Viceroy in India, to moor in Table Bay so that they might go ashore in search of fresh water. It was a disastrous decision. In a skirmish with a handful of Khoikhoi who fought with hardened fire-sticks using their oxen as shields, the viceroy and at least twelve captains were killed. The defeat of these aristocrats by men regarded as primitive savages was a shock long remembered by the Portuguese, who subsequently concentrated their African efforts on the eastern seaboard of the continent.

For the rest of the century many caravels laden with spices, silks and gold bullion were driven by storms onto the shifting sands off the eastern coast of southern Africa. Among the accounts of shipwreck which reached Europe was that of the wreck of the São João in 1553, with the news that local savages had butchered the nobleman, Manoel de Sousa, his wife and children. The Portuguese read with horror of the last hours of Dona Leonor who, left naked:

> flung herself on the ground immediately and covered herself completely with her hair, which was very long. She made a hole in the sand in which she buried herself up to the waist and never arose from it again. (Ley, 1947, p. 257)

Accounts of shipwrecks and of the sufferings of those few who survived and returned home were printed in cheap pamphlets tied together with cord (string literature) and sold in the streets of Lisbon. It did not take long before these inhabitants of southern Africa were regarded by Europeans as the most bestial and sordid of all the peoples of the continent. In stark contrast, the Bantu-speaking tribes, who began introducing agriculture south of the Limpopo river from about the first millennium AD and who had become the largest indigenous group by the time Europeans came to colonise Africa, were sometimes regarded as examples of the "noble savage".

> Nevertheless, most of what we consider to be evil is forbidden also in Bantu society and what we hold to be good is also recommended by them (Schapera, 1953, p. 270).

By the mid-seventeenth century, Portuguese domination of the spice trade had been succeeded by Dutch maritime power. The Dutch East India Company became almost a "nation within a nation", legally empowered to wage war and to govern its own territories. In 1652 the

Company sent an official, Jan van Riebeeck, to the Cape with orders to establish a watering-post for its ships on their long hazardous voyage to the Far East. Van Riebeeck's *Dagregister* is the first sustained record, in a European language, of life at the Cape. He records his struggle to persuade the local Khoikhoi to barter cattle, his failure to grow enough food for his own garrison, let alone the crews of passing ships, his problems with the growing dissatisfaction of the men under his command. Indeed, his Dutch outpost proved an expensive venture; some years food even had to be imported from the Company's headquarters in Batavia.

Soon after his arrival, van Riebeeck was visited by a man called Autshumao, or Autshumato, a Khoikhoi chief who had earlier been taken aboard an English ship which called at the Cape for water. The sailors named him Harry and taught him some English on a voyage to the East. At first, Autshumao had welcomed the Dutch on behalf of his people and expressed a wish to barter with the strangers. However, relations between the Europeans and the locals soon deteriorated, particularly once van Riebeeck released a handful of his discontented men from the Company's service, allowing them to leave the vicinity of his small fort to farm land along the banks of the Liesbeek river. These would become the first Dutch settlers, the Free Burghers or *Boers*. This was a permanent settlement the locals had not foreseen. Harry protested at the loss of his tribe's traditional grazing grounds. By this time Harry's people, the Goringhaikonas, had been nicknamed Hottentot, a reference to the alluvial clicks of their language. This word was later to enter the *Oxford English Dictionary* with the secondary and pejorative meaning of "person of inferior intellect and culture". The Goringhaikonas' dietary habits (raw sheep entrails draped round their necks was the Khoikhoi version of a mid-morning snack), social customs, nakedness and unwillingness to part with their cattle, had not endeared them to the Europeans. The Dutchman told Autshumao that the country was big enough for all to share. Despite this declaration, the Free Burghers decided that "a day would be set aside for prayer and fasting, and the weeks thereafter for ridding the surroundings of the Hottentot scourge" (Becker, 1985, p. 46).

The Goringhaikonas proved to be an elusive foe. Sporadic skirmishes continued until 1660 when Autshumao sought to negotiate peace. Van Riebeeck advised him to keep his people well away from Table Bay because the Dutch, he announced, "had won by the sword" and Harry and his people could have no claim either to the lands along the Liesbeek or to the cattle taken as booty. Inevitably, it was not long before European diseases, in particular smallpox, contributed to the decimation of the indigenous peoples of this region. At the same time, and even more appalling to relate, many of them, the San (or Bushmen) in particular, were hunted down like animals by the encroaching Europeans.

By the early nineteenth century, the San arguably occupied the lowest rung in the hierarchy of race as understood by the Europeans, and the *Boesman* woman, in particular, became an icon of degraded female sexuality. Notoriously, in 1810, Saartjie Baartman, a KhoiSan known as "the Hottentot Venus", was exhibited, naked or nearly so, in London and in Paris. Her exhibition evoked scandal and outrage, both from those campaigning for the abolition of slavery and from those appalled by her nudity. Saartjie Baartman herself died in Paris at the age of twenty-five. However, in 1992, her genitalia and buttocks were still on display in the Musée de l'homme in Paris. In 1817, the French pathologist Georges Cuvier, who had dissected her body after her death, published a paper speculating on the supposed anomalies of Saartjie's genitalia: on her protruding buttocks and on her near relationship to the orangutan, an approach which contributed substantially to developing a stereotype of the San as being sub-human, degenerate and sexually deviant, one which was regarded as scientific fact by Europeans in the nineteenth century (Gilman, 1992). Needless to say, this was also a prejudice which permeated South African society since the arrival of da Gama and one of which I have had personal experience.

I remember a so-called "history" lesson as a child at school in the Cape in the 1940s when an elderly *Boesman* (San) with a deeply-lined face, was led like an animal on a lead into the school hall. His evident misery filled me with disquiet and left me wondering what, if anything, I was supposed to learn from such a spectacle. That such an exhibition was deemed suitable is in itself testimony to the views on the San which endured at the Cape from the arrival of Europeans until the post-apartheid era.

Van Riebeek's initial vegetable plot, the outlines of which may still be traced in the Kirstenbosch Botanical Gardens at the foot of Table Mountain, expanded very slowly, eventually becoming a Dutch colony radiating from Cape Town; an attractive rural backwater with its wheat fields and vineyards, its gabled architecture and oak-lined streets. It was a slave economy, for the Dutch imported slaves from the Malay peninsula, thus further adding to the complex ethnic mix of the local population. Some few KhoiSan remained in the south, but, as has been mentioned already, the majority of the San in particular were hunted like wild game. Some fled inland to the Drakensberg mountains, some further north to the Kalahari Desert. The Khoikhoi also intermarried with Malay slaves and Europeans and became the Cape "Coloureds" adopting as their mother tongue Afrikaans, the language of the frontier Boers. Life for the dispossessed KhoiSan changed little when the English took over the Cape. British occupation took place in stages, first in 1795, then again in 1806. It was not until 1815, at the end of the Napoleonic wars, that British sovereignty was formally declared.

In 1820, Lord Charles Somerset, autocratic governor of the Cape Colony, persuaded Westminster to authorise the emigration of about 4,000 English settlers to the eastern Cape frontier, an area constantly plagued by clashes between white frontiersmen and the Xhosa people, both groups competing for grazing land for their cattle. The British cared little about distinctions between San and Xhosa and there is much application of the term "Hottentot" to indicate an indigenous person irrespective of tribe or race. "Kaatje Kekkelbek or Life Among the Hottentots", a popular drinking song at officers' parties in Grahamstown, a frontier garrison town, satirises the mission at Philips Town established especially for the evangelisation of the remnants of these so-called

Hottentots. The ditty stresses the dirt, drunkenness and stupidity of all Hottentots. It was sung to the tune of "Calder Fair" in the Grahamstown amateur theatre; a town which prided itself on its debt to the English settlers of 1820 who had, supposedly, brought with them elements of civilization superior to that of their Dutch neighbours:

> My name is Kaatje Kekkelbek
> I come from Katriver,
> Daar is van water geen gebrek [geen gebrek = of little use]
> But scarce of wine and beer.
> Myn ABC at Ph'lipes school
> I learnt a Kleine Beetje [= a little bit]
> But left it just as great a fool
> As gekke Tante Meitje [meitje = foolish, half-witted].[2]

The doggerel accurately represents the attitude of most white settlers not simply towards those remaining, semi-acculturated San, or even Xhosa, but more generally towards those people of mixed race (the descendants of San, Malay slaves, Europeans and other tribes and races) who came eventually to be officially designated "Coloured" by a later Nationalist government.

The only favourable account of a Hottentot (and here I use the term as loosely as it was employed at the time) in the frontier literature of South Africa is a description of a soldier in the Cape Corps written by the novelist Harriet Ward, who was also an officer's wife, although there are verses sympathetic to the Xhosa people on the eastern Cape in Thomas Pringle's *African Sketches*. Pringle, one of a party of 1820 settlers, eventually clashed with Lord Somerset over the question of press freedom. Somerset, in his turn, regarded Pringle as seditious and dangerous (Pringle, 1834). Mrs Ward, for her part, offers the following description of a "Hottentot soldier":

> There he is, in his bush-coloured jacket, clay-coloured leather trousers, seated on his sturdy little steed, as though nothing had ever parted, or could ever part, the horse and his rider [...] When it is remembered that the average height of a Hottentot soldier is five feet one, and that he is slight in proportion, it may be imagined what a figure he cuts when accoutred for the field; but he is the most efficient soldier for this colony for all that. He is keen-witted and intelligent, patient of hunger, thirst and fatigue, active as a monkey, and possessed of a perfect knowledge of the country, and occasionally of the Kaffir language. (Ward, 1848, p. 173)

Despite this sympathetic portrait, which nevertheless does not avoid the tell-tale phrase "active as a monkey", Harriet Ward concluded categorically that: "All the miseries of the Colony arise from the mistaken philanthropy displayed towards the coloured inhabitants, who are as insolent as lazy [...] A treadmill is much wanted in Graham's

---

[2] *Sam Sly's African Journal*. Vol.14, 20 August, 1846.

Town [sic]" (Ward, 1848, p. 75). Needless to say, the virtues which she was at pains to point out previously were characteristics which made the Cape Corps soldier useful to his colonial master.

By the mid-nineteenth century, London publishing houses were cashing in on the popularity of books about Southern Africa. Explorers, missionaries, administrators and their wives recorded their experiences in great detail. The Cape was a lodestone for hunters, particularly for soldiers and administrators serving in India who often spent months enjoying the mild climate and unlimited opportunities for big game hunting. An added attraction was the fact that time spent at the Cape was not regarded as "home leave", that is leave spent in England, which was usually granted every five years. Understandably, for example, the Cape became a favourite resort for convalescents from India. *Notes on the Cape of Good Hope* by "A Bengali", which appeared in 1847, lists prices for almost everything a visitor might need, from the cost of a ticket from Bombay to Cape Town, to the price of South African beer – for the servants, of course. For those among their masters with the leisure to indulge a philosophical bent, on the other hand, in the same account, it is reported that books were sold at the Cape "at the London prices".

Among the most popular of these accounts of life at the Cape was *The Wild Sports of Southern Africa* by William Cornwallis Harris. By 1852, it had run to its fifth edition. Cornwallis Harris appears to have been obsessed by the wild animals of Africa, who are portrayed unfailingly as being "noble and majestic" while, in contrast, "uncultivated man is a compound of treachery, cunning, debauchery, gluttony and idleness". Cornwallis Harris, naturally, was too conscious of his status as "an officer and a gentleman" to pay much attention to other human beings unless he recognised them as being of his own tribe. However, he did note that his arrival at the Cape, on leave from India, coincided with the "migration of a large body of Dutch farmers [...] to effect an establishment in the wilderness". This movement north into the interior which had begun, centuries previously, with da Gama's Free Burghers, gathered momentum after 1837 with the publication, in the *Grahamstown Journal*, of Piet Retief's *Manifesto* which listed the grievances of those Boers in the frontier district of Albany. "We quit this colony, under the full assurance that the English government has nothing more to require of us, and will allow us to govern ourselves without its interference in future" (de Klerk, 1976, p. 24).

The motives for the Great Trek, an exodus which became the sustaining myth of Afrikaner nationalism, did not, all the same, interest Cornwallis Harris. He was rather more appalled by the notion that those Boers already in residence in the interior with whom he came into contact as he hunted big game might for an instant be under the inglorious misapprehension that he himself had anything to do with "trade":

> The profession of a gentleman being quite unknown in the colony, we were constantly taxed with being itinerant pedlars, the tea and snuff-loving vrouws never failing to rush out as we passed [...] to enquire what we had in the wagon. (p. 153)

The Restitution of Indigenous Identity in South African Fiction

It is one of the ironies of history that these trek Boers, the descendants of those first colonising farmers in the Liesbeek valley who had helped construct the negative stereotype of the San and the Khoi, had by the mid-nineteenth become, themselves, an object of scorn and contempt to the imperious English.

The Boers are first encountered in South African English fiction in Harriet Ward's two volume novel, *A tale of Kaffirland* when a British officer, Ormsby and a companion officer encounter a Boer community:

> The captain of the bivouac, Lodewyk, a hunter with a face almost covered with hair, arms bared to the elbow, but garnished kaffir fashion with bangles of brass, and a ring of ivory, a large straw hat on his head, and equipped with leather trowsers, girded with a belt containing immense pistols and carrying besides an elephant gun, stepped forwards. (p. 10)

The Boers are described as if they were white tribesmen, who have so closely identified themselves with the savages of Africa that their faces are hairy like those of monkeys, and their bodies are ornamented with bangles and ivory like the Hottentots. They repulse the British officer, Ormsby, who is reluctant to shake their hands. The text further suggests that his reluctance is justified because when Ormsby and his companion are shown inside the Boer farmhouse, they find that:

> The aspect of the principal apartment and only sitting room of the house did not strike the travellers as inviting [...] the slaughtered sheep suspended from the roof, with his head downwards, and dripping with blood, was particularly revolting. Turning his back to it in disgust, he found himself face to face with two enormous people, the grandfather and grandmother of the family. (p. 10)

Thus, half a century before the outbreak of the Anglo-Boer war, it appears the paradigm for the Boers is already drawn; they are dirty, uncouth, indolent, gross and a little weak in the head. Except for their *kombuis taal* or kitchen-Dutch and their white skin there is nothing to differentiate them from the indigenous savages; in the eyes of the English thus there is little to choose between Boer and Boesman.

Forty years later, in 1883, Olive Schreiner's Victorian best seller, *The Story of an African Farm,* fixed the portrait of the Boer woman for the English reader:

> In the farmhouse, on her great wooden bedstead, Tant Sannie the Boer-woman rolled heavily in her sleep. She had gone to bed, as she always did, in her clothes; and the night was warm and the room close, and she dreamed bad dreams. (p. 35)

Schreiner informs her reader that this 250 pound woman, Tant Sannie, stuffed not only with the pig's trotters which disturbed her sleep, but with credulity, avarice and the most *verkrampte* racism, believed that her kaffir servants need not attend Sunday service as they "were descended from apes and needed no salvation" (Schreiner, p. 69). *Verkrampte* is an Afrikaans word which has been used to describe those of an ultra-conservative stance, especially in politics. In mitigation, it must be said that

Schreiner was a young woman working as a governess on a Karoo farm in the northern Cape when she wrote this novel. Later in life she became, particularly during the Anglo-Boer War, a passionate advocate of the Afrikaner cause and of the Boer woman in particular.

Indeed, when *The Story of an African Farm* was published, Schreiner's former employer, Mrs Fouche, the Boer farmer's wife for whom she had worked as a governess was deeply offended by the portrait of Tant Sannie, believing her to be a caricature of herself. This was an accusation which Schreiner strongly denied. Indeed it is perhaps evident to a disinterested eye that both Blenkinsop and Tant Sannie in Schreiner's novel owe more to a comic tradition stemming from Hogarth and Sterne than they do to any prejudice against Boer women on the part of Schreiner herself.

Schreiner's letters record much that was pleasant about her early life in a remote Dutch community. However, her own mother was fiercely antagonistic to Afrikaners. Indeed, Schreiner never forgot the fierce beating her mother gave her as a child for polluting her English with Afrikaans words. This prejudice may perhaps have had something to do with John Barrow's *An Account Of Travels Into The Interior of Southern Africa,* published in 1804. Long before Tant Sannie's appearance, John Barrow had concluded that all the white inhabitants of the Cape (especially those in the interior living in close proximity to the black tribes) were indolent, over-fed, excessively given to sleep, gross in their persons, vulgar in their manners. He wrote:

> I believe that there is no country in the world that affords so large a proportion of unwieldy and bulky people: and I am certain there is none where the animal appetites are indulged with less restraint [...] or where the powers of the mind are capable of less exertion. (p. 97)

Not only were the Boers said to be physically gross and intellectually torpid, they even lacked normal human affections. At first Barrow distinguished between the Trek (interior) Boer and the wheat and wine farmers of the Cape. Later he observed that even among the wealthier Burghers there was "a great want of affection among near relations", while the women abandoned their children "to scrabble as well as they can among the slaves" (p. 105). He also gave graphic accounts of torture inflicted by the Trek Boers on their Hottentot slaves. He describes an eight-year-old boy who had been chained for more than ten months "with a pair of iron rings clenched upon his leg of the weight of ten or twelve pounds". The irons had been in place so long that they had sunk into the leg "so that the lamed boy was forced to crawl upon the ground" (p. 97). These accounts contributed to the stereotype of the Boer as being not only idle, slovenly and stupid but also excessively brutal into the bargain. Influenced, no doubt, by such scenes, Barrow went on to generalise about the Afrikaners, particularly their women and their family life, constructing an enduring stereotype of the white tribe, one which was later to be further enlivened by the caricature of Tant Sannie in Schreiner's novel. Yet these were the same degenerate, scarce-literate Boers who, on the outbreak of the Anglo-Boer War, were mysteriously able to inflict hitherto unheard-of casualties on the forces of a great imperial power.

During the Anglo-Boer War English newspapers, both at home and at the

Cape, were fired by a rabid jingoism, a virulent racism that eerily foreshadows Nazi propaganda in its stress on "racial purity". While Kipling's stories and poems on the South African campaign often reveal a grudging admiration for the enemy, in 1902 "Coldstreamer", in his *Ballads of the Boer War,* expressed a far more typical view of the Boer:

> But You're hail the same, you blooming Dutch,
> With a hinnersent look in your childlike heyes,
> An it's nothing but lies, an lies, an lies.
> Twill we find you hout – when you doesn't care
> But you lies some more, just to make things square.
> An I looked at the treacherous lead, an guessed
> Wot 'ad made that 'ole in the trooper's chest.

The influence of the Little Englanders, that is the Pro-Boer party who were opposed to the war (dubbed The Screamers by Lord Milner, then High Commissioner for Southern Africa), is reflected only occasionally in English writing of the period. In 1904, a slim collection of verses dramatising the suffering of the Boer women, their courage and their faith in their cause, was published by A. M. Buckton:

> Under the wild moon
> A rough stone stands.
> Raised too soon.
> Marked by alien hands.
> Glimmering white afar
> In the dead lambs' fold -
> "Jaapie – prisoner of war -
> Ten years old".

After the war, the legacy of the concentration camps and of Milner's scorched earth policy fuelled the animosity between English and Afrikaans-speaking whites in South Africa and diverted attention from the enslaved situation of the mass of the African people. "Race relations" in the new Union of South Africa, created in 1910 after the Peace of Vereeniging, often meant relations between the victorious *Rooineks,* Rednecks or English, and the defeated Boers. The *Vryheid's Oorlog* (the war for freedom) as it was called by the Boers left them a poor and divided people. Some drifted to the towns in search of work, others struggled to survive as *bywoners* (tenants) on the lands of luckier neighbours. As late as the 1940s, in isolated places, deep in the Outeniqua forest for example, in hamlets dotted round the Knysna lakes and in country areas known in South Africa as the *platteland* there still existed communities of Afrikaans speakers who were known as "Poor Whites", a derogatory term in a country where to be white was then normally to be prosperous.

The lives of such people were pictured with sensitivity and power in *The Little Karoo,* a collection of short stories by Pauline Smith whose English father had been a doctor in Oudtshoorn, the only town of any size in this arid area of what was then the Cape Province. Pauline Smith accompanied her father as a child when he called on his patients, mostly Poor Whites scraping a precarious living from the dry soil of the *Karoo*. When she was twelve she was sent to England to be educated. Years later, with the encouragement of Arnold Bennet, Smith published *The Little Karoo* and a novel, *The Beadle*. Smith's fiction recreates the narrow, oppressive society of these isolated Calvinist communities with an understanding of Afrikaner life rare in English writing.

In *The Beadle,* Pauline Smith constructed a contrasting stereotype to Tant Sannie in Alida van der Merwe, a mother of eight children who is mistress of the prosperous Boer farm Harmonie. Alida alone holds a key to the spacious kitchen: a beautiful room, gleaming with copper, brass and polished yellowwood, a room which unites the values of Western Europe with the colonised African land. At one end of the room was a low brass stand, brought out from Holland by the first van der Merwe who, as Landrost in the service of the Dutch East India Company, had settled at the Cape. Alida radiates love, comfort, hospitality; her generosity and compassion extend beyond her own family to all her white neighbours. She is a wise woman, who, like the San, distils her own medicines:

> There was no plant or herb, no veld root or leaf or berry, whose virtues she did not know...Her medicine chest, a small brown box with a leather strap, was kept in a corner cupboard in the dining room. (p. 168)

Europeans were astonished by the herbal knowledge of the KhoiSan. As François Leguat reported in 1698:

> However ignorant or rather how bestial soever the Hottentots are [...] Let one be bit with any venomous Creature, be one Wounded or Ulcerated, or let there be any Swelling or Inflammation, they know how to go exactly to the Plant that will cure them, and administer the Remeday with greater Success that we oftentimes do ours" (Moisert, p. 112).

Surely among the servants at Harmonie there was a San woman to whom Alida was indebted for her knowledge of the indigenous plants. This woman has no voice; neither have any of those whose labour made gracious living at Harmonie possible even in the semi-desert of the Karoo. As J. M. Coetzee has pointed out:

> Silence about the place of black labour is common not only to Schreiner and Smith but, by and large, to the Afrikaans *plaasroman* [farm novel] and represents a failure of the imagination before the problem of how to integrate the dispossessed black man into the idyll (or in Schreiner's case the anti-idyll) of African pastoralism. (1988, p. 77)

Alida van der Merwe's world is built on a hierarchy of obedience. "Make me obedient to my mistress" is the prayer of one of the indentured children on the farm.

Nearly thirty years later Alan Paton is still recreating both the pure-hearted Boer matriarch and the stereotype of the San or Coloured woman who is sexually dangerous. His novel *Too Late the Phalarope* was written at a time when personal tragedies were multiplying in South Africa as a result of prosecutions under the notorious Immorality Act which made sexual intercourse between the races a criminal offence. Pieter van Vlaanderen, a married war veteran, rugby hero and respected policeman makes love to Stephanie, a prostitute and woman of mixed blood. The couple lie among weeds in a plot of vacant grounds. These weeds are:

Kakiebos which makes his body and clothes stink; which stinking was a symbol of his corruption, so that in his going he feared that the stench of it would go through the town and bring men and women from every house, to find him and know what he had done. (Paton, 1955, p. 148)

Pieter's wife, Nella, believes that sexual pleasure is sinful. This suspicion of the world and the flesh, stemming from a particular reading of Genesis and fostered by that brand of Calvinism nurtured by the Dutch Reformed Churches in South Africa, drives Pieter to "go to his home, and boil tins of water on the stove, and pour them into the bath, and wash himself clean of his corruption" (p. 149).

Within the parameters of Paton's liberalism, the novel examines the consequences to Boer society of an ideology which harnesses the power of the religious, administrative and judicial system to control the sexuality of the individual, with the aim of maintaining the myth of blood purity and, with it, the power of Afrikaner nationalism. Paton mentions, but does not stress, the poverty and love of her child which have driven the "Coloured" woman Stephanie to prostitution. She remains a symbol of stinking corruption whose sexuality brings about the downfall of the hero.

On the other hand, the stereotype of the Boer woman, whether caricatured as in Tant Sannie or idealised as angel-in-the-house in Alida, is not on the whole questioned in colonial texts. Indeed, it is not until the novels of Nadine Gordimer that we begin to meet Afrikaner women who are uncomfortable in such strait jackets. Gordimer's female characters are often, partly at least, of Afrikaans descent or, like Maureen in *July's People*, married to Afrikaners.

Another model for the Boer *vrouw* may be encountered in Magda, the madwoman of J. M. Coetzee's novel *In the Heart of the Country*. This demented spinster, who alternately cares for and harbours murderous thoughts about her father, stands at the farmhouse window wondering "What are pain, jealousy, loneliness doing in the African night?" However, despite her suffering, Magda can claim "I have uttered my life in my own voice throughout [...] I have chosen at every moment my own destiny". Though she has retained her voice, she appears to have done so at the price of her own sanity and the novel invites one to ask, on many levels, what the part of the now-detested colonial father, may have had to play in this.

While it is nearly two centuries since Governor Somerset's Language Proclamation of 1822 which declared English the official tongue in the Cape Colony with effect from 1827, and despite the increasing integration of English and Afrikaans speakers since South Africa became a Republic in 1960, South African English still retains remnants of that vocabulary which expressed the old British imperial disdain for the Boers. They were hairy backs, rock spiders, ropes (narrow-minded and twisted), *plaasjapies* (country bumpkins) or Tant Sannies. For example, the contemporary popular novelist, Wilbur Smith repeatedly puts this language in the mouths of his characters. In his novel *Rage*, for instance, Shasa and Manfred provide the following exchange of pleasantries:

> "Do you remember how once you called me Soutpiel?" Shasa asked.
> "Ja," Manfred chuckled. "'Salt Prick': with one foot in Cape Town and the other in London and the best part of you dangling in the Atlantic Ocean. Ja. I remember." (p. 386)

Withal, images of Boer men and women appear to have changed little for the English reader over the past century. If Wilbur Smith's *Boerevrouw* is no longer as crude as Tant Sannie she is still blonde (of Nordic stock), broad-hipped, fecund and submissive to her husband. Heidi, wife of the same Manfred, is described as follows:

> "You will stay to lunch, Meneer" she asked demurely.
> "I don't want to be a nuisance".
> "You are welcome".
> She was a handsome woman, with large high bosom and wide fruitful hips. Her hair was dense and golden blonde and she wore it in a thick plaited rope that hung almost to her waist... (p. 110).

Would Kitchener, in 1902, have given such scant attention to the administration of the camps set up for Boer women and children if his knowledge of the Afrikaner had been formed by a different discourse, a discourse less imperialist in its assumptions about the inferiority of the Boer? He, and others like him, accepted the lie which was later repeated in South African school texts that the Boer women and children were dying in such numbers because they were unclean in their habits. It was left to the Quakers and the Little Englanders to expose the truth of the camps: women and children left in crowded tents in blazing sun and freezing cold, with no sanitation except buckets stinking in the heat, without soap, with very limited water, starvation rations and no milk for the babies. About twenty-five thousand Boer women and children died in the concentration camps of the Anglo-Boer war. For this Colonial Discourse must bear some responsibility.

The destructive images of Boesman and Boer are all pervasive in English writing in Southern Africa. From the early descriptions of travellers like Barrow and Cornwallis Harris to the popular blockbusters of Wilbur Smith, the same stereotypes prevail. Until the publication of Mark Behr's first novel, *The Smell of Apples*, with its powerful critique of Afrikaner nationalism based on an understanding of the effect of history on the formation of apartheid ideology, Pauline Smith's sympathetic portraits of the *Bywoner* class remained a landmark in the history of English writing about Afrikaner culture.

Curiously, it was an Afrikaner, Laurens van der Post, writing in English, who delivered the San from the opprobrium heaped on them by colonial discourse. *The Lost World of the Kalahari*, the first of van der Post's travel books recording the lives and culture of those remnants of the San still roaming the northern desert, rescued these people from the dehumanisation which had begun with the Portuguese. Van der Post himself had grown up in an educated Afrikaner family on a remote farm in the part of South Africa which the Boers had called The Orange Free State. Early in his life, when he was about to apply for a job on an English newspaper in Durban, one of his brothers had warned him that the Natal English "were people who had the greatest reservations about those of us who lived in the interior, and they had strong feelings of superiority, even scorn, for our supposed deficiencies" (1984, p. 34).

Aware of English attitudes towards Boers from the *backveld*, van der Post was even more sensitive to the stereotypes of the San. In *The Heart of the Hunter*, he recorded many of the myths through which these ancient people interpreted the natural world. In van der Post's writing, the stone-age hunter is transformed from a sub-human creature whom the colonist could kill without remorse to a philosopher, poet and artist who has left his paintings on innumerable rock faces all over southern Africa.

Attractive San characters, at one with the natural world, opposed in every way to the destructive forces of twentieth-century life in Africa, are also central to van der Post's novels, *A Story Like Wind* and *A Far Off Place*. Van der Post's fiction owes much both to his childhood memories and to his Jungian understanding of the importance of dream in the creative unconscious. It may be, in the end, that this fiction tells us more about the author than it does about the San themselves but it is nevertheless true, as Michael Chapman has said, that "the value of van der Post's empathies is to take seriously the literary culture of people who bore the brunt of colonial hostility" (1996, p. 30).

In the late 'eighties, the contemporary writer, Zoe Wicomb, in her collection of short stories, *You Can't Get Lost in Cape Town*, recreates for us the emotions of Freda, a young girl of KhoiSan ancestry growing up in the Cape flats during the apartheid years. Ambitious for her daughter, Freda's mother constantly attempts to straighten her child's hair and she insists on her speaking English, which alienates Freda from other children in her community. Eventually Freda Shenton escapes both her mother and the nightmare of apartheid South Africa by travelling to England. When she returns to visit her family, her mother persuades Freda to drive her to the Gifberge, the mountains from where her ancestors came. "We know who lived in these mountains when the Europeans were still shivering in their own country", her mother says.

In an abandoned shepherd's hut the pair find a bush flourishing in the earth floor. Freda asks her mother about it:

> "Is it ghanna?" I ask.
> "No, but it's related, I think. Look, the branches are a paler grey, almost feathery. It's Hotnos-kooigoed."
> "You mean Khoi-Khoi-kooigoed."
> "Really, is that the educated name for them? It sounds right doesn't it".
> And she repeats Khoi-Khoi-kooigoed, relishing the alliteration.
> "No, it's just what they called themselves." (p. 180)

In this brief exchange Zoe Wicomb has condensed much of the tragedy of the South African past. The KhoiSan have lost everything, even their name, since the arrival of the Europeans. They have come to be known as *Boesman* or Hottentots, (*Hotnos* as used here is a related word in Afrikaans). They have become so acculturated that they now use the language of the Afrikaner white tribe to describe an indigenous plant, the *kooigoed*. Freda's generation is more empowered than her mother's, so she partly recovers the old tribal name, using Khoi-Khoi in conjunction with *kooigoed*.

The stories in this collection are profoundly sad, weighted as they are by the intolerable pressures of life in so blatantly racist a society, albeit one only a couple of years away from the end of apartheid. Yet, this passage answers the call of the South African critic Njubele Ndebele for a rediscovery of the ordinary in South African English writing, particularly in writing by black South Africans, so much of which has understandably been, as Ndebele puts it "the history of the representation of spectacle" (p. 41).

Ndebele's call for a restitution of the ordinary in South African writing is more than fulfilled in Wicomb's creation of Freda Shenton and her mother. Their essential ordinariness contributes both to the rewriting of southern African history and to the development of a southern African literature in English able, at last, to confront and shed the hitherto all-pervasive stereotypes. South African writers have suffered not only the persecutions of the apartheid years but also the restrictions of protest fiction – the moral obligation to use their art in the service of a cause. Few writers have been able, as J. M. Coetzee has, to combine the ethical and the aesthetic. Inevitably, therefore, much talent has been cramped and lost over the years of revolution. There is now a great need, as Ndebele has pointed out, for contemporary writers in South Africa to take up the latitude the absence of governmental discrimination permits them: the liberty to explore individual consciousness, as it comes to them, in its unique and complex southern African setting.

References

Buckton, A.M. (1904) *The Burden of Engela*: *A Ballad-Epic*, London.

Chapman, M. (1996) *Southern African Literature*, London, Longman.

Coetzee, J.M. (1977) *In the Heart of the Country*, London, Secker and Warburg.

--------------. (1988) *White Writing*, Yale, Yale University Press.

Coldstreamer. (1902) *Ballads of the Boer War*, London, Grant Richards.

Cornwallis H. (1852) *William, The Wild Sports of Southern Africa*. London, Henry G. Bohn.

Cuvier, G. (1817) "Extraits d'observations sur le cadavre d'une femme connue à Paris et à Londres sous le nom de Venus Hottentote". *Mémoires du Museum d'histoire naturelle* 3, pp. 259-74.

Gilman, S. L. (1992) "Black Bodies, White Bodies: Toward and Iconography of Female Sexuality in Late Nineteenth-Century Art, Medicine and Literature", in *Race, Culture and Difference*, ed. James Donald and Ali Rattansi, Milton Keynes, Open University, pp. 171-197.

Klerk, W.A. de. (1076) *The Puritans in Africa: A History of Afrikanerdom*, London, Penguin.

Ley, D. C. (ed.). (1947) "A Journal of the First Voyage of Vasco da Gama in 1497-99", *Portuguese Voyages 1498-1663*. London, Dent.

Moisert, N. (1992) *Frontiers*. London, Pimlico.

Ndebele, N. and G. Pechey (eds.). (1994) *South African Literature and Culture: The Rediscovery of the Ordinary*, Manchester, Manchester University Press.

Paton, A. (1955) *Too Late the Phalarope,* London, Prentice and Hall.

Post, L. van der. (1974) *A Far-Off Place*, London, Hogarth Press.

------------------. (1972) *A Story Like the Wind*, London, Hogarth Press.

------------------. (1961) *The Heart of the Hunter*, London, Hogarth Press.

------------------. (1964) *The Lost World of the Kalahari*, London, Hogarth Press.

------------------. (1984) *Yet Being Someone Other*, London, Penguin.

Pringle, T. (1834) *African Sketches*, London, Edward Moxon.

Ross, R. (1999) *A Concise History of South Africa*, Cambridge, Cambridge University Press.

Schapera, I. (ed.). (1953) *The Bantu-speaking Tribes of South Africa*. Cape Town, Maskew Miller.

Schreiner, O. (1982) *The Story of an African Farm*, London, Penguin.

Smith, P. (1925) *The Little Karoo,* London, Jonathan Cape.

----------. (1927) *The Beadle*, London, Jonathan Cape.

Smith, W. (1987) *Rage*, London, Heinemann.

Ward, H. (1851) *A Tale of Kaffirland*, London.

--------------- (1848) *Five Years in Kaffirland*, 2 vols., London.

Wicomb, Z. (1987) *You Can't Get Lost in Cape Town*, London, Pantheon Books.

"La canción más hermosa del mundo":
Joan Manuel Serrat, the "Reactionary" in his Fortress of Solitude

Álvaro J. Vidal Bouzon

*To Carmen,
who with J.M.S., P.R. and warm, mad complicity,
called me, back in February 1983 or 1984,
an outlandish person – that is to say, a free man:
I've learnt from you, sister.*

Pecado, maior, é tentar traduzir a música
[A sin it is, and mortal, to try to translate music]
(Manuel de Freitas)

Ni tú ni yo somos nadie, ni hacemos historia
pues somos la escoria
que aún puede quemar.
[You and I are nobodies, and we don't make history
for we are but the cross
that can still burn]
(Luis Eduardo Aute)

Inútil escrutar tan alto cielo
inútil cosmonauta el que no sabe
el nombre de las cosas que le ignoran
el color del dolor que no le mata
inútil cosmonauta
el que contempla estrellas
para no ver las ratas
[It's useless to search the distant skies
useless cosmonaut if he doesn't know
the name of things that ignore him
the colour of the suffering that doesn't kill him
useless cosmonaut
that contemplates stars
so as not to see the rats]
(Manuel Vázquez Montalbán)

At the end of his "Introducción" to *Cancionero Serrat* Santiago Alcada writes that "Serrat, like his songs, is an open book written in both the first and the third person" (Alcada, 2000, p. 33). What follows, thus, might be *listened to* as an attempt at *reading* Serrat's lyrics as a book. I would not say open, however. That will be my task – to compose it as such. I would not say, either, that its first person would be other than a hinge for articulating our perspective. Or, in other words, to clarify this obvious requirement from the very beginning – it should be noted that such a book would not be a biography. Less, even, an (always spurious) autobiography. Contrary to the immense majority of what has been written on his work, I am not interested in Serrat's life. Well, of course *I* am, but *that I* should be silent, here, and the pronoun used in what follows aspires only to be a textual marker: the first person of anyone and nobody. Because even when Joaquín Sabina sings about him –

> Tengo yo un primo que es todo un maestro
> de lo mío, de lo tuyo, de lo nuestro,
> un lujo para el alma y el oído,
> un modo de vengarse del olvido.
> [I have a cousin who is a total master
> of what's mine, what's yours, what's ours,
> a luxury for the soul and to the ear,
> a way of avenging oblivion.]
> (Sabina, 1996).

– he is not only talking about his friend. And, for our purposes, he is not primarily doing so. That luxury, that way of taking revenge, are effects. Modulated in an artistic form. And such effects are part of a major enterprise, a gigantic effort. The strategies through which such effects are created and produced will be the main focus of these lines. For only those strategies made justifiable Sabina's portrait of Serrat as:

> [...] un primo que es primo de todos,
> cada cual a su forma y a su modo,
> loco hidalgo con yelmo de Mambrino
> que no teme a gigantes ni a molinos.
> [(...) a cousin that's a cousin to all,
> each in his own manner and mode,
> a mad noble with a Mambrino's helmet
> who fears neither giants nor windmills.]
> (Sabina, 1996).

Joan Manuel Serrat, then, as an object (though, as we shall see, in a subject position). And a signifier, an artifact and a device[1] through which a textual/musical creation/production articulates meaning. Or, in Sabina's terms – *an (anti)hero*. And a Quixotic one.

The articulation I am aiming at will operate as a book, as said before. What sort of book then? The universe of Serrat's songs composes a set of paths that, frequently, intersect. Think about the structure of Quentin Tarantino's *Pulp Fiction* (1994) and try to reconstruct Serrat's *Cancionero* in a similar way. Anecdotes, landscapes, objects, people, characters, types, archetypes even, that will keep appearing in different

---

[1] "[T]he proper name, here, is precisely not a reference to a particular person as author or subject of ennunciation; it refers to one or several assemblages; the proper name brings about an individuation by 'hecceity', not at all by subjectivity" (Deleuze and Parnet, 2002, p. 120)

compositions, under different circumstances, in different contexts. But those contexts are going to be crucial here. As one of the characters in *Reservoir Dogs* (1991) put it, they are the details that sell the story. And Serrat is famous for his magical handling of details, "aquellas pequeñas cosas" ["those little things"] (Serrat, 1971) that give atmosphere and, above all, life to a picture. That animate it. Because Serrat's songs, in the tradition of the troubadours, are a spectacle. Poetry in the mode. But not always lyrical in the genre. On the contrary, they picture quite dramatic situations. They stage, so, a little (melo-cum-neorealist) drama. It would be fairer to them to consider their discourse as a reflection of that speech represented by the utterance of a teller. Not of a story/history, however. No direct relation here with a beyond (or before, it does not matter) the text. These songs operate in the manner of that friend who tells us what the last film she saw was about. It is, therefore, the rearticulation of a story in which images (both tropes and picture composition) are crucial. The verbal representation of a storyboard, then. Or a comic; a graphic novel. With heroes of pulp fiction.

Indeed, were the terms "popular" and "hero" to be applied together in a single qualification to a singer-songwriter holder of a Spanish passport, Joan Manuel Serrat would be, most probably, one of the two or three preferred candidates. The articulation of his work, his performances, the reception he has enjoyed since the beginning of his career back in the sixties,[2] under the yoke of a Francoist Spain (whose shadow is still conditioning cultural life in the non-Portuguese Iberia), and his political interventions in the public arena would place him firmly in a position not that far away from the one expected of an engaged, progressive, left-wing intellectual… Him. What about "his" songs? Is there any common ground, in ideologico-political terms, being the unifying territory of their meaning? Or, coming at the issue from a different, and not necessarily complementary level: any giants or windmills to face there?

Quite early on, Manuel Vázquez Montalbán chose to approach Serrat ethics and aesthetics under the following parameters:

"Changer la vie" (Rimbaud) or "change history" (Marx) is a false option. To change life helps towards changing history, although historical changes have a greater influence on vital changes. Our era has situated this option at the forefront of its concerns, because there is a vital appetite for change which has not always run in parallel to obvious historical changes. The songs of Serrat have a great deal of the ideological struggle in them at the leading edge of vital change; yet we can hardly speak of him as a "civil" singer, in the conventional sense of that term (Vázquez Montalbán, 1973, p. 46).

---

[2] Serrat recorded his first disc, the EP *Una guitarra*, in 1965; his last one to date – and his first recording of original materials in Catalan for 18 years – is *Mô* (2006). Before that, he recorded *Serrat Sinfónico* (2003), an "anthology" of some of his most popular songs arranged to be sung by himself accompanied by the Orquesta Simfònica de Barcelona i Nacional de Catalunya.

Long after these words were written, it is not difficult to verify that most of Serrat's production has been concerned with those details I was referring to above. Any macro-political point would have to be reconstructed as embedded in the well constructed micro-situation story. It would be, quite clearly, an effect of reading rather than a condition of writing. There are exceptions, though, songs which tend to articulate general socio-political points and progressively reduce to a minimum the story-telling focused on a character/object that has been Serrat's trade-mark: "Por las paredes (mil años hace...)" ["On the walls (one thousand years on...)"] (Serrat, 1978), "Temps era temps" ["Once upon a time"] (1980), "A quien corresponda" ["To whom it may concern"] (1981), "Algo personal" ["Something personal"] (1983), "Plany al mar" ["Mourning the sea"] (1984), "Detrás está la gente" ["Behind, the people"] (1987), "La gente va muy bien" ["People are doing fine"] (1994), "Buenos tiempos" ["Good times"] (1998), "África" ["Africa"] (2002) are amongst the most obvious.[3]

I shall pick out two songs, first, that could be considered the limits (or thresholds, it depends on the perspective) of Serrat's way of dealing directly with political issues in, and through, artistic ways. Both come from his most explicitly political album (*Utopía*, 1992). One dialogues with the other, framing a quite apparent (but are not appearances deceptive?) progressive political message. The first one, "Disculpe el señor" ["Forgive me, sir"], is channelling/articulating a political discourse through a short story with a number of archetypes as characters interacting (and negotiating, even) in a given spatio-temporal context.

The second song, which gives name to the album, is "Utopía". The story is clearly *reduced* here to its basic allegoric dimension, subordinated in all its elements to the ideological meaning which constitutes *the message* of this song/fable.

In my view one of the less accomplished of Serrat songs, "Utopía", presents the three most characteristic components of what would constitute utopia as an (ideological) notion – the realisation of the limits of the present ("que no tiene bastante con lo posible" ["which doesn't find the possible enough"]), the postulation of a new future which would surpass those limitations ("hasta que lleguen mejores días" ["til better days arrive"], "que alumbras los candiles / del nuevo día" ["that lights the candles / of the new day"]), the fragile condition of utopia itself as the threshold to such a future. Even the religious or, perhaps better, sacred connotations of any utopian project are referred to here through the use of a quite recognisable line of the central Christian prayer ("el

---

[3] I am leaving aside, of course, the clearest area of Serrat's work where a "civil singer" would be easier to find – his musical interpretation of the lyrics of poets such as Antonio Machado, Miguel Hernández, Rafael Alberti, Eduardo Galeano or Mario Benedetti. It is worth noting here that it is easier to find this particular form of engagement in his compositions in Spanish than in his compositions in Catalan, and that this most explicitly engaged position began to flourish once Serrat decided to write/compose in Spanish and to put music to, first, Spanish and, later, Spanish American poets as well.

pan nuestro de cada día" ["our daily bread"]) and the consignation of utopia's miraculous capacities ("que hace que el ciego vea y el mudo hable" ["that make the blind see and the dumb speak"]). The feminisation of utopia in this anthropomorphic representation – inextricably linked both to the already traditional modern representation of the bearer of freedom, equality and fraternity as a woman guiding the people and to the frail condition associated with her by the song – is making her explicitly dependent upon a male carer ("será un buen hombre / el que la encuentre / y la cuide hasta que lleguen mejores días" ["who'll be a good man / one who finds her / and looks after her 'til better days arrive"]). Carer, only. Not catalyst of her potential. It is, however, from here where we can collect the three original takes on the topic that the song stages. First of all, in its allegoric scenery, it enacts a very specific sequence: *Utopía* is hunted down *as an animal*. And a female, as we have already seen. The articulation of such a becoming is made possible under the evocation of an uncanniness of extreme tensions: strange familiarity and absolute otherness, the symptom of a lack which is *elsewhere* (Albiac, 1995, pp. 98-100). But, secondly, added to the fact that *Utopía* is here a female human (that is to say, a [reflection of] non-completeness, then) and not a location or even a project, *Utopía* is not the deliverer nor the space of those "mejores días" ["better days"] or "el nuevo día" ["the new day"] either. She is, on the contrary, just the device to provoke ("que levanta huracanes" ["raises hurricanes"]) "rebeldía" ["rebelliousness"], particularly through a quite humorous (in the Deleuzeo-Bergsonian sense) take on her most dangerous, prototypically "feminine" characterisation as "aurora" ["dawn"], yes, but also as "embaucadora" ["trickster"], "hechicera" ["bewitching"] and "incorregible" ["incorrigible"]. Not a hybrid Nietzschean-Marxian superhuman, superproletariat here, then. Nor a beyond proposed either – as the agent (*Utopía*) is properly passive (she will not bring the new day, she will be taken care of until that happens) and already existent in the present day. Our hero is an incomplete human, or Other than hu/man, firmly inscribed in an *uchronistic* here. For no sign of a new day is, in fact, made possible, even thinkable, by the materiality of the song: she will remain always against. Never incorporated into a new order she has only, at most, helped to create, if at all; perpetually being "subversiva / de lo que está mandado, *mande quien mande*" ["subversive / of what has been ordained, *whoever ordains it*"), in a clear allusion to a religious conception of human power as always, and humanely, sinful, demoniac even (in fact, many of the female-like elements of the figure of the Christ are, quite probably, being conjugated here).

I referred above to a third, original take on the issue of utopia as enacted by the song. And the fact is that this last point of *Utopía*'s permanent subversiveness refers us back to its beginning, the moment when the very condition of the sequence to be enacted is defined: "Se echó al monte la utopía"[4] ["utopia took to the hills"], persecuted not

---

[4] Without a capital U: female, but common despite her being later described as a proper noun, because only by virtue of such commonness/sameness is her

just by any humans (a man will only be mentioned as "un buen hombre" ["a good man"] that will find and take care of her) but by cold murderers ("lebreles *que se criaron* / en sus rodillas" ["greyhounds *which were nursed* / at her feet"]). Traitors to her and, today, "funcionarios / del negociado de *sueños dentro de un orden*" ["functionaries / in the department of *controlled dreams*"]. Eternal return? Utopia engenders dystopia that engenders utopia that...? Not at all: dystopia, as the landscape we inhabit, is always, is everywhere. The sombre, painful music simply underlines this third, most essential take on the topic: the consciousness that *Utopía's* children (in functional not biological terms) will end by hunting down not revolutionaries (those do not even get mentioned), but their own bearer – the "aurora" ["dawn"], "embaucadora" ["trickster"], "hechicera" ["bewitching"] and "subversiva" ["subversive"] that makes their current position tenable in the first place. *Utopía* is saved ("Sin utopía / la vida sería un ensayo para la muerte" ["Without *Utopía* / life would be an attempt at death"]). Utopia is never.

By contrast, "Disculpe el señor" ["Forgive me, sir"] is probably one of the most accomplished OF Serrat songs. It might be put in dialogue with "Utopía", nonetheless, in a quite specific way. Less obviously charged with concepts and notions, I propose to *read* (rather than *listen to*, of course, in this case) the former within the ideological framework provided by the latter. Not as an actualisation of the model (as the model is actualised itself through the popular form of a fable in "Utopía") but as the scene of its consequences. Because there is an enormous precariousness in what "Disculpe el señor" enacts. Let me show my interpretative card from the very beginning: Utopia, as I said above, is never. But here, furthermore, *Utopía* is, still, missing. Let us see. Let us listen.

The situation is presented through a quite recognisable dichotomy whose tension is underlined by the music and the tone of the interpretation: "el señor" ["sir"] (singular and, above all, masculine – the situation would have been very different if it were a "señora" ["madam"]) / "pobres" ["poor"] (as plural as plurally articulated because not fixedly determined by the song – "un par de pobres" [" *a couple of* poor people"], "pobres" ["poor"], "*más y más* pobres" ["*more and more* poor people"] and, only at the end, "*los* pobres" ["*the* poor"]). The haves and the have nots. Those are the terms. Of the injustice of the situation we know only through the humorous butler's voice, it is implied in each of his utterances and is progressively building up.[5] It is, precisely, this third term of the butler's voice that is the interesting one here. He inhabits the sphere (in more than one sense) of *el señor*, though he is as well, and above all, the ambiguous ("le dejo con los *caballeros*" ["I'll leave you with the *gentlemen*"] but "que *ésos* no se han enterado" ["for *that lot* are not aware"]) border, filter and

---

specificity communicable... and this is all she will do: communicate to others.

[5] In some of his performances, Serrat would minimalistically appear on stage dressed in a characteristic butler's waistcoat and white gloves *clearly addressing the audience as "el señor"*.

interface of the *outsideness* represented by the "pobres" ["poor"]. An *outsideness*, of course, upon whose exploitation the very articulation of *el señor's* spatio-temporal dimension is possible (delinquency is even evoked by the use of the expression "han dado con su paredero" ["they have found your whereabouts"]). This butler is a waged worker. Those *pobres* outside are not ("Son pobres que no tienen nada de nada" ["They're the poor who have nothing at all"]). We are told (and we are addressed either as in the place of *el señor* or as specta[c]tors of the scene) in the second stanza that they have nothing to sell so when immediately in the third the butler's voice says "No entendí muy bien / si nada que vender o nada que perder" ["I didn't understand very well / if it was nothing to sell or nothing to lose"], the humour is evident and evidently used to introduce the crucial point "pero por lo que parece / tiene usted alguna cosa que les pertenece" ["but it seems / that you have something belonging to them"] further emphasising it with the use of the old Spanish sayings "`Santa Rita, Rita, Rita, / lo que se da no se quita'..." ["Once gifted, never returned"] and "`Bien me quieres, bien te quiero, / no me toques el dinero'" ["Friendship and money don't mix"]. In this last case, making explicit the representation of the material bases of the opposition organising the dichotomy and invoking its symbolic centrality by using a syntagm which evokes the powerful expression "no me toques los huevos/cojones" ["Don't break my balls"]. Humour is further channelled through each of the ludicrous (ludicrous?) butler's suggestions to get rid of the *pobres* and underlined by the suspension (dots) at the end of each of them.

So, do we know who – or, even, *what* – the *pobres* are? We know they are not workers, nor are they the immigrant Africans who, in many Spanish cities' streets, sell "alfombras de lana" ["wool carpets"] or "elefantes de ébano" ["ebony elephants"]... or if they are, their situation is now quite different. I am considering here that they might *as well* be included because what is important in terms of the meaning is the general archetype of the have nots. With nothing to lose because they possess nothing (a totally different situation to that presented by Marx in *Das Kapital*: waged labour *has*, indeed, something to lose...). They are, therefore, nobody. Or, in other terms – they are (defined by) what they do not have. They lack. They are... *things*... Or are they?

These songs were recorded in the quite bleak times of the Spanish early 1990s, under a not just disappointing and deceptive but essentially criminal Socialist administration. Let us go back, now, to a Spain still enthused, in general terms, by the possibility of "cambio" ["change"]. And to a song, "Cada loco con su tema" ["To each his own, each to his own"] (Serrat, 1983) included in the album of the same title.

Through its optimistic music and tone of interpretation, Serrat is using his most critical device, as already seen – humour. In the Deleuzean sense (Deleuze and Parnet, 2002, pp. 68-69) alluded to: these are the conditions and the rules ("Cada loco con su tema, / contra gustos no hay disputas; / artefactos, bestias, hombres y mujeres, / cada uno es como es, / cada quién es cada cual / y baja las escaleras como quiere" ["Every fool has his obsessions, / there is no accounting for taste; / objects, animals, men and women, / each as each is, / each one is any one / and comes downstairs as he or she wants"]), let us play with them, let us see where they leave us if used both to their letter and to their limits. If I am free to choose, I shall do it ("pero puestos a escoger, soy partidario" ["but given the choice, I'm in favour"]). It is up to the structure that allowed me to do so to deal with the consequences... especially if that choosing, and its consequences, shows not just the limits of the structure but the threshold to a different one. My proposition is to take the objects and actions preferred by the voice speaking to us in the song as the ones embedded in the characters not simply preferred but, most crucially, *being in favour of, partisan* ("soy partidario"). And, finally, to take these characters, and those objects, and those actions as belonging to the same *nature* of the *pobres* in "Disculpe el señor".

"Las voces de la calle" ["voices of the streets"], "los barrios" ["neighbourhoods"], "los artesanos" ["artisans"], "la razón" ["reason"], "el instinto" ["instinct"], "un *sioux*" ["a sioux Indian"], "los caminos" ["the roads"], "una mariposa" ["a butterfly"], "el farero de Capdepera" ["the lighthouse keeper of Capdepera"], "un buen polvo" ["a good fuck"], "un bombero" ["a fireman"], "crecer" ["to grow"], "la carne" ["flesh"], "las ventanas" ["windows"], "el lunar de tu cara" ["the mole on your face"], "el tiempo" ["time"], "el perro" ["the dog"], "las nueces" ["the walnuts"], "el sabio por conocer" ["the wise man to know"]... all in a (at times highly contradictory) reflective relation (because it is a relation, under the potentially conflicting terms of *preference* and *partisanship*) to those which/who would imprison, curtail, exterminate, regulate or reduce them to a subsumptive logic: "el diccionario" ["the dictionary"], "el centro de la ciudad" ["the centre of the city"], "la factoría" ["the factory"], "la fuerza" ["force"], "la urbanidad" ["urbanity"], "el Séptimo de Caballería" ["The Seventh Cavalry"], "las fronteras" ["frontiers"], "el Rockefeller Center" ["The Rockefeller Center"], "el vigía de Occidente" ["the watchman of the West"], "un rapapolvo" ["a telling-off"], "un bombardero" ["a bombarder"], "sentar cabeza" ["to settle down"], "el metal" ["metal"], "las ventanillas" ["the kiosk windows"], "la Pinacoteca Nacional" ["the National Art Gallery"], "el oro" ["gold"], "el sueño" ["dream"], "el collar" ["the collar"], "el ruido" ["noise"], "los locos conocidos" ["the known madmen"]. And, finally, of course, "revolución" ["revolution"] facing "pesadillas" ["nightmares"]. But, what revolution is that? Could it not be that revolution gives birth to nightmares? Is not that the assumption in "Utopía"? Revolution, then, facing itself on a mirror? Or, revolution *through the looking-glass*?

What are, first of all, the things and people of the first list? I have the distinct impression that, particularly in "Cada loco con su tema" but not only, Serrat is drawing the ruinous landscape of the specific post-modernity that Antonio Negri and Michael Hardt (2000) call Empire and think is only the privileged effect of the aporetic colonisation of all life by the sphere of (capitalistic) production – the only real giant, the only real windmill that these songs are facing, tilting at. Or, in the words of Santiago Alba Rico:

That is to say, our public sphere is not a World: it is a market [that] has been in operation for at least two hundred years as a system, not of exchange, but of generalised destruction [...] whose vital death sentence, against men and things, has only accelerated and extended its process in recent decades through the yeast that we call globalization and which demands, as in the 19th Century, the imposition of the "natural law of supply and demand" with armies and canons. From the economic point of view this order is a massacre: of men, of trees, of animals and of objects. From the point of view of culture, this order of things is a form of nihilism. Recalling reflections that I have made elsewhere, what characterizes capitalist society *qua* society is that it does not distinguish between things to eat, things to use and things to look at; that is to say, between consumer objects, perishable goods and things of wonder (Alba Rico, 2003, p.7).

Ruins, then, which need to be built up in order to allow us the time and the space to contemplate, at least, their spectacle. But, why bother? What is both fascinating and disturbing in those ruins? Perhaps just that, with them,

we recuperate, then, men themselves, uprooted from the post-modern city. Ruin is the ultimate, the only place still inhabited, where poverty or rebelliousness conserve the most ancient culture. [...] ruins boil down bodies. [...] Ruins are not *romantic*; they are the last refuge of anthropology (Alba Rico, 2004).

Ruins, thus, are those places where the most important residue of capitalism (Fernández Vítores, 1997) inhabits, the things and people in the first list above: [6] those who, at the limit, "no tienen nada de nada" ["who have nothing at all"]; those who are not, even, waged labourers; those who remain just human... but those, also, who are still able to distinguish between objects for consumption, objects for use, objects to marvel at. Those, then, and finally, who *prefer* "querer" ["to desire"], "palpar" ["to touch"], "ganar" ["to win"], "besar" ["to kiss"], "bailar" ["to dance"], "disfrutar" ["to enjoy"], "volar" ["to fly"], "hacer" ["to do"], "amar" ["to love"], "tomar" ["to take"]... "vivir" ["to live"], "antes que nada" ["above all"] because, without all those actions, all those "artefactos, bestias, hombres y mujeres" ["objects, animals, men and women"] life would be "un ensayo para la muerte" ["an attempt at death"].

What about the revolution, then? Is it legitimate to ask such a question in such a "conservative" context? But, is that context actually "conservative"? I do not think so. The important thing here is the action... or, to put it better – the *re*action, as many of those ruinous effects are the result of a revolution, proper. A political category like left/right, conservative/progressive which belongs to the conceptual arsenal of the bourgeoisie and which is a moment required by the self-regulation, self-enhancement of capitalism (Fernández Vítores, 1994,

---

[6] But, those in the second as well, of course; although under different conditions.

p.120). Perhaps "ésos no se han enterado / de que Carlos Marx está muerto y enterrado" ["those, that lot have not noticed that Karl Marx is dead and buried"]. Certainly, the remapping of ruins made by Serrat's songs is *alongside, in the margins of Capital... beyond Marx.*

He is not contemplating stars to forget about the rats. In his songs, the stars are the rats. Popular heroes, ordinary people, like Eleanor Rigby or Nowhere Man, friends, family and lovers, places... "There are places I'll remember / all my life, though some have changed..." *Memory*, that most preferred – and most untrustworthy in its umbilical dependency upon oblivion ("Después, inflexible, el olvido / irá carcomiendo la historia" ["Although, inflexible, oblivion will gnaw away at history"] Serrat, 2002) – amongst Serrat's textual devices, the incarnation of his hero, *lonely voice* in the Fortress of Solitude that is melancholy (in its plain philosophical sense) where Kal-El is not Superman anymore, but a Clark Kent *with enhanced sight.* And never nostalgic. A hero telling the stories of residues just because "Art, the last resistance against astonishment, custodian and administrator of what is visible, cannot pretend to create new things amidst mercantile excess that makes everything invisible; it ought simply to relocate them in space so that they might be seen" (Alba Rico, 2004). The hero, the artist, *the reactionary.*

In what I see as the most achieved (even if unintended) tribute to Serrat's artistic procedures, this precise use of such raw materials is going to be done by Joaquín Sabina in the best song from his album *Dímelo en la calle* [*Let's take it outside*] (2002). Like Sabina, Serrat "quería" ["wanted"], only, "escribir la canción más hermosa del mundo" ["to write the most beautiful song in the world"] (Sabina, 2002).

References
Alba Rico, S. (2003) "Los intelectuales y el apocalipsis cultural", *Rebelión*, available online at **http: //www.rebelion.org/cultura/ 031127sal.pdf** (posted 27 November 2003).
------------. (2004) "Instrucciones para construir una ruina", *Rebelión*, available online at **http: //www.rebelion.org/cultura/040123** (posted 23 January 2004).
Albiac, G. (1995) *Caja de muñecas*, Barcelona, Destino.
Alcada, S. (2000) "Introducción" to Serrat (2000), below, pp. 21-33.
Deleuze, G. and C. Parnet. (2002) *Dialogues II*, London, Continuum.
Fernández Vítores, R. (1994) *Maquiavelo: la política*, Madrid, Libertarias/Prodhufi.
----------------------. (1997) *Teoría del residuo*, Madrid, Endimión.
Negri, A. and M. Hardt. (2000) *Empire*, Cambridge, MA, Harvard University Press.
Sabina, J. (1996) *Yo, mí, me, contigo*, BMG Music Spain/Ariola.
Sabina, J. (2002) *Dímelo en la calle*, BMG Music Spain/Ariola.
Serrat, J. M. (1971) *Mediterráneo*, BMG Music Spain/Ariola.
------------. (1978) *1978*, BMG Music Spain/Ariola
------------. (1980) *Tal com raja*, BMG Music Spain/Ariola.
------------. (1981) *En tránsito*, BMG Music Spain/Ariola.

-------------. (1983) *Cada loco con su tema*, BMG Music Spain/Ariola.

-------------. (1984) *Fa vint anys que tinc vint anys*, BMG Music Spain/Ariola.

-------------. (1987) *Bienaventurados*, BMG Music Spain/Ariola.

-------------. (1992) *Utopía*, BMG Music Spain/Ariola.

-------------. (1994) *Nadie es perfecto*, BMG Music Spain/Ariola.

-------------. (1998) *Sombras de la China*, BMG Music Spain/Ariola.

-------------. (2000) *Cancionero Serrat*, Madrid, Taurus.

-------------. (2002) *Versos en la boca*, BMG Music Spain/Ariola.

-------------. (2003) *Serrat Sinfónico*, BMG Music Spain/Ariola.

-------------. (2006) *Mô*, BMG Music Spain/Ariola.

Vázquez Montalbán, M. (1973) *Serrat*, Barcelona, Júcar.

Paternity, the Postal Principle and Exile
in Michael Radford's *Il Postino*

Colin Wright

Michael Radford's 1995 film, *Il Postino*, explores multiple interlocking themes. Firstly, by subtler means than mere word association, the film invokes what Jacques Derrida, in *The Post Card: From Socrates to Freud and Beyond* (1987), calls the "postal principle". This factor, but never *facteur*, refers to a necessary contingency in the very operation of language which results from the claim that, contra Jacques Lacan, a letter may always *not* arrive at its destination.[1] The postal principle insists on the gap between interlocutors as a condition of the very dialogical possibility which nonetheless threatens communication with an exorbitant dissemination, even within the putatively intimate discourse of lovers. Secondly then, in its exploration of the intersections between poetry and the condition of exile, the film narrates the melancholic effects of this postal principle on a model of happiness centring on the trope of "home", as the imaginary dwelling place of relations without difference. I shall also be gesturing towards a third effect, and an effect of thirdness, which relates to the relevance of a post-conflict context within the novel of which Radford's film is the less than "faithful" adaptation: *Ardiente paciencia* by the Chilean author, Antonio Skármeta. (The novel was re-titled *El cartero de Neruda* after the success of *Il Postino*). After all, it is precisely situations of serious conflict that shake to the ground the "home" (national, regional, ethnic, social, familial) in which are usually housed pre-existing economies (*oikonomos*: *oikos*, house or home, and *nomos*, law and/or custom) of happiness.

The Text of the Father: Four Signatures
Insofar as the father is the head of the household, and insofar as it is (assumed to be) down to "fathers" to restore order after conflict situations have rendered the home *unheimlich*, it will have been necessary to begin by focusing on the theme of paternity. The two fathers dealt with by Derrida in *The Post Card* – like parentheses without exteriority for the history of Western metaphysics – are Socrates and Freud. The former is supposed never to have written: it is only through his "son", Plato, who wrote, that we are apparently able to "listen" to the plenitude of his "speech". Similarly, Freud is perceived as the founding father of psychoanalysis, a therapeutic practice and hermeneutic theory apparently indelibly marked by, and carried out

---

[1] In his seminar on Edgar Allen Poe's "The Purloined Letter", Lacan insists on the materiality of the signifier as a vehicle of jouissance by arguing that the letter always reaches its destination. Derrida, in his critique of Lacan's position entitled "The Purveyor of Truth", emphasises instead the structure of writing which, in its reliance on difference, renders the possibility of mis-communication, or non-arrival, *a priori*, irrespective of any attempted control by the signifier, phallic or otherwise. For a sustained discussion of this debate, see Muller and Richardson (1998).

under, Freud's proper name. Derrida passes the offspring of these founding fathers through a complicated paternity test. For example, could Plato have preceded Socrates: "Socrates writing, writing in front of Plato, I always knew it" (Derrida, 1987, p.9)? And does Freud suppress the Nietzschean lineage of psychoanalysis: "He [Freud] never misses him [Nietzsche] within the grasping movement of a denegation" (*ibid.*, p.263)? Already at issue here are problematics of inheritance and debt, origin and originality, property and the very possibility of the proper. The postal principle traverses all of these fields. The father, as patriarch, would have the resultant dissemination reigned in: happiness as unchallenged right of ownership.

In investigating these Derridean motifs in *Il Postino*, it seems logical to begin with Antonio Skármeta, who can surely claim paternity rights over this story? Yet if Skármeta is the father of an originary text, we shall see that Radford is quick to ignore his paternal authority. Moreover, if Plato can be before Socrates, is Skármeta really the *first* father, or does the postal principle begin even before his burning missive, the novel, is sent? His very title is itself second-hand: "burning patience" is a phrase borrowed, or stolen, from Arthur Rimbaud. If the title already adverts to an indelible intertextuality then the narrative of Skármeta's novel weaves itself through and around two interlocking and pre-existing narratives. Firstly, the strikes, civil unrest, American intervention and finally the military coup that led, in September 1973, to the end of Allende's socialist and populist presidency of Chile and the beginning of Augusto Pinochet's military dictatorship. Secondly, the personal exile from Chile of the renowned poet and communist, Pablo Neruda, the central paternal figure on the diegetic level. These two narratives form the implicit backdrop to Skármeta's novel, providing its events with a special piquancy enabled by the informed reader's retrospective awareness of the character's fates. Historical, political and personal threads therefore constitute the intertextual weave of Skármeta's novel before it has even begun: every father is also always a son. Yet, if anything, Radford's adaptation of the novel foregrounds this *mise en abyme*, insofar as these historical and political threads are cut by its dramatic relocation: Radford literally uproots Skármeta's narrative from its native Chilean soil and re-pots it on a provincial island off the coast of Italy which, although it is never identified, we assume is Sicily. Homes are being rendered *unheimlich* on multiple levels already. Within Skármeta's novel, we have Chile's bloody rejection of (or eviction from?) populist socialism as an implicit dramatic backdrop, Neruda's prior political exile from Chile precisely for his communism, and the main character's feverish and disorienting *amour fou*. Yet Radford chooses to compound these forms of homelessness by removing the story from the very (historical, political) home by which the "original" text is intertextually accommodated – a spatial transition we shall examine later.

Turning to the diegetic level of *Il Postino*, the locus of paternity is to be situated with and within the figure of Pablo Neruda himself, specifically in his condition as an exile and as a poet. The central axis of the narrative is the master-protégé relationship between Neruda, –

world famous poet, pacifist, diplomatic ambassador and Communist – and Mario Ruoppolo, – shy and unsophisticated fisherman's son turned postman (and the filmic son of Skármeta's more Latin-American "Mario Jiménez"). The companionable pedagogy that blossoms between them institutes a hierarchical relation essentially identical to that of father and son. Susan Handelman employs this father-son relation (albeit within a Judaic thematic) to articulate the tension in deconstruction between identification with and the displacement of the already written text upon which it (re)writes:

> The writing, the text as gift, is the father's presence-in-absence. Through the text, the subject is taken and possessed – the son is possessed by the voice of the father. (Handelman, 1987, p. 108)

It is in this sense – of text, and the subject in thrall to that text – that Neruda becomes the father, Ruoppolo the son. Ruoppolo's *biological* father is notable for his taciturnity: Ruoppolo admits of him that "he doesn't talk much". Without a voice, his claim to paternity goes unheard. Neruda, on the other hand, is a consummate craftsman of words. Thus, there is a familial transference analogous to adoption: Ruoppolo leaves his home within a silence patriarchal in tone for another space. It is Neruda who introduces Ruoppolo to this other poetic space, to text and, I am arguing, to textuality, to a pleasure of the text irreconcilable with the patriarchal economy of orderly "happiness".

The hypothesis of Neruda's paternity is supported by the role of his signature, which appears in the film on four significant occasions. I want to suggest that all four signatures represent demonstrations of writing in its dimension as a support, or seal, or stamp (timbre) of authority. Then, departing from *The Post Card* briefly, I want to look at what Derrida says about the signature in *Margins of Philosophy*, in order to problematise this paternity.

Neruda's first signature is the most innocuous: we do not actually see it. And yet, it *is* important. It occurs on Mario Ruoppolo's first day in his new job as postman: upon receiving his mail, Neruda signs the form to attest to the success of the exchange. Significantly, Neruda's is the only address on Ruoppolo's route, the only destination to which he must send himself. Therefore, Neruda's signature *alone* can confirm or authenticate the transmission of the messages, and ratify the role of the messenger: Ruoppolo is not a postman until Neruda's signature says so. Already, the signature functions as a mechanism of positionality, situating Ruoppolo in a specific context – on this occasion, broadly, that of waged labour. This contractual confirmation in its turn inserts Ruoppolo into the ambit of Neruda's prefigured Communism, already destining him towards the fateful Communist rally with which the film ends. The signature operates in this positioning capacity in all four autographic moments.

The second act of signing testifies to the division of influence characteristic of the father-son topology. Hoping that, by association, some of Neruda's charm over women will "rub off on him", Ruoppolo asks Neruda to sign a copy of one of the latter's collections of poetry. However, instead of the kudos of suggested friendship, the dedication is coldly impersonal: "Regards, Pablo Neruda". Lamenting the misfiring of his intention, Ruoppolo wonders if it might be rewritten: "It means nothing ... You think he can cross it out and write it better so you can see it's for me, that we're friends?" (Radford, 1995). It is as if Ruoppolo hopes, *via* Neruda's signature, to be inscribed within the poetics of happiness as fulfilled desire, from which he feels exiled: the opening shot of the film shows him wistfully contemplating a postcard from the United States, melancholically suggesting that life is perpetually elsewhere.

The third act of signing – making good the debt incurred by its predecessor – simultaneously inaugurates Ruoppolo into both poetry (as the desire of discourse), and love (as the discourse of desire). Ruoppolo finds himself blighted by aphasia in the presence of his new love, "Beatrice Russo". He goes to Neruda for help, imploring him to write an ode to her beauty with which to win her over. Neruda refuses, and the two fall out. Neruda's third signature resolves these conflicts. He goes down into the village to drink with Ruoppolo at the inn where Beatrice works. He calls her over and, making her stand by as a witness, he signs the notebook he has *already* given to Ruoppolo, saying: "You already have your poetry. If you want to write it down, here's your notebook" (*ibid.*). This phrase enacts an embrace which, again, adopts Ruoppolo into the bosom of Neruda's family of poets. However, it is a rhetorical conceit, performed for the benefit of Beatrice. The purported anteriority is the nexus of a sophistic inversion: Ruoppolo does not already have poetry (he has written nothing), but does already posses the notebook being ceremonially (re)bequeathed to him. The theatricality is successful: on seeing Neruda's signature, Beatrice glances at Ruoppolo with an unprecedented glimmer of interest.

The fourth and final signature, then, seals the libidinal teleology first set into motion – that is, given birth to – by this same patrilineal script. Neruda is the witness whose signature ratifies the marriage certificate of Beatrice and Mario, both endorsing and enabling their union in the eyes of the law (of the Father).

These four signatures seem to establish the code of Neruda's benevolent, because giving, paternity and to underpin the economy of Ruoppolo's newfound happiness. They become hierograms of illocutionary force: when Neruda signs, the constellation of the world shifts. But between the inauguration of love with the third signature, and its conjugation with the fourth, there is not a firm causality. The signature, even Neruda's, is incapable of this remote authority.

Derrida, in *Margins of Philosophy*, has pointed out the contradictoriness of the signature by laying bare the structure of iterability which is its operative but concealed *a priori*.

> In order to function, that is, in order to be legible, a signature must have a repeatable, iterable, imitable form; it must be able to detach itself from the present and singular intention of its production. (Kamuf, 1991, p. 107)

The signature alleges a pure self-identity which, as a *representation* of the author-scriptor's presence, it cannot have.[2] For Derrida, all representation inhabits this logic of supplementarity, a logic fractured by the schism between a simultaneity of addition *and* replacement.

The insubordinate polysemia implied by this necessary threat of iterability would be, to authorial intention, as the rebellious son is to the stern patriarch. Looked at closely, the position of pure paternity is revealed as an impossible structure that thinks itself, in line with identitarian logic, as a circle. This metaphysical mode of happiness posits a line that meets itself without break or rupture in a continuity of pure presence which a certain romantic tradition, indeed, calls love: love as the joyful encounter that creates an indestructible unity. Ironically, it has been Freud's "son", psychoanalysis, that has debunked this romantic image of happiness most systematically.[3]

The Name Returning to Itself: Pablo meets Pablito

Yet Derrida discerns in Freud's relation to psychoanalysis, as it is conveyed in *Beyond the Pleasure Principle*, a similar paternal circularity that conflates the addressor with the address. As the title suggests, it was in *Beyond the Pleasure Principle* that Freud was forced to challenge his own previous model of the economics of instinctual satisfaction, or happiness, in the light of clinical evidence that suggested the existence of the repetition compulsion. Significantly, this clinical material, and this theoretical shift within Freudianism, has as its backdrop another post-conflict context: Freud was reacting in large part to the pathological complaints of shell-shock victims returning from the trenches of WWI. The pleasure principle, insofar as it posited a fundamental avoidance of unpleasure (which from Freud's economic perspective of the mind is excessive psychic excitation), was unable to account for the flash-backs and recurrent nightmares these soldiers suffered. Yet the form of Freud's new theoretical elaboration, the death-instinct, which asserts an even more fundamental instinctual and violent tendency towards absolute equilibrium, stasis, or lifeless stagnation, surely owes some of its tone to the deep existential disorientation of the post-war years?

---

[22] The baroque curlicues of a signature's paraph might be seen as the paradigmatic mark of this alleged singularity, a complexity of ornamentation one also finds, not coincidentally, on bank notes. The contradiction is identical: a repetition which denies its own possibility, and yet gains its power, its *exchange value*, precisely from its repeatability. Recognising this, US artist J.S.C. Boggs draws money and then attempts to "spend it" by exchanging it as art work, frequently obtaining a value far in excess of the denomination of the particular note. Even as he exposes the iterability which is the operative condition of abstract exchange, Boggs also runs up against the structures that repress this condition: he is currently being sued by the US government for fraud. In a ruse that suggests the power of deconstruction, Boggs intends to pay for the legal bills incurred by his trial with his own art works (see Weshler, 1999).

[3] Freud's other son, Jacques Lacan, arguably takes this psychoanalytic insight into love further than anyone, not only in his analysis of courtly love as an articulation of the unattainability of *objet a*, but in his re-conceptualisation, in *Seminar XX*, of love in general as the experience of the real of desire, including the fact that there is no sexual relation (see Lacan, 1998).

Deemed "clinically silent", the death-instinct seems to threaten the very economy of happiness, or at least pleasure, and the therapeutic approach predicated on that economy, that Freud had theorised hitherto. However, far from demonstrating the capacity of psychoanalysis to think outside its own restrictive models of instinctual pleasure and happiness, Derrida's deconstructive interpretation, in exposing the postal principle within the repetition compulsion, shows that the death instinct merely prepares the way for a larger reinscription of psychoanalysis' domain. The sending of the death instinct out into the world of institutionalised psychoanalysis, despite the controversy with which it was greeted there, has the shape of an arching return to its point of departure. Peggy Kamuf explains that

> only a persistent determination of signs as exclusively ideal (and therefore indivisible) can permit the notion of their circulation within, precisely, a closed circuit of meaning. The detachment of the sign would, according to this ideal schema, merely allow it to circle back to the place of its emission. (Kamuf, 1991, p. 460)

Freud, in attempting to rein in the dissemination of psychoanalytic discourse – of which he feels himself the originator, despite Nietzsche and, through him, Schopenhauer – holds it tightly to himself, even as he pretends to give it. Freud (the father) does not want psychoanalysis (the son) "playing" beyond the confines of his proper name. Derrida recognises this tension as "the structure of an impossible bequest of the name to itself, the name inheriting from itself" (*ibid.*, p. 517). This kind of giving, in its circularity, only ever gives to itself. It is the mode of sending Heidegger describes in *On Time and Being* as "[a] giving which gives only its gift, but in the giving holds itself back and withdraws" (*ibid.*, p. 460). The double nature of this bestowal plays itself out in the limping non-steps of Freud's supposed speculations about a "beyond" of the pleasure principle – a non-movement Derrida terms the "thesis of the athesis" (Derrida, 1987, p. 262).

Freud pretends to speculate about the presuppositions of his own discourse and yet, how can one speculate within a circle without exteriority? One is doomed to the "origin", to tautology: Freud's letters are addressed only to himself.[4] For a singular paternity, the speculative *fort* movement can only ever be the preparation for a recuperative *da*. Ernst's repetition compulsion of the throwing and retrieving of the spool is thus mirrored in Freud's speculation, which only "repeats itself in place" (*ibid.*, p. 296). Nor is it insignificant to point out here that Ernst

---

[4] Another text which plays with the consequences of a letter returning to itself (in this case to the eponymous Don Juan) is José Zorilla's play, *Don Juan Tenorio*. Using this conceit of the errant epistle, Zorilla inverts causality (Juan, apparently alive, manages to witness his own funeral) creating the same collapsed temporality that Derrida's notion of "the name inheriting from itself" implies. For an excellent discussion that brings out this problematisation of causality (albeit within a theoretical framework not poststructuralist but Bakhtinian) see the opening chapter, entitled "The Spirit of the Letter", of Firmat (1986).

is Freud's own grandson, son of his own daughter, Anna Freud, herself an analyst, a circular repetition upon which the institutionalisation of orthodox psychoanalysis depended.

This figure of the circle, and its corollary economy of the enclosed circuit, also makes its appearance in *Il Postino*. Faced with the blank page of the notebook (the same notebook which has been given, withdrawn, and given again), and with the prospect of writing his first poem, what does Ruoppolo write? Nothing. Devoid of inspiration, he breaks up the daunting *tabula rasa* by simply marking it, with a circle.

On one level, he is drawing the table football, memento of his meeting with Beatrice. On another, he is delineating the trajectory of metaphysical desire, governed by the One, and the fantasy of wholeness. And yet, what if he is also describing a claustrophobia felt in relation to Neruda's poetry? What if the circle is a panopticon suffused by the inescapable shadow of the father, an emblem of the "anxiety of influence" of which Harold Bloom has written?[5] If Neruda is, for Ruoppolo, the father and origin of *all* poetry, would he not represent a black hole whose gravitational pull would drag every nascent iambic into its orbit? This may sound excessive, yet Ruoppolo, succumbing to this very pull of influence, resorts to using *Neruda's* poetry, *not* his own, to woo Beatrice. In effect, this is a deconstructive citation that challenges the law of the father that governs the patriarchal economy: the precocious son quotes the text of the father deliberately out of context. This citation extends the logic of the exception – by which, as Freud argued in relation to the "primordial father" who *can* have his mother (and anyone else) as his sexual partner, the Oedipal law is both inaugurated and guaranteed (Freud, 1967) – to every instance of the invoking of the law itself. Insolently, Ruoppolo reminds Neruda that "*You* taught me to use my tongue for more than licking stamps" (Radford, 1995). Skármeta's Neruda is particularly irked by this: "let's not get so carried away that we have to vote on who the father is in a family!" (Skármeta, 1988, p. 63). And yet, the paternal circle is neither transported, nor displaced, let alone erased by this citation.

Later, when Neruda has returned to Chile, Ruoppolo opens the same notebook and turns past that first page on which he drew the circle. Pen poised over the next clean page, it is possible to discern that the page is not virginal after all: the indentation, the impression, dent, brand, or indeed *stamp*, of the circle remains, ready to form and distort subsequent inscriptions. One can imagine that every page of The Book

---

[5] Bloom posits in the book of this name something like a master-slave dialectic operative between, respectively, tradition and the would-be-poet. Bloom's poet revises tradition under the guise of correction and purification, but only to create enough space to be able to become a poet in his or her own right. And yet, ultimately, Bloom describes this usurpation in exactly the terms of paternal circularity which I am here opposing to Derrida's horizontality, as Susan Handelman suggests: "Through this revisionary interpretation, the poet can then see himself as his own father" (1987, p. 110). In Bloom's model of poetic development the son only overthrows the father in order to become in turn a father. In contradistinction, the slant I am giving to Derrida here represents the perpetual suspension of paternity.

is similarly marked, which is another way of recalling that Derrida does not allow himself the illusion of a transcendental exteriority unstrictured by metaphysics. The necessity of this theological structure (and structuration) perhaps affords a certain fatherly comfort, yet it also inspires a claustrophobia that scandalously lays bare the mania of absolute faith. The definitive proof of God's existence comes in the unsolicited debt always already incurred by my own, belated and degraded-because-secondary existence, irrespective of how hard I attempt to etch my own discourse onto, into, over His Word. By the same token, there is a suggestion in *Il Postino* (evinced by lingering looks and prolonged moments of contact), that Ruoppolo's citation backfired, that, even in his absence, it was *Neruda's* influence – via the telecommunication of his poetry – which obtained Beatrice's desire, not Ruoppolo himself, who was present, but only, again, in his capacity as a delivery man. Such an authority *in absentia* of writing is also Freud's ambition for psychoanalysis, even if within Freud's own writings there is an apparent secularisation of God-the-Father as a projection of the superego.

This circle of identity finds its apotheosis when Neruda returns from Chile and comes face to face with, literally, his own name-as-offspring. Pablo meets Ruoppolo's son, "Pablito". And what does little Pablito hold in his hand? It is the table football, the circle, which has acted as a trope for metonymy itself ever since Ruoppolo took it from Beatrice's mouth (locus, of course, of the "plenitude" of speech).

For Derrida, this circular thought deceives itself: writing, in its horizontality and its indelible difference, both traverses, and *constitutes* the relay. The trace necessarily contaminates every enunciation, *différance* forever suspending the consummation of metaphysical happiness. All modes of sending, including Neruda's and Freud's, surrender themselves to a space in which the threat of drifting is ineradicable. Once outside the tautologous insularity of the circle, the concepts of origin and origination become untenable, discourse itself apparently unmoored. Thus, the giving, which we have seen in Freud and Neruda, is not autochthonous, unprecedented, generous in the largest sense. Rather, anteriority-without-beginning is the very structure of inheritance:

> I specify in passing: no legacy without transference. Which also gives us to understand that if every legacy is propagated in transference, it can get underway only in the form of an inheritance of transference. Legacy, legation, delegation, *différance* of transference. (Derrida, 1987, p. 339)

The Postal Relay: Privacy, and "Beatrice" as Palimpsest
This suffocating legacy, which is simultaneously also a dissemination, cuts across inheritance and thereby problematises the transmission of property (and propriety) by which families and homes are held together following a death, a divorce, or, indeed, a conflict. I want to characterise this problematisation as a spatial "opening-out", one moving from an enclosed realm of privacy (home), to an expansive

public plane of disseminated letters. For in its condition of legibility, writing is visible, exhibitionist, even promiscuous. "Envois", the extended introduction to *The Post Card*, explores this opening-out, taking the form of a fragmented yet intimate correspondence between lovers. The reader initially becomes a voyeur of this intimacy because the postcards have been delivered to the wrong address, but also because the adulation which they communicate is necessarily *legible*: "The singular address divides, fragments, goes astray, and, like a misdelivered post card, lays itself open to anyone's reading" (Kamuf, 1991, p. 485).

With the postal principle, even the most clandestine of whispered desires can become public, because privacy – at the limit of its horizon – ceases to be possible. Every surreptitious message of love is already potentially exposed, because the modality of the announcement is public: iterability is, inescapably, a form of consensus. Thus, no encryption is immune to being de-ciphered.

Ruoppolo falls foul of this same communicative promiscuity when his own letter fails to reach its address. The poem he has stolen from Neruda and sent to Beatrice, is stolen again when intercepted by Beatrice's despotic aunt. Hoping to redouble its intimacy, Beatrice had concealed the letter in her cleavage. Yet, as we have seen, space is a condition of *trans*mission, difference a provision of desire: no closeness is so intense as to become identity. Her aunt is therefore able to (re)steal the letter, to *cleave* the communication. This concatenation of levels of theft again indexes the problematic relation between the proper, propriety and property. It also evokes the idea of communication-as-currency, of utterances exchanged according to approximate valuations within an economy. Beatrice's aunt is the first to recognise the iniquity inherent in all exchange, the influence of the profit motive which obfuscates any putative transparency: "those words are no better than a bad cheque" (Skármeta, 1988, p. 44).

Of course, the aunt's concern is for the *purity* of her niece, her virginity, for, in other words, the condition of her hymen (earlier she had quizzed Beatrice with: "What words did he *do* to you?"). For Derrida, the hymen is an undecideable: irreducibly *both* virginity and consummation.[6] The aunt's rage is levelled against exactly this shuttling undecideability. Skármeta has Beatriz's mother expressing an awareness of the common thread between metaphor and euphemism.

"Don't be a fool!" her mother exploded. "*Now* your smile is like a butterfly, but tomorrow your tits are going to be two cooing doves, your nipples two juicy raspberries, your tongue the warm carpet of the gods, your behind the sails of a ship, and that thing burning there between your legs the furnace where the proud, erect metal of the race is forged. Now, good night!" (Skármeta, 1988, p. 47)

---

[6] On the *hymen* see especially "The Double Session", pp. 173-286 in Derrida (1997).

It is in response to this rage that Neruda warns Ruoppolo that he, too, is susceptible to the duplicity of language:

> You won't save yourself from the widow's fury with adjectives [...] She'll say you threatened the virginity of her damsel: with a metaphor hissing like a dagger, as sharp as a canine, as lacerating as a hymen. (Radford, 1995)

Whether Ruoppolo's intentions are honourable (hymeneal), or scandalous (hymenoid), poetry is not robust enough to act as a singular rhetoric which might dissuade Beatrice's aunt from her ire.[7] Her anger is born of the very fragility of communication that led to the misappropriation of the letter in the first place:

> the letter makes its return after having instituted its postal relay, which is the very thing that makes it possible for a letter *not* to arrive at its destination, and that this possibility-of-never-arriving divides the structure of the letter from the outset. (Derrida, 1987, p. 324)

However, there is a more primordial sense in which Ruoppolo's libidinal investments in Beatrice are made public, a sense so absolute that privacy is dissolved, desire dispossessed. This dispossession operates at the level of the wanton iterability of the proper name of "Beatrice".[8]

With his new love of words, Ruoppolo treats this name as a sacred chalice brimming with the uniqueness of her presence. On meeting her, he is unable to say anything but her name. Later, when Neruda asks him to choose something beautiful about the island, the answer comes – with a relish of the rolling vowels and susurrating consonants that foregrounds the anthroponym ahead of its owner – "Beatrice Russo". And yet, very quickly, this sacred chalice is shown to be one of a number, what presence it may have, less than unique (it is already an

---

[7] What Neruda is saying here maps onto Derrida's own humility regarding the "truth" (as in eternal fixity) of his own deconstructive interpretations. Derrida continually disavows the possibility of exhaustive mastery in his own texts, underscoring them as deconstructions perpetually open to further deconstructions. Echoing the Judaic tradition of hermeneutics, this strategy indefinitely defers paternity through a processal interpretative activity (writing) which, staying with the familial trope I have been using, is the remit of the "son".

[8] This dispossession of the name of Beatrice has its parallel in *Of Grammatology*, where Derrida treats of a similar chaining of desire around the name "Thérèse" in Rousseau's novel *Emile*. In both cases, the very "properness" of the proper name is incongruous with a system predicated on the operation of difference:

> To think the unique *within* the system, to inscribe it there, such is the gesture of the arche-writing; arche-violence, loss of the proper, of absolute proximity, of self-presence, in truth the loss of what has never taken place, of a self-presence which has never been given but only dreamed of and always already split, repeated, incapable of appearing to itself except in its own disappearance. (Derrida, 1998, p. 112).

Italianisation of Skármeta's "Beatriz González"). Neruda[9] warns him that the name of "Beatrice" has been the subject of another poet, Dante Alighieri. To Ruoppolo's displeasure, Di Cosimo extends this divine comedy of metonymic regress yet further:

Di Cosimo: I held the splendour of your eyes secretly within me, blissful Beatrice.
Ruoppolo: What's Beatrice got to do with it?
Di Cosimo: It's a poem.
Ruoppolo: Mm, Dante Alighieri.
Di Cosimo: No, Gabriele D'Annunzio, my poet.
Ruoppolo: Your poet wrote something for Beatrice? ... I don't like it (Radford, 1995).

A jealous lover learning of his partner's former affairs, Ruoppolo is forced to reconceive her name not as a sacred, unique, virginal signified, but as an overdetermined, derivative, and sullied signifier. The object of Ruoppolo's veneration has always already been deflowered: he is last in line behind a queue of other poet-lovers who

---

[9] Pablo Neruda (not the name attached to the face of the actor Phillippe Noiret, but the name under which certain poems are gathered) displays an awareness of the connection between naming and owning in his poem "Demasiados Nombres" (Too Many Names):
>   Nadie puede llamarse Pedro,
>   ninguna es Rosa ni María
>   [No one can be called Pedro,
>   None is Rosa or Maria]
He refuses the territorialization hidden in nominalism:
>   Me han hablado de Venezuelas,
>   de Paraguayes y de Chiles,
>   no sé de lo que están hablando
>   [They have spoken to me of Venezuelas,
>   of Paraguayes and of Chiles,
>   I don't know what they are speaking of]
And in the penultimate stanza:
>   que no nos llenemos la boca
>   con tantos nombres inseguros,
>   con tantas etiquetas tristes,
>   son tantas letras rimbombantes,
>   con tanto tuyo y tanto mío,
>   con tanta firma en los papeles.
>   [let us not fill our mouths
>   with so many uncertainties,
>   with so many sad labels,
>   with so many resounding words,
>   with so much mine and so much yours,
>   with so many signatures on papers.]
>   (Neruda, 1970, pp. 362-364).
Neruda obeyed his own imperative, publishing *Los Versos del Capitán* anonymously, despite being at the height of his fame. More fundamentally than this, the name "Pablo Neruda" is constitutively impure, divided, simulacral: it is, of course, merely the pen name of Neftalí Ricardo Reyes y Basoalto.

have had "intercourse" with that name, have coupled with it to make their couplets. When Skármeta's version of Ruoppolo, Jiménez, is finally about to sleep with Beatriz, this contamination is temporarily forgotten in the throes of passion: "Words had returned to their roots" (Skármeta, 1988, p. 67).

But the fullness of this consummation is delusional, writing, as we are about to see, precisely a kind of uprooting. As against a private, singular appellation, the name "Beatrice" becomes radically public, ranging across an entire discursive field: it becomes a palimpsest, the site of a mutiny of metalepsis.

Diasporic Writing: Homesickness and Exile
The gap that is constitutive of the addressor-addressee relationship, but which is ideologically obfuscated by a metaphysical discourse of the home as the natural dwelling place of happiness, is therefore challenged by the structure of writing. Indeed, and recalling Freud again, happiness seems to have a neurotic structure which transforms the notion of home into the phantasmatic symptom of a more primordial homesickness: the space between interlocutors registers the incessant homesickness which nonetheless motivates the desire for an impossible homecoming.

There seem to be two modalities of homesickness operative in *Il Postino*. Firstly, Neruda's conventional nostalgia for the fatherland from which he has been expropriated. Skármeta's Neruda laments: "I desperately need something, even if it is only a shadow, from my home. I am not well physically. I miss the sea. I miss the birds" (Skármeta, 1988, p. 82). The two obvious moments of nostalgia felt by Radford's Neruda are both evinced by recordings: firstly by a record of Latin American music (not actually Chilean, but Argentine tango), and secondly by a tape-recorded message sent from home. It is the *intimacy* of sound, the apparent closeness of voice, of breath, that succeed in plunging him into reverie. And yet, the recording is a telecommunication embedded in writing like any other: even analogue tape is a form of magnetic inscription. While the recordings may seem to *trans*mit the pure presence of the referent Latin America (or, for Neruda, "home") they actually operate, like any writing, by differential relations, spacings, absences. Homesickness is thus the *structural* cost of signifying the desired home, signification being predicated upon absence.

The second modality of homesickness, belonging primarily to Ruoppolo, seems closer to a Derridean self-consciousness of this aporia. This is because it is not a homesickness which tends to its yearning with the palliative of a projected return, but – as a sickness *of* home, *here* and *now* – it resembles an unbounded nostophobia. Immured in monotony, Ruoppolo is utterly indifferent (because *habituated*) to the beauty of the island, even jaded: Neruda: "What are the nets like? Mario, I need an adjective". Ruoppolo: "The fishing nets? ... Sad" (Radford, 1995). This nausea of familiarity drives Ruoppolo to want to escape, to fly the nest, as he laments to Beatrice: "We have to leave here, no one understands us here" (*ibid.*).

For both Neruda and Ruoppolo, it is space (respectively capacious and claustrophobic) that generates anxiety, distance (respectively excessive and lacking) that motivates their respective nostomania and nostophobia – the Latin root *nostra* here should recall the continuing thread of property, of belonging. With the operation of Derridean *différance*, this yearning for belonging becomes endemic to writing in its expanded sense.

Derrida's thinking makes the home, which homesickness holds up as its desired object, constitutively *unheimlich*. I have pointed out that the move from Skármeta's text to Radford's film is also one from Chile to Italy. This transition has ramifications far beyond mere aesthetic questions about backdrop, since it is also a transvaluation from one constellation of discourses to another. Where Skármeta's text recounts the military junta, obviously specific to Chile, which deposed Allende's Socialist government in 1973, Radford's film must portray a completely different brand of Socialism (marginalised, oppressed, powerless) because Italy's relationship with that political theory and social movement has been utterly different. Radford must inflict substantial contortions upon the original plot in order to retain Skármeta's thematics. Why, then, does Radford choose to relocate the events of a narrative inextricably interwoven with the political history of a particular nation, in an entirely different one? And does this choice inflict a violence on the Latin American culture in which Skármeta's novel is rooted, roots which Radford tears out?

The Derridean reading I have been offering already has an answer to this: there never was such a thing as a fully present, fully "homely" Chile, nor a metaphysical essence of Italy, only second-hand signs (including narratives of both individual biography and political history). On this view, *Il Postino* does not represent a neat transition from one binary to another, from one home to another, but is a hybrid third term in which Skármeta's Chile and Radford's Italy come together in an oscillating, undecideable aesthetic space which is at once both and neither. This third term does not enact the violence of the Hegelian *Aufhebung*, which subsumes difference, but rather blocks differences together in a cloven temporality and a schizophrenic spatiality which nonetheless maintains their particularities. In *Il Postino*, neither Chile (it is never shown) nor Italy (Sicily is never named) is given priority as the home of the narrative. Instead that narrative is endlessly pulled between the two locales, defining its own liminal space in relation to the perpetual non-actualisation of their respective poles. None of its characters will arrive at the homes they pine for, since this state of pining *is* their home.

Both Neruda and Ruoppolo are doubly inscribed in this economy of a yearning-for-elsewhere (which-is-nowhere), since it is also the condition of the poet,[10] as Derrida describes in *Writing and Difference*:

[10] This is also the condition of the Jew. Derrida, however, is rarely addressing the historico-political Jewish subject specifically, even as he uses notions of exile and displacement. Rather, he is proposing a model of language predicated upon a radicalised *différance* that the Judaic tradition, with the Talmudic and infinitely

> For this site, this land, calling to us from beyond memory, is always elsewhere. The site is not the empirical and national Here of a territory. It is immemorial, and thus also a future. Better: it is tradition as adventure. (Derrida, 1981b, p. 66)

Adventure implies exploration of foreign lands. The poet is by definition a self-imposed exile: an outsider, banished from the "home" of language. Within the discourse of poetry itself, as we have seen, this "home" – which belongs to the father – is built from a traditional configuration of proper names from which the poet must be exiled *in order to become a poet*: "The poet, in the very experience of his freedom, finds himself both bound to language and delivered from it by a speech whose master, nonetheless, he himself is" (*ibid.*, p. 65). The poet must leave the father's home so that he can in turn become a father of poems – a relation to tradition which Derrida here describes as deliverance: "In question is a labour, a deliverance, a slow gestation of the poet by the poem whose father he is" (*ibid.*).

As well as writing around Edmond Jabès' *Le Livre des questions*, Derrida is here articulating the tension of inheritance and displacement between the textual strategies of poststructuralism, and the texts upon which these strategies are parasitic (a tension I have tried to trace between Neruda and Ruoppolo, and between Skármeta and Radford). To those who would accuse Derrida of a neo-Nietzschean reification of unreason,[11] his use of Jabès' trope of the root and the flower in this essay might provide a piquant retort: " ...freedom must belong to the earth, to the root, or it is merely wind" (*ibid.*, p. 66). Deconstruction is a rigorous *working through* of tradition, not an irrational or Dadaist repudiation of it. Analogously, while Ruoppolo only manages to write his first and last poem when Neruda is distant in both space and time, he nonetheless entitles it "Ode to Neruda".

But this site or land, this earth, is not amenable to territorialisation: despite their patriarchal claims to land rights, *all* the poet-inhabitants of tradition are nomads, outcasts, wanderers. Writing is the very peripatetic activity which enacts this rupture from, that is also a suture to, the cannon of tradition, that reservoir of melancholic odes to past happiness as well as heartache. The poets' interpretative creativity with the text of the father *is* the displacement, *is* the diaspora. And this

---

differed nature of its proximity to an unnameable God, is peculiarly equipped to articulate. In this, Derrida is in consonance with certain aspects of Jean-François Lyotard's thinking. Lyotard's strategy of a provisional, lower-case "the jews" aims to both despecify and reassert this movement of occlusion, as his explicit qualification suggests:

> I use lower case to indicate that I am not thinking of a nation. I make it plural to signify that it is neither a figure nor a political (Zionism), religious (Judaism), or philosophical (Jewish philosophy) subject that I put forward under this name [...] "The jews" are the object of a dismissal with which Jews, in particular, are afflicted in reality (Lyotard, 1990, p. 3).

In my concluding remarks on poetry, diaspora, and exile, I also am concerned with "the jew", rather than the Jew.

[11]Jürgen Habermas (1987) makes such an accusation.

applies to my own ludic, Derridean manipulation of *Il Postino*, and Radford's reading of *Ardiente paciencia* before it. The postal principle – which rocks the foundations of the father's home, problematises the policing of the borders of his land, and depresses the happiness of origins – testifies to the "breathing spaces" within the seeming monolith of tradition, preventing that tradition becoming a tyranny of patriarchal (over)determination: neither Socrates, nor Freud, nor Neruda can shore up a determinant, eternally grounded meaning in their texts, nor guarantee the serene happiness of plenitude this might enable.

But this insight comes at a cost, and it is the cost that psychoanalysis faced up to long ago when Freud admitted that its role was merely to transform neurotic misery into an ordinary, everyday human unhappiness that we must understand as structural, and therefore necessary. Home is said to be where the heart is but *Il Postino*, in its various textual avatars, suggests that the home is in fact constituted in and through an indelible homesickness. Pablo Neruda himself evokes this relation between exile, writing, and a structural melancholy when, in his poem "La Palabra" ("The Word"), he describes the very material of his creativity as coming:

> de padres muertos y de errantes razas,
> de territorios que se hicieron piedra,
> que se cansaron de sus pobres tribus
> [of dead forebears and errant races,
> of territories that turned to stone,
> that tired of their poor tribes]
> (Neruda, 1970, p. 430).

References

Bloom, H. (1973) *The Anxiety of Influence*, Oxford, Oxford University Press.

Derrida, J. (1982) *Margins of Philosophy*, trans. Alan Bass, London, University of Chicago Press.

------------. (1981) *Writing and Difference*, trans. Alan Bass, London, Routledge and Kegan Paul.

------------. (1988) *Limited Inc abc*, trans. Samuel Weber, Evanston, Illinois, Northwestern University Press.

------------. (1987) *The Post Card: From Socrates to Freud and Beyond*, trans. Alan Bass, London, University of Chicago Press.

------------. (1995) *On the Name*, trans. David Wood, John P. Leavy, and Ian McLeoud, Stanford, CA, Stanford University Press.

------------. (1997) *Of Grammatology*, trans. Gayatri Chakravorty Spivak, London, Johns Hopkins University Press.

------------. (1997) *Dissemination*, trans. Barbara Johnson, London, University of Chicago Press.

Freud, S. (1967) *Moses and Monotheism*, New York, Vintage Books.

Freud, S. (2003) *Beyond the Pleasure Principle and Other Writings*, London, Penguin.

Habermas, J. (1987) *The Philosophical Discourse of Modernity*, trans.

Frederick Lawrence, Cambridge, Polity Press.

Handelman, S. (1987) "Jacques Derrida and the Heretic Hermeneutic", in *Displacement: Derrida and After*, ed. Mark Krunick, Mark, Bloomington, Indiana University Press, pp. 98-129.

Kamuf, P. (ed.) (1991) *A Derrida Reader: Between the Blinds*, New York, Harvester Wheatsheaf .

Krupnick, M. (ed.) (1987) *Displacement: Derrida and After*, Bloomington, Indiana University Press.

Lacan, J. (1998) *Seminar XX, On Feminine Sexuality, the Limits of Love and Knowledge, 1972-1973,* trans. Bruce Fink, London, Norton.

Lyotard, J.-F. (1990) *Heidegger and "the Jews",* trans. Andreas Michel and Mark Roberts, Minneapolis, University of Minnesota Press.

Muller, J. P., and W.J. Richardson (eds.). (1998) *The Purloined Poe: Lacan, Derrida and Psychoanalytic Reading*, Baltomore, Johns Hopkins University Press.

Neruda, P. (1977) *Memoirs*, trans. Hardie St. Martin, London, Souvenir Press.

------------. (1970) *Selected Poems*, trans. Anthony Kerrigan, W. S. Merwin, Alastair Reed and Nathaniel Tarn, London, Jonathan Cape.

Pérez Firmat, G. (1986) *Literature and Liminality: Festive Readings in the Hispanic Tradition,* Durham, N.C., Duke University Press.

Radford, M. (dir.). (1995) *Il Postino*, Miramax.

Skármeta, A. (1988) *Burning Patience*, trans. Katherine Silver, London, Methuen.

Weshler, L. (1999) *A Comedy of Values*, London, University of Chicago Press.

Wolfreys, J. (1988) *Deconstruction: Derrida*, Basingstoke, Macmillan.

Wood, D. (ed.) (1992) *Derrida: A Critical Reader*, Oxford, Blackwell.

In Search of Love Past
The Dirty War of Erri De Luca's *Tre cavalli*

Bernard McGuirk

In his *Six Walks in the Fictional Woods*, Umberto Eco penetrates the undergrowth of fiction's relationship with fact in a manner peculiarly pertinent to analysis of much of the imaginative literature written on the Falklands-Malvinas conflict in general; and, in particular, of one of the few fictional narratives to have drawn successfully on the violent confrontation in the South Atlantic, namely, the Neapolitan Erri De Luca's 1999 novel *Tre cavalli*. And he does so by fathoming "the Argentine press's coverage of war":

On March 31, 1982, two days before the Argentine landing in the Malvinas and twenty-five days before the arrival of the British Task Force in the Falklands, the Buenos Aires newspaper *Clarín* published an interesting item: allegedly, a London source claimed that Britain had sent the Superb, a nuclear submarine, to the Austral area of the South Atlantic [....] Who invented that Yellow Submarine? The British secret services, in order to lower the spirits of Argentines? The Argentine military command, in order to justify its tough stance? The British press? The Argentine press? Who benefited from the rumour? I am not interested in this side of the story. I am interested in the way the whole story grew out of vague gossip, through the collaboration of all parties. Everybody cooperated in the creation of the Yellow Submarine because it was a fascinating fictional character and its story was narratively exciting [....] The Yellow Submarine was posited by the media, and as soon as it was posited everyone took it for granted. (Eco, 1998 pp. 97-100)

Eco disingenuously, or is it craftily, denies interest in what he himself has, in fact, further elaborated in his five complicit questions; for he has (re-)mythologized a mist-shrouded episode in the reporting of the Task Force in adding the essential if carnivalesque epithet "Yellow" to "the" submarine, and has even attributed to "everybody" its being taken "for granted". Before moving on to his favoured topic of the "fascinating fictional character" of the "story [which] was narratively exciting", he has already inserted a second fictional submarine into a first fictional submarine-*story*, and one most readily associated with another, a prior, England – a fictional, or wonder, land not so much of icon-clad 1980s' Thatcherism as of a (very Eco) 1960s' cultural imaginary. A Beatles-suited narrative is cut and tailored to the other worlds of reader expectation. Which side do you (ad)dress, sir?

Eco's strategic response is to hang to neither left nor right, but to play it down the middle; preferring to the *reportage* of war, and to its ideologies, the ever less obtrusive style of narrative excitement:

This story – that is, the real story of a fictional construction – in the first place, shows that we are continually tempted to give shape to life through narrative schemes [....] Second, it demonstrates the force of existential presuppositions. In every statement involving proper names or definite descriptions, the reader or listener is supposed to take for granted the existence of the entity about which something is predicated [....] What happens when in a fictional text the author posits, as an element of the actual world (which is the background of the fictional one), something that does not obtain in the actual world? (*ibid.*, p. 99)

Time and again, in the focusing of the conflict, and from whichever side or sides of the story the ordering perspectives emerge, it is the representations more than the realities of war that confront the reader or viewer. Whether in the press reporting or in the novel writing, characters take precedence over protagonists; both facts and factions are rapidly fixed as fictions. There will be goodies and baddies, with little place for anyone caught in the cross-fire. And, in any narration, the cultural aura of an era will ever obtrude.

"Blue Meanies" are the very stuff of tabloid headlines; yet to be written, perhaps, but appetising stereotypes easily adaptable to, say, the image of "true blue Tories", *à la* Margaret Thatcher, from a populist Argentine perspective; or, in a bluer shade of pale, to flag-waving *Galtierista* jingoists, from Buenos Aires to Patagonia, from a snooty Saxon angle. Even prior to the conflict's outbreak, the press and other media on both sides had already situated the *kelpers*[1] of the islands themselves as virtual "Nowhere Men", "living in a nowhere land, making all their nowhere plans for..."; which is where the analogy with the Beatles song runs out.[2] For, in war, or even in the preparation of the public imaginary for either the invasion or the re-taking of the Islands, appropriation *is* the name of the game. When it becomes politically convenient, the plaintive "isn't he a bit like you and me?" can readily turn – or be turned – nationalistic, ever to convoke patriotic slogans on the duty to defend "kith and kin", or to prove that "las islas son nuestras".[3]

Fiction's relationship with fact, however, is particularly resonant in press coverage of the Falklands-Malvinas conflict on both sides, notoriously in the Manichean tabloidism of *The Sun's* headline, *Gotcha!*,

---

[1] *Kelpers*: a native of the Falklands/Malvinas. The term evokes the main occupation of the islanders, gathering and processing kelp, large seaweeds, or "oarweeds", of the genus *Laminaria*.

[2] The Beatles' 1968 animated psychedelic adventure film *Yellow Submarine* took the Fab Four to combat the Blue Meanies who had invaded Pepperland, there to restore to its grateful inhabitants the sovereignty of music and happiness. They were k/helped, and occasionally hindered, by one Jeremy Hillary Boob, PhD, a real "Nowhere Man". See **oak.cats.ohiou.edu/~ms538596/ys.html**.

[3] See for example: "Whose kith and kin now?", Peter Godwin's cover-story on how the slogan had turned sour for post-UDI "Rhodesians" in Zimbabwe, *The Sunday Times Magazine*, 25 March 1984; and the McLean refrigeration company's opportunistic take on the "las islas son nuestras" in an advert that appeared in *Clarín* on 14 May 1982: "Fabricamos frío... pero estamos calientes por nuestras Malvinas", reproduced in Blaustein and Zubieta, 1999, p. 488

on the sinking of the *General Belgrano*, or in *Revista Tal Cual*'s demonising cover series on "La Thatcher Peor que Hitler", "Más Mala que El Diablo" and "La Thatcher Está Loca";[4] but also generally in what the novelist Julian Barnes has categorised as "the worst reported war since the Crimean [....] The fact that the rest of the world viewed the war as a brainless squabble between nostalgic imperialism and nostalgic fascism was irrelevant; we didn't care what the rest of the world thought except to imagine that it was impressed".[5]

If "the two sides to every story" cliché is predictably ignored in, especially, the popular press's adversarial coverage of the conflict both, imaginative literature is generally considered by critics to have performed little better, particularly in Britain. A succinct and judicious situating of the Falklands conflict's appearance in and ostensibly slight impact on the novel in the UK is provided, in 1992, by Nigel Leigh in his "A Limited Engagement: Falkland's Fictions and The English Novel" (1992, pp. 126-127). Readers interested in the sub-genre of "Combat Fiction" will find here a quick-fire guide to the mini-spate of popular novels in which "Argies" are the stereotyped fodder of predictable "Brit" up-and-at 'em action cum victory. Leigh is scathing but objective and contextualising in his assessment:

> As we can now see, with few examples to the contrary, the Falklands War has not, so far, permeated the consciousness of Britain's most prominent writers. Its main influence has been on exploitation literature and, to a lesser degree, the popular novel, where its handling has been, almost without exception, trivial, incidental and stereotyped [....] There have been remarkably few attempts among British writers at what Walter Holbling calls, in the context of Vietnam literature, "literary sense-making", and the Falklands novels discussed here are in no way an attempt to "understand a specific historical situation" [...] they are nothing more than what Bruce Merry calls "readable evasions". Clearly, there is no such phenomenon as the Falklands Novel and it is unlikely that any such genre should emerge, although this is not to say that we will not see in the next 20 years or so the emergence of a Falklands novel equivalent to *The Red Badge of Courage* (1893), or *The Naked and the Dead* (1948), or even *Gravity's Rainbow* (1973). (Leigh, pp. 126-27)

In Argentina, the panorama is less bleak, but still problematic. In "De cómo la literatura cuenta la Guerra de Malvinas", subtitle of their seminal meditation "Trashumantes de neblina, no las hemos de encontrar",[6] Martín Kohan, Oscar Blanco and Adriana Imperatore, already in 1993, and in a rhetoric characteristically more theoretical

---

[4] *The Sun*, 4 May 1982; and *Revista Tal Cual* of 14 and 28 of May and 4 July 1982, reproduced in reproduced in Blaustein and Zubieta, p. 471
[5] Barnes, 2002.
[6] "Trashumantes de neblina" is an untranslatable pun; it plays on the famous patriotic anthem: "Tras su manto de neblina/no las hemos de olvidar/Las Malvinas argentinas/clama el viento y ruge el mar", *Marcha de Las Malvinas*.

than the pragmatic analysis of Leigh, felt able to look back as follows:

> The Malvinas conflict, like all wars, is a confrontation of bodies and, at the same time, a confrontation of discourses [....] The war unfolds a construction of versions ever struggling to impose themselves, even when the fight between bodies has been concluded. Two ways of recounting the Malvinas war have predominated in the dispute for the terrain of collective memory: one, that we might call the triumphalist version; the other, the version of lament [....] What is certain is that both are inscribed, finally, in one and the same frame, participating in one and the same logic: the logic of the Great National Narrative, that is the Great Argentine Narrative [....] A symbolic system: name, flag, anthem, coat of arms, pantheon of heroes and deeds [....] This story is effective when it succeeds in dissolving internal differences, making them converge and coincide in the values of national unity. (Kohan, Blanco and Imperatore, p. 82, my translation)

The point is that, whether or not the pro-war or the anti-war discourses predominate at any one moment, neither "version" can escape the entrapment in its own logic of this "Gran Relato Argentino". Thus, while situating the mainstream literary tropings of the conflict as either veering nationalist or going transcendental (to use a Rortian term), Kohan, Blanco and Imperatore establish the ideological and the discursive limitations of most writings on the war: "everything can be said, except that the problem of sovereignty over the islands lacks relevance" (*ibid.*, p. 83). Guilefully, the authors are thus setting up both a patently inadequate binary and a man-of-straw fall-guy – the Nation and its representations – before indulging their crucial, and irrefutable, claim that, already from within the period of the war itself to the time of their writing eleven years on, a differential discourse has existed: "other narratives that, yes, deconstruct *El Gran Relato* and that belong to the discursive field of the literary" (*ibid.*, p. 83).[7]

Their analysis of why, in Argentina, critics are unsettled by, and require an alternative to, a tired national narrative (paradoxically seeking, perhaps, a literature of exhaustion) serves as a crucial Argentine perspective into the style and tenor of much of the literature they praise. They strike a keynote of subversion that might apply to both the Argentine writers they single out and, as I shall now argue, to De Luca's *Tre cavalli*:

> Their operation consists of deconstructing and of not destroying: what destruction triggers is a logic that attacks from outside of the system

---

[7] They go on to cite *La causa justa*, by Osvaldo Lamborghini, *Los Pichy-cyegos* (sic), by Rodolfo Fogwill, *A sus plantas rendido un león*, by Osvaldo Soriano, "El aprendiz de brujo" and "Soberanía nacional", in *Historia argentina* by Rodrigo Freśan, "Memorandum Almazán", in *Nadar de noche*, by Juan Forn, or "Impresiones de un natural nacionalista", in *El ser querido*, by Daniel Guebel (*ibid.*, p. 84).

in question; its objective is to overcome and to replace that other system, therefore it bombards but does not dynamite it. To dynamite it, to deconstruct it, assumes acting from the inside: recognising the internal logic and structure in order to locate the key points, the pillars that support the system and that will bring it down: a task of the spy, of the saboteur. (*ibid.*, p. 84)

They finger, of course, the pressure points of the "Gran Relato Nacional" at precisely its most vulnerable junctures: causes are not just *per se*; jokes are more serious than the purportedly real; investment is outperformed by inversion. Classically, in deconstructive parlance, between the inside and the outside there is ever less difference than *différance*:

A soldier goes to the Malvinas, but his family is English, and his brother is in London. An ex-combatant reports to an Argentine Embassy but turns out to be a Chilean who has usurped the latter's place. And even when it comes to volunteering, which in the case of war encapsulates the national as desire (to fight for the fatherland as if exercising one's will), it is a Japanese who appears; he is enlisting in the anti-imperialist cause, guided by the principles learned in the name of the Emperor during the Second World War [....] But all national identity, not only the Argentine, is similarly deconstructed: even that of the enemy [....] And the Argentine kids in the Malvinas are astonished because the English are "Escot", "Wels" or "Gurjas" and wonder if there are any real English. And it is precisely the idea that there is a national authenticity that is thrown into question; the English, too, are not themselves, there is no pure centre that is not impregnated by otherness (*ibid.*, p. 84).

The work from which they take their cue that, in the Malvinas/Falklands novels most liable to "literary sense-making" in attempting to "understand a specific historical situation", as referred to by Nigel Leigh, is *Los Pichiciegos*. Written during the conflict, Rodolfo Fogwill's inspired meditation on not the dogs but rather the moles of war, tunnelling and trading as they inhabit the black market of the conflict in both literal and metaphoric intensity, exploits however a very different if established genre of dystopian narratives, drawing brilliantly on classic evocations of underground man or survival narratives such as H.G. Wells' *The Time Machine* or William Golding's *Lord of the Flies*. There is a sense, still, that Fogwill is indulging a however ingenious act of "readable evasion" from the "Gran Relato Argentino", by inverting it, burying it only to see it living on in the subterranean gloom of its own other.

Perhaps it was necessary not only "to wait nearly 20 years or so [for] the emergence of a Falklands novel equivalent to [...] *Gravity's Rainbow*", but also to look outside and beyond the binary of an Argentine or a British "national" narrative for the phenomenon of a fiction that works on the difference; that will shuttle between Italy and Argentina, and even towards Africa, with English and Irish encounters on the way, for a vision wherein any and all national authenticity is creatively to be thrown into question... and continually re-broached as a phantasm, an ineluctable haunting, a wager, a third term... or horse.

The close analysis that follows will propose that one of the most successful instances, in literary terms, of the fictional embracing of the Malvinas/Falklands conflict is De Luca's *Tre cavalli*. Thematically, it could be said that the Argentina of the first-person narrator's imaginary is the dominant mover of the action even though it is set in a contemporary Italy of shadowy *camorra* or *mafia* menace. The reader will find no easy access to what is, stylistically, the most subtle and habitually indirect meditation on *el proceso* and the Malvinas moment. The minimalist plot is borne on the memory of an older man, working now in his native Italy, as a gardener; finding a self (again) falling in love, (again) lapsing into reminiscence. De Luca's style reflects a terse and elliptical stream of consciousness preoccupation with capturing inseparably from the unfolding plot the way the body feels, the memory weaves, the *libido* drifts and identities merge and re-separate. Thus, the long Argentine Patagonia and Malvinas sequences of the narrative are interwoven with short memories of the narrator's early twenties and his present middle-age lingering solitude and mistrust of almost everything and everyone not spontaneously associable with the refuge he has taken in nature. His flight to the Argentina of the 1970s prompted the determining actions of his life; his flight from the Argentina of the post-Falklands era would appear to guarantee an escape from the consequences of his involvement with a country that is pervasively characterised by him as much as a person as a militarist state.

The novel is preceded by a strangely tell-tale *premessa* – a single page that operates as both preface and premise. The opening words both situate and structure the obsessive imaginary that will haunt and shape the narrative:

Argentina è un triangolo rettangolo che ha per cateto grande le Ande a occidente, per minore il cateto irregolare dei fiumi a nord e per smangiata ipotenusa l'Oceano Atlantico a est. [Argentina is a triangle rectangle which has for its long side the Andes to the west, for its short side the irregular rivers of the north and for its ragged-edge hypotenuse the Atlantic Ocean to the east.] (De Luca, p. 9)

A personal geometry based on the play of three- and four-sided relationships will come to dominate this peculiar fusion of private memory and cultural memoir; for the narrator is drawn ever back and down towards the Horn of the Americas' mystical reaching out for the anonymous relief of Antarctica. Yet the novel is to be as violent as it is poetic, socially bound up no less with an Italian psychography of 1970s terrorism than with an Argentina of the dirty war, *el proceso*, and the occupation and loss of the islands. The *premessa*'s six brief and staccato paragraphs remind the reader not only of the millions of Italian immigrants who had settled in Argentina by 1939 but also of the inescapable bilateral awareness of a shared political inheritance. For De

Luca creates a first-person narrator who, in his ideological uprootedness and unfailing stalking of the violence of terror or criminality is forever caught between rather than within continents:

> Argentina è lunghezza di tremilasettecento chilometri, tra ventuno e cinquantatré gradi di latitudine sud. L'ultimo zoccolo d'America, condiviso col Cile, sta a soli dieci gradi dalla terra di Graham, corno del continente Antartide.
>
> Argentina ha accolto quasi sette milioni di emigranti fino al 1939. Circa la metà erano italiani.
>
> Dal 1976 al 1982 Argentina ha scontato una dittatura militare che ha prosciugato una generazione. Al termine mancheranno all'anagrafe circa quarantamila persone quasi tutte giovani, senza una tomba.
>
> La dittatura collassa dopo la fallimentare invasione delle isole Falkland/Malvinas, circa mezza Sicilia, a più di trecento chilometri dalla costa. È la primavera del 1982.
>
> Queste immensità di luoghi e di vicende riguardano accidenti occorsi a persone di questa storia.
>
> [Argentina is three thousand seven hundred kilometres in length, between twenty-one and fifty three degrees latitude south. The last plinth of America, shared with Chile, is only ten degrees from Graham Land, horn of the continent of Antarctica.
>
> Argentina welcomed almost seven million immigrants up to 1939. About half were Italians.
>
> From 1976 to 1982 Argentina served its sentence under a military dictatorship that drained a generation. In the end, state records will be missing about forty thousand persons, almost all of them young, without a grave.
>
> The dictatorship collapses after the failure of the invasion of the Falkland/Malvinas Islands, about half a Sicily, more than three hundred kilometres from the coast. It is the Spring of 1982.
>
> This immensity of places and of episodes has to do with occurrences that befell people in this story.] (*ibid.*, p. 9)

In the *premessa*, the standard Italian definite article of "l'Argentina" is missing, rendering personal, prior to the opening of the narrative itself, a relationship that will intermittently draw on history and on facts but is one that reflects a markedly ideological perception of a broader war. Eventually, the conflict of 1982 will serve simultaneously as release for a repressed Italian psyche and as the cleansing of a repressive Argentine dictatorship. The second-handness of everything to be gleaned or understood is caught by the narrative's opening words: "Leggo solo libri usati [I read only used books]" (*ibid.*, p. 11).[8]

The minimal plot and, not least, the enigmatic title of *Tre cavalli* are hardly rendered explicit to the reader until almost the end of the novel. Only when the narrator, in his early fifties and falling in love with the thirty-something call-girl Laila, talks to her obsessively about his

---

[8] At the time of writing there is no published English version of *Tre cavalli*. All translations are mine.

"South", do the nature and consequence of his near twenty-year experience of Argentina emerge. Before that point, we know only of another North-South relation, the ideological Torino-Calabria trajectory that first brought him into contact with his present employer, twenty years before; he a southern worker, Mimmo the student son of a Calabrese father, communists both in the turbulent 'seventies. But to Mimmo he is reluctant to divulge anything of "i miei malanni di Argentina, i tori scatenati, la caccia alla vita [my ill-fated Argentine years, the raging bulls, the hunt for life]" (*ibid.*, pp. 16-17). Such a confession would not fit the triangle-rectangle geometry promised at the outset and confirmed throughout the novel. It will spill out shortly after the narrator glimpses, and raises his wine to, Laila: "Alzo allo stesso punto il bicchiere e lo lascio sospeso prima di berlo. L'allineamento mi spinge a un principio di sorriso agli zigomi. La geometria delle cose intorno fa succedere coincidenze, incontri [I raise my glass at the same height and hold it out before drinking from it. The coincidence of glasses draws from me the flicker of a cheekbone smile. The geometry of things around one prompts coincidences, encounters]" (*ibid.*, p. 12). Yet his spontaneous lapse leads ever into solipsism: "Cosa chiede una donna coi fiocchi a un giardiniere di cinquant'anni seduto al fondo di un'osteria? Mai incontrati prima, è giovane e io vengo da venti anni di America del sud [what can a special woman like that ask of a fifty-year old gardener sitting in the back of an eating house. Never met before, she is young and I come from twenty years in South America]" (*ibid.*, p. 13).

It is in the characteristically poetic prose of a hesitant narration that the apparently mystical gardener sows the seeds of his ever-tentative dependency on what turns out to be the third seminal but childless relationship of his life:

> Ora con te aspetto il sonno e penso a quel cielo del sud.Quale sud, chiede. Quello del mondo, dico: il saggittario, il lupo, il centauro, la vela, la croce.
> Se conosco le stelle? Le chiamo per nome, mi piglio la confidenza, ma non
> le conosco, solo una presentazione da lontano. Sorride: e perché là? Guerra. Quale? Una, ce n'è sempre una.
> [Now with you I wait for sleep and think of that southern sky. Which south, she asks. The south of the world, I say: Sagittarius, the Wolf, the Centaur, the Sail, the Cross. Do I know the stars? I call them by name, I allow myself that familiarity, but I don't know them, it's only an introduction from afar. She smiles: and why there? War. Which war? A war, there's always a war.] (*ibid.*, pp. 33-34)

Suddenly, the constellations of Antarctic skies unfurl a reason not for being but for being *there*. Yet was it really a war, just another war, that drew so fatefully southwards this man of the soil who claims that he can identify, wherever he is, the points of the compass? No. His first love had been "Dvora, argentina, sta viaggiando l'Europa in premio del diploma [Dvora, an Argentine girl, travelling in Europe as a reward for graduation]" (*ibid.*, p. 43). Virginally, he had waited: "Aspettare. Questo è il mio verbo a venti anni [...] Amore di nozze tra noi succede solo in Argentina" (*ibid.*, pp. 41,45). [To wait. To wait is the verb of my twenties [...] Consummated love ("amore di nozze") between us happens only in Argentina.]

In the arms of Laila, he is, at the same time and always, elsewhere: "Ce n'è un'altra in cui sto, che ascolta la voce andare, senza governo" (*ibid.*, p. 46) [There is another part of me, where I am, that hears my voice fade away, ungoverned]. There follows the fatal, snatched, shift across the Atlantic, in uncontrollable pursuit of a woman, delivered with the convulsive beauty of Breton's chase of a Nadja.[9] What starts as libidinal fascination turns into a brutally violent reality; for a self, for a generation:

Ci ammazzano tutti, noi della rivolta. Schizziamo da un nascondiglio all'altro. Portiamo addosso l'odore della paura. In strada i cani lo fiutano e ci vengono dietro. Nella fuga cerchiamo qualche vendetta. L'Argentina strappa dal mondo una sua generazione come una pazza fa con i capelli. Ammazza i suoi ragazzi, vuole fare senza. Noi siamo gli ultimi. Sto qui da anni per amare una donna e ora sto in guerra. Al posto di blocco succedono spari. Ci fermano, abbiamo armi. Siamo due, lui ferisce un poliziotto e subito una scarica gli trapassa la gola e muore sui miei piedi. La sua faccia è spalancata da uno sforzo. La sua faccia mi dà forza. Sento il rilascio delle sue viscere ed è quel puzzo che mi spinge fuori. Da dietro la macchina esco allo scoperto, punto verso il riparo dei due poliziotti, la loro raffica s'inceppa, gli sono addosso, sparo a un corpo che cade su quell'altro ferito, vedo la faccia sbigottita di un ragazzo, non è più un nemico, non sparo su di lui, scappo. Così sono i giorni, di corse.Si afferrano soldi in una banca per continuare a correre. Prima di smettere, vado a sparare a un colonnello, un solo colpo in mezzo alla folla di un marciapiede di domenica. Ancora oggi non so se è vivo o morto. Poi vado a sud, dove le terre si stringono, dove è stupido scappare. Cercano altrove gli ultimi di noi.

[They massacre us all, all of those in revolt. We dart from one hiding place to another. We carry the smell of fear upon us. In the street, the dogs sniff it out and come up behind us. In fleeing, we seek some revenge. Argentina snatches one of its generations from the world as a madwoman tears out her hair. She kills her young, she wants to do without them. We are the last. I've been here for years to love a woman and now I'm at war. At a road-block there are shots. They stop us, we're carrying arms. We're two, he wounds a policeman and at once a volley of gunfire cuts through his throat and he dies at my feet. His face is agape from his efforts. His face gives me strength. I smell his intestines relax and it is the stench that flushes me out. I break cover behind the car, I aim at where the two

---

[9] De Luca's self-conscious high literary style evokes the comparison with André Breton's *Nadja* and the pulse of convulsive beauty or total loss: "la beauté sera convulsive ou ne sera pas".

policemen are hiding, their firing jams, I'm upon them, I shoot at one body that falls on top of the other wounded, I see the astonished face of a boy, he is no longer an enemy, I don't shoot at him, I escape. That's what the days are like, on the run. Money is stolen from a bank to carry on running. Before stopping, I'm going to shoot at a colonel, a single shot in a crowd on a pavement on a Sunday. Even today I don't know whether he's alive or dead. Then I go south, where the land narrows, to where it is stupid to flee. They look elsewhere for the last of us.] (*ibid.*, pp. 47-48)

Bloodshed has burst into the fiction with the speed and unstaunched flow of a lost virginity; the lover who waited could not be awaited by war. Chance involvement with an Argentine has become a stark engagement with Argentina.

The pace of the narrative, previously pulsing with the measured quietude of the aging gardener, now conveys the panic of the *proceso* years through the footfalls of a man on the run:

C'è un peschereccio di balene che va alle Malvinas. Sto in fondo al sacco della mia stessa vita, ogni giorno è buono per essere scosso fuori. L'oste vuole che me ne vada. Forse mi sta aiutando. Mi combina un imbarco di mozzo sopra un battello irlandese. Prima di salire a bordo mi disfo delle armi [....] Senz'armi non peso più niente [....] Non penso alla ragazza amata, seguita fino a essere parte del suo paese. Ora sto che sta in fondo al mare buttata al largo giù da un elicottero con le mani legate. Vissuta per me, morta per regalare occhi ai pesci.

[There's a whaler that's Malvinas bound. I'm at the bottom of the sack that is my own life, one day's as good as another to be tipped out. The landlord wants rid of me. Maybe he's helping me. He fixes me up with a passage as a deck-hand on a little Irish boat. Before boarding, I get rid of my weapons [....] Without weapons I no longer weigh anything at all [....] I don't think about the beloved girl, followed to become part of her country. Now I know she's at the bottom of the sea, thrown out of a helicopter, her hands tied. Lived for me, died to gift her eyes to fish.] (*ibid.*, p. 48)

A classic case of a *desaparecida*; but a loss treated with absence of memory, of recuperability, of a past inseparable from a writing present, characteristic of Erri De Luca's style, and counter to predominating patterns of thinking cultural memory. Perhaps a search for cultural – and personal – oblivion. The writing here is elliptical in Italian: "vissuta", "morta", "per" – heavily charged absolutes with an ambivalence of agency... or purpose? Escape into sleep and anonymity entails the interplay of the real with the metaphorical:

"Mi chiamano il morto, nessuno dorme dove riesco io. Nessuno sa da quanta vita non dormo [....] Qualcuno di loro dev'essersi battuto prima di mettersi in mare. Mi portano con loro perché anch'io puzzo di guerra. Mi pago il viaggio lavorando, ma non hanno bisogno di me. È inteso che mi lascino alle isole." [They call me the dead man, no one sleeps where I manage to do so. No one knows the length of life I've not been sleeping [....] Some of the men must have been fighting before turning to the sea. They take me with them because I also stench of war. I pay my passage working, but they don't need me. It's understood that they'll leave me on the islands.] (*ibid.*, p. 49)

Even the echoes of Ireland, and of its own men on the run, are understated, broached as a whiff... and without commonality, let alone comradeship:

> Non credo agli scrittori, ma alle loro storie, questo rispondo a un marinaio impestato di lentiggini che mi chiede se ho fede in Dio.
> [I don't believe in writers, but in their stories, is what I reply to a too-freckled sailor who asks me if I've got faith in God.] (*ibid.*, p. 49)

This moment of excess, of meta-language, is but a rare concession De Luca makes to his recalcitrant narrator. No ties.

The graphic participation of the narrator in urban guerrilla warfare and his flight from Argentina's so-called "process of national reorganisation" operates ostensibly as in a bubble. No more tellingly than in the but one-page initial treatment of his arrival on "the islands". The tightly structured geometry of the sexual relations in *Tre cavalli* filters the experience of the man on the run, perforce, through his experience of solitude... and of woman:

> Sbarco a Soledad che non so camminare [...] Sto sopra suolo inglese. Mi fermo a una locanda, la donna è vedova di un pescatore di balene, Maria, Maria Delsol si chiama. Faccio per lei il cuoco, aggiusto l'orto, bado alle pecore gonfie di lana. Di notte facciamo rumore. Maria è forte come una scialuppa che piglia mare contrario, io sto in piedi e spingo i remi [...] Il labbro delle pecore è forte per strappare il pelo corto e duro del pascolo [...] Aspetto. Non ho niente da chiedere al tempo. Ci sono più bestie che uomini, più donne che uomini, tutto è più numeroso di un uomo. E succedono anni, io lavoro, do pace a Maria, non tocco un soldo, non ci penso. Alla radio risento una canzone di Argentina, il giorno dopo è l'invasione.
> [I disembark at Soledad and I no longer know how to walk [....] I'm on English soil. I stop at an inn, the owner is the widow of a whaler, Maria, Maria Delsol is her name. I do her as cook, fix up the vegetable garden, tend the sheep fluffed up with wool. And at night we make sound. Maria is as strong as a life-boat that strives against the tide, I am upright and I pull on the oars [....] The sheep's lip is strong from tugging at the short and hard hair of the pasture [....] I wait. I've nothing to ask of time. There are more animals than men, more women than men, everything is more numerous than man. And the years pass, I labour, I give peace to Maria, I don't touch a cent, I don't think of it. On the radio I hear again a song of Argentina, the day after it's the invasion.] (*ibid.*, pp. 50-51)

Stereotype is cultivated as a resource of impersonality: Soledad is solitude; Maria is an empty space to be filled.[10] The dispassionate pulse of a 'seventies Italy (make love *and* war) is caught in the rutting rhythm of a frantic rowing to and fro; involuntary involvement in terror... or error. A disengaged male narrator spectates, as if not active; a female – a port of call – figures only as the protagonist slips in and out, keeps her cervixed. A floating commitment to cause, but rarely if ever to person, is captured, untranslatably perhaps, in the highly stylised Italian: "Di notte facciamo rumore [....] E succedono anni, io lavoro, do pace a Maria, non tocco un soldo, non ci penso". Denial but re-affirms the subconscious – whore and peace? *At night we quake love... the years slip by, I toil, pacify Maria, don't touch a cent, don't think of it*. Or, less flippantly, might this particular form of maleness, projected onto Argentina, be but a discursive re-enactment of the cyclical Italianising of the country and the cult(ure)?

The Malvinas have been, in the first instance, a sphere of suspension, of escapism, for a protagonist becalmed before the storming of April 1982. Within the collapsed temporal sequence of the narrative present, for him to lie now in Laila's arms is forever to re-take the (un)occupied fucklands: "Sto con lei come in Argentina, senza giorno dopo. Nei suoi abbracci mi torna al naso la torba dell'isola di Soledad [I'm with her as I was in Argentina, with no tomorrow. In her embraces comes again to my nose the turf of the isle of Soledad]" (*ibid.*, p. 54). In text time, however, there is no escape from present into past or from past into present:

> Nemmeno so se mi cercano ancora per il conto di quegli anni. Non ci sono più soldatini al governo, ma le leggi sono buffe e magari se le dimenticano in vigore, così per distrazione. Chissà se Maria paga una taglia per i miei testicoli o se le basta di maledirmi [...] È notte anche quando lascio l'isola di Maria, salendo sul battello per risalire i paralleli del ritorno [....] Vomito alle prime onde, questo è tutto l'addio. Si monta verso la pancia d'equatore...
>
> [I don't even know if I'm still being pursued to account for those years. There aren't any toy soldiers in government now, but laws are funny and one probably forgets that they still apply, just like that, distractedly. Who knows if Maria's put a price on my testicles or if it's enough for her just to curse me [....] It's night time too when I quit Maria's island, taking ship through the parallels of return [....] I vomit from the first waves, that's all the farewell there is. Up towards the belly of the equator...] (*ibid.*, p. 54)

No escape either from remorse, from guilt. The persona shifts constantly across zones of time, of place, of woman, a subjectivity unified but at the same time frozen by violence or the expectation of

---

[10] De Luca's imaginary does not go so far as to give to this Maria the explicit particularity of Di Stefano but moves to his inside right Del Sol. A 'fifties childhood and a 'sixties youth culture infuses the *tiffoso* psyche of the *macho* narrator, notwithstanding the prose's often gentle style.

it.[11]

Non ho niente di Dvora perché senza di lei mi tengo il niente [....] So che sta in fondo al mare con le mani legate [....] Penso a questo sotto le parole di Laila e per una volta di più so che di me non avanza niente [....] Non ho neanche un rantolo di rammarico per gli spari, la piccola guerra, la parte di vendetta presa e non pagata. Perché io sono illeso [....] Ascolto male Laila, piccolo ritorno di Argentina feroce [....] E invece Laila dice: "Anch'io cogli ammazzamenti."

[I've nothing left of Dvora for without her I hang on to nothing [....] I know she's at the bottom of the sea with her hands tied [....] That's what I think under Laila's words and once more I know that there's nothing left of me [....] I haven't a scrap of regret for the gunfire, the little war, the bit of revenge taken and not paid for. Why am I safe and sound [....] I hardly hear Laila, a little return of Argentina, ferocious [....] And yet Laila says: "Me too with murders."] (*ibid.*, pp. 78-9).

Tre cavalli, according to Luce Irigaray, tells a different story of the Malvinas/Falklands conflict.[12] But it also tells a different Irigaray:

Giving oneself, that giving – a transition which undoes the properties of our enclosures, the frame of envelope of our identities. I love you makes, makes me, an other. Loving you, I give myself you. I become you. But I remain as well to love you still. And as an effect of that act. Unfinishable. Always in-finite. (Irigaray, pp. 73-4)

An "I" indeed remains, but only as an effect; an effect of that act – of involvement in *el proceso* – which, for De Luca's narrator, is unfinishable. Dvora – Maria – Laila... Always in-finite. Always the collapsed triangle. Always the different yet the same story:

Fa schifo ammazzare Laila. Non te lo togli più di dosso il grasso della morte [...] mentre più sei lontano da quel sangue, quello torna perché tu sì, tu respiri, sei un vivo, un maledetto vivo [...] è ancora lì, appiccicato a te, l'ammazzato [...] E quando ammetti questo, senti pure sollievo. Quanti assassini si lasciano ammazzare. E continuo, continuo a dire a Laila il mio sgangherato scongiuro per amore.

[It's disgusting, to kill, Laila. You never get rid of the grease of death [...] just when you're the furthest from that blood, it comes

---

[11] "Dopo la pubblicazione del *Nome della rosa*, rispondendo ad una domanda di un giornalista che gli chiedeva dove nel suo romanzo si poteva trovare la soggettività dell'autore, Umberto Eco rispondeva: 'il soggetto è negli avverbi.'"["After the publication of *The Name of the Rose*, responding to a question from a journalist who asked him where in his novel the subjectivity of the author was to be found, Umberto Eco replied: 'the subject is in the adverbs.'"] See Violi (2006).

[12] Luce Irigaray, in private correspondence, drew my attention to, and sent me the gift of, *Trois chevaux*; whence the challenge of my reading, in counterpoint to her lover's discourse, De Luca's novel as *spécule-homme... de l'autre femme*.

back because you, yes, you breathe, you're alive, alive but cursed [...] it's still there, sticking to you, the one you murdered [....] And when you admit that, you even feel relieved. How many assassins let themselves be killed. And I continue, I continue to tell Laila my ramshackle exorcism for love.] (*ibid.*, pp. 80-81)

The lover's discourse erupts into a revelation of violence inseparable from the epiphany of sexual surrender, a trope used often in war fiction generally and, in Falklands fact, in the recalling of a soldier's reality, by Ken Lukowiak, "a backstreet Wilfred Owen", in his most literary of memoirs, *A Soldier's Song*.[13]

In *Tre cavalli*, however, a peculiar gender inversion intervenes in the unravelling of the plot and of the in-built geometry of three- cum four-play. The revelation that the life of Laila herself is threatened by the criminal *camorra* group that she has frequented – she knows too much – prompts in the narrator, inscribed as he is about to become in a present mortal danger, a convulsive outpouring of his own Malvinas trauma:

> Finisce qua, Laila. Mentro lo dico si seccano gli occhi, tocco il libro in tasca per appoggio, sento sulla fronte un vento di altre onde. È l'Atlantico del sud, dentro il corpo fuga e furia di non farmi acciuffare dagli argentini sbarcati a occupare l'isola di Soledad. È aprile, autunno, scappo via da Maria senza dire niente, lei è dei loro e io sto da capo in terre di caccia e di cattura. Mi nascondo in un frastaglio di costa in un punto dell'isola detto "passo di aquile", il punto più a sud, tempeste e uccelli marini e onde e vento da consumare orecchie. Pesco, bevo acqua piovana, rubo uova ai nidi, faccio fuoco di torba la notte e sento la trappola che morde dappertutto e resisto, tanto per vivere [....] Resto di giorno al coperto a guardare il mare. Sento indurirsi la mia vita per assorbire il colpo e accettarlo [....] Vedo la linea rossa del tramonto che separa giorno da notte, penso che il mondo è opera del re del verbo dividere e aspetto la linea che viene a staccarmi dai giorni [...] e ogni uovo deposto è solitudine. E io faccio al buio di brace una frittata di solitudini e mi sfamo [....] Pensiero d'oltrevita Laila, so che li stai ascoltando.
>
> [Laila, it is finished here. While I'm speaking my eyes dry, I touch the book in my pocket for support, I feel on my forehead a wind of other waves. It is the South Atlantic, within my body flight and fury not to let itself be caught by the Argentines who had landed to occupy the Island of Soledad. It's April, autumn, I run away from Maria without saying anything, she is one of them and I am once again in lands of hunt and snare. I hide in a cove on the coast at a point of the island called "Eagle's Pass", the southern-most point, storms and seabirds and waves and wind to slice off your ears. I fish, drink rainwater, steal eggs from nests, make a turf fire at night and feel the trap that bites into everything and I resist, just to live [....] By day I

---

[13] Ken Lukowiak, "a backstreet Wilfred Owen", according to *The Mail on Sunday* (cover blurb of Lukowiak, 1993).

remain under cover looking out to sea. I feel my life hardening to absorb the blow and to accept it [....] I see the red line of the sunset which separates day from night, I think that the world is the work of the king of the verb divide and I await the line which will come to cut me off from my days [....] Each new laid egg is solitude. And I, in the ember-glow of darkness, make an omelette of solitude and sate my hunger [....] Thoughts from an afterlife life, Laila, I know that you are listening to them.] (*ibid.*, pp. 82-83)

Withdrawal from sex, flight from death; loss of woman, theft of life; the *fort-da* compulsions of a politically uprooted, ideologically displaced, (non-) protagonist of psychological warfare draw on the South Atlantic as might a sucker of eggs. But the sustenance drawn is solitude in its raw state. Even the cooked alternative betrays an unfulfilled subject's struggling to break into a social reality and out of a curiously isolating amorphousness. His is but a presence in the islands, an absence of engagement with, much less commitment to, what is the ever-alien two-sided conflict of the Malvinas-Falklands theatre. Yes, Lacanians, the set-up here does invite, ostensibly, a reading according to the structures and strictures of the Symbolic Order. The narrator is – as throughout – a third man, an agent trapped between a *them* and an *us*; a "little" male, an *hommelette*, soft-centred as yet, even when seeking to gel, when trying to be hard. That geometry of the fourth term, hinted at in the *premessa* but thus far projected from within a triangle of females, is but immanent. A case, will it turn out, of *cherchez l'homme*?

   Dura qualche settimana, mi scoprono a forza di frugare e scappo sugli scogli, sparano contro il vento e c'è un sassolino di piombo che infila il polmone e io credo di vederlo mentre mi esce davanti e scappa più lontano e io gli corro dietro finché il fiato smette tutto insieme e finalmente una bonaccia nelle orecchie e sento i calci come da un portone e uno mi vuole finire lì e gli altri dicono che fanno bella figura a spedirmi in terraferma e mi mettono sul cofano di una camionetta come si fa con la caccia e girano la città sparando in aria che hanno preso un terrorista e mi chiamano l'aparecido e mi mettono in carcere e un medico inglese mi cuce l'uscita e l'ingresso e mi dice buonafortuna e anche di resistere che i suoi stanno arrivando. E io non so chi sono i suoi, ma dopo qualche notte sento i cannoni a mare. E io sto sulla branda della cella e intorno non ci sono più guardie e gridano di fame da altre celle e niente cibo per giorni e poi arrivano ad aprire e sono tutti pazzi felici e io non respiro, però so che la morte mi sputa in faccia anche per questa volta. E tutte queste storie stanno a un centimetro dalla testa di Laila [...] e io sento ancora le mie parole andarsene da me. Le vedo mentre le pronuncio. "C'è una casa su un viale a siepi di bougainville. Lì dentro un uomo indossa l'uniforme e un altro in strada aspetta di sparare. C'è la minima scorta di un autista. Mentre quello esce io sbuco da un intrico di siepi col vantaggio di essere veloce, solo e nella bocca stringo le redini dei nervi. E una radio attacca una canzone [...] e vedo il fianco destro di una divisa e una mano che va tardi in cerca dell'arma e l'autista che cerca qualcosa, poi scappa dietro un riparo e io salgo sulla macchina e parto e sento qualche colpo, ma soprattutto sento la canzone della radio lasciata accesa nella macchina" [....] Laila ride, le Americhe, dice, mi hanno svitato [....] È America di sud, Laila, giorni senza giorno dopo, si resta in pochi [...] non dipende da se stessi di vivere, durare.

[It lasts for several weeks, they discover me by foraging and I escape on to the rocks, they fire against the wind and there is a lead pebble that passes through my lung and I believe that I see it as it comes out in front of me, as it takes flight from me, and I run after it until all at once my breath gives out, until finally all is becalmed in my ears. I feel their kicks as if they are forcing an entrance and one of them wants to finish me off there and then, but the others say they'll make a bigger impression if they despatch me on the mainland. And they put me on the bonnet of a van as if I was hunted game, they tour the town shooting into the air that they've captured a terrorist, they call me the *aparecido* and put me in prison where an English doctor sews up the entry and exit and wishes me good luck, also saying to resist because his side are coming. I don't know who his side are, but after several nights I hear shelling out at sea. I'm on the bunk in my cell and there are no longer any guards about. Cries of hunger come from the other cells and there is no food for days on end, then they come and open up for us, everyone's mad with joy and I can't breathe but I know that this time again death is spitting in my face. All these stories take place just a centimetre from Laila's head [....] Again I hear my words leaving me. I see them in the very moment I pronounce them. "There is a house on a bougainvillea-lined avenue. Inside a man is putting on his uniform and another waits in the street to shoot. There is a chauffeur as his only escort. While he comes out, I emerge from a clump of hedge, with the advantage of being quick, alone and having the reins of my nerves between my teeth. And a radio launches into song [...] and I see the right side of a uniform, a hand that drops too late towards a weapon and the chauffeur who attempts something, then runs for shelter and I jump into his car, I leave and hear shots, but most of all I hear the song of the radio that's still on in the car" [....] Laila laughs, says that the Americas have made me a little crazy [....] That's the America of the south, Laila, todays without tomorrows, only a few left, it's not up to us to live, to endure.] (*ibid*., pp. 82-86)

Hardness, when it is achieved, comes in the form of a bullet and, for all the poetic prose, there can be no escape, no dream sequence, once the doors of the self are kicked in. Abruptly, a soldierly violence, indissociable from the inhumanity of a brutalising regime, invades the narrative. A fleeing neutral's view of the looming Argentine-British confrontation is momentarily skewed, and hardly restored by the disingenuous disclaimer "I don't know who his side are". Distraction it may be; but from a death-wish unfulfilled for an *aparecido* as yet unwelcome on the last islands of *Thanatos* ... though still close to Laila, *donc* Dvora; and, inseparably, to his memoir of terror, and to the

Americas that have made him a little crazy, tomorrowless.

When he records Laila's passionate interruption of his self-exorcising disclosure, it is the narrator who now hears a lover's discourse in tones germane to the Irigarayan terms to which I have drawn premonitory attention and which now help situate – and differentiate – De Luca's calculatedly doubled narrative perspective:

> Ti voglio, dice, mi spetti e a te spetta di allargare braccia e tenermi. Ti amo per amore e per disgusto di uomini, ti amo perché sei integro anche se sei avanzo di altra vita, ti amo perché il pezzo che resta vale l'intero e ti amo per esclusione degli altri pezzi spersi.
>
> [I want you, she says, you're mine and it's yours to open your arms and hold me. I love you out of love and of disgust for men, I love you because you're whole even if you're left over from another life, I love you because the bit that's left is worth the whole and I love you even without all the other lost pieces.] (*ibid.*, p. 86).

However, it would seem that he is beyond the rescue of any "transition which undoes the properties of our enclosures"; he cannot feel "unfinishable":

> Non chiedermi, Laila, non sono più io quello, nessuno può essere quello a lungo, perciò le guerre smettono e una generazione successive prende fiato davanti e cancella di dietro. Via di fuga, dici, ricordo la fuga, ma nessuna via. Sono l'ultimo e corro fino in fondo all'Argentina, non mi fermo più [....] Cerco il fondo, il vuoto.
>
> [Don't ask for anything, Laila, I'm no longer him, no one can be the same for long, that's why wars stop and the next generation draws its breath from in front and cancels out from behind. An escape route, you say, I remember the escape but not the route. I am the last one and I run all the way to the end of Argentina, and stop no more [....] I seek the bottom, the void.] (*ibid.*, p. 87)

Least of all can he conceive of saying – or believing – "I give myself you. I become you". The "frame of envelope" of *his* identity is that unwillingness to risk transition "which undoes the properties" of his self-enclosure as terrorist. He runs until he can run no more, runs until he smells again the Mediterranean odours of his childhood. As he escapes into a primal scene, he pushes open the door of an inn; and of an insight:

> Vedo occhi viola di venuzze esplose. Ha sessant'anni almeno e capelli imbiancati come ghiaccio."Una vota di uomo dura quanto quella di tre cavalli e tu hai già sotterrato il primo" [....] "C'è ancora del buono in te. Ti metterò su una nave e te ne andrai. Sarai salvo. Ti costerà i figli: non ne avrai. Quelli come te vanno lasciati senza" [....] Sul muro dirimpetto c'è una carta geografica del mondo. È capovolta, con l'Antartide in alto. Si accorge che la fisso. "Sei del nord", dice, "quelli del nord restano scemi a guardare il loro bel pianeta sottosopra. Per noi invece il mondo sta così, col sud in alto". Me ne

sto a occhi persi sulla carta [....] Il nord disegna carte false col suo bel polo in cima, mentre è il fondo del sacco. E poi per voi conta l'oriente e l'occidente, mentre per noi è solo acqua sbattuta, oceani di ponente e di levate. Stiamo sul corno appuntito del mondo, accovacciati al suolo per non farci staccare dal vento [....] La carta capovolta ora mi sembra giusta, m'insegna a stare sull'antipodo. La fuga creduta verso il fondo, si rovescia in alto. Sto in cima a uno scoglio e aspetto il tuffo.

[I see eyes veined bloodshot violet. He is at least sixty and his white hair is like ice. "A man's life lasts as long as that of three horses and you have already buried the first one" [....] "There's still some good in you. I'll put you on a ship and you'll get away. You'll be safe. It'll cost you your offspring: you'll have none. Those like you must be left without" [....] On the wall facing there is a map of the world. It is upside down, with the Antarctic at the top. He notices that I am staring at it. "You're from the north" he says, "those from the north are dumbstruck to see their beautiful planet bottom up. But for us the world's like that, with the south on top". I stay staring emptily at the map [....] The North designs false maps with their beautiful pole on top, while it is the bottom of the sack. And for you it's the orient and the occident which count, while for us it's only choppy water, oceans of sunset and sunrise. We're at the pointed horn of the world, huddled on the ground so as not to be blown away by the wind [....] The upside down map now seems right to me, it teaches me how to be in the antipodes. The flight I thought of as downwards turns upwards. I stand on a rock and await the plunge.] (*ibid.*, pp. 90-92)

Within a short sequence, both the title of the novel and the topsy-turvy cartography of memory are rendered explicit. With the insistent resignation of a folk-wisdom instilled since the skipping-songs of childhood, the narrator counts not his chickens but his horses: [14]

Tre anni una siepe,	[Three years a hedge,
tre siepi un cane,	three hedges a dog,
tre cani un cavallo,	three dogs a horse,
tre cavalli un uomo.	three horses a man.]

In the process, however, he recounts a singular version of *el mundo al revés*, a time-honoured Hispanic tradition of popular literature's expressing – often didactically – a vision of the world upside-down. De Luca's prose concisely captures a peculiar remapping of the world; and of many an Argentine's sense of cultural displacement.

But what lessons does the dumbstruck northerner bring back from his mission south? Populism ("for us")? Smugness ("the world's like that")? Triumphalism ("with the south on top")? Resentment ("the North designs false maps")? Exposure ("choppy water")? Isolation ("oceans of sunset and sunrise")? Abjection ("huddled on the ground")? Vulnerability ("so as not to be blown away")? Solidarity... or

---

[14] From an Emilian Appennine *filastrocca* or nursery rhyme.

acquiescence ("now seems right to me")? Disorientation has come to *seem* right for this resigned, un-northed, Italian; returned with lost optimism from South America, he cultivates the garden... and is candid with Laila; he awaits only death – from whichever compass-point, now, that it might come.

> Laila mi abbraccia, versa vino, me lo porta al sorso [....] Dice che non conosce nessuno che parla del passato col tempo del presente. Che me ne faccio delle girandole dei verbi? Non sono il padrone del tempo sono il suo asino. Va bene per gli scrittori il passato e il suo ceraunavolta [....] Al futuro non servono verbi, vuole nomi [....] Il mio futuro, dice, sta in un maledetto verbo pratico e sporco. Ammazzare, chiedo, lei mette giù la testa e toglie le braccia dalle mie spalle. Non dico niente. Quel verbo una volta usato resta in corpo così, all'infinito.
>
> [Laila embraces me, pours the wine and brings it to my sip [....] she says she knows no one who speaks of the past in the present tense. What do verbal weather vanes matter to me. I'm not the owner of time, I'm its donkey. The past tense and its "once upon a time" are all very well for writers [....] The future isn't served by verbs, it wants names [....] My future, she says, is a verb that's cursed, practical and dirty. To kill, I ask her, she lowers her head and takes her arms from around my shoulders. I say nothing. That verb once used remains like that in the body, infinitely.] (*ibid.*, p. 93).

Is this his chance? To kill and to die? "And as an effect of that act. Infinitely"... to love?

> Uno di noi due è già morto e adesso a me non importa sapere chi. Attraverso la strada e entro nel giardino [....] Al cancello Selim è allegro per il caldo e ha una camicia nuova. "Primavera, uomo, bisogna avere il nuovo addosso". È alto robusto, un albero di uomo [....] Vengo con te, dice. Meglio di no, Selim. Meglio di sì, uomo. Lo dice così certo che sto zitto [...] poi mastichiamo insieme sardine e pane all'aria di aprile.
>
> [One of us is already dead and now it's not important for me to know which one. I cross the road and go into the garden [....] At the gate, Selim is happy because of the heat and he has a new shirt. "It's spring time, man, you've got to have something new on your back". He is tall, robust, a tree of a man [....] I'm coming with you, he says. Better you don't, Selim. Better I do, man. He says it so firm that I stay quiet [...] then we down sardines and bread together in the April air.] (*ibid.*, p. 98).

The April onset of crisis is exploited for the triggering of violence. A male subjectivity for so long blocked in its development, arrested, spoiled, yet never quite able to be (self-) obliterated, still resists entry into common, shared, action with another man. At best, he can acquiesce and join the African, Selim, in – or is it for? – sustenance. As the promised release of an alternative geometry looms, the land-locked gardener turns away, and in upon himself, in search not of a man, of an other – *l'homme cherché* – but of manhood.

> Mi calmo e mi indurisco [....] Scanso per strada le persone che vengono incontro. Ho paura di sfiorarne una e solo così ferire. Incrocio una donna, cambio marciapiede prima che lo faccia lei. Un assassino deve stare in un vuoto [....] E so di essere un uomo adesso perché sono la più pericolosa delle bestie. Non è caccia la mia, ma solo attacco per distruggere. Quando arrivo a sentire questo, sono pronto. Quanti soldati cadono se non arrivano in tempo a questo.
>
> [I calm down and harden up [...] In the street, I avoid the people who come towards me. I'm afraid of brushing against one of them and just like that, of wounding them. I walk past a woman, I change pavements before she can do the same. A killer must stay in a void [....] And I know that I'm a man now because I am the most dangerous of beasts. For mine is not the hunt, it's the attack to destroy. When I get to feel that, I'm ready. How many soldiers fall if they don't get to that in time.] (*ibid.*, p. 103).

To see (to psyche?) the self into soldiery, into fighting for a cause, the terrorist must view himself as man and beast, or man as beast; a question less of military training than of feeling. Hardness is on parade as if in front of a mirror – a state, a stage, of development? Or a textbook case: where id was will ego be... even if denied entry into the (uniform-ed) superego?

> E mi giro di colpo [...] e sento un soffio di zolfo che sfiata dal naso ed esce un caldo e cola per la faccia e mi accorgo che è sangue e le narici spruzzano schizzi a terra a colpi di arteria e un uomo mi offer un fazzoletto e mi dice di tenere la testa all'indietro e io obbedisco e chiudo gli occhi e sento una voce di donna che parla di un negro e io penso a Selim con la sua bella camicia nuova e mi appoggio a un muretto e mi siedo per terra e forse dormo [....] È ancora da farsi la cosa decisa e il tempo perso stringe intorno a Laila [....] Ma il sangue perso mi procura sollievo [....] Qualcuno, una donna vede un negro afferrare un uomo che esce dalla macchina e sgozzarlo. E vede che va via senza neanche uno schizzo di sangue addosso, sulla camicia [....] E poi arrivo io e siccome ce n'è poco, aggiungo anche il mio al sangue della strada [...] mi succede di intendere la cenere di Selim, il suo saluto e quello che capisco non riesco a trattenerlo. Il sangue perso mi fa vuoto [....] Io torno dal sud di un'ora di Argentina, navigo i cento paralleli in una sera, mi separo da Laila e non voglio pensare all'amico che riscatta un debito con un abbraccio e una gola tagliata [....] Mi tocco il punto del proiettile passato senza portarmi via.
>
> [I turn suddenly [...] and I sense a sulphurous smell coming from my nose, a hot liquid flows across my face and I realize that it's blood and that my nostrils are haemorrhaging on to the ground as if from an artery and a man offers me a handkerchief and tells me to keep my head up and I obey and close my eyes and I hear a woman's voice that speaks of a black man and I think of Selim with his beautiful new shirt and I lean against a wall and sit on the ground and

perhaps fall asleep [....] What's been decided is still to be done and the time lost is squeezed around Laila [...] but the spilt blood gains me relief [....] Someone, a woman, sees a black man grab a guy who's getting out of a car and slit his throat. And she sees him go off without a blood stain on him, on his shirt [....] And then I arrive and as if there's not enough of it already, I add my own blood to that of the street [...] at last I understand the ashes of Selim, his farewell, and I can't hold back what I've understood. The loss of blood leaves me empty [....] I return from the south of an Argentine hour, I sail through the hundred parallels in a single evening, I am separated from Laila and I do not want to think of the friend who repays a debt with an embrace and a slit throat. I touch the point of the projectile that passed through me without taking life away.] (*ibid.*, pp. 104-07)

Screwing his courage to the sticking place has taken its toll. The compulsion to act in order to continue to be with a woman is inextricably linked with the drive to perform as a real man. But the real is ever other; *the* other, the other man, the "other" (incomplete) Self... Sel/im. Out of an all-too-familiar triangle of relating exclusively to a Dvora-Maria-Laila, the possibility of completing the rhombus emerges; of achieving a personal geometry sketched from the outset in the "doubling" of Argentina in the "triangle rectangle" of the *premessa*. Experience, however, has confounded structure, ideology, fulfilment. Premise has been the doubled life; promise has been the failed threat of consummation.

The shame of "I do not want to think" merely underscores the abject, the letting of the wrong blood, the spilling of the wronged self; living-cum-dying always vicariously. Selim has acted quickly and decisively, while the self-staging protagonist "in action" sways ever to and fro. Towards and then away from woman; southwards to Argentina then northwards to Italy... ever drawing attention to the parallels on the way. Fingering near-death; lingering near life.

Le ragazze si preparano a scendere, io seguo ultimo. Sul marciapiede alzo il naso al cielo e sento l'odore del mio sangue secco. Ci sono sere in cui il cielo è un uovo e lo si può guardare dall'interno [....] Non sono innocente, non è questo il sollievo, ma solo quello fisico di un mestruo dal naso. Un altro uomo sta al mio posto di assassino senza togliermi colpa, solo la mossa toglie [....] So che porta via con sé il coltello per continuare a tagliare pane, a fare mazzi di fiori, a spaccare un frutto. Chi ama le cose e sa il valore di usarle, non le abbandona a un ultimo servizio maledetto. Nel buoi della cucina muore il mio secondo cavallo [...] Se anch'io sono un altro è perché i libri più degli anni e del viaggio spostano gli uomini [....] Mi rado in poca luce la faccia bagnata e il rasoio prova un altro verso di passare la pelle. Metto il libro nella tasca di dentro della giacca, me l'appunto sul petto dall'interno. Nel vecchio posto dell'arma ora c'è il tutt'altro.

[The young girls prepare to get off the train, I follow. I'm the last. On the pavement, I raise my nose skywards and I sense the smell of my dried blood. There are evenings when the sky is an egg and you can see it from inside [....] I am not innocent, that's not the relief, but only the physical sensation of menstruating through the nose. Another man is in my murderer's place but without taking the blame from me, only sparing me the gesture [....] I know that he is taking his knife with him to carry on cutting bread, making bouquets of flowers, slicing a fruit open. Anyone who loves objects and knows the value of using them doesn't abandon them to a final cursed usage. In the darkness of the kitchen my second horse dies [....] If I too am an other it's because books more than the years and travel displace men [....] I shave with a feeble light, my face wet and the razor tries to pass over my skin in a different direction. I put the book in the inside pocket of my jacket, pin it against my chest from within. In the old place of the weapon there's now everything that is other.] (*ibid.*, pp. 107-09).

Where have all the young girls gone? And why am "I" the last man? The non-coagulating of *l'hommelette*, at the end of the novel, is hardly disguised; especially when "the sky is an egg and you can see it from the inside". A male "I" menstruates differently, protesting no innocence but taking blame; for inhabiting, rather than co-habiting with, woman, woman, woman; being spared the gesture, but not the curse. Whence, it is "in the darkness of the kitchen [that] my second horse dies". The final wager, on the last horse, will be on an inactive "I". For the projected man of action, embryonic within the narrated self, was another. Now passive, except for the feeble gesture of the counter shave, an end-self prefigures its rectangular coffin... with its third horse substitute, the book. *Ipse non dixit. Scrivet. Perdet*?

3 singles, 3 doubles and a treble...
William McGuirk

Coda

> What it comes to is that an artist doesn't merely exemplify an ultimacy; he employs it.
>
> John Barth

"The Literature of Exhaustion" was one of the most influential concepts of the decade in which I took my first tentative steps into engagement with that invitation which we call academic literary criticism. In his essay of that title, the US novelist John Barth laid out in starkly accessible terms the proposition that, when other referentialities have fallen into futility, the most characteristic recurrent resource of literature is the text's referring to its own limitations. In short, we have come to take it for granted that meta-textuality is the frame of many a creative solipsism, of an ever-more intricate self-referring literariness. Mimesis exhausted, theology dethroned, philosophy word-bound, poetics navel-gazing, such is the paradigm under the sign of which the meta-fictions of Jorge Luis Borges, Franz Kafka and their inheritors are seen to perform. Imitatio naturae, imitatio Christi, imitatio Freudi, imitatio linguae, however, is not a series of substitutions, but rather an enchainment. In John Barth's "homelier terms, it's a matter of every moment throwing out the bath water without for a moment losing the baby". Let us refresh our memory (and our bath water), as we re-situate De Luca's end of millennium novel, by hearing again Barth's assertions regarding literary creativity and "ultimacy":

> One of the modern things about these two [Beckett and Borges], is that in an age of ultimacies, in everything from weaponry to theology, the celebrated dehumanization of society, and the history of the novel – their work in separate ways reflects and deals with ultimacy, both technically and thematically [....] What it comes to is that an artist doesn't merely exemplify an ultimacy; he employs it [....] Borges writes a remarkable and original work of literature, the implicit theme of which is the difficulty, perhaps the unnecessity, of writing original works of literature. His artistic victory, if you like, is that he confronts an intellectual dead end and employs it against itself to accomplish a new human work [...] an artist may paradoxically turn the felt intimacies of our time into material and means for his work – *paradoxically* because by doing so he transcends what had appeared to be his refutation [....] Borges defines the Baroque as "that style which deliberately exhausts (or tries to exhaust) its possibilities and borders upon its own caricature" (Barth, pp. 22-30).

As critics, as contemporary literary historians, as cultural commentators, we are constantly challenged to dismantle the easy continuities of successive eras, movements, "-isms", in order to reconceive the inherited wisdoms of our disciplines.[15] Thus, I have chosen to ponder, and echo, Barth's age of ultimacy, not merely as

---

[15] cf. "Nei nostri scritti mancano gli 'ismi' anche se sia 'modernismo' che 'post-modernismo' sono termini che vengono in mente alla lettura degli scritti 'compatti' e 'asciutti' di uno scrittore consapevole della compattezza dell'ebraico biblico che si scriveva originariamente senza vocali, e nel quale il dire ('daber') condivide le consonanti per la parola per 'cosa' ('davar'), proprio quel dire che fece la creazione. Ma gli scritti di De Luca [...] non vanno versati attraverso un particolare filtro critico, anche se dobbiamo subito ammettere che non ci siamo potuti sottrarre dalla nostra 'condition postmoderne', quel modo di essere nello spazio e nel tempo in cui i limiti e le frontiere sono cancellati e che ci lascia in uno stato di fluttuazione in cerca di ciò che abbiamo perso lungo la strada. E il ritorno è impossibile". [Missing from our writings are "isms", even if both "modernism" and "post-modernism" come to mind as we read the "compact" and "dry" writings of an author who is aware of the compactness of the biblical Hebrew which originally was written without vowels, and in which the saying ("daber") shares the consonants with the word for "thing" ("davar"), that very saying which made Creation. But De Luca's writings [...] are not to be poured through a particular critical filter, even if we must immediately admit that we have not been able to subtract ourselves from our "condition postmoderne", that way of being in space and time in which limits and borders are erased and which leaves us in a floating state, seeking what we have lost along the way. And no going back is possible" (Ruthenberg, 2004, pp. 10-11).

exemplified but as subtly employed by De Luca, whereby the technical *is* the thematic and vice-versa – but not just in terms of the history of the novel. For cultures, and cultural studies, too, require a (non-)sense of an ending; and one by no means confined or confinable to epochal, even centenary, markers.

Far from chronologising modernity and its discontents, its conflicts, its wars, its terrors, its defeats, this case study has wagered on an Italian horse-race; at the risk of an intellectual dead end employed against itself, the transcending of what has appeared to be its refutation. By inference, De Luca's tactics can be construed, too, as a shuttle that operates between Argentina and Italy, between Barth's Borges and Borges's Baroque...modernity unconfined; and multivocal.

Tre anni
una siepe...

Hedging one's bets... but for how long?

References
Barnes, J. (2002) "One of Britain's leading novelists recalls how the conflict unfolded back home. The worst reported war since the Crimean", *The Guardian*, "Falklands Special: The Television War", 25 February.

Barth, J. (1967) "The Literature of Exhaustion" *Atlantic Monthly* 220, pp. 29-34.

Blaustein, E. and M. Zubieta (eds.). (1999) *Decíamos ayer*: *La prensa argentina bajo el Proceso*, Buenos Aires, Ediciones Colihue.

De Luca, E. (1999) *Tre cavalli*, Milan, Feltrinelli.

Eco, U. (1998) *Six Walks in the Fictional Woods*, Cambridge, Mass., Harvard University Press.

Irigaray, L. (1992) *Elemental Passions*, trans. Joanne Collie and Judith Still, London, Athlone Press.

Kohan, M., O. Blanco and A. Imperatore. (1993) "Trashumantes de neblina, no las hemos de encontrar: De cómo la literatura cuenta la Guerra de Malvinas", *Espacios* 13, pp. 82-86.

Leigh, N. (1992) "Falklands Fictions and the English Novel" in James Aulich (ed.), *Framing the Falklands War: Nationhood, Culture and Identity*, Milton Keynes, Open University Press, pp. 117-128.

Lukowiak, K. (1993) *A Soldier's Song*, London, Phoenix.

Ruthenberg, M. S. (ed.). (2004) *Scrivere nella polvere: Saggi su Erri De Luca*, Pisa, Edizioni ETS.

Violi, P. (2006) "'Il soggetto è negli avverbi': Lo spazio della soggettività nella teoria semiotica di Umberto Eco", **www.associazionesemiotica.it/ec/pdf/violi**.

Notes on Contributors

Neal Curtis is Director of the Centre for Critical Theory in the Department of Cultural Studies at the University of Nottingham. He is the author of *Against Autonomy: Lyotard, Judgement and Action* (Ashgate) and *War and Social Theory: World, Value and Identity* (Palgrave).

Macdonald Daly is Associate Professor in the Department of Cultural Studies at the University of Nottingham. His books include *A Primer in Marxist Aesthetics*, *Crackpot Texts: Absurd Explorations in Modern and Postmodern Literature*, and a volume of short stories, *Engels on Video: a Joint Production*, written with Ellis Sharp. He has also published editions of novels by H.G. Wells, Elizabeth Gaskell and D.H. Lawrence, and is the General Editor of the multi-volume series *Documents on Marxist Aesthetics* (CCC Press, 2006-).

Cristina Demaria is Lecturer at the University of Bologna, Department of Communication. She was a Leverhulme Fellow and is currently Special Professor in the Department of Cultural Studies at the University of Nottingham, in the School of Modern Languages. She has worked on media and television and is the author of *Teorie di genere. Femminismo, critica post-coloniale e semiotica* (Bompiani), *Semiotica e memoria. Analisi del post-conflitto* (Carocci) and, with Colin Wright, editor of *Post-Conflict Cultures: Rituals of Representation* (Zoilus).

Constance Goh has recently completed a Ph.D in Critical Theory and Cultural Studies at the University of Nottingham. The thesis explores the intricate philosophical relations pertaining between the two superficially demarcated areas called the East and the West, with particular focus on the multiple conflicts which occurred at Tiananmen Square in the twentieth century.

Roberto Grandi is Professor of Mass Communications and Public Communications at the University of Bologna, where he is Vice-Rector for International Relations. His most recent publications are: *Elementi di comunicazione politica*, *La comunicazione pubblica*, *L'impresa che comunica*. From 1996 to 1999 he held the office of Deputy Mayor for Culture in the Municipality of Bologna.

Nicholas Hewitt is Professor of French and Head of the Department of Cultural Studies at the University of Nottingham. He is a specialist in French literary, intellectual and cultural history in the first half of the twentieth century and is the author of books on Henri Troyat, Louis-Ferdinand Céline, interwar "malaise", and the culture of the French Right. He is Editor of *French Cultural Studies* and is currently working on a cultural history of Marseille in the nineteenth and twentieth centuries.

269

Bernard McGuirk is Professor of Romance Literatures and Literary Theory at the University of Nottingham where he is also Director of the Centre for the Study of Post-Conflict Cultures. He has published widely on literatures in English, French, Spanish, Portuguese and Italian and his books include *Latin American Literature: Symptoms, Risks and Strategies of Poststructuralist Criticism* (Routledge), *Poesia de Guerra* (Memo) and *Falklands-Malvinas An Unfinished Business* (New Ventures).

Rui Gonçalves Miranda is a PhD student in the Department of Hispanic and Latin American Studies at the University of Nottingham. His thesis focuses on the writings of the Portuguese poet Fernando Pessoa, whose vast work also includes a significant number of texts relating to Portuguese national identity. His research interests include late nineteenth and twentieth century Portuguese literature and philosophy as well as Lusophone films and popular music.

Michelle Pépin was born in South Africa and holds a PhD in International Relations. She is a Principal Lecturer at Nottingham Trent University (UK) in the School of Architecture, Design and the Built Environment. Her field of research reflects her personal, enduring concern with peace and conflict, focusing on the relationship between human identity, conflict and shelter. She has published and spoken in the USA, Europe and the Far East.

Elena Pirazzoli took her Ph.D. in the History of Art at the University of Bologna in 2005. Her research focuses on the nexus between memory and art, paying particular attention to the theme of destruction and reconstruction of the urban form. She has recently worked on the form of the archive in the fields of art and architecture, specifically in artists' work and museum practices, often involved in themes of memory and identity.

Stephen Roberts is Lecturer in Spanish Literature at the University of Nottingham. He has written widely on the literature, philosophy and politics of Miguel de Unamuno and has just published the monograph *Miguel de Unamuno o la creación del intelectual español moderno* with the University of Salamanca Press. He has also published on other Spanish and Spanish American intellectuals and poets, such as Ortega y Gasset, Rodó, Juan Ramón Jiménez, García Lorca and Neruda.

Stanislaw Rzyski is Research Assistant at Department of Economic Geography, University of Gdansk, Poland. His research focuses on contemporary socio-spatial changes of post-socialist cities, quality of life and residential mobility issues in urban areas and new migration trends in borderlands after European Union enlargement. He is a leader of the research project investigating quality of life patterns in two post-socialist cities, Gdansk (Poland) and Klaipeda (Lithuania).

Elizabeth Taylor began her academic career at Grahamstown University, in South Africa, and produced a doctoral thesis on nineteenth-century literature in English written in and about South Africa. She then moved to the University of Nottingham where she enjoyed a long career in the Department of English and the Department of Critical Theory and Cultural Studies where her teaching evolved from the canonical texts of the English seventeenth, eighteenth and nineteenth centuries to feminism, particularly black and post-colonial feminisms, women's writing and her chief specialism, South African literature in English. She is currently working on a primer on South African writing in English, from Olive Schreiner to the post-apartheid era.

Álvaro J. Vidal Bouzon is Lecturer in Lusophone and Hispanic Studies at the University of Nottingham. His main research interests focus on the interfaces between language(s), (literary) writing, art, culture and politics in contemporary Iberian societies.

Patrizia Violi is Professor of Semiotics at the University of Bologna, Department of Communication, and Coordinator of the PhD Programme on Semiotics, Italian Institute of Human Sciences. Her main areas of research are semantic theory, text analysis, the semiotics of culture, language and gender, on which she has published numerous books and articles.

Colin Wright is Lecturer in Critical Theory in the Department of Cultural Studies at the University of Nottingham. His general areas of research interest include French Critical Theory, Continental Philosophy, Psychoanalysis, and Political and Postcolonial Theory. He is the author of *Philosophy, Rhetoric, Ideology: Towards a Sophistic Democracy* (Magnolia), *Psychoanalysis* (Zoilus) and, with Cristina Demaria, editor of *Post-Conflict Cultures: Rituals of Representation* (Zoilus Press).

Index